LEX FAMILY WELCOME GUIDE 1996

Jill Foster was a professional actress until her retirement at the age of seventeen. She has been a literary agent for over twenty years and has run her own agency for most of that time. In 1970 she married Malcolm Hamer and they have a daughter, Polly.

Malcolm Hamer was educated at Shrewsbury School and Trinity College, Cambridge. He worked in marketing for various multi-national companies and then formed his own agency to represent sportsmen and television journalists. He is now a full-time writer and his fifth novel is about to be published. His non-fiction includes a study of golf's Ryder Cup and the *Guinness Continental Europe Golf Course Guide*.

GW00566363

LEX
FAMILY WELCOME GUIDE
GUIDE

To
Hotels, Pubs and
Restaurants

1996 Edition

Jill Foster and Malcolm Hamer

HEADLINE

ISBN 0 7472 5261 0

Typeset by Palimpsest Book Production Limited,
Polmont, Stirlingshire

Printed and bound in Great Britain by
Cox & Wyman Ltd, Reading, Berks

HEADLINE BOOK PUBLISHING
A division of Hodder Headline PLC
338 Euston Road
London NW1 3BH

ACKNOWLEDGEMENTS

Our thanks to Cyril Carter and David Lemmon, who helped us greatly with our research.

CONTENTS

FOREWORD

by Sir Trevor Chinn
Chairman and Chief Executive, Lex Service PLC

Lex Service is delighted to be sponsoring the 1996 *Family Welcome Guide*, particularly at a time when there appears to be increasing recognition of the need for 'family-friendly' hotels, pubs and restaurants in the UK.

Our own research earlier this year revealed that families are keen to holiday in Britain, the biggest advantage being the ability to drive to their destination. However, many parents claimed to be put off holidaying at home by the poor service they receive from many hotels, restaurants and pubs. Lack of suitable facilities and amusements for children was cited as a real problem by over half of the parents we interviewed.

The *Lex Family Welcome Guide* is based on the actual experience of the authors who have spent the past year travelling the UK to complete their research, ensuring that only those facilities which extend a true family welcome have been included. The establishments included in the *Guide* meet the needs of the families we interviewed, providing both practical help for parents in the form of cots, high chairs and baby-listening facilities, and amusements such as play areas for their children.

Like the *Family Welcome Guide*, Lex Service aims to be the leader in its market. As well as being the UK's largest car retailer, Lex provides a complete range of services to make life easier for motorists in the UK. Our goal is to make sure that the name Lex stands for trust and value for money for all your motoring needs.

Lex Retail is the leading retailer of cars in the UK, with over 90 outlets. Cars sold include: Ford, Hyundai, Isuzu, Jaguar, Jeep, Kia, Land Rover and Range Rover, Mazda, Mercedes-Benz, Nissan, Peugeot, Porsche,

Renault, Rolls-Royce and Bentley, Rover, Saab, SEAT, Subaru, Toyota, Vauxhall, Volkswagen Audi and Volvo.

Lex Autocentres is a chain of over 80 specialist service centres which provide servicing and repairs for vehicles of all makes and ages.

Lex Autosales is a growing network of specialist all-makes used-car centres offering a wide range of three- to five-year-old cars at fixed prices.

Lex also imports and distributes Hyundai cars, which combine high specification with excellent value for money, through a network of 150 UK dealers, five of which are owned by Lex.

Lex Vehicle Leasing provides full service contract hire for cars and vans, with a fleet of over 67,000 vehicles representing most makes of cars and vans.

We hope that, with the help of Lex Service and the *Lex Family Welcome Guide 1996*, you will enjoy your next family holiday or meal out in Britain.

INTRODUCTION

In the 13th year of the *Family Welcome Guide*'s existence, we welcome a sponsor in the form of Lex Service, who recently carried out some research into parents' attitudes and concerns when on holiday or eating out in Britain. Amongst other data, it showed that parents of younger children often have difficulty in finding restaurants with enough high chairs and with nappy-changing facilities; and that those with children aged from 6 years upwards regard the availability of a children's menu as a priority when choosing a place to have a meal.

From the first edition of our *Guide* in 1984, our aim has been to allay such concerns by directing our readers to hotels, pubs and restaurants which offer a real welcome to families and which provide the appropriate facilities – and never more so than in the 1996 edition which recommends well over 500 establishments throughout Britain. Our researches have taken many different directions over the last decade and a half. We have looked at facilities in stores and supermarkets, airports, bus stations and railway stations; in museums, stately homes, zoos and theme parks; and have surveyed the self-catering market in Britain. In the *Lex Family Welcome Guide 1996* we are concentrating on hotels, pubs and restaurants, listing more than ever before.

We should stress that since we first set out on our researches at the beginning of the 1980s, new parents with crusading lights in our eyes, the attitudes to families have changed radically, and particularly during the last few years. The impetus for change has sprung from several sources. First, public opinion has been a major factor; parents, their views perhaps coloured by the comparatively civilized way that families are treated in European and American resorts, will no longer tolerate 'second-class' status. The days of families being put upon by snooty British hoteliers and restaurant owners or by aggressive publicans are numbered. That sort of establishment would not, of course, find its way into our *Guide*.

This 'wind of change' has been sniffed and identified by the media and many other pressure groups, and they have encouraged families to demand proper treatment and essential facilities. For example, a 'family-friendly' campaign was supported a few years back by the *Daily Telegraph*, and the blessed Esther Rantzen hosted the Tommy's Campaign awards on her show in 1994.

Another factor has been the Government's attempts to liberalize the licensing hours. A public house can, if the management desires, stay open throughout the day, every day, and many in the *Lex Family Welcome Guide* have chosen to do so. This is good news for the consumer and particularly for families who, when having a holiday or merely a day out together, do not necessarily want the irritating restriction of having to break for lunch between 12.30 and 2pm.

For years we have been making the obvious point that pubs have taken on the role of the family restaurant, and especially now that they can offer food throughout opening hours. We list over 300 pubs and at least two-thirds of them keep their doors open through the day.

The Government has also loosened the regulations governing the presence of children in pubs. The Children's Certificate, recently introduced in England and Wales (it has been in force in Scotland since 1991), allows children into any part of a pub until 9pm. There are other basic rules; for example, there must be a suitable environment for children, meals and soft drinks must be available, and children must be accompanied by an adult. As the 1995 report of the Brewers and Licensed Retailers Association accurately says, it's really a *family* certificate, not a children's certificate, since there is no question of a child being allowed in a pub without an accompanying adult. There are stringent rules to be met, too, but brewing trade estimates suggest that between 3,000 and 4,000 pubs have successfully applied for the certificate. Many of the larger pubs (with restaurants which are open all day) simply admit children to all areas except the immediate bar area. Many pubs in the *Guide*, and they have been recommended by us for years, have such good facilities that they have no need to apply for a Children's Certificate: and they are no doubt grateful to escape all the red tape that such an application involves.

Another powerful force in changing attitudes to families in the 'leisure market' has been the interest shown by some of the major brewery companies. Somewhat belatedly in our view, they have identified the importance of the family market. Their marketing gurus have told them that the traditional smoke-filled old boozer, dominated by dartboards and burly men swilling pints of beer, has had its day. They must now 'get their share of the leisure pound' via the family. Whitbread, with their ever-expanding Brewers Fayre chain, have led the way in converting their properties to family pubs and restaurants; they serve food all day, provide plenty of high chairs, nappy-changing facilities, baby food and children's menus, and indoor and outdoor play areas. Scottish and Newcastle, with their Homespreads pubs, the Boddington Pub Company, Greenalls and several other operators are following suit.

We have a selection of such outlets in the *Guide*, alongside the more traditional pubs run by tenants and independent owners.

Nearly 150 hotels are recommended and they range from simple farmhouses with a few rooms to splendid seaside and country hotels with wide-ranging amenities. The one thing they have in common is the provision of the basic facilities which families need: cots and high chairs, and a free baby-listening service. In fact they provide a great deal more – a warm and friendly welcome, for a start. Many of them also have a great array of extra facilities: swimming pools, play areas, tennis and squash courts, fishing, and even golf courses.

Many of the pubs and restaurants in our *Guide* provide accommodation, and we mention this where appropriate. Some of the pubs owned by the big brewers have Travel Inns or Lodges attached to them. These tend to have thirty or forty bedrooms, which are available at very reasonable prices: £30–£40 per room. For a family on the move, an overnight stop in a spacious bedroom (which might sleep two adults and a couple of children) for under £50 makes economic sense.

THE ENTRIES
We try to present the information in the simplest form, without any of those confusing codes or symbols.

Name of the town or village, and its county or region.

Name of the establishment, and whether we recommend it as an hotel Ⓗ, a pub Ⓟ or a restaurant Ⓡ. Sometimes establishments are entered in more than one category.

Directions.

Description: we try to give you an impression of what the place is like and why we have included it and we summarize its facilities.

Food: we give you the serving times, and an idea of the price range and (if possible) type of food on offer. For restaurant meals (as opposed to bar snacks) we quote the price of a three-course meal and again an extract from a typical menu. Since prices are hard to forecast we have quoted to the nearest £, and have rounded figures upward. We tell you if special menus or smaller portions are available for children.

Opening and closing times: except for pubs which, with rare exceptions, are open every day of the year. Pubs often remain open throughout the day, and when they do, we tell you in our report.

Ale means real ale and we name the brands available.

Hotel information includes:

Price of rooms: we give two sets of information; first the lowest price for bed and breakfast for two people for one night, graded thus:

£ Low = up to £45
£ Medium = from £46 ro £65
£ High = over £65

Best Bargain Break: every hotel offers bargain breaks, especially at weekends, and we have given these prices when they are available. There are great advantages in hunting these breaks out, since they really are bargains, especially out of season.

Children: we give you the terms for children and these are always on the basis that a child is sharing a room with its parents.

Facilities: we tell you how many cots and high chairs are available, and to what extent a baby-listening service is offered.

Number of rooms: we give the total number of rooms in hotels, and the number of family rooms (ie, which can sleep at least three people). We also mention suites, and interconnecting rooms. Apart from these, most hotels have other rooms which will take cots and/or extra beds.

We are writing this introduction in the middle of August 1995. We have made every effort to check the facts in our reports – invariably with the help of the management of each establishment recommended. However, managements change and prices are altered. We cannot be held responsible for changes which are made after we have gone to press. It is essential, therefore, that you check basic information, such as the cost of accommodation, before you book.

We thank all those people who wrote in to us with recommendations and with comments about places already in the *Guide*. These are invaluable; and we take your comments very seriously. Many establishments have been excluded, and many added, as a result. Please keep writing to us (the forms are at the back of the book).

ENGLAND

ALDEBURGH, SUFFOLK   Map 6
Ⓗ **WENTWORTH HOTEL, Wentworth Road**
Tel: 01728 452 312
Next to the beach, near the town centre.

....

This very appealing hotel has a splendid position overlooking the sea
across a pebbled beach, where the fishermen still sell their catch in the
morning. Many of the bedrooms have lovely views, as have the attractive
restaurant and the sun room, which is a delightful spot in which to relax.
The main lounge is alongside, an elegant room with comfortable sofas
and some good antique furniture. There is also a reading room cum
library on the ground floor.

On one side of the hotel there is a sunken terrace and it is a sun trap
on warmer days; on the other side is a small lawned garden. The wide
expanses of sea and beach lie before you and you can walk for miles in
either direction.

Although there are no permanent family rooms here, fourteen of the
bedrooms can be set up to take two adults and a child.

Nearby: Although the beach is shingle, Aldeburgh lies on the Suffolk
coastal path which runs from Felixstowe to Lowestoft. Just to the north
you can visit Minsmere Nature Reserve and the interesting village of
Dunwich with its museum. A music festival is held every June at
Snape Maltings and there are castles at Orford and Framlingham.
Adults with an interest in wine might try visits to Brandeston Priory
and Bruisyard Wines.

....

✖ Bar lunch (12pm to 2.30pm) £2–7: moussaka, fried skate, cottage
   pie, grilled lamb's liver;
   Lunch (12pm to 2pm) £14: smoked chicken & grapefruit salad,
   grilled whole plaice, pudding or cheese;
   Dinner (7pm to 9pm) £17: dressed crab, beef casserole, pudding
   or cheese
   Children: high teas, half portions
   £ High
✓ Best Bargain Break: £99 per person, 2 nights – dinner, b&b

Children: free to age 2; £7.50 thereafter
Facilities: 2 cots and 2 high chairs; baby-listening system
31 rooms
Closed 2 weeks after Christmas
⌶ Ale: Adnams
🅿 Own car park and on street

ALDERMINSTER, WARWICKS   Map 4
🅿 BELL INN AND BISTRO
Tel: 01789 450 414
On the A34 near Stratford-upon-Avon.

On the main road to Stratford, you cannot miss this smart, white-painted pub with its bright window boxes. It has been converted to become a large and busy pub/bistro; the cream-painted walls, brick pillars and bar, and nice wooden furniture make for a cheerful and relaxing atmosphere.

Families are welcome to use the area at the far end of the pub, well away from the bar, and French windows lead out to an enclosed and lawned garden with white furniture and parasols.

This is an enterprising family pub with the emphasis very much on food, of which there is an extensive and interesting range on offer, including always a wide selection of fresh fish. On weekdays a two-course lunch is great value at £5.95. There are two high chairs on the premises.

✗ (12pm to 2.30pm and 7pm to 11pm) £2–15: curried parsnip soup, courgette bake, garlicky king prawns, rogan josh, lamb & almond casserole
Children: own menu
⌶ Ale: Flowers, Marston's
🅿 Own car park

ALDWORTH, BERKS

Map 5

P THE BELL

Tel: 01635 578 272

Just off the B4009 south-west of Streatley.

This is a real village pub, with dark-red brick walls crowned with a deep roof, and it looks out to its tiny hamlet on one side and open countryside on the other. A few yards from the front door is the village well, 'sunk in 1868 with monies raised in this parish'.

Inside there is one bar, L-shaped with a low-beamed ceiling and with an alcove where a bread oven used to be. Photographs of past village cricket teams decorate the walls. The family room is off to one side, and is also a low-beamed, wood-panelled room with a few tables and benches and a huge and splendid open fireplace. The room houses the dartboard too. On warmer days you can sit at ease in a large and beautifully kept lawned garden, which is enclosed by hedges and dotted with trees.

Very little, if anything, seems to have been done to change this unpretentious and delightful pub during the last few decades. The landlord likes it that way, and so do we – long may it remain so.

✕ (12pm to 2pm and 6pm to 10pm): hot crusty rolls (Stilton, ham, turkey, etc)

◑ Ale: Arkell's, Hall & Woodhouse, Morland

P Own car park

ALFRISTON, EAST SUSSEX

Map 3

P R DRUSILLAS PARK

Tel: 01323 870 234

Just off the A27 near Alfriston.

It was no surprise that Drusillas won one of the English Tourist Board's top awards in 1991 (the Family Welcome of the Year Award), since adults and children of all ages can have a lot of fun at this excellent park; the focal point is the zoo, but there are many more attractions available, including a pub and a restaurant.

There is a good range of food and drink on offer, and the restaurant, now called Toucans, has been recommended for many years in the *Family Welcome Guide*. It is open at weekends and during the school holidays and has high chairs, plenty of space and a varied menu; it is especially popular on Sundays when entertainments for the children are laid on, and it is a favoured place for birthday parties. Next door is a spacious pub, the Inn at the Zoo; this has two family rooms and is open every day.

While you are here you should enjoy all the other facilities, of which there are many in the zoo: 'termite mounds' to be climbed, a zoolimpics with jumps and swings, and a huge play area with all sorts of equipment to amuse the children; if the weather turns nasty there is a well-equipped play barn. A miniature train runs through the animal paddocks and it includes a carriage for the disabled.

Adults are well cared for too. Apart from the wide range of birds and animals to see, there are eight shops on the site, including a pottery shop and a garden centre. There are some lovely gardens in which to relax, including the quiet Japanese Garden, and a very large and well-maintained picnic area, a part of which is under cover.

This is an extremely well-run and entertaining place where the whole family can have an enjoyable day. A number of special events are held through the year; family barbecues, an American Indian camp, birds of prey displays, world of owls week, and so on.

....

✕ (12pm to 6pm) £2–6: spaghetti Bolognese, fish & chips, burgers, vegetable crumble bake
Children: own menu
⌑ Ale: Harvey's
🅿 Ample

ALRESFORD, nr WINCHESTER, HANTS   Map 3
PR Percy Hobbs
Tel: 01962 849 631
Three miles from Junction 9 of the M3 on the A31.

....

This agreeable country pub has a good collection of facilities for families, including several high chairs, a family dining room (no smoking), a small indoor play area with Lego tables and toys and a nappy-changing facility.

The Percy Hobbs has a very pleasant interior, with a long bar area with windows on to the paved terrace. Off the bar there is a series of rooms and alcoves with wooden furniture and padded benches and chairs, wooden panelling and screens here and there and Laura Ashley-style wallpaper.

At the back you will find a pretty enclosed garden, shaded by tall trees, and there is a children's play area on a safe bark surface.

....

✕ (11.30am to 10pm; Sun 12pm to 10pm) £2–8: pâté, plaice & chips, sirloin steak, vegetable moussaka, chicken Alexandra
   Children: own menu
◎ Ale: Flowers, Strong's
P Own car park

ALREWAS, STAFFS   Map 4
P The Navigation
Tel: 01283 791 468
Just off the A513.

....

The pub has an interesting location alongside the canal, and Fradley Junction, where several waterways including the Trent and Mersey Canal join, is close.

The Navigation is a pleasant old brick building, with an extension that marries pretty well. The restaurant is an agreeable brick-walled room with a beamed ceiling and it can accommodate about forty diners

7

in comfort. There is a reasonable choice of food and the menu changes according to the seasons.

The sizeable bar has booths with padded benches and wooden settles, and there is a separate area with a television.

The large enclosed garden is mostly lawned and there are several bench tables. It overlooks a playing field and you can walk through to the canal and its pathway. A children's play area has been set up in the garden.

✖ (12pm to 2pm and 6pm to 9pm) £2–11: fresh sardines, plaice fillet, chicken & ham & peach pie, lasagne, steaks
Children: own menu
◑ Ale: Marston's
Ⓟ Own car park

ALSTONEFIELD, nr ASHBOURNE, STAFFS   Map 4
Ⓟ **GEORGE**
Tel: 0133 527 205
Off the A515 from Ashbourne to Buxton.

This old stone building overlooks the village green and its spreading chestnut trees. The grey stone can look drab but even on a wet evening Alstonefield has an ageless charm. It is high above Ashbourne and Dovedale and is a gathering place for walkers and climbers.

The main bar is a charming room with oak beams and an open fire. The long, low-ceilinged family room has six stout tables, and the walls are decorated with copper bric-à-brac. There is a large field enclosed by stone walls at the rear, where children can play; it is also used by campers.

If you are keen on walking and the outdoor life you can recover from your exertions here with a few draughts of Burtonwood, and a substantial plate of food.

✖ (12pm to 2pm and 7pm to 10pm) £2–7: meat & potato pie, chicken & chips, plaice & chips, lasagne, smoked trout

Children: small portions
℗ Ale: Burtonwood
🅿 Own car park

Nr ALTRINCHAM, CHESHIRE   **Map 8**
🅿 **ROPE & ANCHOR, Dunham Massey**
Tel: 0161 929 8217
Off the A56 at Dunham Massey.

....

You must follow your nose past the Dunham Massey estate and you
will find this pleasant and traditional-looking country inn. It has the
benefit of a pleasant lawned garden, with a children's play area and a
barbecue.

Around a central bar are gathered a series of high-ceilinged rooms. The
saloon bar has a dartboard and some fruit machines, and the other rooms
are primarily set aside for people who wish to dine. Families are welcome
in these areas and high chairs are available. Food is served throughout
the day at weekends.

The dining areas are cheerfully decorated – smart and colourful
wallpaper covers the walls and the ceilings – and have the advantage
of wide windows. Padded settles are laid along the walls and one of the
rooms is semicircular in design.

The Rope & Anchor is an inviting village pub in delightful
surroundings. Dunham Massey, the seat of the earls of Stanford and
Warrington, is well worth a visit. Over thirty rooms are open to the
public and there are 250 acres of parkland in which to wander.

....

✗ (12pm to 2pm and 5.30pm to 9.30pm; weekends 12pm to 9pm)
£1–8: black pudding topper, garlic & herb chicken, vegetable Balti,
fillet steak, Barnsley chop
Children: own menu
℗ Ale: Boddington's, Wadworth's
🅿 Own car park

Nr ALTRINCHAM, CHESHIRE   Map 8
P R STAMFORD ARMS, **Little Bollington**
Tel: 01565 830 018
Close to Junction 7 of the M56, on the A56 towards Lymm.

This delightful old building is made of brick, with a half-timbered upper storey. Stained-glass windows add distinction and masses of flowers in pots and hanging baskets are placed around the pub. A small garden at the front has a few bench tables and, at the side, there is an enclosed lawn; a sizeable play area has been made for children at the back and a bouncy castle is erected on summer days.

A traditional bar has heavy beams holding up the ceiling and a brick fireplace. On the other side, the family restaurant (high chairs and baby-changing facilities are available) is sizeable. On the ground floor the big bay window is one of many with leaded panes and coats of arms. The low beamed ceiling, wooden screens and brick pillars are used to create an Olde England ambience. Even more so on the floor above, where the overall effect is that of a medieval banqueting hall: nicely shaped leaded windows, shields on the walls, and drapes over one ceiling. It's good fun and easy on the eye, and the various alcoves even include Merlin's Cavern.

✕ (12pm to 2.30pm and 5pm to 10.30pm; weekends 12pm to 10.30pm); £2–13: prawn sundae, pasta Lucana, sirloin steak, haddock & chips, Indonesian chicken
Children: own menu

◑ Ale: Boddington's, Marston's and guests

🅟 Own car park

AMBLESIDE, CUMBRIA Map 8
🄷 ROTHAY MANOR HOTEL
Tel: 015394 33605
A few hundred yards out of the town on the Coniston Road.

This elegant Regency-style hotel was once the home of a prosperous Liverpool merchant and has a distinct colonial look. The wide windows and terrace on the ground floor overlook the immaculate garden with a fine variety of trees and a rockery; on the first floor there is a veranda with iron railings. Climbing plants and hanging baskets of flowers add to the attractions.

The hotel has been in the care of the same family since 1967 and many antiques have been collected during that time to adorn the main rooms. The restaurant is non-smoking and so is one of the lounges.

The bedrooms are all individually furnished to a very high standard. Three suites are available in the grounds of the hotel, two of which are ideal for families. They are spacious and beautifully furnished and each has one double and one twin bedroom. An adjoining single room can be used by either suite and they have little terraces and enclosed gardens of their own.

Residents have free use of a nearby leisure club (one mile away) with swimming pool, sauna, steam room and jacuzzi. Squash is also available. During the winter the hotel offers music, bridge, art and antiques, painting and gardening courses.

The hotel has an excellent reputation for its food which is freshly cooked from local produce. It is a delightful place to stay in a splendid part of the Lake District.

Nearby: The hotel is situated in the heart of the Lake District with all its attractions. Fishing, golf, riding and water sports are readily available. Brockhole Visitor Centre, the Steam Boat Museum, Sizergh Castle, Levens Hall, Brantwood, the Beatrix Potter Exhibition, Fell Foot Park, Grizedale Forest Centre and the Ravenglass and Eskdale Railway (the 'Ratty') are all within easy reach.

....

✗ Lunch (12.30pm to 2pm) £7: cold buffet or hot dishes of the day;
Dinner (8pm to 9pm), £25: smoked duck breast, soup, rack of lamb, fresh fruit salad
Children: high teas, half portions
£ High
✓ Best Bargain Break: £80 per person per night – dinner, b&b
Children: cot £5; extra bed £10
Facilities: 3 cots and 2 high chairs; baby listening
18 rooms, 5 family, 2 suites
Open Feb to Dec
Ⓟ Own car park

ANSTY, DORSET   Map 2
Ⓗ Ⓟ THE FOX
Tel: 01258 880 328
Signposted in the minor roads near Milton Abbas and south-west of Blandford.

....

In its dual role as both a medium-sized hotel and a pub, the Fox has outstanding facilities for families. The building itself is very appealing with its brick and flint façade, and it has two attractive bars with a remarkable collection of Toby jugs and china plates. Alongside the food service area there is a pleasant dining room with good wooden tables and a little alcove at one end with wide windows which overlook the garden. There is also an attractive restaurant, which is open in the evening, with french windows that lead out to the enclosed garden.

The pub is notable for its large family area (no smoking here) with plenty of tables and chairs, and has a pool table and table football. Alongside is a sizeable playroom with slide, rocking rabbit, toys and children's books, and a skittle alley. High chairs are available.

The bedrooms have excellent standards of decoration and comfort, and the family rooms are very spacious indeed. We looked at several: two with a double bed and two single beds, and another which could accommodate a family of five without any strain at all. The rooms are light and bright and have lovely views.

There is plenty of room in the rear garden, where there is an enclosed lawned area with bench tables and a Wendy House, and a sizeable swimming pool with a surrounding terrace. The front garden, under some mature trees, has another Wendy House and some slides and a few bench tables.

This is an exceptional family inn in a lovely part of Dorset.

Nearby: A number of interesting places are within easy reach, not least the coast, which runs east and west from Weymouth, and the Sea Life Centre. Athelhampton House and Kingston Lacy, Milton Abbey, Hardy's Cottage, the Tutankhamun Exhibition, the Tank Museum at Bovington, Corfe Castle and Brownsea Island are also close by.

✕ Bar meals (12pm to 2pm and 7pm to 9.30pm) £2–8: prawns, pork casserole with dumplings, lamb chops, Madras curry;
Dinner (7pm to 9pm) £12: fish & crab ramekin, steak Marius, pudding or cheese
Children: small portions
£ Medium

✓ Best Bargain Break: £33 per person per night – dinner, b&b
Children: free up to 3 years; £10 from 4 to 11; £12 from 12 to 16
Facilities: 4 cots, 3 high chairs; baby-listening system
14 rooms, 5 family
Open all year

◠ Ale: Hall & Woodhouse, Tetley and guests

▣ Own car park

APPLEBY, CUMBRIA   Map 8
Ⓗ **APPLEBY MANOR HOTEL**
Tel: 017683 51571
Off the A66. Follow the signs to the hotel.

....

This imposing manor house, made of rose-coloured Westmorland stone, overlooks the village of Appleby and the castle. The hotel was extended a few years back and is an excellent mix of old and new, and there is a notable pitch-pine staircase in the hall. The attractive public rooms include a stately and elegant sitting room, a pleasant bar and a light and airy dining room with wonderful views over the gardens to Appleby and the distant hills.

The same views will delight the eye from the splendid gardens which are shaded by some fine old trees. Other facilities include the games room, which has pool and table tennis, and the leisure club, which has a plunge pool, sauna, jacuzzi, solarium and some exercise machines.

The family bedrooms are well designed and offer plenty of space; four of them have either double or twin beds and bunk beds, and the others have various combinations of double and single beds.

With the eight family rooms, the interconnected rooms, a good supply of cots and high chairs and the excellent all-round facilities, this is a first-class family hotel and a good base for exploring this part of England.

Nearby: there is superb countryside all around, a great area for walking, fishing and riding. Golf is available in the vicinity. Appleby is a delightful town and the children will enjoy a visit to the conservation centre based at the castle. Lowther Park, with its nature trails, adventure playground and miniature railway, is close and it is easy to reach all the attractions of the Lakes and the Yorkshire Dales.

....

✗ Dinner (7pm to 9pm) £19: crab & prawn terrine, roast shoulder of pork, pudding or cheese
   Children: own menu, half portions
   £ High
✓ Best Bargain Break: £99 per person, 2 nights – dinner, b&b

Children: free to age 15
Facilities: 6 cots and 4 high chairs; baby-listening system
30 rooms, 8 family, 4 sets interconnecting
Open all year
P Own car park

APPLEBY, CUMBRIA   Map 8
P ROYAL OAK INN, Bongate
Tel: 017683 51463
Half a mile off the A66.

This delightful old coaching inn, long and low, is an attractive sight with its colourful hanging baskets and window boxes. It enhances an already appealing town, which used to be the county town of Westmoreland. Parts of the building may date back to the 12th century, and the River Eden is nearby.

You will not be disappointed with the inside, with its wealth of brasses, old furniture, and low dark beams. Families can use a spacious room just inside the front door and it is comfortably furnished. There is an equally agreeable dining room alongside.

The long and varied menu doubles up for both bar meals and dinner, and also includes vegetarian dishes and daily specials. A high chair is provided, and the children's menu is enterprising: pork & apple burger and cheesy sausages are on offer, for example.

There is always a very good choice of real ales here; as many as ten are on the go at any one time.

✗ (12pm to 2pm and 6.30pm to 9pm; Sun from 7pm) £2–10: hot green pancakes, savoury crumble, prawn & queenie gratin, Cheddar chicken, steaks
Children: own menu
◐ Ale: Yates, Theakston's, Younger's, Bongate Special
P On forecourt

ARNOLD, nr NOTTINGHAM   Map 7
P R THE SEVEN MILE INN
Tel: 0115 926 6595

On the A60, seven miles from Nottingham city centre near Newstead Abbey.

....

This red-brick building has a grassed area at the side with several bench tables. At the rear of the building is a small stone-flagged patio, once again with bench tables, and alongside there is a play unit on a safe bark surface.

The restaurant is an agreeable place, with its brick walls and oak beams. It has a raised area which seats up to thirty diners, whilst the main restaurant is split into four alcoves. It is carpeted throughout, and has wooden tables and chairs and comfortable padded benches.

To the left of the entrance is the main bar where families can enjoy a drink, and this is in the same style as the restaurant: there are alcoves, settles and dark wooden farmhouse-style chairs and tables. There are two exits on to a raised patio, below which is the play area.

Meals are served throughout the day in the bar (the restaurant times are shown below) and high chairs are provided. There is a nappy-changing unit.

....

✗ (12pm to 2.30pm and 5pm to 10.30pm; weekends all day) £2–13: Greek dip, three-bean feast, ocean bake, peppered steak, beef & Boddington's pie
Children: own menu, half portions

◑ Ale: Boddington's, Marston's and guests

℗ Own car park

ASCOT, BERKS   Map 5
🅿🅡 Royal Foresters Hotel
Tel: 01344 884 747
On the A329 towards Bracknell.

The appealing, low-slung building has a mass of flowers adorning its façade, and an extensive lawned garden, equipped with many bench tables and parasols, lies in front of the hotel.

The bar extends the full length of the building; its low ceiling and the cottage-style bay windows with curved settles fitted to their contours give it an agreeable atmosphere. There are lounges at each end, both maintaining the general style of this pub: open fireplaces, wood-panelled walls, beamed ceilings, comfortable wall benches and nice wooden furniture.

The spacious restaurant has a racing motif, an appropriate one since the famous Ascot racecourse is less than a mile away. The room has a wooden ceiling and wooden rails, race results boards, prints of horses and jockeys on the walls, and even some racing silks. It's good fun.

Families are firmly in mind here, with the provision of high chairs and nappy-changing facilities. The pub is open all day and food (bar snacks when the restaurant is closed) is served throughout opening hours. The hotel contains thirty-three rooms.

✗ (12pm to 2.30pm and 5pm to 10.30pm; weekends all day)
£2–13: prawn sundae, sirloin Oscar, ocean bake, three-bean feast,
Normandy pork
Children: own menu

✿ Ale: Morland's

🅿 Own car park

ASHBY ST LEDGERS, nr RUGBY, NORTHANTS   Map 7
Ⓗ🅿 THE OLDE COACH HOUSE INN
Tel: 01788 890 349
Off the A361 north of Daventry, close to Junction 18 of the M1.

This fine old pub sits in a delightful village of stone buildings with
thatched roofs. Robert Catesby hatched the Gunpowder Plot in
Ashby Manor, an elegant mansion next door to the church of St
Leodegarius.

When Sir Edwin Lutyens restyled the village, a stone Victorian façade
was added to a farmhouse of an older vintage to make a pub for the
villagers, originally called the Coach and Horses. It is a superb pub of

great character with several areas where families can settle down to enjoy the excellent food and the various real ales, which include St Ledger Ale. Up some stairs at one end of the pub is a handsome room with cross beams and rafters, wood panelling and stone walls. Down below there is another pleasant room with an alcove, good wooden tables and a large open fireplace. The rest of the pub is taken up by two excellent bars and a games room.

On summer days the garden is wonderfully inviting. The patio is shady under its trailing plants and there are plenty of bench tables on the spacious lawn. There is a new and business-like barbecue in the garden and people with young children can use the parents and baby room. A children's garden, with an activity centre, is safely enclosed and the village playground is next door.

We looked at all six bedrooms and were impressed by the high standards of decoration and the excellent furniture (pine in general). All the bedrooms have their own bathrooms and there is a very spacious family room with a double and two single beds; two other rooms have sofa beds and could therefore accommodate a family of four. A bonus is the lovely views of the surrounding countryside.

✕ Snacks (12pm to 2pm and 6pm to 9.30pm) £2–12: Whitby scampi, cold buffet, lasagne, steaks, range of vegetarian dishes;
Dinner (6pm to 9.30pm) £14: salad niçoise, supreme of chicken, pudding or cheese
Children: own menu, half portions
£ Medium
✓ Best Bargain Break: £57 per person, 2 nights – dinner, b&b
Children: free up to 5 years; £5 up to 11 years
Facilities: 2 cots and 2 high chairs, baby listening
6 rooms, 1 family
Open all year
⌂ Ale: Everard, Flowers, Jennings, Chiltern, St Ledger
Ⓟ Own car park

ASHCOTT, nr BRIDGWATER, SOMERSET　　　　　Map 2
P THE ASHCOTT INN
Tel: 01458 210 282
On the A39 west of Street.

Much of this cream-painted building with its red-tiled roof dates from the 14th century and it sits by the main road through the village.

The main entrance takes you into a small bar with a beamed ceiling and a large inglenook fireplace, and you should look out for the bread oven here. It is at a table next to this fireplace that one might encounter the ghost of the 'Grey Lady'; she places spoons under this table and moves the candles in the main restaurant.

A striking feature of the lounge bar is a fine stained-glass window, which dates from the 14th century.

Between the bar and the main restaurant there is an annexe where families may sit and enjoy a quiet drink. Its brick walls are adorned with pictures, plates and copperware, and it is a homely and welcoming place. Families are also welcome to dine in the main restaurant, which is tastefully decorated in cream; the flower print curtains enhance the cottage-like atmosphere of this room. The large wood beams here were imported from Spain and there is certainly a touch of the 'galleon' about the ceiling. An extension is proposed for 1995, and it should be noted that there are both smoking and non-smoking areas.

Outside the restaurant there is a paved and grassed patio area with bench tables from which to enjoy the garden and the open air. Beyond this is a grass paddock and there are plans to install an adventure play area here.

The pub is open all day from Monday to Saturday during the summer months (May to Sept).

✖ (12pm to 2pm and 6.30pm to 9.30pm; Sun 7pm to 9pm) £2–10: leeks & Stilton, lasagne, mixed grill, cauliflower & tuna bake, pork Dijonnaise
Children: own menu, half portions

⊙ Ale: Butcombe, Flowers
Ⓟ Own car park

ASHINGTON, nr PULBOROUGH, WEST SUSSEX   Map 3
ⓅⓇ RED LION
Tel: 01903 892 226
On the A24 in the village of Ashington.

This large family pub and restaurant is housed in a substantial three-storey building, which is partly faced with tiles in the traditional Sussex manner and also has a good covering of Virginia creeper.

The façade gives one very little idea of the vast amount of space inside the pub, but sensibly the designers have split the interior into a series of small interconnecting rooms and alcoves. They are divided by screens of wood and glass, and wood is much in evidence in the form of beams and pillars. Comfortable padded seats and benches, wooden tables, nice brick fireplaces, prints on the walls and baskets of dried flowers add to the agreeable atmosphere.

Families are very well catered for, with their own no-smoking dining areas, and there is a sizeable children's play area indoors with Lego, videos, a ball swamp and other equipment. There are several high chairs and a baby-changing facility. In addition, there is an enclosed outdoor play area with a bouncy castle and various rides, including a seesaw.

The Red Lion is a well-equipped family pub which is open throughout the day and serves food from morning through to evening.

✖ (11.30am to 10pm; Sun 12pm to 10pm) £1–8: onion bhajis, steak & kidney pie, sirloin steak, fish pie, vegetable crumble
Children: own menu, half portions
⊙ Ale: Boddington's, Flowers
Ⓟ Own car park

ASKHAM, CUMBRIA   Map 8
P PUNCH BOWL INN
Tel: 01931 712 443
Two miles off the B5320 and the A6. At the bottom of the village.

....

This delightful pub is situated in the pretty village of Askham, alongside Lowther Park and its impressive castle.

You enter a spacious and low-beamed bar, comfortably furnished and welcoming, and families are able to use a room at the far end. It's two rooms really, on different levels, with several tables and chairs. It's pleasantly cosy in there, and an alternative is a tiny little room, off the bar, with a padded bench running along the walls. A real snug. There is also a games room in the pub, which now has a children's certificate.

On warmer days you can sit on the terrace at the side of the pub and watch the world go quietly by.

An enterprising range of bar meals is served lunchtime and evening, seven days a week, and on Sunday lunchtimes you can have a two-course meal for under £6.

....

✕ (12pm to 2pm and 7pm to 9pm) £2–9: shrimp bake, salmon en croute, fisherman's pot, cashew & pepper loaf, steaks
   Children: own menu
◗ Ale: Castle Eden and guests
P Own car park

AUST, AVON   Map 2
P BOAR'S HEAD
Tel: 01454 632 278
Follow the A403 to Avonmouth (at Junction 21 of the M4 by the Severn Bridge) and turn left to Aust village.

....

Only a few seconds from the M4, this attractive 17th-century pub has a sizeable lounge with low ceilings and a large stone fireplace complete with iron stove. The main bar is also very appealing, with its stone walls, large open fireplace and various wooden tables and settles. On warmer days the children will perhaps be interested in the collection of rabbits and guinea pigs in the charming garden, which also has a swing and a climbing frame on the lawn.

There's a wide range of food and, with a couple of exceptions, it is all home-made. Snacks are available every day except Sunday and the buffet lunch from Monday to Friday offers around thirty different salads and pickles to accompany quiches, cold meats, salmon, game pie, turkey, etc. There are two high chairs on the premises.

This pub has excellent facilities for all the family in a very accessible place close to the M4.

X (12pm to 2pm and 7.30pm to 9.45pm) £2–9: buffet lunch, ploughman's, potato & cheese & onion hotpot, fresh plaice, braised oxtail
  Children: half portions
P Ale: Courage
P Own car park

AVEBURY, WILTS   Map 2
R STONES RESTAURANT
Tel: 01672 539 514
Off the main street of the village.

The village is encircled by the famous Neolithic stones which brood across the landscape in their twin circles and were thought by John Aubrey in the 17th century to be of more historical importance than Stonehenge. He wrote of the stones as looking 'like a flocke of sheep. One might fancy it to have been the scene, where the giants fought with huge stones against the gods.'

The restaurant is housed in a fine old stone barn next to the National Trust Shop and the Tourist Information Centre. There's a cobbled patio outside, a large grassy area with a pond, a dovecote, a backdrop of lime trees, and across the way is the manor house. Inside, the restaurant is long and spacious, plainly and attractively furnished with pine tables, chairs and settles.

All the food is home-made, including the bread and cakes (from organic flours), the jams and the chutneys. The herbs and much of the organic produce are grown in the village and do not contain any artificial additives. There are plenty of morning snacks available, including rolls, quiches, salads, cakes and various savouries; afternoon teas are served from 2.30pm, and there is an excellent choice of teas.

A chair and a table have been provided in the Ladies, but the space is limited.

✗ £1–5: soup, salads, hot savoury dishes, cream tea
    Children: smaller portions
    Open 10am to 6pm every day during summer; weekends only in winter; closed in Jan
    No credit cards accepted
℗ Ale: Bunce's
P In the village

BAGSHOT, SURREY
Map 3
Ⓡ Notcutts Garden Centre
Tel: 01276 472 288
On the A30 on the south-west side of Bagshot.

....

Like the other Notcutts Garden Centres, this is a spacious and well-organized establishment where you will find everything necessary to maintain and improve your garden.

It also has an excellent restaurant where families are made welcome. Several high chairs are available and there is a wide range of food, both hot and cold, enticingly laid out at the self-service counter. The restaurant has an attractive look, with its wooden tables and fresh flowers. It is set out on two levels and the upper level is a no-smoking area.

....

✕ (9.30am to 5pm) £2–5: lasagne, cold buffet, beef in ale pie, baked potatoes, cottage pie
Children: own menu, half portions
Unlicensed
Ⓟ Lots

BAMFORD, DERBYSHIRE
Map 7
Ⓟ Derwent Hotel
Tel: 01433 651 395
In the centre of the village, just off the A57.

....

This imposing country inn, with a half-timbered façade, dates from the late 19th century. There are several rooms off the central bar area and the staff are clearly used to dealing with families and welcome them.

The spacious and bright family room is adorned with bric-à-brac and has plenty of tables, comfortable padded benches and a bay window at one end. It is a nice relaxing room, and families are also welcome in the pleasant dining room with its pine panelling.

There is a large garden with tables and umbrellas, walled off from

25

the road so the children can play in safety, and a little terrace in front of the pub.

The pub is open throughout the day from Monday to Saturday. The three-course Sunday lunch is excellent value at just under £7.

....

✗ (12pm to 2.30pm and 7pm to 9.30pm) £2–9: cauliflower cheese, fillet steak, halibut mornay, plaice & chips, chicken tikka
Children: own menu, half portions

⚲ Ale: Boddington's, Ward's, Stone's and guests

Ⓟ Own car park

BANTHAM, DEVON   Map 1
ⒽⓅ Sloop Inn
Tel: 01548 560 489
West of Kingsbridge off the A379/B3197.

....

Bantham is a pretty village in one of the loveliest parts of south Devon and the Sloop Inn fits in well, a 16th-century building which was once owned by a notorious smuggler and wrecker called John Widdon. It is a spacious pub with a separate family room where adults and children can eat and drink together, and on warmer days, you can head for the patio at the rear of the pub. Food is available every day and includes a good choice of local fish; there is a choice of real ale too, including Bass.

There are two family bedrooms, which have their own bath-rooms and include a double and a single bed. In addition, there are three self-catering flats, each with two bedrooms and equipped to a high standard. They offer lovely views of the bay and Burgh Island. The rents range from £205 to £570 a week; short breaks are available, too.

Nearby: There is an excellent stretch of sandy beach a few hundred yards from the inn, which is patrolled by lifeguards during the summer because of the currents, but is safe as long as the warning notices are heeded. It is also a marvellous beach for surfing and there are other pleasant beaches, including Thurlestone, nearby. If you prefer dry land, the south Devon coast path goes from Bantham towards Hope Cove and offers a walk with some spectacular views. There are two golf courses, at Bigbury and Thurlestone, and there is plenty of sea and river fishing to be had, plus water sports of all kinds. There are many other attractions within reach: the National Shire Horse Centre and the Dartmoor Wildlife Park, the Torbay Aircraft Museum, Buckfast Abbey and the Dart Valley Railway.

....

✖ (12pm to 2pm and 7 to 10pm) £2–9: local smoked salmon, plaice & chips, steaks, fresh crab salad, grilled lamb steak
£ Medium
Children: cot £2; half price thereafter up to 11 years
Facilities: 3 cots and 2 high chairs
5 rooms, 2 family
◖ Ale: Bass, Blackawton, Usher's
Open all year
ℙ Own car park

BARNGATES, nr AMBLESIDE, CUMBRIA   Map 8
ℙ THE DRUNKEN DUCK
Tel: 015394 36347
Off the B5286.

....

Standing alone at a crossroads in a lovely part of the Lakes, and not far from Tarn Hows, you will find this welcoming 16th-century pub. The name derives from some ducks which, in Victorian times, were inadvertently given ale with their usual feed. Modern visitors will not be disappointed by the range of beers available.

It's not ducks but a row of foxes' heads on one of the low beams which greets you as you enter. Various hunting trophies, brasses, pewter mugs and stuffed birds are a feature of the inn.

Families are welcome to use a small room with pine settles, or the dining room, which is divided by beamed stalls.

A little veranda at the front of the pub gives you a wonderful sight of rolling countryside, and at the back is a patio.

✕ (12pm to 2pm and 6.30pm to 9pm) £2–8: lamb & apricot casserole, gammon steak, lasagne, beef Stroganoff
Children: half portions
▢ Ale: Marston's, Tetley's, Theakston's, Jennings
▣ Own car park

BARRINGTON, CAMBRIDGESHIRE   Map 6
▣▣ ROYAL OAK, High Street
Tel: 01223 870791
Off the A10, south of Cambridge.

This is an inn and restaurant of great beauty in a delightful village. The thatched roof reminds us that there has been an inn on this spot since the time of the first Elizabeth, and there is some Tudor brickwork above a mantel beam in the large central chimney. The pub is fronted by a charming open garden with family benches and parasols which looks across the wide main road to a vast village green. Next to the green is the well-maintained cricket ground of the local club, and there are thatched cottages in the centre of the village which were built by Oliver Cromwell.

The restaurant is extensive, and the recently added conservatory, an annexe of charm, gives dining space for non-smokers. Children are catered for in the large room next to the bar which was once the restaurant. Vegetarian food is a speciality.

✕ (12pm to 2pm and 6.30pm to 10.30pm) £2–8: chestnut & cashew pâté, moussaka, steak & kidney pie, king prawns, beef in stout
Children: half portions
▢ Ale: Adnams, Greene King, Eldridge Pope
▣ Own car park and on road

BASINGSTOKE, HANTS

Map 3

PR DOWN GRANGE, Winchester Road
Tel: 01256 461 149

On the A30, on the south-west side of Basingstoke, close to Junction 7 of the M3.

This splendid country house, located in several acres of parkland, is said to have been built by one of George III's mistresses; he must have put up the money in one of his many moments of madness. The place has a chequered history since Sir Oswald Mosley led rallies of his British Union of Fascists here. It is said that the infamous William Joyce (Lord Haw-Haw) was present.

However, Down Grange is now a family pub and restaurant, operated by the Brewers Fayre chain. Splendid bay windows lend great style to the various rooms, beginning with a comfortable bar where you can sit at ease on one of the padded settles. There are two dining rooms. The first is a well-proportioned room with prints on the wall, and the large one has two of those delightful bay windows; one of them overlooks a stretch of parkland and the other a paved terrace. An enclosed play area for children has been sited here.

The family dining area (no smoking) has plentiful supplies of high chairs and a nappy-changing facility. There is also a Fun Factory for young children: one wonders what Sir Oswald would have made of it.

✕ (11.30am to 10pm) £2–8: onion bhajis, fish pie, chicken escalopes, marinated lamb steak, tagliatelle carbonara
  Children: own menu
◻ Ale: Boddington's, Flowers, Marston's
P Own car park

Nr BASINGSTOKE, HANTS   Map 3
PR THE HATCH
Tel: 01256 473 077
On the A30, east of Basingstoke, at Basing.

....

If you approach The Hatch from the car park you will walk straight into a very attractive stretch of garden. A stream runs through it and you might choose to sit in a lawned area to one side. Several trees provide shade on a sunny day. There is another expanse of lawn alongside, and no fewer than three children's play areas, including swings and an adventure playground.

This rambling old pub, its façade smartly painted white, has been revamped with the family market in mind. There are half a dozen high chairs available, and a nappy-changing unit.

There is plenty of space inside to cope with all manner of diners and drinkers. For example, the latter might head for the appealing lounge at one end of the pub. It has brick walls with some wood panelling, and a stuffed pike decorates the space above the large fireplace. The bar itself has wide windows and an eclectic array of wooden tables.

The various eating areas start here and the family dining room is a splendid place, with windows overlooking the terrace and the stream. Brick pillars and walls, a high wooden ceiling, and a nice dresser with a good collection of plates ensure a welcoming atmosphere. There is a smaller room alongside, with a skylight. An indoor play area, with a ball swamp and games machines, will help to amuse the children.

....

✕ (12pm to 3pm and 5pm to 10pm; weekends 12pm to 10pm)
    £2–9: moules marinières, peppered steak, lasagne, lemon chicken, mixed grill
    Children: own menu

⬭ Ale: Courage, John Smith's, Theakston's

P Own car park

BASSENTHWAITE, nr KESWICK, CUMBRIA   Map 8
Ⓗ ARMATHWAITE HALL HOTEL
Tel: 017687 76551
Off the A591 – don't go to Bassenthwaite village but follow the signs for the Lake. Turn off at the Castle Inn.

This is a splendid 18th-century stone building very much in the 'baronial' style, and set in 400 acres of parkland; its lawns flow down to Bassenthwaite Lake, where guests can fish, and Skiddaw Mountain looms dramatically in the background.

Sir Hugh Walpole wrote of it: 'Speaking of Romance, is there anything more romantic than Armathwaite Hall. With the trees that guard it and the history that inhabits it, it is a house of perfect and irresistible atmosphere.'

There are some wonderful rooms here, including a huge lounge with a grand marble fireplace, wood-panelled ceiling and walls and leaded windows – all glassily surveyed by the stags' heads on the walls.

In addition to its beautiful situation, there are splendid facilities within the hotel: a leisure centre with indoor heated swimming pool, gymnasium, a hard tennis court, a pitch and putt course, and a croquet lawn. A snooker table (for over-16s) is in a remarkable panelled room with walls covered with scores of original Punch cartoons. The hotel also has an Equestrian Centre with fully qualified instructors and over twenty horses and ponies.

The hotel makes a considerable effort to look after and entertain all members of the family and, in addition to the excellent facilities mentioned above, there are special treats for the children. 'Trotters & Friends' is an animal farm park (open from April to October) with many animals to make friends with and feed; there is a Farm Trail Quiz every day; and Family Treasure Hunts are held several times a week.

The Armathwaite Hall Hotel is an outstanding hotel in delightful surroundings where families will find all they need for an enjoyable stay.

Nearby: From this base you can reach any part of the Lakes with ease, including Grasmere, Hardknott Roman fort, Brantwood, the Lake District headquarters at Brockhole. The children will no doubt vote for Fell Foot Park which has facilities for all types of water sports, or the Grizedale Forest Visitor Centre. Railway buffs have several choices, including the famous Ravenglass and Eskdale, known as 'Ratty', and all the family will love a trip on it.

⚔ Leisure Club (12pm to 5.30pm and 6.30pm to 10pm) £2–9: garlic mushrooms, spaghetti Napoli, chicken curry, sirloin steak;
Lunch (12.30pm to 1.45pm) £14: smoked salmon & cucumber salad, roast leg of pork, strawberry pavlova;
Dinner (7.30pm to 9.30pm) £29: galia melon, lemon sole fillet, breast of guinea fowl, pudding or cheese
Children: own menu, half portions
£ High
✓ Best Bargain Break: £148–182 per person, 2 nights – dinner, b&b
Children: free
Facilities: 6 cots and 6 high chairs; baby-listening system for each room
42 rooms, 4 family, 2 sets interconnecting
🅿 Own car park

BATCOMBE, nr EVERCREECH, SOMERSET   Map 2
🅿 **BATCOMBE INN**
Tel: 01749 850 359
At Batcombe, by the church, off the A359 south of Frome.

This superb inn is only about a mile from the main road and you will be amply rewarded for your minor detour since the Batcombe Inn, as we all agreed as we sat at peace in its garden, truly is an archetypal English country pub. It sits alongside the magnificent 15th-century church of St Mary's, Gothic in style and resembling a small-scale minster, and the pub itself dates from around 1600, as its mellow stone walls might suggest.

The licensees, Derek and Claire Blezard, have accomplished a programme of refurbishment with great aplomb. The terrace, which

EVERY YEAR WE SPEND MILLIONS DEVELOPING CARS TO GO SOMEWHERE YOU'VE NEVER BEEN BEFORE. THE NEXT CENTURY.

Hyundai has invested £2.5 billion in research and development projects such as the HCD-11 concept car pictured above. And another £2.5 billion in the latest facilities to ensure we're in the world's top ten car manufacturers by the year 2000. We're already the 14th largest car manufacturer in the world and by far the biggest in Korea, with an annual production capacity of 1,150,000. You see, at Hyundai we're not just concerned with what people will be driving this time next year, but what they will be driving in the next century.

LEX **Autocentres**

Lex Autocentres provide fixed price service and repairs for all makes of cars

- Servicing
- MOT Testing
- Computerised Engine Tuning
- Brake, Steering and Suspension work
- Clutch Replacement

is like a courtyard with one open side, is a pleasant place to sit on a summer day, or you can seek the shade of the trees in the delightful lawned garden, which now has a little pool, complete with fish and newts. Alongside the garden there is a splendid children's play area, with sturdy wooden equipment: slides, climbing frames, tree houses and a miniature roller-coaster.

Inside the pub you will find a very attractive bar, which is notable for the huge inglenook fireplace at one end; there is a wood-burning stove at the other end. Off the bar, the play room has a good selection of toys for younger children, a television and a video (with a library of Disney and National Geographic videos) and an ice-cream bar. There is a bar billiards table in here as well.

Part of the building was once the toll house on the main wool route to Frome (Batcombe was one of the five major wool villages) and this now houses the delightful dining room which retains its original stone walls. Part of the room is open to the rafters, and the walls and the beams are entwined by plants. High chairs can be provided and there is a well-equipped baby-changing area in the Ladies.

With a choice of real ales and food that has been commended by other guidebooks, we wholeheartedly recommend the Batcombe Inn.

✗ (12pm to 2pm and 7pm to 9pm) £3–11: stuffed quail, supreme of sea bass, orange & ginger pork, chicken piri piri, roast poussin
 Children: own menu, half portions
◯ Ale: Butcombe, Wadworth's
▣ Own car park

BATH, AVON   **Map 2**
Ⓡ **SALLY LUNN'S HOUSE, 4 North Parade Passage**
Tel: 01225 461 634
In the town centre, not far from Abbey Green.

This is one of the oldest houses in Bath and dates from 1482. Excavations in the cellar revealed items such as pottery, pieces of mosaic from Roman times, and a series of figures which depict people through the ages: these are on display in the little museum, along with an ancient oven. Sally Lunn started baking her famous buns in the latter part of the 17th century, and buns made from the same recipe are still sold here – both the savoury and the sweet variety.

The café is on two floors: there is a pretty, chintzy room on the first floor with a large fireplace; and the larger ground-floor room is an attractive beamed area with an archway in the middle. Dinners are now served from six o'clock in the evening and the early sittings are popular with families. It is advisable to book ahead.

Space is at a premium here, and there is nowhere to change a baby.

....

✗ £1–5: Sally Lunn buns – Welsh rarebit, chicken curry, smoked salmon pâté, baked beans, salads;
Dinner (6pm to 11pm) £14: crudités, stuffed breast of chicken, apple pie & cream
Open 10am to 11pm; Sun from 12pm; Mon until 6pm
P Public car parks

BATHFORD, nr BATH, AVON   **Map 2**
P THE CROWN, 2 Bathford Hill
Tel: 01225 852 297
At the junction of the A4 and A363 east of Bath.

....

This stately stone pub dates back to the 18th century but was substantially altered in the early years of this century. Its fine Georgian façade is enlivened by lovely displays of flowers.

There is plenty of space inside, with a large bar area, but the interior is well designed to give the effect of a number of small rooms. One of these is for families: the smartly furnished Garden Room is a no-smoking area; a door leads out to a terrace and on to a large lawned garden, which is safely enclosed. There are plenty of bench tables and in summer toys are put out for young children.

An alternative to the Garden Room for families is the Burgundy

Room on the other side of the pub. This is a spacious and well-proportioned room with plenty of tables and chairs and it particularly comes into play at weekends. There are several high chairs available and a changing table in the Ladies.

It is good to report that the enterprising range of food is freshly prepared, so you must expect to wait at busy times (weekends, for example). Even better to report that chips do not sully the premises, and that children are offered smaller portions of the adult dishes – not the inevitable things and chips. They also have their own range of cocktails: Blue Lagoon, Dragon's Blood, Purple People Eater and so on.

This is an admirable and very welcoming pub where the licensees hold a balance between their various customers with great success; it is a real pub in the traditional sense (good food and a choice of real ales) and it also has excellent facilities for families.

....

✕ (12pm to 2pm and 7pm to 9.30pm, not Mon lunch) £2–9: rump steak, Thai chicken & brown rice, steak & mushroom & ale pie, lentil nut casserole, Indian chicken parcel
  Children: own menu, small portions
🍺 Ale: Bass, Marston's, Usher's
🅿 Own car park

BEACONSFIELD, BUCKS   Map 5
P R WHITE HART TOBY HOTEL
Tel: 01494 671 211
In the centre of the town.

This fine 16th-century coaching inn sits at the centre of this pleasant town. G. K. Chesterton, the author of the Father Brown stories and a great deal more, lived in Beaconsfield and it is said that he frequented the bar of the White Hart. He would still feel at home in the spacious L-shaped room with its brick walls, ancient wooden beams and central fireplace. There is a lovely pubby atmosphere. On the other side, the lounge bar is more intimate, with a low beamed ceiling and several leather sofas.

The restaurant, which provides several high chairs, is a well-proportioned room, with a central fireplace and brightly coloured lampshades, and with prints and photographs of bygone Beaconsfield on the walls.

The restaurant times are listed below, and when it is closed, bar food is always available, since the pub is open throughout the day.

The hotel has thirty-three bedrooms, mostly in a modern block, but there are five in the original building itself.

✕ (12pm to 2pm and 6pm to 10pm; Sun 12pm to 10pm) £2–11: cod smoky, mixed grill, Brie & courgette crumble, fish & chips, steaks
Children: own menu
◗ Ale: Bass
P Own car park

BEAUWORTH, nr ALRESFORD, HANTS   Map 3
P THE MILBURY'S
Tel: 01962 771 248
About two miles south of the A272, and one mile beyond the hamlet of Beauworth.

Standing alone on top of the hill, this 17th-century pub is built in soft, warm Hampshire brick with hung tiles, flint walls and dormer windows set in a many-angled roof line. It is good to report that families are welcome in various areas, so that adults can still enjoy the real ales which are available and the excellent range of food. A notable feature of the pub is the well in the bar. It is three hundred feet deep and an ice cube, dropped from the safety grid, takes eight seconds to hit the water. There is also a huge treadmill to be seen.

The two family rooms sit one above the other alongside the large mill wheel. There are several tables on the ground floor and up above you will find the gallery, an interesting room with a beamed sloping ceiling and wooden tables. There is also a skittle alley with several tables.

There is a grassy garden with superb views of the wide-open countryside. There are plenty of picnic tables, and barbecues are held during summer weekends. Two swings make up a play area in a corner of the garden.

X Bar snacks (12pm to 2pm and 7pm to 10pm) £1–10: smoked salmon, cod fillet Mornay, steaks, plaice, chilli con carne
Children: own menu, half portions
D Ale: Courage, King Alfred, Milbury Special, Pendragon and guests
P Own car park

BEDFORD, BEDS   **Map 5**
P R **PRIORY MARINA, Priory Country Park**
Tel: 01234 352 883
Off the Cambridge road (A428). There are signs to Priory Country Park.

Two hundred acres of woods, grass and water are set within a curve of the River Great Ouse – and it's only a mile or two from the centre of Bedford.

This huge family pub and restaurant was opened less than ten years ago and, on summer days, customers can sit in the garden and look out over the wide expanses of water and enjoy the wildlife. There is also a children's play unit on a safe bark surface.

Inside, there is a great amount of space under the high vaulted roof. Naturally, boats and boating is the theme of the pub and there are skiffs suspended on beams above the main bar area, lifebelts and nautical prints on the walls, fishing nets, and a pond with a fountain in one corner.

There is loads of room in the two bar areas, which are comfortably furnished, and the restaurant has masses of space under its high ceilings. Wide windows give views of the garden and of the lake beyond.

High chairs are made available and there are baby-changing facilities in the Ladies.

Although the restaurant closes during the afternoon, the pub stays open and bar snacks are served.

✕ (12pm to 2.30pm and 5pm to 10.30pm; all day at weekends) £2–13: pork satay, marinated chicken, haddock & chips, scampi, steaks
Children: own menu
◊ Ale: Boddington's, Flowers and guests
P Ample

Nr BEDFORD, BEDS

Map 5

Ⓟℝ RED LION, High Street, Elstow
Tel: 01234 359 687

Just south of Bedford. From the A421 take the signs to Elstow Village.

No doubt this was once an unremarkable village pub, its façade marked by its large bay windows. It has been transformed into a spacious family pub and restaurant and offers a children's menu, several high chairs and baby-changing facilities in both of the Ladies' toilet areas. The manager told us that he serves at least 250 children's meals a week.

The pleasant bar, with its large central fireplace, overlooks the street. It is comfortable with its padded benches and settles, and wood and glass screens form booths.

The restaurant is divided into three main areas, although there are alcoves here and there. One area is intended mainly for families with small children, since there is a play area in one corner. Alongside is a much larger dining area, and beyond a garden room with a wall of windows on to the enclosed garden. There is a lawn with many bench tables and a play unit with a safe bark surface. A bouncy castle is also on view during the summer.

✕ (11.30am to 10pm) £2–8: hot mushrooms, vegetable crumble, chicken Balti, haddock & chips, marinated lamb steak
Children: own menu
Ⓞ Ale: Boddington's, Flowers, Castle Eden and guests
Ⓟ Lots

BEELEY, DERBYSHIRE

Map 7

Ⓟ DEVONSHIRE ARMS
Tel: 01629 733 259
On the B6012, north of Matlock.

An absolute beauty of a pub which nestles in a charming village only a couple of miles from Chatsworth House and close to Haddon Hall.

Three cottages were converted in 1741 and the original thick stone walls and mullioned windows remain; with the river meandering by it is a perfect spot.

Neither will you be disappointed inside, since the low ceilings and blackened beams, flagstones and open fires confirm the age of this splendid hostelry. The family room has a few wooden tables and the unusual feature of a stone wishing well; beyond it there is a food and coffee bar, where there is ample space for families since they can also use another room upstairs away from the bar.

....

✖ Bar meals (12pm to 2pm and 7pm to 10pm) £2–9: devilled whitebait, garlic chicken, haddock & chips, Barnsley chop, steak & ale pie
   Children: own menu, half portions
🍺 Ale: Black Sheep, Boddington's, Theakston's and guests
🅿 Own car park

BELBROUGHTON, HEREFORD & WORCS   Map 4
🅿🆁 BELL INN, Bell End
Tel: 01562 730 232
On the A491 between Bromsgrove and Stourbridge.

....

The old brick building is covered with Virginia creeper and inside there are four agreeable rooms clustered around the bar. Families can settle in those away from the bar: one with heavy black ceiling beams, and another with a large stone fireplace, or in a sizeable room with brick walls and ancient cross beams. Bar meals are served, and the two-course Sunday lunch sounds a bargain at £4.95.

The restaurant is in a separate building and its bar is housed in an old barn with a very tall vaulted roof. It is an interesting room with a wood-burning stove at one end. The dining room is more intimate and there is also a conservatory in which you can dine. The Sunday specials are good value at £8.95 and £11.25.

There is a garden on each side of the pub: a small one with a couple of bench tables and a bouncy castle, and a larger lawned garden which has a children's play area.

....

✗ Bar meals (12pm to 2pm and 6pm to 9.30pm) £2–5: cottage pie, lasagne, chicken chasseur, plaice & chips, burgers;
Restaurant (12pm to 2.30pm and 6pm to 10pm) £2–11: cod smokey, fettucine primavera, fish & chips, steaks, sesame chicken
Children: own menu

P Own car park

BELLINGHAM, nr HEXHAM, NORTHUMBERLAND   Map 9
H RIVERDALE HALL HOTEL
Tel: 01434 220 254
On a minor road just west of Bellingham on the north bank of the River Tyne. Bellingham is on the B6320, 16 miles north of Hexham.

....

The core of the hotel is a Victorian country house which overlooks the North Tyne River. It is the nearest hotel to Kielder Water and has recently undergone a major programme of refurbishment. It has excellent facilities which include an indoor swimming pool and a games room.

The owner is a cricket enthusiast and has his own cricket field which also doubles for other sports. There is a putting green, croquet and petanque; you can fish in the adjoining river for salmon and trout and the golf course lies opposite. So sports fans are well catered for. Alternatively you can simply relax in the five acres of garden; from the terrace you have splendid views over the cricket ground to the hills beyond. The same views will also please you from the stately bar, the lounge and the pleasant dining room. The bedrooms are very well turned out and we were impressed by a spacious family room which has a four-poster bed and a single bed.

Nearby: Kielder Water, with its wide variety of water sports, can be enjoyed by the whole family; and the castle is the starting point for many walks and nature trails through the Kielder Forest. To the south you can follow the line of Hadrian's Wall with its chain of forts. Within easy reach you will find Belsay Hall, Wallington House, Cragside House and the ruins of Brinkburn Priory.

✕ Bar snacks (12pm to 2pm) £2–11: garlic mushrooms, steaks, tuna & Brie bake, mixed grill;
Dinner (6.45pm to 9.30pm) £17: devilled whitebait, soup, roast Northumberland lamb, pudding or cheese
Children: own menu, half portions
£ High

✓ Best Bargain Break: £84 per person, 2 nights – dinner, b&b
Children: free up to 5 years; one third of adult rate from 5 to 8; two thirds from 9 to 14 years
Facilities: 3 cots and 2 high chairs; baby-listening system
20 rooms, 5 family
Open all year

⏝ Ale: Ind Coope Burton, Tetley

Ⓟ Own car park

BERKSWELL, WEST MIDLANDS   Map 4
Ⓟℝ THE GEORGE IN THE TREE, **Balsall Common**
Tel: 01676 533 118
On the A452 north of Kenilworth at Balsall Common.

The façade of this extensive pub and restaurant is painted an odd shade of yellow, but it offers good facilities for families in the shape of high chairs, baby-changing facilities, play areas both inside and out, and an eclectic choice of food.

There is plenty of space inside the pub and the restaurant is split into several areas. It has a good atmosphere by dint of the wood panelling, the comfortable furniture (which includes some dressers with books on the shelves) and the cheerful décor. A sizeable play area for young children includes a ball swamp.

The large lawned garden has plenty of bench tables and parasols and is an excellent place to settle on a warm day. There is a children's play unit here, with a safe surface.

✕ (12pm to 2.30pm and 5pm to 10.30pm; weekends 12pm to 10.30pm) £2–13: prawn sundae, three-bean feast, hot chicken salad, steaks, scampi
   Children: own menu
◑ Ale: Boddington's, Flowers
Ⓟ Own car park

BERRYNARBOR, nr ILFRACOMBE, DEVON   **Map 1**
Ⓟ Yᴇ Oʟᴅᴇ Gʟᴏʙᴇ
Tel: 01271 882 465
Off the A399 east of Ilfracombe.

This is a picturesque village of stone cottages, brightly decorated with flowers, which has a handsome church, St Peter's. The pub has been here since 1675 and was probably converted from a row of cottages of an even earlier vintage. It now has pink-washed walls, and the various rooms, which run off the bar, are packed with antiques and curios –

horse brasses and tackle, copper flasks, cases of miniatures, etc. The beamed ceilings and timbered walls testify to the age of the building, and there is a surprising amount of room inside.

The family room is very large, with French windows at one end which open on to the garden. There are plenty of wooden tables and wheel-back chairs, a Wendy House, toys for younger children and books and puzzles for older ones. There is an alternative, smaller family room which has an open fireplace and a few wooden tables. A couple of Christmases ago, we spent several enjoyable lunchtimes here: the beer was excellent and the food of good quality and generously served.

There is a small terrace at the front of the pub and, to the rear, a fairly large enclosed garden with many bench tables on the lawn, and a playhouse. A marvellous array of flowers greets your eyes: dahlias, fuchsias, sweet peas, petunias and many others. We were not surprised to learn that the pub has won its brewery's 'best kept garden' award.

....

✖ (12pm to 2pm and 7pm to 10pm) £2–12: spaghetti Bolognese, Cornish pasty, plaice & chips, steaks, lasagne, pizzas
  Children: own menu, half portions
♉ Ale: Courage Directors, Usher's
Ⓟ Limited, but large public car park nearby

Nr BILLINGSHURST, WEST SUSSEX   Map 3
Ⓟ BLUE SHIP, The Haven
Tel: 01403 822 709

Off the A29 just north of the junction with the A264. There is a sign to The Haven and you should then take the turning to Garlands and Okehurst.

....

This 15th-century pub is a lovely sight with its half-tiled brick walls, and dormer windows above, all festooned with Virginia creeper. There is a timeless look to the place, especially as you see the superb low-ceilinged bar, with a collection of wooden tables, scrubbed white, the old brick floor, and the large inglenook fireplace. There is just a serving hatch, and the beer is served direct from the barrels.

There are a couple of rooms away from the bar where families can sit; one has a pool table and the other is comfortable enough with its various wooden tables.

There is a very large grassy garden at the back of the pub and it includes some swings and a climbing frame for children. From here you will see some of the landlord's Newfoundland dogs. There is more garden alongside the pub, with bench tables and a pretty display of roses, snapdragons and other flowers, plus a small patio at the front.

....

✕ (12pm to 2pm and 7pm to 9.15pm, not Sun or Mon pm) £2–5: scampi, ham & eggs, plaice & chips, cheesy cottage pie, steak & kidney pie
Children: half portions
◔ Ale: King & Barnes
ℙ Own car park

BISHOP'S FROME, HEREFORD & WORCS   **Map 4**
ℙ **GREEN DRAGON INN**
Tel: 01885 490 607
Just off the B4214 north of Ledbury.

....

This is an excellent pub with all the right basic ingredients – a good choice of food and of real ales, which are augmented by guest beers. There are two large bars. Both have beamed ceilings, ancient stone floors and good wooden furniture; one has a huge open stone fireplace and the other a wood-burning stove. They are congenial and relaxing rooms.

The pub has been extended at one end and the sizeable room is in keeping with the rest of the pub. It has various roles: as a pool room, a function room, or a family room, for instance.

Families are also very welcome in the attractive little dining area off the bar. There are half a dozen tables here.

The lawned garden at the rear has a few bench tables and there is a small stretch of garden at the front.

....

�X (12pm to 2pm and 7pm to 9.30pm) £2–10: whitebait, plaice & chips, vegetable curry, cider chicken, venison pie
Children: own menu

◖ Ale: Wadworth's, Tetley, Timothy Taylor's, Robinson's, Wood's and guests

ℙ Own car park

BISHOP'S LYDEARD, SOMERSET　　　　　Map 2
ℙ **BELL INN**
Tel: 01823 432 968
In the village, off the A358 north-west of Taunton. Head for the church.

The lovely garden gives visitors a good introduction to this old pub. It has a terrace with some bench tables and is ringed with bright flowers and greenery. The pub, built in the 15th century, is alongside the ancient village church.

Inside, the stone walls and beamed ceilings give an appealing atmosphere to the place and families are welcome either in the Cellar Bar, which has a pool table and various amusement machines, or in the restaurant area, a lovely bright room on the far side of the lounge bar.

Food is served every day and includes an extensive choice of fresh fish. Sunday lunch is good value and there is an excellent range of real ales.

✗ (12pm to 2pm and 6pm to 10pm) £2–12: devilled whitebait, chicken Kiev, steaks, mixed grill, plaice & chips
Children: own menu, half portions

◖ Ale: Marston's, Golden Hill, Wadworth's, Websters and guests

ℙ Own car park

BLACKBURN, LANCS

Map 8

ℙℝ BODDINGTON ARMS, **Balderstone**

Tel: 01254 813 900

On the A59 at Balderstone and close to Junction 31 of the M6.

A long and low building (next door to another pub), the Boddington Arms comprises a pub, a restaurant and a Lodge Inn with twenty bedrooms. Away from the road there is a central area with some stretches of lawn, and bench tables are set out on a paved terrace.

The long bar area has a series of alcoves opposite, divided from each other by brick and stone walls. Padded settles are covered in cheerful materials; and the open fireplaces contribute to the congenial atmosphere. A line of windows looks over the lawns.

The restaurant area is designed in the same style and is, in effect, a series of rooms with stone walls and low beamed ceilings. There are small cottage-type windows and a big fireplace at one end with a wood-burner.

The pub and restaurant has a very pleasing design and a welcoming atmosphere. There are high chairs, nappy-changing can be done in the disabled toilets, and the restaurant serves food throughout the day on Sunday. The pub is open all day and the restaurant hours are shown below.

✕ (12pm to 2.30pm and 5.30pm to 10.30pm; Sun 12pm to 10pm)
£2–12: Thai chicken, broccoli tempura, sirloin steak, grilled plaice, Mexican bake
Children: own menu
◐ Ale: Boddington's, Flowers
ℙ Ample

BLACKBURN, LANCS   Map 8
Ⓟℝ Spread Eagle Hotel, **Mellor**
Tel: 01254 813 033
North of Blackburn, just off the A6119, at Mellor.

From the garden alongside the pub you can sit and enjoy the most splendid of views – the full sweep of the Ribble Valley to the north. The old stone pub, in its location on the top of a hill, looks towards Blackburn in the other direction and, on a clear day, you can see Blackpool Tower as well.

The Spread Eagle has been extended to become a family pub and restaurant, and there is plenty of space inside. The large open-plan bar has wood panelling on the walls and a smart, Laura Ashley-style wallpaper above, plus a nice brick fireplace. Prints, black-and-white photographs and china plates decorate the walls, and there is a pleasant lounge area at one side with padded settles.

Skylights of coloured glass are a feature of the interior, and there are two dining areas. From the conservatory room, which is wrapped around two sides of the building, you can delight in the views of the undulating countryside.

Families are well looked after here; high chairs are provided and there is a nappy-changing unit. At the back of the pub you will find a terrace and a children's play area.

✖ (11.30am to 10pm) £2–8: fried scampi, chicken masala, sirloin steak, vegetable moussaka, fish pie
   Children: own menu
◑ Ale: Boddington's, Castle Eden, Flowers
Ⓟ Lots

Nr BLACKBURN, LANCS

Map 8

ℙℝ **The Gamecock, Great Harwood**
Tel: 01254 883 719
East of Blackburn, on the A680 at Great Harwood.

....

This handsome stone pub sits by the roadside, a well-proportioned building with black and white cladding on its upper storey.

Inside you will find an open-plan design, with a series of eating areas facing the bar. When the pub was expanded to encompass a family restaurant, an effort was made to maintain the atmosphere of a country inn. Therefore, stone walls, wooden beams, prints, willow-pattern china plates and horse brasses are much in evidence.

The family dining area is a pleasant room, on a different level to the others, with a large stone fireplace. Padded benches line the walls and there is a Fun Factory for the children in a separate room. It has lots of playthings and its own soft drinks bar. High chairs are available in quantity, and there are baby-changing facilities.

....

✕ (11.30am to 10pm) £2–8: onion bhajis, fillet of plaice, Teviotdale pie, lasagne verdi, sirloin steak
  Children: own menu
◖ Ale: Boddington's, Castle Eden, Flowers
ℙ Own car park

BLAKENEY, NORFOLK

Map 6

Ⓗ **Blakeney Hotel, The Quay**
Tel: 01263 740 797
Just off the A149 between Cromer and Wells.

....

This fine old building, made of flint and brick, sits in a marvellous situation overlooking the harbour, which is owned by the National Trust. The rooms are spacious, many of them with lovely views, and the family rooms contain extra bunk beds.

There are excellent facilities for families, beginning with the splendid and sizeable garden, with its smooth lawns. It is beautifully maintained, safely enclosed, and has a children's play area at one end. The games room has a pool table, table tennis and darts, and there is a full-sized snooker table as well (for over-16s only). In addition there is a heated indoor swimming pool, a sauna, a jacuzzi and a fitness room.

The public rooms are comfortable and relaxing and the spacious bar area looks out over the harbour, as does the attractively decorated restaurant.

All in all, this is a very agreeable hotel in a lovely part of the country. One of our readers described it as 'superb all round' and we agree with that summary.

Nearby: Blakeney Point is an area of outstanding natural beauty, over 1000 acres of it, and has a great wealth of bird life. There are two observation hides and a nature trail for children. Holkham Hall, the Norfolk Shire Horse Centre, Felbrigg Hall and the North Norfolk Railway, Blickling Hall and the Norfolk Wildlife Park are all within easy reach. If the area is a paradise for naturalists, so it is for golfers, with Hunstanton, Brancaster and Sheringham close by. Boat hire is easily arranged, as are horse riding and fishing.

✕ Light lunch (12.30pm to 2pm) £2–9: seafood lasagne, Norfolk trout, cold buffet, brochette of lamb;
Dinner (7pm to 9.30pm) £15: game terrine, grilled whole plaice, pudding or cheese
Children: own menu, half portions
£ High
✓ Best Bargain Break: £56 per person per night – dinner, b&b
Children: £5 up to 12 years
Facilities: 8 cots and 4 high chairs; baby-listening system
60 rooms, 6 family
Open all year
⼝ Ale: Courage
Ⓟ Own car park

BLEDINGTON, OXON   **Map 5**
P **KINGS HEAD INN, The Green**
Tel: 01608 658 365
Off the B4450, to the east of Stow-on-the-Wold.

Situated in a charming Cotswold village, this pub is in a marvellous position by the immaculate village green, with its stream and attendant ducks. There are even some swings and a see-saw on the green quite close to the pub and within easy shouting distance of a small garden at the front.

It's a superb 15th-century stone inn, with steep slate roofs; you enter directly into a delightful bar, with black beams and pillars, wooden settles and a big open fireplace at one end. As well as the bar menu, there is a full *à la carte* menu. It is worth a trip for the imaginative food alone, and everything is home-made. Apart from the regular real ales (see below) the guest beers are rotated on a weekly basis.

Families are welcome in the garden room, which is furnished in the same style as the rest of the pub, with wooden tables and chairs, stone-flagged floors, a wooden screen and wooden beams. There is a pleasant atmosphere here, and smoking is forbidden. Doors lead out to the courtyard and the garden.

There are six bedrooms at the Kings Head, all with *en suite* bathrooms.

✕ (12pm to 2pm and 7pm to 9.45pm) £2–6: basil & mozzarella pancake, lasagne, smoked salmon & dill pasta, braised kidneys, casserole of the day
Children: own menu, smaller portions
O Ale: Hook Norton, Stanway, Wadworth's and guests
P Own car park

BLEDLOW, BUCKS   Map 5
P LIONS OF BLEDLOW
Tel: 01844 343 345
Off the B4009 near Chinnor. Look out for West Lane – the pub's at the top of the hill.

The pub is housed in a long and low-slung white 16th-century building, with dormer windows set in a steep roof, and is situated in lovely countryside at the foot of the Chilterns. When the sun shines you might sit on the patch of green which fronts the pub and be quite at peace with the world; and there is also a large garden at the rear.

The interior has all the delightful attributes of a classic English pub: low beamed ceilings, huge open fires, alcoves here and there with padded wooden settles and wooden tables. It's a busy and cheerful place, with a really pubby atmosphere. At one end of the pub there is a sizeable and comfortable family room.

At weekends families have the use of the restaurant.

✕ (12pm to 2pm and 7pm to 9.30pm, not Sun pm) £3–5: steak & kidney & mushroom, spare ribs, salads, fresh mussels and seasonal seafood
Children: own menu, small portions
Ale: Ruddles, Wadworth's, Courage, Gale's and guests
P Own car park

Nr BOLTON, LANCS   Map 8
P R KING WILLIAM IV, Egerton
Tel: 01204 303 484
North of Bolton on the A666.

The road winds steeply upwards towards Turton Moor, and just beyond the Last Drop Village, you will find this fine old stone building, its façade covered in ivy and sparkling with baskets of gay flowers.

The entrance hall, with an adjoining food servery, has stone walls, a sloping wooden ceiling and tall windows. There are some tables here. On a higher level, the restaurant has a heavily beamed ceiling and padded wall-benches. It has a nice central table for eight people.

There is a good pubby atmosphere in the bar, whose semicircular serving counter has four separate areas around it. One has a central stone fireplace with a wood-burning stove, and there are stone walls and brick arches between two of the rooms. Low beams, wooden screens and open fireplaces complete the traditional look – and very pleasant it is too.

Families are made welcome with the provision of high chairs, nappy-changing facilities, and a small enclosed play unit at the side of the pub.

....

✕ (11.30am to 10pm) £2–8: onion bhajis, fish pie, chicken escalopes, tagliatelle carbonara, steak & kidney pie
   Children: own menu
☼ Ale: Boddington's, Castle Eden, Flowers and guests
ℙ Own car park

BOLTON ABBEY, NORTH YORKS   Map 9
Ⓡ Cavendish Pavilion and Tea Rooms
Tel: 01756 710 245
Look for the stone archway in the village and then for the tea rooms sign. You will find the Cavendish Pavilion at the centre of the Bolton Abbey Estate picnic area.

....

In its setting of unrivalled beauty within the bounds of the Bolton Abbey Estate and by the River Wharfe, the Cavendish Pavilion has excellent facilities for the whole family.

It has recently been completely rebuilt but still maintains its general appearance as a pavilion with a terrace under its awnings and plenty of colourful flowers. The interior is designed on a generous scale with plenty of good wooden tables and wicker chairs, a tiled floor, lots of pot plants and a collection of china plates on the walls. There are plenty of high chairs, a children's menu and a new mother and baby room.

On a summer's day it is an idyllic place to have a meal and you can enjoy all the natural beauty of the estate.

....

✕ (10am to 7pm Mar to Oct; open Fri, Sat and Sun in winter until 6pm) £2–10: filled Yorkshire pudding, burger with salad & chips, grilled haddock, savoury pie, fillet steak
Children: own menu, half portions

Ⓟ £2.50 at nearby car park refunded if meal is pre-booked

BORROWDALE, CUMBRIA   Map 8
Ⓗ STAKIS LODORE SWISS
Tel: 017687 77285
On the B5289, south of Keswick.

....

Many of our readers have praised this hotel, which 'nestles close to the shores of Derwentwater and is shadowed by beautiful waterfalls'. These are the words of the manager, and we endorse his excellent description.

It is indeed a splendid hotel: a traditional-looking Cumbrian slate façade gives way to an interior which is modern and very comfortable. The list of facilities on offer for families would be hard to surpass – even by the grandest hotel.

There is an indoor swimming pool, a well-equipped gym and a sauna; the priceless bonus of a supervised nursery with trained nannies from 8am to 6pm each day (and where children's meals are served); a games room; an outdoor play area; and tennis and squash courts.

The hotel actually stands in forty acres of grounds, which include the famous falls, and there are a couple of acres of lawned garden, where several thousand geraniums are planted each year.

The fine, and difficult, balance is struck here between the needs of children, and the comfort and relaxation of adults. One of the compromises is that children under six have their evening meals in the nursery and this leaves the adults and the older children free to enjoy their dinner together at a later hour in the dining room.

To quote one of our readers: 'extremely comfortable, wonderful food, and very friendly staff'. It is a marvellous place to stay.

Nearby: A short drive will take you to the heart of the Lake District – to Grasmere, the Hardknott Roman Fort and the Ravenglass and Eskdale Railway; to Windermere and the Lake District headquarters at Brockhole, where the children can see, amongst many other things, a Beatrix Potter exhibition. Fell Foot Park has all sorts of water sports (as have the other lakes), and the Grizedale Forest Centre is the starting point for many interesting walks.

....

✗ Bar snacks (12pm to 5.30pm) £2–6: hors d'oeuvres, chicken Madras, pizzas, vegetable stir-fry;
  Dinner (7.30pm to 9.30pm) £21: pheasant terrine, soup, noisettes of lamb, pudding or cheese
  Children: own menu
  £ High
✓ Best Bargain Break: £50 per person per night – dinner, b&b
  Children: from £13 to £43 depending on age (includes meals)
  Facilities: 10 cots and 10 high chairs; baby-listening to every room
  70 rooms, 10 family
Ⓟ Own car park

BOURNEMOUTH, DORSET   Map 2
Ⓗ **HINTON FIRS HOTEL, Manor Road, East Cliff**
Tel: 01202 555 409
Follow the signs for East Cliff.

....

This welcoming hotel, built in the late 19th century as a seaside villa, occupies a corner site in the heart of the hotel area of the town, and is just a hundred yards or so from the cliff top. Lifts and paths go down to the beach.

The hotel is in pristine condition and one of its merits is the large amount of space at the guests' disposal: a large and smartly decorated dining room, a very comfortable large lounge which overlooks the garden, a no-smoking television lounge and a very agreeable cocktail bar, rich in colour with padded green furniture.

The facilities are excellent here. There is a heated outdoor pool with a children's play pool in a sheltered spot in the attractive lawned garden, which is enclosed and has some fine trees, a rockery and rhododendron bushes. It is a real sun trap and lunch can be enjoyed on the terrace. Sliding doors lead to the indoor pool, there is also a sauna and spa pool, and the games room has table tennis and a pool table.

Just as the public rooms are spacious and bright, so are the many family rooms, usually equipped with a double and a single bed (every bedroom has its own bathroom). The decorations and furnishings are first class. The annexe also contains two family rooms, including a large family suite which has a double and a single bed in one room and a separate single room.

The Hinton Firs is a very appealing hotel which offers excellent value in a popular holiday area.

Nearby: Apart from the many attractions of Bournemouth itself you have easy access to the rest of Dorset: to Corfe Castle, the Swanage Railway and Durlston Country Park; to Brownsea Island and Merley Bird Gardens, and to Kingston Lacy and Wimborne Minster. A bit further afield you can visit the Tank Museum at Bovington Camp, the Tutankhamun Exhibition, Clouds Hill and Hardy's Cottage.

....

✗ Bar lunch (12.30pm to 2pm) £2–6: grilled plaice, stir-fry rice with vegetables, chicken goujons, ham & turkey pancake, French bread pizza;
Dinner (7pm to 8.30pm) £14: cannelloni Rossini, soup, grilled sirloin steak, dessert & cheese
Children: own menu
£ Medium

✓ Best Bargain Break: £38 per person per night – dinner, b&b
Children: babies free; one third up to 5 years; half price from 5 to 11 years; two thirds over 11 years
Facilities: plenty of cots and high chairs; baby-listening system

52 rooms, 12 family
Open all year
P Own car park

BOURNEMOUTH, DORSET   Map 2
P R THE RIVERSIDE, Tuckton Bridge
Tel: 01202 429 210

On the outskirts of Christchurch. Take the A3059 (off the A35) and head for Southbourne.

The Riverside is a charming building, low-built, with bay windows and a steeply pitched roof with dormer windows; and it has a splendid position by the water at Tuckton Bridge.

Customers can take full advantage of the river views, particularly from the large terrace below the pub. Inside, there are wide windows at one end of the bar, an agreeable room with brick walls and wood panelling. The spacious restaurant also looks out to the water on one side. It is a bright and comfortable area, where smoking is prohibited. At one end there is a children's play area, with things to ride on and climb on and a ball swamp.

Food is served all day and every day, and several high chairs are made available.

✗ (11.30am to 10pm; Sun from 12pm) £2–8: hot mushrooms, chicken Alexandra, steak & kidney pie, marinated lamb steak, haddock & chips
Children: own menu
⊃ Ale: Boddington's, Flowers and guests

BOYDEN GATE, nr CANTERBURY, KENT   Map 3
P THE GATE INN, Marshside
Tel: 01227 860 498

North-east of Canterbury on the minor roads between the A28 and the A299.

....

This attractive building houses a friendly pub with a charming bar with a large open fire. The pub manages to be one of the hubs of local life while still welcoming tourists and families, who are usually very much in evidence in the garden and the family room. All sorts of events are arranged at the pub: from a Burns Night supper to quiz nights, folk evenings, bell-ringing, and all manner of traditional pub games.

It is a relaxing and 'pubby' place and the family room echoes the character of the inn. It has an eccentric collection of odds and ends on the walls, and several easy chairs, books and board games. There is a small and pleasant garden with a river alongside which is home to great numbers of loquacious ducks, geese and chickens.

It is good to report that food is available throughout opening hours; and that this pub was one of the first to receive a 'Heartbeat' award for its menu.

The pub also has a place in sporting history since it was once the home of William Webb Ellis, the founder of rugby union.

....

✗ (12pm to 2pm and 6pm to 9pm) £1–5: ploughman's, vegetarian pie, black pudding, bean & vegetable hotpot, cheese vegeburger
   Children: portions of any size
Ɵ Ale: Shepherd Neame
P Own car park

Nr BRADFORD-ON-AVON, WILTS   Map 2
Ⓗ **WOOLLEY GRANGE**
Tel: 01225 864 705
At Woolley Green, off the B3105 north-east of Bradford-on-Avon.

This 17th-century manor house is an engaging sight, built as it is from a warm-looking limestone and with its pointed gables and tall chimneys. It was a family home for several hundred years until Mr and Mrs Chapman adapted it a couple of years back as a country house hotel. Style is the keynote from the moment you step into the wood-panelled hall with its patterned plaster ceiling and comfortable chairs and sofas.

The original décor is maintained in the sitting rooms and the attractive dining room; the Long Room, which is part library, part television room and part games room, is a delight. So are the bedrooms, which are all differently furnished and decorated but in every case reflect the owners' wishes to provide their guests with comfortable and elegant surroundings.

The huge Victorian conservatory, with its excellent cane furniture, is a lovely place to sit over coffee or something stronger. Outside, there are stretches of garden and a stone-paved terrace where you can have alfresco meals. Through a gate, you will find a heated swimming pool, a croquet lawn in an enclosed area, two grass tennis courts (by this year more all-weather courts will have been added), and a badminton court. There are fourteen acres of garden in which to relax, and children can enjoy the 'Bear Garden', which has swings, a slide, a climbing frame and a small enclosed football pitch. As well as the Moulton bicycles provided at the hotel, guests can try an authentic Indian trishaw.

Amid all these comforts and excellent facilities it has been remembered that many adults have young children who also have to be cared for. This is done with a will, too. There are plenty of cots and high chairs and certain rooms are interconnecting and can form family suites.

Woolley Bear's Den occupies a large barn and is packed with Little Tikes toys and games for younger children; there is also a pool table, table tennis and table football for older children. A nanny is in attendance every day (from 10am to 6pm) and the children can be fed in the nursery off the playroom; lunch is at noon and tea at 5pm. What a boon for parents, who can enjoy their food in peace!

The hotel has a notably good chef and the same attention to detail goes into the buying of the raw ingredients for the dining room. The hotel has a two-acre kitchen garden which provides the fruit and vegetables.

This is a really splendid hotel which provides marvellous facilities, and a proper welcome, for all the family. It well deserved its 1992 'Parent Friendly' Award.

Nearby: If you can tear yourself away from the comforts of Woolley Grange there is a range of places to visit. The beautiful city of Bath is very close, as are Corsham Court, Sheldon Manor, Lacock Abbey and Bowood House, which has a wonderful adventure playground. Longleat Safari Park is also within reach, with Stourhead a little further south. Riding and clay pigeon shooting can be arranged and the hotel provides bicycles and local maps to guide you. The route along the Kennet and Avon Canal is recommended.

....

✗ Terrace menu (12pm to 3pm and 7pm to 10pm) £4–12: chicken & vegetable stir-fry, smoked salmon, hamburger, griddled fish & salad; Dinner (7pm to 10pm) £28: seared scallops with pea purée, roast pigeon, rhubarb & orange crème brûlée or farmhouse cheeses

Children: own menu
£ High
✓ Best Bargain Break: £58 per person per night – dinner, b&b
Children: free
Facilities: 15 cots and 12 high chairs; baby-listening system; nursery
with a nanny
20 rooms, 8 family, 5 sets interconnecting
Open all year
P Own car park

BRAITHWAITE, nr KESWICK, CUMBRIA   Map 8
Ⓗ COLEDALE INN
Tel: 017687 78272
Just off the A66 at the top of Braithwaite village.

Set snugly up a small hill, towards the top of this picturesque
village, you will find the Coledale Inn, which is a small country
hotel and pub. It was built in the early 19th century as a woollen
mill, became a pencil mill and was then converted to an inn.
The building commands superb views of Skiddaw at the front,
while to the rear, the panoramic Grisdale Pike rises steeply into
the sky.

It is a particularly welcoming pub with two roomy bars and an
attractive dining room, nicely decorated, and with a bay window which
overlooks the garden. Families are made very welcome and the adults
will find an excellent choice of real ales.

The bedrooms are all very well furnished indeed with the sort
of facilities you would normally associate with more pretentious
establishments. The family rooms, three of them with a double
and a single bed, and one with a double bed and bunk beds for
children, are spacious and well organized. Upstairs, there is also a very
smart residents' lounge with a splendid Victorian fireplace. Scattered
through the hotel you will find plenty of Victorian prints, furnishings
and antiques.

Apart from the other normal hotel facilities, guests also have the bonus of two convivial bars at their disposal which serve real ale and a good range of meals and bar snacks. There is also a children's menu.

There is an attractive garden with colourful shrubberies and lawns and bench seats and tables where you can take your ease in fine weather. If you fancy more active pursuits, the proprietor can offer membership of the nearby tennis and bowls club.

Nearby: The wonderful Lakes scenery is all around you and Keswick is well worth a visit for its interesting shops and other attractions. The birthplace of William Wordsworth is very close and the many sights of the Lake District lie to the south: Grasmere and Windermere, the Grizedale Forest, Fell Foot Park, Brantwood and so on.

....

✗ Bar snacks (12pm to 2pm and 6.30pm to 9pm) £2–19: filled baked potatoes, Cumberland sausage, scampi, steaks;
Dinner (6.30pm to 9pm) £10: smoked mackerel, chicken Kiev, pudding or cheese
Children: own menu, half portions
£ Medium
✓ Best Bargain Break: £54 per person, 3 nights – b&b
Children: under 4s £5; half price thereafter
Facilities: 2 cots and 2 high chairs
12 rooms, 4 family
Open all year
☺ Ale: Coledale XXPS, Jennings, Yates, Younger's
Ⓟ Own car park

BRANSCOMBE, nr SEATON, DEVON   **Map 1**
Ⓗ **THE BULSTONE, Higher Bulstone**
Tel: 01297 680 446

Off the A3052. Turn at the junction called Branscombe Cross. It is signposted to Bulstone.

We continue to receive highly favourable reports of this hotel, which is run specifically for families by the charming and indefatigable Mr and Mrs Freeman. When we called in at the tail end of the season a year or two ago, the hotel looked in pristine condition.

The hotel has been extended and the new stone walls fit in very well with the rest of the building, part of which dates back to the 16th century. The delightful sitting room with its fine fireplace testifies to the age of the original building – this is the only room which is for adults only.

The children have a large play room of their own and it is very well provided with toys and games, including a very snazzy (and robust) Lego table. The garden has loads of space for children to play and they can help to look after the chickens, the cats and Barney the rabbit. A large grassy play area contains slides, climbing frames, a sandpit, and a football net; the nature garden, in the paddock and part of the orchard, is now established. This is a long-term project to attract the local wildlife into the grounds.

There is a pleasant conservatory in which to sit, and parents on holiday will be glad of the laundry room and the well-equipped kitchen in which they can prepare drinks or snacks. Glad, too, of the way the family rooms are designed with separate bedrooms for the children.

Everything at this hotel is geared to the needs of families on holiday and this includes the provision of a cot for every room in the hotel and as many high chairs as could be required. It's a superb family hotel, which offers remarkable value, and makes you realize how poorly equipped are most other hotels to cope with the needs of families.

The food here is always made from fresh local produce; and artificial flavourings and colourings are avoided. The children have their high teas between 4.45 and 5.30pm, so that the adults can enjoy their meals together later.

Nearby: The sea is very close with pleasant beaches, although some have pebbles underfoot. There is, however, a sandy beach at Sidmouth. It is a delightful part of the world with many benefits for holiday makers: the Donkey Sanctuary near Sidmouth, the Farway Country Park, Bicton Park, Killerton House, the nature reserve at Dawlish Warren, Castle Drogo, Powderham Castle, Pecorama and Crealy Working Farm are all an easy drive away.

....

✕ Dinner (7.45pm to 8.45pm) £13: devilled avocado, beef Stroganoff, pudding or cheese
   Children: own menu
   £ Low
✓ Best Bargain Break: £125 per family, 2 nights – dinner, b&b
   Children: free up to 12 years
   Facilities: 12 cots and 8 high chairs; baby-listening system
   13 rooms, all family
   Closed mid-Nov to mid-Feb
   No credit cards accepted
🍺 Ale: Branoc
🅿 Own car park

BRETFORTON, HEREFORD & WORCS   Map 4
🅿 **THE FLEECE**
Tel: 01386 831 173
In the centre of the village off the B4035 east of Evesham.

....

This is one of our favourite pubs, a gem of a medieval building, which started life as a farmhouse, became an inn in 1848, and was left to the National Trust by Lola Taplin, who ran the pub for over thirty years. Her bequest stipulated that there should be no crisps, music, fruit machines, pool tables, or advertisements: a lady of great taste and perception! It is beautifully furnished throughout with old oak tables, high-backed settles, dressers, brass and copper pub measures and so on.

Families are welcome in a room next to the servery; this houses a superb collection of pewter, which dates from the Cromwellian period and may indeed have been left there by the infamous Oliver.

There is a very large garden with a swing, a climbing frame, and a log Wendy House. There are tables and benches to seat up to sixty people.

At weekends, if the weather is kind, a barbecue is set up in the garden; and this is supplemented by a salad bar in the restored barn. Prices range from £1 to £4. There is a beer festival in mid-July and Morris dancers visit on most Sundays.

....

✕ (12pm to 2pm and 7pm to 9pm, not Mon pm) £1–6: gammon steak, plaice & chips, Gloucester sausages & chips, steak & kidney pie
   Children: own menu
◑ Ale: Everard's, Uley and guests
ℙ In village square

BRIGHTON, EAST SUSSEX   **Map 3**
ℝ **Browns Restaurant, 3/4 Duke Street**
Tel: 01273 323 501
On the western side of The Lanes, not far from the Old Ship Hotel.

....

This is very much in the same style as their Cambridge and Oxford restaurants (qv) and is a busy, gregarious place in the centre of a seaside town which continues to retain its charm and style.

The restaurant serves an excellent range of food, with the emphasis on pastas, salads and grills. We have invariably enjoyed our meals here, as well as the lively atmosphere. Families are well cared for: for example, there were over half a dozen high chairs at the last count; the toilet area is spacious and a pull-down shelf has been installed in the Ladies.

....

✕ (11am to 11.30pm; Sun from 12pm) £2–11: pasta with various sauces, fisherman's pie, sirloin steak, burgers, poached salmon
   Children: own menu, half portions

Closed at Christmas
P Multi-storey nearby

Nr BRIGHTON, EAST SUSSEX   Map 3
P R DEVIL'S DYKE, **Poynings**
Tel: 01273 857 256
North of Brighton off the A23. Follow the signs for Devil's Dyke.

Follow your nose right up to the top of the hill and you will be rewarded by fantastic views over miles of Sussex countryside; and there is the bonus of being able to watch the hang-gliders launch themselves, foolhardy souls, into space.

This family pub and restaurant was built about five years ago and is an extremely popular spot – especially at weekends. It's a huge place, with windows on all sides to take advantage of the wonderful views. It's cheerful and bustling, with Laura Ashley wallpaper, wooden pillars, padded benches, lots of prints on the walls, alcoves here and there to induce a feeling of intimacy and a long curved bar which has a selection of real ales.

The pub is firmly aimed at the family market – there are a dozen or more high chairs, a mother and baby room and an indoor play area. On a fine day you can sit on the paved terrace or the grass outside and luxuriate in the rolling expanse of countryside below you.

X (11.30am to 10pm) £2–8: oriental prawns, haddock & chips, steak & kidney pie, chicken Alexandra, vegetable crumble
   Children: own menu
O Ale: Boddington's, Flowers and guests
P Lots

BRISTOL, AVON   Map 2
Ⓗ Aztec Hotel, Almondsbury
Tel: 01454 201 090
Close to Junction 16 of the M5 on the Aztec West business park.

Located close to both the M5 and the M4, this hotel is convenient
to the city of Bristol and the splendid countryside of the surrounding
area. Ostensibly a modern business hotel, situated on the outskirts of
a technology business park, the management and staff are more than
welcoming to families. On arrival all children are given an activity pack
and there are special children's packages during holiday periods.

The rooms at the Aztec are large and generously furnished, with *en
suite* bathroom facilities second to none. You may even find large, ornate
four-poster beds in some of the executive-style family suites.

The food reaches a high standard and you may dine in the
Quarterjacks restaurant. It is constructed from 200-year-old oak beams
taken from Lancashire mills and is designed to resemble a light and airy
barn. This restaurant overlooks two stone terraces where you can sit if the
weather is kind. These in turn overlook some attractive landscaped gardens in the middle of which is a small lake with a cascading waterfall.

Within the hotel there is a comprehensive leisure complex, complete
with swimming pool, whirlpool, sauna, gymnasium, solarium, squash
courts, steam room and snooker room. It should be noted that the pool
is supervised at all times by competent lifeguards. The hotel also has its
own pub, The Black Sheep, a spacious and open-plan place with its
own terrace; food is served morning and evening.

Those planning to tour the surrounding area will find this hotel an
extremely comfortable and well-appointed base.

Nearby: Bristol itself is a lively city with many attractions, including
a zoo, the Exploratory and the Harbour Museums, where you can see
Brunel's great ship, the *Great Britain*. The delights of Bath are close,
as is the nature reserve at Chew Valley Lake and Dyrham Park. A little
further afield you will find the Westonbirt Arboretum, Berkeley Castle,
Cheddar Gorge, and Wookey Hole Caves.

✕ Lunch (12.30pm to 2pm; not Sat) £16: carvery;
  Dinner (7.30pm to 9.45pm) £20: crab & avocado gratin, escalope
  of pork, pudding or cheese
  Children: own menu, half portions
  £ High
✓ Best Bargain Break: £57 per person, per night – dinner, b&b
  Children: free up to 16 years
  Facilities: 4 cots, 4 high chairs; baby-listening system
  109 rooms, 13 family
  Open all year
◯ Ale: Thwaites
Ⓟ Own car park

BRISTOL, AVON   **Map 2**
Ⓡ **BROWNS RESTAURANT, 38 Queens Road**
Tel: 0117 930 4777
Next to the Bristol Museum and opposite the triangle.

This is the most recent offspring of the excellent Browns chain (there
are others in Brighton, Cambridge and Oxford, qv) and it is housed in
a wonderful and stately building which began life as the town library
and then became the Students' Union refectory. There are tables on
the terraces at the front among the substantial stone pillars and inside
you will find a huge high-ceilinged room with tables set out on two
different levels.

Plenty of space is left around a long wooden bar and there are alcoves
here and there, one with padded benches and Lloyd Loom chairs.
The main restaurant has ceiling fans, wide windows, a profusion of
potted plants and nice wooden furniture. It is a lively place, with
youthful and cheerful staff, and it offers an excellent range of food
at reasonable prices.

Families are made very welcome and there are plenty of high chairs,
a children's menu and a well-equipped mother and baby room.

✗ (11am to 11.30pm; Sun from 12pm) £2–11: Caesar salad, pasta with various sauces, fisherman's pie, roast pork ribs, fresh vegetable bake
Children: own menu, half portions

P Meters or public car parks

BROCKENHURST, HANTS   Map 3
H WATERSPLASH HOTEL, The Rise
Tel: 01590 622 344
On the B3055.

....

This hotel is situated in a quiet road, and the various extensions do not hide the original Victorian building with its high roofs and dormer windows. The elegant dining room overlooks the garden, as does the welcoming lounge bar; another comfortable lounge, with a bay window, is nearby.

The family bedrooms (usually with a double and two single beds) are at the top of the house and have the benefit of plenty of space. With their sloping ceilings and wide dormer windows, they are light and bright and furnished in an appealing style.

The large gardens are sheltered by mature trees and are beautifully kept. The sizeable heated outdoor swimming pool has a terrace with picnic tables and is located by the kitchen garden, which supplies fresh fruit and vegetables for the hotel, and there is a children's play area. Other facilities include a games room with a snooker table; and a cards and board games area can be used by guests.

The Watersplash is an excellent family hotel in a most attractive area of the country.

Nearby: This is the heart of the New Forest, with beautiful countryside and pleasant villages all around; a lovely place to walk and browse. There are many places to visit within easy reach: the famous motor museum and stately home at Beaulieu, the Bucklers Hard Maritime Museum, the New Forest Butterfly Farm, the Bolderwood Arboretum with its delightful walks, Paultons Park which offers splendid entertainment for families, and Broadlands, the home of Palmerston and later of Lord Mountbatten. In addition, there are some excellent sandy beaches less than half an hour's drive away.

....

✗ Bar snacks (12pm to 2pm) £2–5: scampi & chips, fried chicken & chips, ploughman's, filled baked potatoes;
Dinner (7.30pm to 8.30pm) £17: home-made soup, fresh local duckling, pudding and cheese
Children: high teas, half portions
£ High

✓ Best Bargain Break: £80 per person, 2 nights – dinner, b&b
Children: cots free; one third of adult rate from 4 to 10 years; half the adult rate from 10 to 16 years
Facilities: 3 cots and 3 high chairs; baby-listening to all rooms
23 rooms, 5 family
Open all year

ℙ Own car park

BROSELEY, SHROPSHIRE   Map 4
Ⓗ CUMBERLAND HOTEL, Jackson Avenue
Tel: 01952 882 301
On the B4373 – look for the sign to the hotel.

....

You would be hard pushed to find more charming examples of 18th-century architecture than the two buildings which comprise the Cumberland Hotel. It is a pleasant shock to find them – just off a main road through the town – and realize just how peaceful the hotel is.

The main building was extended in Victorian times and has a couple of bars on the ground floor, where you will always find a good choice of real ales. The dining room is attractively decorated and is notable for its collection of Coalport china. At the front there is a large lawned garden, a peaceful place with lots of flowers.

The annexe is another superb Georgian building which has a direct connection with the Industrial Revolution. It was at a meeting here in

1775 that the decision was taken to build the famous Iron Bridge. It also has a delightful and tranquil garden.

The bedrooms are comfortable and quiet and very nicely decorated, and most of them overlook the various gardens. This is a really excellent hotel which offers value for money to families.

Next to the annexe there is a small two-bedroomed cottage which can be used for self-catering, or for bed and breakfast or full board at the hotel. Part of a terrace of stone cottages, it has central heating, a large and comfortably furnished lounge and two large, twin-bedded bedrooms on the first floor with ample room for cots.

Nearby: It is a good spot if you wish to visit Ironbridge, which has a marvellous museum. The exhibits are spread over six sites, including the Museum of Iron, the Coalport China Museum, the Jackfield Tile Museum, and so on. South Shropshire is a delightful area, and there are many other attractions, including the Midland Motor Museum, the Severn Valley Railway, Carding Mill Valley and Wilderhope Manor.

....

✘ Bar meals (11am to 2pm and 6.30pm to 9.30pm) £2–4: fennel goulash, vegetable Stroganoff, mixed grill, smoked haddock pasta, chicken & ham crumble;
Dinner (6.30pm to 9.30pm) £11: chilled melon, rump steak, pudding or cheese
Children: own menu, half portions
£ Low
No Bargain Breaks
Children: £5 approx.
Facilities: 3 cots and 2 high chairs; baby-listening system
14 rooms, 3 family
Open all year
◐ Ale: Ruddles, Bass (also mild)
🅿 Own car park

BROXBOURNE, HERTS   Map 5
P R THE CROWN, Old Nazing Road
Tel: 01992 462 244

Very close to Broxbourne station: left out of the station, first right.

This ancient public house is adjacent to Lee Valley Leisure Centre, which offers many pleasures, such as the Paradise Wild Life Park, the boating centre, fishing and river trips. It is a delightful inn with Victorian-style décor and tiled fireplaces. There are plans to develop the restaurant with an open grill and to extend the play rooms for children.

Changing facilities are available in the ladies' toilet, and five high chairs are provided. There is a children's menu and specials for the under-sevens.

There is a large tree-filled riverside garden with an attractive children's play area which offers a bouncy castle, slides, climbs and rides. There are family benches and arbours where barbecues are held in summer.

✗ (12pm to 2pm and 6pm to 10.30pm) £2–11: garlic prawns, sesame chicken, steaks, fish & chips, cashew nut paella
   Children: own menu
◐ Ale: Bass, Stone's
P Ample

BROXBOURNE, HERTS   Map 5
P R NEW RIVER ARMS, High Road, Turnford
Tel: 01992 462 807

Off the A10 south of Broxbourne. Turn off for Turnford and it is near the Hertford Regional College.

The New River Arms stands on a main junction, and there has long been an inn on this site. Celebrating its closeness to the river and to farmland, the pub is decorated with the bows of boats and with agricultural implements. There are secluded alcoves lined with books which give a feeling of welcome and comfort.

Children have ample space within the pub, but they are not allowed in the bar area. There is a separate mother and baby room, and the restaurant has five high chairs. There is a special children's menu, and food from the bar may be had at any time. The garden is pleasant, with family benches and a children's play area with slides.

✕ (12pm to 2.30pm and 5pm to 10.30pm; weekends 12pm to 10.30pm) £2–13: prawn sundae, steaks, chicken tikka masala, seafood tagliatelle, beef & Boddington's pie
   Children: own menu
☞ Ale: Boddington's, Tetley
Ⓟ Ample

BUCKFASTLEIGH, DEVON   Map 1
Ⓡ BUCKFAST ABBEY
Tel: 01364 642 519
Just off the A38 between Exeter and Plymouth. Follow the brown signs.

This Benedictine monastery was originally founded early in the 11th century but foundered after Henry VIII's dissolution of the monasteries in 1539. Several monks took it upon themselves to rebuild it and started work in 1907. They finished in 1938.

The building is a monument to their devotion, and some of its notable features are the mosaic floors, the stained-glass windows and the remarkable high altar. In the crypt, there is an exhibition which traces the history of the Abbey, and there are concerts every month.

Families are well catered for, especially in the restaurant, the Grange. The self-service area is bright and airy under a high dome, and all the food is freshly made on the spot. The dining room is also spacious and appealing, with its high, curved ceiling and its glass wall. Doors lead to a delightful stone terrace, where there are plenty of bench tables. Whether indoors or outdoors, you will have splendid views of the gardens and of the great Abbey itself.

The well-equipped mother and baby room, close to the entrance, has a changing table and chairs, and there are several high chairs in the restaurant.

....

✕ (9am to 5pm, Easter to Oct; otherwise 10am to 4pm) £2–5: soup, steak pie, lamb hotpot, lasagne, chicken chasseur

Children: own menu

Ⓟ Ample

BURNSALL, nr SKIPTON, NORTH YORKS   **Map 9**

Ⓟ RED LION HOTEL

Tel: 01756 720 204

On the B6160, in the centre of the village.

....

A wonderfully traditional old inn set in one of the classic Yorkshire Dales villages. Dating from the mid-17th century, this old building enjoys a perfect setting only a stone's throw from the attractive village green which goes down to the River Wharfe. With the magnificent Burnsall Fell and the rolling Dales countryside as a backdrop, it's a perfect spot in which to spend a few hours.

The pub is geared up to cater for its many tourists and you will find a comprehensive bar snack menu plus lunch and dinner menus, which always include a choice of fresh fish; there is a good range of wines, too. Several high chairs are made available.

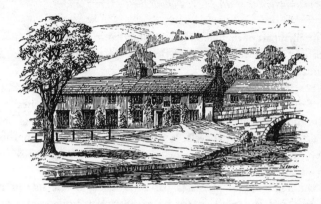

There are two rooms where families may sit; a small room just across from the main bar or up some stairs a larger room which is furnished in attractive style. It was originally an old barn and some of the stonework has been retained. It has plenty of tables with comfortable chairs to match, and overlooks the garden, which comprises a terrace, a rockery and a patch of lawn. There are other stretches of lawn alongside the peaceful river, and you can also sit on the cobbled forecourt at the front of the pub.

....

✗ (12pm to 2.30pm and 6pm to 9.30pm) £3–9: smoked chicken & avocado salad, steak & kidney pie, Cumberland sausage with red cabbage, supreme of salmon, sirloin steak
   Children: half portions
◗ Ale: Theakston's, Tetley's and guests
ℙ Own car park

BURSLEDON, nr SOUTHAMPTON, HANTS Map 3
P R **WINDHOVER MANOR**
Tel: 01703 403 500
Close to Junction 8 of the M27. Follow the signs to Hamble.

....

The original part of the building is a grand, half-timbered manor house which was once owned by one of Britain's great aviation pioneers, Sir Edwin Alliott Verdon Roe.

It now houses a very large pub and restaurant. The sunroom was part of the old building and is a very pleasant spot to have a meal. Off the sunroom, the ground floor is broken up into a number of areas and alcoves on different levels. It is pleasantly decorated with Laura Ashley-style wallpaper, wood panelling, a beamed ceiling and screens of wood and coloured glass.

A children's indoor play area has been made to one side of the restaurant and is complemented by a substantial outdoor play unit with slides and swings. A pretty stretch of lawned garden is shaded by mature trees.

There are high chairs in numbers and a baby-changing facility. The pub serves food throughout the day.

....

✗ (11.30am to 10pm; Sun from 12pm) £2–8: oriental prawns, chicken Balti, steak, Teviotdale pie, vegetable crumble
   Children: own menu
◑ Ale: Boddington's, Flowers and guests

BYWORTH, WEST SUSSEX Map 3
P **BLACK HORSE**
Tel: 01798 342 424
Close to Petworth – look for the sign off the A283.

....

This fine old pub was built on the site of an ancient friary and has a charming tall brick front. Inside, the overwhelming impression is of wood: wooden floors, scrubbed wooden tables of varying shapes and sizes, and black pillars and beams. The interior has great charm because it has not been messed about.

Families are welcome to use the three interconnecting rooms at the rear of the pub, a delightful spot which is primarily intended for eating and where an enterprising range of food is available seven days a week and includes a Sunday lunch for under £6. The menu changes every two months.

The garden is also a lovely spot to spend some time. Little verandas and grassy areas go in steps down a slope (keep a wary eye on young children here) and you look across a valley to the woodlands beyond. At the bottom of the hill is a large lawned area.

The pub is only a mile or so from Petworth House with its magnificent collection of paintings by Turner, Van Dyck, Holbein, Rembrandt, Gainsborough et al., and is a good place to repair to after the rigours of sightseeing.

....

✗ (11.30am to 1.45pm and 6pm to 9.45pm) £2–10: spicy crab pot, Stilton & onion bake, lemon sole, braised steak Bordelaise, roast rack of lamb

☊ Ale: Young's, Ballard's, Eldridge Pope and guests

Ⓟ Own car park

CADEBY, SOUTH YORKS   **Map 7**
Ⓟ **CADEBY INN**
Tel: 01709 864 009
Off the A630 between Rotherham and Doncaster.

....

Be careful you don't drive past this former farmhouse because at first glance, surrounded by outbuildings, it looks as though matters agricultural are still its prime concern. However, on closer inspection the long lawn with tables and chairs leading up to the front door and the swing in the garden give a clue that this is a pub geared to families.

Inside you could spend so long looking at the walls, you might run out of time to order. All sorts of things, from mounted fish to cricket caps, are on display.

The family room is simple and cheerful (and a no-smoking area), and an added bonus is that there is ample space in the Ladies to change a baby.

The carvery offers excellent value and the Sunday lunch for around £5 is extremely popular.

....

✘ (12pm to 2pm and 6pm to 10pm) £1–7: gammon steak, half chicken, Cumberland sausage, seafood platter
   Children: own menu and half portions
◖ Ale: varying range
Ⓟ Own car park

CAMBRIDGE, CAMBS   Map 6
ⓅⓇ THE TRAVELLERS REST, Huntingdon Road
Tel: 01223 276 182
On the A14 north from Cambridge to Huntingdon. The Travellers Rest is on the left, on the outskirts of Cambridge before Girton.

....

The Travellers Rest occupies a site where once stood a coaching inn, and that past era is celebrated in the recent refurbishment. A green phaeton is set nobly on a ledge above the diners, and agricultural implements provide pleasing decoration.

The restaurant is open all day on Saturdays and Sundays, and is a spacious place constructed on different levels and with a number of secluded alcoves. Children are welcome anywhere in the restaurant, but an area on a higher level is reserved for smokers. The large car park at the rear of the building is decorated with trees, flowers and shrubs, and this attractive setting is carried into the patio area where there are family benches and a children's playground which is fenced for safety. A rocking panda and a springing duck complement the slides and climbs.

Five high chairs and booster seats are available, and cushions are also provided for the young diner, who has various options from which to choose his or her meal. Baby food is offered free for those under 15 months, and there are nappy-changing facilities in the ladies' toilet.

....

✕ (12pm to 2.30pm and 5pm to 10.30pm) £2–13: pork satay, rump steak, seafood tagliatelle, ocean bake, Indonesian chicken
   Children: own menu
◗ Ale: Boddington's and guests
🅿 Lots

CAMBRIDGE, CAMBS   Map 6
Ⓡ **BROWNS, 23 Trumpington Street**
Tel: 01223 461 655
In the town centre.

....

Part of a small chain of restaurants (see the entries for Bristol, Oxford and Brighton), this is a huge building opposite the Fitzwilliam Museum. We were told that it was once the casualty department of the old Addenbrookes Hospital. It has the familiar and effective décor of cream walls, bentwood chairs, overhead fans, Edwardian mirrors and converted gas lights.

It is a cheerful place which offers an excellent range of food to suit most palates, including young ones. If you need to change a baby there is a mother and baby room with good facilities and there are plenty of high chairs.

We should warn you that parking is difficult in Cambridge, as it is, strangely, in Oxford. So it is best to park your car in a public car park and enjoy the sights on foot.

....

✗ (11am to 11.30pm; Sun from 12pm) £2–11: steak & mushroom & Guinness pie, toasted olive bread with sun-dried tomatoes, pasta with various sauces, roast pork ribs, fisherman's pie
   Children: own menu, half portions

ℙ Meters and own car park

CAMBRIDGE, CAMBS   Map 6
ℝ HOBBS PAVILION RESTAURANT, **Park Terrace**
Tel: 01223 367 480
On Parker's Piece, and alongside the University Arms Hotel.

....

The restaurant is housed in a brick pavilion which was opened by Jack Hobbs himself in 1930 and faces Parker's Piece where the maestro learned his cricket. Its origins are clearly apparent inside and, under its high ceiling, the restaurant is attractively furnished with pine tables, a dresser and old advertising signs (Wills's Gold Flake, Kops Crisps, Sunlight Soap, etc).

The back room is just as appealing, and especially so to cricket lovers, with its photographs of pre-war cricketers, cigarette cards of cricketers and portraits of Ranjit Sinjhi and of Hobbs, whose career is encapsulated on a wooden plaque.

Amid such sporting nostalgia one must remember that this is a restaurant. You can eat salads and soup but it concentrates on a very full range of pancakes, savoury and sweet. The fixed-price menu at just under £10 for three courses is excellent value, or you can have two courses at lunchtime for under £6. All the food is made, on site, by the owners, and includes a vegan menu; even the ice cream is home-made and, as well as the ever-popular vanilla, includes flavours such as white chocolate, and honey and lavender. The owners, Stephen and Susan Hill, told us that they served their 150,000th pancake on Shrove Tuesday 1994.

There is a small terrace outside with a few tables, and children have the whole of Parker's Piece on which to romp – the perimeter measures nearly a mile. The restaurant has some lavatories and a baby might be attended to there.

....

✖ (Tues to Sat 12pm to 2.15pm and 7pm to 9.45pm; Thurs dinner starts 8.30pm) £3–8: pancakes – Dijon chicken, black pudding & mash & apple, hot chillied lamb, cyclists (steak, mash, spinach and egg), maple syrup, etc
　　Children: own menu, half portions
　　Closed mid-Aug to mid-Sept, Christmas and Easter, Sun and Mon
　　No credit cards accepted
Ⓟ Not easy, mostly street parking

Nr CAMBRIDGE, CAMBS　　　　　　　　　　　**Map 6**
ⓅⓇ THE GREEN MAN, 55 High Street, Trumpington
Tel: 01223 844903
On the southern outskirts of Cambridge, and close to Junction 11 of the M11.

....

Number 55 High Street, Trumpington, is a listed building, for it is one of the oldest in Cambridge. The front entrance leads into the bar, and some of the original beams, very low, remain. From the bar one walks through to the extension at the rear, a splendid restaurant area with open grill. It is a wonderfully attractive barn-like structure on two levels. Its decoration is all related to the local area, and the university and student community is honoured by the number of bicycles that hang from the ceiling, a witty and warm reminder.

There are admirable facilities for children, with ten high chairs available as well as booster seats, and there is a toilet for the disabled and a baby changing room which can be used by either sex. There are several food options for children, and the garden has family benches, springy animals and an excellent play area.

The Green Man has a children's licence so that children may go anywhere in the pub except close to the fruit machines. Opening hours are from 11 to 11, and food is available for most of the day.

....

- ✗ (12pm to 10.30pm) £2–11: prawn sundae, steaks, chicken tikka masala, seafood tagliatelle, beef & Boddington's pie
  Children: own menu
- ⌂ Ale: Boddington's, Flowers, Marston's
- Ⓟ Ample

Nr CAMBRIDGE, CAMBS   **Map 6**
ⓅⓇ **THE PLOUGH, Fen Ditton**
Tel: 01223 293 264
Off the B1047 by the river.

....

The Plough has an idyllic position by the River Cam and from the terrace and the large, grassy garden you can enjoy the peace and tranquillity of the scene. The occasional college boat will row by and you can glance up from your refreshments to check their style.

The pub is now a part of the Brewers Fayre chain, and a fine range of facilities is offered for the family. High chairs are made available, there is a splendid high-tech play unit in the garden, a little playpen with toys and a blackboard in the eating area and space to change babies in the toilet areas. A play leader is in attendance during several afternoons a week and will keep the children amused while the adults relax.

The open-plan bar and restaurant has been designed on two levels and there are good views of the river and the gardens from the wide windows. It is a comfortable and well-organized place, attractively furnished and decorated, and has the great merit of offering reasonably priced food and a good choice of real ales.

✕ (11.30am to 10pm; Sun from 12pm) £2–8: hot mushrooms, fish pie, sirloin steak, vegetable crumble, chicken Alexandra
Children: own menu
◯ Ale: Boddington's, Flowers and guests
Ⓟ Lots

CANNINGTON, SOMERSET   Map 2
Ⓟ Malt Shovel Inn, Bradley Green
Tel: 01278 653 432
Just off the A39 west of Bridgwater. Look for the sign (to Bradley Green).

This friendly and unpretentious country pub has an appealing atmosphere, with wooden tables and settles under the low wooden beams, cream-painted stone walls, on which are hung photographs of the Bridgwater Canal, some window seats and a wood-burning stove.

The three bars provide plenty of space, and families are welcome to use a room separated from the main bar. It has several tables and is furnished and decorated in the same agreeable style as the rest of the pub. A high chair is available and there is a good choice of food.

From the family room you can stroll into the large garden. There is a paved patio and lots of lawn, edged by beds of flowers. From here you have views of the distant Quantock Hills.

There are four bedrooms here, one of which is a family room with a double and two single beds.

....

✗ (12pm to 2pm and 7pm to 9.30pm) £1–9: fisherman's pie, steaks, smoked haddock cheesy bake, pasta & spinach mornay, lamb & potato provençale
  Children: own menu

◧ Ale: Butcombe, John Smith's and guests

ℙ Own car park

CANNOCK, STAFFS   Map 4
ℙℝ LONGFORD HOUSE
Tel: 01543 572 721
On the roundabout at the junction of the A5 and A460.

....

The original Victorian house is a gracious affair, with its prominent bay windows and impressive pillared entrance. It has been much extended to make a large family pub and restaurant and, to the rear, there is a Travel Inn (one of Whitbread's budget hotels).

Inside, those big bay windows are used to good effect. In the bar, one of them overlooks the garden and you can settle in an armchair and enjoy the view. One of the restaurant areas also has the benefit of a bay window and a large central table underneath is ideal for a family group. You can eat in a smaller wood-panelled room with a ceiling fan and coloured lamps, or in the pleasant conservatory room.

The garden comprises a lawn with bench tables, some of them positioned under shady trees. There are two children's play areas and a bouncy castle.

....

✕ (12pm to 2.30pm and 5pm to 10.30pm; weekends 12pm to 10.30pm) £2–13: Cajun prawns, steaks, Louisiana chicken, ocean bake, red snapper Florentine
  Children: own menu
◖ Ale: Boddington's, Flowers and guests
Ⓟ Plenty

CARTMEL FELL, nr WINDERMERE, CUMBRIA   Map 8
Ⓟ MASONS ARMS
Tel: 015395 68486
Two and a half miles off the A5074. Follow the signs to Bowland Bridge.

....

This superb country pub is wonderfully situated on Strawberry Bank overlooking the Winster Valley. Although the Masons is a typically quaint English inn, the cuisine and the remarkable range of beers offered have a distinctly international flavour.

The menu, which is always varied and interesting, includes many unusual vegetarian dishes. Real-ale lovers will enjoy it here – the owners of the Masons offered nearly 200 guest beers last year. They also have their own micro-brewery in operation.

The pub provides a family room just off the main bar with low beams and oak furniture. There is a terrace and patio outside the main door of the pub which is always a popular spot when the weather is fine.

At weekends the pub is understandably busy and in summer it is worth turning up early to get one of the tables overlooking the valley. During summer the pub is open throughout the day.

....

✕ (12pm to 2pm and 6pm to 8.45pm) £2–9: hazelnut & lentil pâté, fisherman's pie, rogan josh, vegetable strudel, beef carbonade
  Children: half portions
◯ Ale: huge selection
ℙ On road and at rear

CASTLE ACRE, nr KINGS LYNN, NORFOLK   Map 6
ℙ OSTRICH INN
Tel: 01760 755 398
Off the A1065 three miles north of Swaffham.

....

In a small and quiet village, you will find this splendid pub, built of brick and flint with a flat front. Its origins lie back in the 16th century. There's a lovely feel to the pub, with its large and unfussy bar, and a notable feature is the large brick-built open fireplace.

It is dwarfed, however, by the fireplace in the family room; it is in the same style and soars high into the vaulted roof. This is a most attractive and spacious room, with a wall at one end which is made of various types of stone and brick. It was once the kitchen, and opens on to the garden.

The garden is a large grassy area, mostly enclosed with flint walls, and has a vegetable patch at the far end. There are bench tables on the lawn, and some caged birds and a few rabbits at the side.

There is an interesting selection of meals available every day – mostly cold food at lunchtimes, and hot in the evenings.

The village is well worth a visit to see the Norman castle and the medieval priory.

....

✕ (12pm to 2pm and 7.30pm to 10.30pm) £2–9: omelettes, pizzas, trout, seafood platter, steaks
  Children: own menu, half portions

Ɖ Ale: Greene King
Ᵽ Own car park

CAWSAND, CORNWALL   Map 1
Ⓗ **WRINGFORD DOWN**
Tel: 01752 822 287
From the B3247 south of Torpoint, follow the signs for Cawsand.
The hotel's brochure gives detailed directions.

Wringford Down is a rare hotel for Britain in that its owners, Harvey
and Andrea Jay, provide only for families; even rarer, their hotel best
suits families with children up to about six years of age. Needless to say,
there are plenty of cots and high chairs and an efficient baby-listening
service. The children all sit down to high tea at 5 o'clock (their meals are
pre-ordered at breakfast). It was a remarkable sight to see nearly thirty
young children, aged from one to five, with their parents in attendance,
all seated at one long table and tucking into their nosh.

This unusual hotel is housed in a nice old stone house, the main part
of which is 18th century, and has been extended over the years. The
facilities include a small bar, a pool table in an adjoining room, and a
restaurant. There is a spacious lounge, which has a TV and a video, and
a playroom alongside; there are plenty of toys and games and blackboards
on which the children can scribble. A very large conservatory has been
built next to the dining room, a pleasant place to snatch some moments
of relaxation with a drink or a book.

The enterprising owners provide loads of amusements both indoors
and out for children. There is a huge play barn which would keep the
children amused for days. It has a ball pool, a huge and very practical
padded playpen, a sandpit, a trampoline and climbing ropes on a special
safety surface, ride-on toys, table tennis, a collection of BMX bikes,
which can be used on the paths outside, and roller skates.

Move outdoors and you can enjoy a large garden with lovely views
over the surrounding countryside with a church spire on the horizon.
There is a children's play area plus chickens, goats, pigs, angora rabbits

and sheep in a walk-in enclosure for them to make friends with. Donkey rides are also organized. An indoor heated swimming pool and a paddling pool have been added to the facilities and were packed with children when we visited. There is also a hard tennis court.

On a practical level, a refrigerator is provided for guests, plus a microwave oven, bottle sterilizers, etc.

This hotel has splendid facilities for young families and if you fancy a gregarious holiday during which you can muck in with lots of other parents with young children in a 'family-friendly' atmosphere, you should visit Wringford Down.

Nearby: There are many sandy and safe beaches and many other attractions within easy reach: Mount Edgcumbe Country Park is just up the road; there is a monkey sanctuary near Looe, the Shire Horse Centre east of Plymouth and Dartmoor Wildlife Park; Morwellham Quay, Cotehele House, Dobwalls Theme Park, Lanhydrock, and Restormel Castle.

....

✕ Dinner (6.30pm to 8pm): wide choice of dishes, always with a vegetarian option
  Children: high teas, small portions
  £ Medium
✓ Bargain Breaks: available in spring and autumn
  Children: free up to 5 years; half price from 5 to 10
  Facilities: 20 cots and 20 high chairs; baby-listening system to every room
  17 rooms, all family, 10 sets interconnecting
  Open all year except Christmas
Ⓟ Own car park

CHAGFORD, DEVON　　　　　　　　　　　　　　Map 1
Ⓗ MILL END HOTEL
Tel: 01647 432 282
On the A382 – not in Chagford itself.

This lovely hotel was once a flour mill and the wheel still turns in the courtyard. You are well shielded by walls in the gardens, and it is very peaceful in the back garden, shaded by enormous trees.

Children are accommodated free to a ripe old age. Indeed, a third person sharing a room with two others does not pay extra – an enlightened policy which more British hoteliers ought to follow.

The charming and hospitable owners now welcome children of all ages into the restaurant in the evenings, provided that reasonable standards of behaviour are met. High teas are still available at 6pm.

It's a lovely part of the country – on the edge of Dartmoor – and Evelyn Waugh wrote *Brideshead Revisited* while staying in the village in 1944.

Nearby: Fishermen are well catered for here. They can fish for salmon and trout in the Upper Teign River which flows past the hotel, and also in some nearby reservoirs. Further stretches of the river are also available. There is a golf course about five miles away, and this is a lovely part of the world for walking and riding. The remarkable Castle Drogo is next door and you can quickly reach Killerton House, Powderham Castle, Becky Falls, Parke Rare Breeds Farm and the nature reserve at Dawlish Warren.

✖ Lunch (12pm to 1.45pm) £14: fresh crab rosti cakes, tarragon chicken, pudding or cheese;
  Dinner (7.30pm to 9pm) £18: Caesar salad, grilled sirloin steak, pudding or cheese
  Children: high teas, half portions
  £ High
✓ Best Bargain Break: £130 per person, 2 nights – dinner, b&b
  Children: free to any age

Facilities: 3 cots and 2 high chairs; baby-listening system to all rooms
16 rooms, 2 family
Open all year
🍺 Ale: Wadworth's
🅿 Own car park

CHAILEY, EAST SUSSEX
🅿 FIVE BELLS

Map 3

Tel: 01825 722 259
On the A275.

....

This lovely roadside inn, built in the 17th century and with a weather-boarded façade, is a handsome building. There are two very attractive interconnected rooms, well away from the bar, where families are welcome. With their low beams, tiled floors, brick walls and smart wooden furniture they are very pleasant places to sit, and there is a huge inglenook fireplace in one of them. The main bar is splendidly in character with its oak beams, and a restaurant has been added to the facilities.

The pub is surrounded by open countryside, and has a large lawned garden with lots of flowers – a good place to be on a warm summer day. There are swings and a climbing frame for the children. But keep a wary eye on them: the garden is enclosed with a low fence, but it might not deter a determined child. Barbecues are held here on summer weekends and there are lots of other activities: country fairs, Easter egg hunts, Morris dancing.

The Five Bells is open all day and every day, and food is available at all times.

....

✘ (11.30am to 9.30pm; Sun 12pm to 9pm) £2–10: mushroom & broccoli bake, mackerel pâté, steaks, supreme of chicken, steak & Guinness pie
Children: own menu

ⵁ Ale: Boddington's, King & Barnes, Wadworth's

ⵎ Own car park

CHALE, ISLE OF WIGHT   Map 3
ⵀⵎ **CLARENDON HOTEL & WIGHT MOUSE INN**
Tel: 01983 730 431
Just off the A3055 in the south of the island.

The hotel began life as a coaching inn in the 17th century and the stone building, with its dormer windows, is full of character.

The owners, John and Jean Bradshaw, have extended the hotel over the years and offer an excellent array of facilities for families. There are eight family-sized rooms (including two attractive family suites) and they are comfortable, spacious and well furnished. There are always plenty of cots and high chairs available for very young children.

The dining room is nicely furnished with wicker-backed chairs and the hanging plants give it a relaxing look. Large windows give wonderful views out to sea.

The hotel has its own pub, the Wight Mouse Inn, which is also geared up for families with several areas where they can sit together. The rooms are full of character with an eclectic collection of musical instruments, antique bottles, prints, maps and pictures. The pub is open all day and has an extensive menu and a choice of six real ales. The list of whiskies, a different brand for every day of the year, is amazing, and the pub recently won the 'Whisky Pub of the Year' award.

Outside you will find a large and grassy garden which looks out to sea. There are plenty of tables and chairs and a separate play area for children with swings, slides, climbing frames, a petanque pitch and a pets' corner with rabbits, chickens and Arthur, the Shetland pony. There are Punch and Judy shows, rides for the children and entertainments are laid on.

The hotel offers splendid facilities (including live entertainment each evening in the inn) for families and is run in an enterprising and well-organized manner.

Nearby: Sandy beaches are easy to find on the island and there are lovely walks close to the hotel. There is a great deal to see and do and none of the attractions are difficult to reach; the nearest to the hotel is Blackgang Chine. Yafford Mill, Carisbrooke Castle, Arreton Manor, Haseley Manor, the Needles Pleasure Park, Robin Hill Park and Flamingo Park are all within easy reach. Golf, fishing and horse riding can all be arranged.

✗ Bar meals (Mon to Sat 11am to 10pm; Sun 12pm to 3pm and 7pm to 9.30pm) £2–10: gravadlax, steaks, crab & prawn mornay, burgers, vegetable lasagne;
Dinner (7pm onwards) £10: quiche Lorraine, grilled lemon sole, fresh fruit meringue and cheese
Children: own menu, half portions
£ Medium
Children £3 up to 2 years; £7 from 3 to 5 years; half price from 6 to 12 years; two thirds from 13 to 16 years
Facilities: 6 cots and 6 high chairs; baby-listening system
13 rooms, 8 family, 2 suites
Open all year

◌ Ale: Boddington's, Strong's, Marston's, Wadworth's, Castle Eden, Old Speckled Hen

Ⓟ Own car park

Nr CHELMSFORD, ESSEX   **Map 6**
Ⓟ THE PLOUGH AND SAIL, **East Hanningfield**
Tel: 01245 400 276
Four miles south of Chelmsford on the A130.

There has been a coaching inn on this site since the mid-18th century, and The Plough and Sail attempts to give some suggestion of period in its interior design. It has been developed over the last six years, and its low-beamed structure with several intimate alcoves has a cool and calming effect. There is a small Charlie Chalk Fun Factory next to a family dining room, and changing facilities which can be used by a father or mother.

There is a children's menu, and eight high chairs are available as well as booster seats for older children. Children may dine anywhere in the pub, but there are several areas to which adults can escape.

Most attractive to children is the garden area which represents something of a mystery trail. There are benches and tables alongside climbs, slides and bouncy animals, and beyond a delightful ornamental lake, on which ducks breed and which is fenced for safety, lie two more children's play areas. One is occupied by a bouncy castle, the other by swings.

....

✕ (11.30am to 10pm) £2–8: prawn cocktail, steaks, fish pie, lasagne verdi, vegetable moussaka
Children: own menu
⏺ Ale: Castle Eden, Fuller's, Boddington's, Flowers
Ⓟ Plenty

Nr CHELTENHAM, GLOS   Map 4
ⓅⓇ Cross Hands, Uckington
Tel: 01242 233 847
Not far from Junction 10 of the M5 – on the A4019 towards Cheltenham.
....

This purpose-built pub was opened at the end of the eighties and has a Travel Inn alongside, with forty family rooms. It is targeted at the family market and has plenty of high chairs, a baby-changing facility, and loads of space inside. Food is available all day, and the restaurant hours are shown below.

As you enter the building there is an agreeable lounge area with padded settles under the wide windows. Up a few steps you will find a cosy bar with brick pillars and a brick fireplace and there is another small lounge below. Part of the restaurant sits under a low ceiling and the large stone fireplace is obviously only decorative, since two wagonwheels repose in it. Another dining area has a wall of windows on to a small terrace and a lawn, and the upstairs restaurant has a high wooden ceiling, brick pillars and dark wooden panelling. Copper pots and pans, sacks of grain and farming implements emphasize the relaxing agrarian décor.

Bench tables are set out at the front of the pub and a huge tree dominates the area.

....

✖ (12pm to 2.30pm and 5pm to 10.30pm; weekends all day) £2–13: pork satay, ocean bake, three-bean feast, peppered steak, Indonesian chicken
   Children: own menu
◻ Ale: Boddington's, Castle Eden, Flowers
Ⓟ Ample

CHESTER, CHESHIRE   **Map 8**
ⓅⓇ **Royal Oak, Mickle Trafford**
Tel: 01244 301 391
On the A56 (Warrington Road), a few yards from Junction 12 of the M53.

....

This is one of those ubiquitous roadside pubs which sprang up during the fifties, built from brick, its upper storey painted cream and with a gabled roof. It is agreeable enough, especially with the cheerful display of flowers in hanging baskets. There is a terrace at the front and an attractive lawned garden at the rear, half of it taken up by a children's play area.

A large bar on one side of the pub is intended for adults who want a drink, and there is a pool table in one corner. Families can use the restaurant, where there are two high chairs. It is divided into two rooms, one of which overlooks the garden. The larger room, on a lower level, has French windows on to the garden. They are smartly decorated rooms, cheerfully appointed and comfortable.

There is a plush and very agreeable bar on this side, which has sofas, easy chairs and padded benches. A Toby Hotel with thirty-six bedrooms adjoins the pub, which is only a couple of miles from the centre of Chester.

✕ (12pm to 2pm and 6pm to 10pm; Sun 12pm to 10pm) £2–11: tiger prawns, mixed grill, peppered steak, fish & chips, cashew nut paella
Children: own menu

Ale: Bass, Stone's

P Own car park

Nr CHESTER, CHESHIRE **Map 8**

P R NAGS HEAD, Bridge Trafford

Tel: 01244 300 206

On the A56 north-east of Chester.

The Nags Head has the look of an archetypal English roadside pub. Smartly painted white, it has a steeply pitched roof with gables, dormer windows and tall chimneys. Below, there are wide windows and the façade is enlivened by hanging baskets of flowers.

It is a welcoming place and the interior is just as agreeable. The long bar has one area at the end for drinkers who enjoy traditional pub surroundings, and there is a dartboard here and bar billiards. The lounge area has plush wallpaper, padded benches, thick carpets, prints on the walls and display cupboards.

The restaurant is spacious, with windows overlooking the garden and a nice brick fireplace. A little play area for young children has been set up at one end. Several high chairs are made available, as is a nappy-changing facility. The pub is open all day and serves food from noon until 9pm from an enterprising menu with plenty of vegetarian dishes.

The enclosed garden has bench tables on the lawn and a large play area. From here, you can see farmland stretching away on all sides.

....

✗ (12pm to 9pm) £2–9: bacon & cheese wedges, tuna melt, fajitas, lemon chicken, sirloin steak
Children: own menu
◻ Ale: Greenall's, Tetley
ℙ Own car park

Nr CHESTERFIELD, DERBYSHIRE   **Map 7**
ℙℝ HIGHWAYMAN, **Baslow Road, Eastmoor**
Tel: 01246 566 330
On the A619 west of Chesterfield.

....

Up on the moors, four miles outside Chesterfield, this large, recently modernized pub is a useful stopping-off point for families heading for Chatsworth House, particularly since the pub is open throughout the day.

Great care has been taken to provide the facilities which any family would welcome. The family room itself is on two levels and has plenty of comfortable seating. There are plenty of high chairs, a baby-changing facility, a little indoor play area with toys and Lego sets, and a very spacious Fun Factory with a ball pool and all sorts of diversions for the children.

There is a sizeable garden at the back of the pub which overlooks lovely countryside. Partly paved and partly lawned, the garden has a children's play area and a barbecue. An extra facility during the summer months is a bouncy castle. There is another lawned area at the front of the pub where you can sit and have a drink and a meal.

The spacious interior can cope with large numbers of families and is an agreeable place with its comfortable furniture, wood and stained-glass screens, pot plants and coloured lights.

The stone pub dates back to 1620 and is mentioned as the New Inn in a Sherlock Holmes mystery. It has unrivalled views of some beautiful countryside through large picture windows.

....

✖ (11.30am to 10pm; Sun from 12pm) £2–8: fish dippers, sirloin steak, plaice & chips, vegetable crumble, chicken escalopes
   Children: own menu, half portions
◑ Ale: Boddington's, Marston's, Whitbread
ℙ Own car park

CHICHESTER, EAST SUSSEX   Map 3
ℙℝ Selsey Tram, **Donnington**
Tel: 01243 783 672
On the A286, just south of the A27.

....

The Selsey Tram is an extensive purpose-built pub and restaurant, constructed in stone, brick and wood; it has a nice glass-porticoed entrance.

The owners have certainly gone for the family market with a will. There is a very large play area at the front, with a sizeable play unit and a little go-kart track; the karts are battery-driven and coin-operated. Inside, children will find all manner of things on which to climb, slide and swing in the Fun Factory, which has its own snack and soft drinks bar. The spacious family restaurant is alongside and it is a no-smoking area.

The other restaurant area (for adults and older children) has stone walls and wood panelling, decorated with numerous prints and horse brasses. The windows overlook the garden.

Plenty of high chairs are provided and there are nappy-changing facilities. Food is served all day and every day.

....

� (11.30am to 10pm) £2–8: onion bhajis, haddock & chips, chicken
Alexandra, sirloin steak, tagliatelle carbonara
Children: own menu
⊙ Ale: Boddington's, Flowers and guests
℗ Lots

CHIDHAM, WEST SUSSEX   Map 3
℗ THE OLD HOUSE AT HOME, Cot Lane
Tel: 01243 572 477
Off the A259 west of Chichester. Don't try to reach it from the A27.

The pub is situated on one of several flat but interesting pieces of land
which jut into Chichester Harbour; and it is a handsome flat-fronted
building which looks Georgian. The interior looks much older with its
ancient beams, collection of old farm implements, and open fireplaces.

Families are welcome to use a room at one end of the pub: a pleasant
spot with low beams, wooden settles and sloping ceilings. At the back
of the pub there is an enclosed grassy garden with a few bench tables
and a shady tree.

The menu is extensive and includes a children's menu and a Sunday
roast for under £6.

✗ (12pm to 2pm and 6.30pm to 10pm) £2–10: Dover sole, fresh
plaice, fisherman's pie, steaks, liver & bacon
Children: own menu, half portions
⊙ Ale: Hall & Woodhouse, Ringwood and guests
℗ Own car park

CHIGWELL ROW, ESSEX   Map 6
🅿🆁 THE RETREAT, Retreat Way
Tel: 0181 500 2716

Turn off the A1112 (Romford Road) into Lambourne Road. Retreat Way is the third turning on the right.

The Retreat is exactly what its name implies, a resting and eating place at the end of a quiet cul-de-sac in a small village which is a strange mixture of ancient wooden cottages and modern commuter dwellings. It is within a quarter of a mile of attractive open country.

Once a nightclub, the pub itself is, in effect, a bungalow. There is a small but attractive children's play area in the garden, which offers slides and climbs, and where children can be supervised by adults sitting at nearby tables. There is also a large field which the new managers plan to develop as an extensive fun area with barbecues, bouncy castle and a variety of entertainments. This area will also provide space for private functions, parties and receptions under canvas.

The interior of the pub is low-beamed and welcoming. There are alcoves and divisions where adults can escape for a quiet meal and drink, while the family eating area is immediately outside the room given over to Charlie Chalk's Fun Factory, which abounds with activities for young children. The children have their own 'bar' which sells sweets, crisps and soft drinks.

High chairs are provided and there are baby-changing facilities close to the family dining area. The pub is open from 11am to 11pm and families will find food available throughout the day.

✗ (11.30am to 10pm; Sun from 12pm) £2–8: hot mushrooms, fish pie, chicken masala, sirloin steak, vegetable moussaka
   Children: own menu
🍺 Ale: Boddington's, Flowers and guests
🅿 Spacious

CHINGFORD, ESSEX   Map 6
P R **THE ROYAL FOREST, Rangers Road, Chingford Green**
Tel: 0181 523 7246
On the A1069, half a mile from Chingford Station, towards Epping Forest.

....

It is not difficult to understand why The Royal Forest won the Brewers Fayre Family Pub Award in 1995. Situated in the midst of Epping Forest, yet easily accessible, it offers a host of entertainments for children and comfortable facilities for parents. There is a spacious garden with family benches and tables for eating and drinking, and an array of slides and climbs for children.

The main part of the pub consists of a long bar and a large dining area divided into alcoves which offer privacy to parties of various sizes. The first floor is given over entirely to Charlie Chalk's Fun Factory, a wonderful maze of adventure activities for children: climbs, slides, balls, ropes, cars and much else. No alcoholic drink or hot food may be taken into this area, but the children have their own 'bar' which serves crisps, sweets and soft drinks.

The Royal Forest is a large, impressive building with a welcoming exterior. The style of decoration is Elizabethan, for an inn of some kind has stood here since Tudor times, and the pub stands next to Queen Elizabeth's Hunting Lodge, an historic building which is now the Epping Forest Museum. The forest itself is a beckoning attraction.

Good news for families is that food is served throughout the day. A baby-changing room is provided (which can be used by both father and mother) and there are some dozen high chairs available.

....

✗ (11.30am to 10pm) £2–8: onion bhajis, turkey fillet, haddock & chips, steak & kidney pie, vegetable crumble
   Children: own menu
◑ Ale: Boddington's, Flowers, Young's, Wethered's, Wadworth's
P Lots

CHISWORTH, CHESHIRE   Map 8
Ⓡ **Woodheys Farm Restaurant, Glossop Road**
Tel: 01457 852 704
On the A626 between Marple and Glossop.

It would be difficult to find a restaurant with a more enchanting outlook than Woodheys. From the wide picture windows which run along two sides of the smart restaurant you can look over a remarkable panorama which includes Etherow Country Park and Werneth Low. The Peak National Park is also very close. From the comfortable and welcoming lounge bar you also have commanding views over the countryside.

A beautiful garden surrounds the restaurant: twenty acres of sloping lawns, rockeries and woodland. It is a delightful place, especially on a fine day.

The food is based on a cold buffet and hot carvery and children under 12 are charged half price. The weekend family buffet lunch is very good value and deservedly popular. Throughout the week the restaurant is available for party bookings. The Ladies has plenty of room in which a baby can be changed.

✗ Lunch (Sat and Sun 12pm to 2.30pm) £11 (Sat), £13 (Sun): 3-course carvery menu (price includes coffee);
Dinner (Tues to Sat 7pm to 9.30pm) £18–19: wide range of seasonal dishes
Children: half portions (when possible)
Ⓟ Own car park

CHOLLERFORD, nr HEXHAM,   Map 9
NORTHUMBERLAND
Ⓗ **George Hotel**
Tel: 01434 681 611
On the B6318.

If you follow the magnificent Roman road, arrow-like alongside Hadrian's Wall, you will find this charming old stone hotel, parts of which date back to the 17th century. It has a peaceful location on the bank of the North Tyne, where guests can fish. The gardens running along the river are a mass of flowers in summer, and you can sit on the terraces at that time of year.

There are some excellent facilities at the George, including a sizeable indoor swimming pool with a sauna, solarium and a whirlpool bath; it has a large conservatory with exercise equipment and a terrace area where you can sit in the sun. Alongside there is plenty of space which includes a children's play area, a golf driving net and a pitch and putt course. Mountain bikes can also be hired.

The views over the river from the very comfortable and well-furnished lounges, and especially from the attractive dining room with its wide windows, are a great bonus. Many of the bedrooms have the same vistas and they are furnished and decorated to a very high standard; the family rooms are notably spacious and many of the rooms are big enough to accommodate an extra bed or a cot.

This is a very pleasant hotel with excellent facilities, and it is deservedly popular with families.

Nearby: The B6318 follows the line of Hadrian's Wall and you can visit several of the forts, the Roman Army Museum and the Roman site near Corbridge. There are many other attractions within reach, including Belsay Hall, Wallington House and the Beamish Open Air Museum. Kielder Water has an array of water sports and Kielder Castle is the starting point for walks through the surrounding forest.

....

✗ Lunch (12pm to 2pm) £13: prawn & mushroom galette, chicken supreme, pudding or cheese;
  Dinner (7pm to 9.45pm) £20: poached trout, soup, sirloin steak, pudding or cheese
  Children: own menu, half portions
  £ High
✓ Best Bargain Break: £98–140 per person, 2 nights – dinner, b&b and one lunch
  Children: free up to 14 years
  Facilities: 6 cots and 6 high chairs; baby-listening system

50 rooms, 2 family, 3 sets interconnecting
Open all year
P Own car park

CHOLMONDELEY, nr MALPAS, CHESHIRE   Map 8
HP CHOLMONDELEY ARMS
Tel: 01829 720 300
On the A49 five miles north of Whitchurch.

Guy and Carolyn Ross-Lowe converted this Victorian school (it was the local school until 1982) and have made a really splendid job of it, so much so that it was named the 1994 'Pub of the Year' by the *Morning Advertiser* (the licensed victuallers' trade paper).

The original building has not been altered, but the interior has been opened into three attractive high-ceilinged rooms; in the centre is a bar and the other two rooms are intended mainly for food. Families are welcome to settle here.

The high schoolhouse windows have candy-striped internal shutters, and there is a fine array of scrubbed wooden tables of various shapes and sizes. China plates, prints and old photographs are scattered on the walls. It all hangs together very well.

There is a huge lawned garden with plenty of bench tables, and a children's play area with swings and a large wooden climbing frame.

This is a very appealing and well-organized family inn which has the great merit of offering an enterprising choice of freshly cooked food. There are some interesting wines to sample as well.

Nearby: You are close to both the Shropshire and the Welsh borders, with lovely countryside within reach. There are many interesting castles on the borders: Erddig and Chirk, for example; and you can see the lovely Dee Valley by taking the Llangollen steam railway. The fascinating town of Chester is not too far away, while Bridgemere Wildlife Park and Stapeley Water Gardens are close at hand. Cholmondeley Castle Gardens are open on Wednesday, Thursday, Sunday and Bank Holidays.

✕ (12pm to 2.15pm and 7pm to 10pm) £2–10: grilled green shell mussels, noisettes of lamb, ribeye steak, chicken piri piri, gratin of Arbroath smokies
Children: own menu, half portions
£ Low
Children: £6 for cot or extra bed
Facilities: 1 cot and 4 high chairs; 2 baby-listening lines
4 rooms, 1 family
Open all year
◑ Ale: Boddington's, Flowers, Marston's and guests
Ⓟ Own car park

CHORLEY, LANCS   Map 8
Ⓟⓡ HARTWOOD HALL
Tel: 01257 269 966
On the A6, very close to Junction 8 of the M61.

The pleasant old stone building is partly obscured by a single-storey extension at the front but the interior has retained its stately appearance. The bar, for example, has wide windows and lovely panelling of dark wood. Wallpaper in rich colours and settles covered in plushly patterned material add to the effect. An elevated lounge area has windows on two sides and a nice central fireplace. There are prints on the walls, cases of medals, and black-and-white photographs (including one of the King's African Rifles of 1939, pictured in Nairobi).

The restaurant comprises a series of elegant rooms, marked by pillars and broad windows. The decorations encompass an array of prints, plates and other china ornaments and bookshelves. It was a pleasure to see real flowers on every table.

Hartwood Hall is a welcoming place with excellent facilities for families, including high chairs. Food is served throughout the day.

� (11am to 10.30pm) £2–12: mushroom & Stilton bake, steak Diane, mixed grill, grilled salmon, chicken tikka masala
Children: own menu
◰ Ale: Boddington's, Flowers and guests
🅿 Own car park

CHRISTCHURCH, DORSET

Map 2

🄿🅁 THE ROESHOT, Lyndhurst Road
Tel: 01425 273 202
On the A35 just east of Christchurch.

A few decades ago this would have been called a roadhouse; and it looks very smart and welcoming with its pink-washed façade, topped by dark weatherboarding.

There is a terrace at the front with a few bench tables and, as you enter, a long bar with a low wooden ceiling and brick walls. The spacious restaurant has a similar wooden ceiling with heavy beams and comfortable padded chairs. Several high chairs are made available.

The bar closes during the afternoons but the restaurant is open throughout Sunday, when a two-course menu is good value at just under £9.

✗ (12pm to 2pm and 6pm to 10pm; Sun 12pm to 10pm) £2–11: cod smokey, chicken tikka, steaks, fish & chips, mixed grill
Children: own menu
◰ Ale: Bass
🅿 Lots

CHRISTCHURCH, DORSET   Map 2
P R THE SOMERFORD
Tel: 01202 485 376
Take the signs to Somerford off the A35 as you approach Christchurch.

Made of brick, with a black and white upper storey, this very large pub is rather imposing. There is a terrace to one side with several tables, and a Travel Inn, Whitbread's chain of budget-priced hotels, to the rear.

Families are very much in mind here. There is a play area with a safe surface and plenty of high chairs inside, as well as a mother and baby room, and the restaurant is open all day at weekends.

The restaurant is done up like a miniature village and you can take your choice where you eat: in the store, blacksmith's forge, railway station, pottery or wheelwright's. Another choice is the handsome semi-circular garden room with its wooden walls and curved ceiling. There is a pleasant bar area and a lounge.

✕ (12pm to 2.30pm and 5pm to 10.30pm; all day at weekends) £2–13: seafood tagliatelle, Greek dip, marinated chicken, burgers, salmon fillet
Children: own menu

🍺 Ale: Boddington's, Flowers and guests

CHURCHSTOW, DEVON Map 1
P **CHURCH HOUSE**
Tel: 01548 852 237
On the A379 west of Kingsbridge.

....

This building was a rest home for Cistercian monks in the 13th century. It was renovated in the 16th century and its basic structure remains to this day.

The delightful bar is long and narrow, with a large inglenook fireplace, black wooden beams holding the ceiling up and a number of wooden settles. There are three alcove rooms at one end of the bar.

The family room is a stylish conservatory, a very pleasant place to sit. There is loads of space, a tiled floor and marble-topped tables. The landlord asks that children be properly supervised – and so say all of us. Two high chairs are available.

The large terrace at the side of the pub is well provided with bench tables and sun umbrellas, and is bright with trailing flowers and greenery. When we called in last summer it was packed with families enjoying their food and drink together.

You will always find some food on the go, including a carvery at Sunday lunchtimes at around £8 for two courses. This is also in operation from Wednesday to Saturday in the evening.

....

✗ (12pm to 1.30pm and 6.30pm to 9pm) £1–8: whitebait, fish pie, devilled chicken, mixed grill, rump steak
  Children: own menu
◑ Ale: Bass, Dartmoor
P Own car park

CLOPHILL, BEDS   **Map 5**
PR FLYING HORSE
Tel: 01525 860 293
At the junction of the A6 and A507.

The original building dates back to the 18th century; the façade sports several dormer windows, and behind there is a steeply pitched roof. The first glance gives no hint of the great amount of space inside, made possible by a long, single-storey extension, where the restaurant is housed. It is reminiscent of a barn, with its vaulted ceiling held in place by heavy cross-beams. The restaurant is on two levels and is a congenial spot, with its brick walls, wooden pillars and panelling, horse brasses and old prints decorating the walls.

Families are very much the Flying Horse's market and there are plenty of high chairs (and booster seats), and baby-changing facilities in the Ladies; bibs and children's cutlery are also available.

The bar is in the original building, and the plaster and timbered walls, huge open fireplace, low ceilings, cottagey windows and padded settles all add to its charm. It is split up into several areas, in one of which there is a dartboard.

The garden, shaded by mature trees, runs around the car park. There is a stream on one side (with attendant ducks) and plenty of bench tables. Swings have been installed for children.

✕ (12pm to 2.30pm and 5pm to 10.30pm; Sat and Sun all day)
£2–13: prawn sundae, sirloin Oscar, marinated chicken, salmon fillet, vegetable mornay
Children: own menu
☐ Ale: Boddington's, Flowers, Marston's and guests

COLCHESTER, ESSEX

Map 6

Ⓟ THE ROVERS TYE

Tel: 01206 845345

From the centre of Colchester, follow the signs to Ipswich to the north of the city. The Rovers Tye is on a roundabout on the Ipswich Road.

Little more than twenty years ago, The Rovers Tye was a farmhouse, and one area of the bar was an adjacent barn. Centuries before that, the farm formed part of an estate belonging to Henry VIII, and, in another period of its history, it accommodated Daniel Defoe, who wrote part of *Robinson Crusoe* during his time there.

The rural character has been maintained in the tasteful decoration, and the restaurant, an extension to the original buildings, gives no hint that it is of a later period. Children are, of course, welcome in the restaurant, but there is also a special family room with an exciting indoor adventure play area. This family room leads out into the garden where there is a games cabin, an enclosed play area and a bouncy castle. The garden also has a patio, a barbecue area and many family benches.

There are eight high chairs for use in the restaurant, and special baby-changing facilities. The area in which children may be taken is clearly defined so that adults also have plenty of room to themselves. The pub is open from 11am until 11pm, but food is served only within certain hours (see below).

✕ (12pm to 2.30pm and 5.30pm to 10pm; weekends 12pm to 10pm) £2–9: moules marinières, seafood pie, peppered steak, lasagne, lemon chicken
Children: own menu

◑ Ale: John Smith's, Theakston's, Webster's

Ⓟ Ample

COMPTON MARTIN, AVON   **Map 2**
P RING O'BELLS
Tel: 01761 221 284
On the A368.

This excellent family pub – long, low and white-painted – sprawls welcomingly against a backdrop of wooded hills, and has a large and splendid garden. It is well grassed, with plenty of log tables and benches, and has a slide, a log climbing frame, an activity unit, swings (all on safe bark surfaces) and a scattering of apple trees. There is also a boule pitch for the adults. It is a delightful spot, which we singled out for special praise in the very first edition of the *Guide*.

The interior of the pub is spacious and welcoming. The main bar has good wooden tables and pews and wooden screens, and there is a huge inglenook fireplace in the other bar.

The family room, a no-smoking area, is extremely well organized: spacious and attractive, with stone walls topped by a high vaulted ceiling and with a good array of wooden tables, chairs and settles and a rocking horse.

It is a rare pub which boasts more than one token high chair – but this one has three.

There's a very extensive menu for the adults, and a particularly good choice of salads. There is always a good range of real ales, too.

X (12pm to 2pm and 7pm to 10pm) £2–9: Somerset smokies, ham & eggs, plaice & chips, sirloin steak, mariner's pie
  Children: own menu, half portions
O Ale: Bass, Butcombe, Wadworth's and guests
P Own car park

110

CRANFORD ST ANDREW, NORTHANTS Map 7
Ⓗ DAIRY FARM
Tel: 01536 330 273
Off the A14 (A604) just east of Kettering. The farm is off the High Street of the village.

This thatched manor house, which was built in the early 17th century, is full of character. Underneath its steeply pitched roof, with its dormer windows and tall Northamptonshire chimneys, you will find charmingly furnished rooms. The comfortable lounge has a large ceiling beam and a recessed window which overlooks the garden, and the dining room is just as agreeable with its inglenook fireplace. The family room has a double bed and its own bathroom, and either a cot or a single bed can be set up as well.

The bedrooms all have lovely views of the gardens and the countryside and include a very spacious room with a four-poster bed and *en suite* bathroom. There is plenty of room here for a cot or an extra bed. The stable block also houses a suite with a double room, an interconnecting twin room and a bathroom. It is a functional, no-frills unit which is only rented out during the summer.

There is half an acre or so of delightful garden, with some fine mature trees, smooth lawns and a notable medieval stone dovecote; you can see the village church through the trees. The grounds are mostly enclosed and children can play in safety, and there is also a swing and a croquet lawn. Guests are welcome to wander around the farm, as long as they stay well clear of any machinery.

Nearby: This is an interesting part of the country and, apart from the pleasant walks which you can enjoy, there are many other diversions. The children will no doubt be keen to see the nearby Wicksteed Leisure Park, while Guilsborough Grange is a bit further away and has a wildlife park. Boughton House, Lamport Hall, Lilford Park, and Rockingham Castle are all within easy reach, as are Burleigh House and Rutland Water.

✘ (7 pm) £10: celery soup, chicken casserole, fruit pie

111

Children: half portions
£ Low
Children: half price under 10 years
Facilities: 1 cot and 1 high chair; baby patrol by arrangement
4 rooms, 1 family
Open all year except Christmas
No credit cards accepted
Unlicensed
P Own car park

CRANTOCK, NEWQUAY, CORNWALL — Map 1
H CRANTOCK BAY HOTEL
Tel: 01637 830 229
Off the A3075 south of Newquay.

The hotel is along the road from Crantock and is probably in West Pentire. But no matter: suffice to say that the hotel has one of the best coastal positions we have seen. Its long grassy gardens, complete with hedges forming wind breaks and suntraps, slope down towards the sea and afford you a magnificent view of the lovely Crantock Bay – a good place to swim and loll, but you must be careful at low tide (obey the signs). It is patrolled by lifeguards during the summer; and is a great spot for surfers too.

The hotel is very much geared up to family holidays, with plenty of facilities to keep young and older occupied. The children have an activity area with a very substantial wooden fort, swings and climbing frames; there is a hard tennis court, and croquet and putting on the lawns.

The excellent indoor swimming pool (plus paddling pool for young children) is enclosed by a curved glass roof, and outside there is a sun terrace. The exercise room has some serious equipment, including a static bicycle, jogging machine and multi-gym, and you can recover on the sun terrace, in the sauna or in the spa bath.

In the field alongside the hotel there are donkeys, pigs and chickens which belong to the hotel, and it is pleasing to report that the owners grow a lot of their own vegetables (as well as providing their own free-range eggs). Children are encouraged to eat smaller versions of the adults' food – mini-dinners are served at 5pm.

Many of the rooms have fine views of the bay and beach, and some of the ground-floor rooms lead directly out to the gardens.

This is a delightful place and the prices charged are very reasonable indeed; the hotel represents outstanding value for families on holiday.

Nearby: As well as Crantock Bay, there are many good beaches for swimmers, surfers and deckchair huggers. There are many attractions around Newquay including the zoo, the Lappa Valley Railway, Dairyland Farm Park, St Agnes Leisure Park and the beautiful Elizabethan house of Trerice.

....

✗ Lunch (12pm to 2pm) £1–3: soup, cold buffet;
  Dinner (7pm to 8pm) £15: fresh salmon mousse, grilled noisettes of lamb, pudding or cheese
  Children: own menu, half portions
  £ Medium
✓ Best Bargain Break: £80 per person, 2 nights – dinner, b&b (winter weekends)
  Children: free up to 2 years; one third of adult rate from 2–5 years; half from 6–8 years; three quarters from 9–12 years
  Facilities: many cots and high chairs; baby-listening
  35 rooms, 6 family
  Closed Dec and Jan
Ⓟ Own car park

Nr CRAVEN ARMS, SHROPSHIRE   **Map 4**
P **SUN INN, Corfton**
Tel: 01584 861 239
On the B4368 north of Ludlow.

This pub has been in business as a roadside tavern since the 17th century and is situated in the lovely Corvedale area of south Shropshire. The great age of the building is apparent when you see the exposed interior beams. The comfortable and appealing lounge bar includes a spacious eating area.

Families are welcome in this room, which is nicely furnished with pine tables and padded chairs and settles. In addition, there is a charming dining room, which is a no-smoking area. On summer days, families can sit on the terrace alongside the pub or head for the garden above the pub, which is enclosed and has some bench tables and various amusements for the children including a slide, an old tractor, swings and other equipment, and ducks and chickens to befriend. The views of the countryside from here are a delight to the eye.

An excellent range of food is available here: it usually includes around ten daily specials and several vegetarian meals. It is all freshly cooked on the premises and the Sunday lunch, at under £6, is great value. A high chair is provided and there are baby-changing facilities.

Lovers of real ale should know that there is always an interesting choice here; the landlord reckons to serve around 150 different brands in a year and the Boddington Mild was proving very popular when we last visited.

....

✗ (12pm to 2pm and 6pm to 9.30pm) £2–12: lamb & leek casserole, steaks, fish pie, vegetable lasagne
 Children: own menu, half portions
◑ Ale: Boddington's, Flowers and guests
ℙ Own car park

DARTINGTON, DEVON   **Map 1**
Ⓡ **Cranks Healthfood Restaurant, Shinners Bridge**
Tel: 01803 862 388
Look out for the Cider Press sign on the A384.

....

Within this very interesting crafts centre you will find a Cranks self-service restaurant, one of the first of the chain of vegetarian restaurants, and it offers a good array of fresh and healthy vegetarian dishes, salads, quiches, fresh orange juice, home-made lemonade, and many other good things. There are many shops in which to browse – Dartington glass, farm food, pottery, clothes, toys, etc, and there is, of course, an old cider press.

There are plenty of grassy areas, with bench tables and shady trees – a pleasant spot to have a picnic.

There is a pull-down shelf for baby-changing in the Ladies in the Cider Press Room.

Cranks have several branches in London: the original one in Marshall Street, W1, and others in Adelaide Street, in Covent Garden, St Christopher's Place, Tottenham Street and Great Newport Street.

....

✗ (Mon to Sat 10am to 5pm; Sun during summer) £1–5: baked potato, mixed salads, pizzas, quiches, cauliflower croustade
 Children: small portions

115

Open all year
P In the complex

Nr DARTMOUTH, DEVON **Map 1**
H **STOKE LODGE HOTEL, Stoke Fleming**
Tel: 01803 770 523
Just off the A379 south of Dartmouth.

A cream-painted Georgian building, with some later additions, it has bay windows on the ground floor and a portico entrance. One of its many agreeable features is the large raised sun terrace with views across the gardens to the pretty village of Stoke Fleming and its fine old church, and beyond to the sea.

The hotel has excellent facilities for families. Three acres of attractive gardens include a pond (once the village pond) where ducks gather, a top-quality all-weather tennis court, a heated swimming pool, a giant chess board, and a children's play area. Indoors you will find another swimming pool, a jacuzzi, a fitness room and a games room with table tennis, darts and a pool table. Reduced fees are available at Dartmouth Golf Club.

There is an abiding impression of space at Stoke Lodge. A long and comfortable lounge, with a bar, overlooks the terrace and the gardens, and there is another well-furnished lounge with lots of easy chairs, books on the shelves and a good selection of boxed games. The dining room, decorated in a dashing shade of pink, has wide windows on to the gardens.

The bedrooms are furnished and decorated to an excellent standard and include spacious family rooms with delightful views.

The hotel has everything a family needs for a relaxing stay in comfortable surroundings.

Nearby: There is a great selection of sandy beaches and bays, and the area offers all kinds of water sports, horse riding, fishing, golf, and many attractions, the National Shire Horse Centre, Dartmoor Wildlife Park and the Parke Rare Breeds Farm among them. You can also visit Buckfast Abbey and the Buckfast Steam Railway, Compton Castle, Morwellham Quay, the nature reserve at Dawlish Warren and of course the beauties of Dartmoor.

....

✕ Lunch (12pm to 2pm) £9: savoury peach & pineapple, liver & bacon, pudding or cheese;
  Dinner (7pm to 9pm) £16: soup, seafood gratin, sirloin steak Lyonnaise, sherry trifle
  Children: own menu, half portions
  £ High

✓ Best Bargain Break: £80 per person, 2 nights – dinner, b&b
  Children: free under 5 years; 25% from 5 to 8; 50% from 9 to 15; 75% thereafter
  Facilities: 4 cots and 4 high chairs; baby-listening system
  24 rooms, 6 family and 2 garden suites
  Open all year

P Own car park

DAWLISH, DEVON   Map 1
H RADFORDS COUNTRY HOTEL, Lower Dawlish Water
Tel: 01626 863 322
In the countryside near Dawlish – the hotel provides an excellent map.
....

This hotel, at the heart of which is an attractive, pink-washed thatched building, has been in the *Family Welcome Guide* since the first edition many years ago, and we have had nothing but good reports of it ever since. It is everything a family hotel should be, and is aimed solely at parents with young children. Many of our readers have told us about the splendid welcome accorded to all members of their families.

Every room is a family room and there are masses of cots and high chairs available. The owners are punctilious about the way in which their guests are cared for: the indoor pool, for example, with its separate children's pool, is always attended by a lifeguard.

Similarly, two of the staff are on duty as baby-sitters every night from 7pm to 11.30pm and the children are monitored on a regular basis.

The facilities are comprehensive: a games room with a pool table, skittles, darts, table tennis, space invaders, etc; a play area with swings, a slide, a large wooden fort, a roundabout and a climbing frame; a play room (open from 9am to 8pm) with a selection of toys; an outdoor badminton court; and, of course, the indoor pool. Entertainments for the children are organized almost every day, including a playgroup three mornings a week, and they have a chance to learn horse riding. The spacious gardens are in the lee of rolling hills and the terrace is a pleasant spot to sit with a drink.

Nearby: Guests have the advantage not only of the hotel's spacious grounds but also of the glorious countryside surrounding it. There are many sandy beaches nearby, including Dawlish Warren, which has a nature reserve adjoining it, where a huge variety of birds can be seen. Nature lovers will also be interested in the Parke Rare Breeds Farm, while the Dartmoor Wildlife Park and the Shire Horse Centre are a bit further away (near Plymouth). Other nearby attractions include Powderham Castle, Bicton Park, the remarkable cottage of A la Ronde, Compton Castle and the Dart Valley Railway – plus the busy resort of Torquay.

✗ Dinner (6pm to 7pm): trout mousse, carbonade of beef, strawberry romanoff
Children: own menu, half portions
£ Medium

✓ Best Bargain Break: £120 per person, 3 nights – dinner, b&b
Children: from no charge to half the adult cost, depending on season
Facilities: numerous cots and high chairs; baby-listening system to each room and baby patrol from 7pm to 11.30pm
37 rooms, all family, 11 sets interconnecting
Closed mid-Nov to Mar (open Christmas and New Year, and in Feb at half term)

Ⓓ Ale: Courage
Ⓟ Own car park

DAWLISH WARREN, DEVON   Map 1
Ⓗ **Langstone Cliff Hotel**
Tel: 01626 865 155
Take the signs for Dawlish Warren off the A379.

....

This is a large and well-organized hotel in a delightful setting amid twenty acres of expansive lawns and woodland. Most of the rooms have balconies which overlook the gardens and the sea beyond. It is a peaceful spot and we were lucky enough to visit on a hot summer's day when the guests were lolling in the gardens.

The public rooms are spacious and appealing, and the long terrace is a good spot on which to enjoy a drink. The facilities are plentiful, with an outdoor and an indoor swimming pool, both with paddling pools, a hard tennis court and a play area for children in the nineteen acres of gardens. You can also play snooker, table tennis, carpet bowls or darts, and there is a golf course next door with concessionary rates for guests. Sandy beaches lie no more than 500 yards from the hotel.

With plenty of high chairs and cots available and forty family rooms (including family suites with two bedrooms), the hotel is firmly in the family market and copes with its demands with great success.

Nearby: Right next door there is the Dawlish Warren Nature Reserve, with a multitude of Brent geese; other wildfowl can be viewed from a hide. There is a host of attractions within reach: Powderham Castle, Castle Drogo, Parke Rare Breeds Farm, Compton Castle, the Dart Valley Railway and Buckfast Abbey. There are many excellent beaches on which to loll, starting with Dawlish Warren, from which dogs are banned, and those around Torquay.

....

✗ Coffee shop (10am to 7pm) £1–3: soup, cottage pie, roast of the day, beef curry & rice, plaice & chips;

Dinner (7pm to 9pm) £15: Brixham crab, navarin of lamb, pudding and cheese

Children: high teas, half portions

£ High

✓ Best Bargain Break: £90–£120 per person, 2 nights – dinner, b&b

Children: free up to 6 years; half price thereafter

Facilities: 20 cots and 20 high chairs; baby-listening system to every room

68 rooms, 40 family

Open all year

⊅ Ale: John Smith

Ⓟ Own car park

DEDHAM, ESSEX   Map 6
Ⓟ **MARLBOROUGH HEAD**
Tel: 01206 323 250
In the centre of the village.

....

The painter John Constable went to school in this lovely village, and it is good to include this ancient and delightful inn, with its wooden-framed upper storey. Inside there is plenty of space in the various bars and eating areas.

The main bar is very comfortable and the timbered beams and pillars are easy on the eye. Past a well-furnished lounge with a huge fireplace with a carved wooden mantel is a large family room with plenty of tables and chairs; it can seat around forty people.

There is a pleasant lawned garden at the side of the pub, enclosed by walls, and with some nice shrubs and trees, and there is also a patio.

A good choice of food is served every day, and includes a Sunday roast at around £6. The pub is open throughout the day.

....

✕ (12pm to 9.30pm) £2–10: herring fillets, lasagne, beef curry, sirloin steak, chilli bean casserole

Ⓒ Ale: Ind Coope Burton, Worthington
Ⓟ Own car park

Nr DERBY, DERBYSHIRE   Map 7
ⓅⓇ Bartlewood Lodge, Dale Road, Ockbrook
Tel: 01332 677 198
On the A6096 near the village of Ockbrook.

....

Located in a most attractive spot in the countryside high above the outskirts of Derby, this is an appealing low-pitched building, surrounded by garden lawns with plenty of bench tables.

The spacious open-plan interior spreads out from a central bar area. It is a comfortable pub with a cheerful décor, where plenty of wood – beams and panelling – is in evidence. The L-shaped conservatory is a pleasant place to sit, whatever the weather.

The facilities for families are outstanding. Plenty of high chairs are made available and there is a mother and baby room; in addition, the Charlie Chalk Fun Factory will keep young children amused for hours with its collection of toys and playthings which include a ball swamp, a slide and cartoons. Alongside there is a pets' corner with goats, rabbits, guinea pigs and ducks, and the outdoor play area is very well equipped.

The pub is open all day and food is available for most of the time. Real ale enthusiasts have a good choice here, too.

....

✕ (11.30am to 10pm; Sun from 12pm) £2–8: onion bhajis, chicken masala, vegetable crumble, fish pie, sirloin steak
   Children: own menu
Ⓒ Ale: Boddington's, Flowers, Marston's, Morland's
Ⓟ Own car park

121

DONCASTER, SOUTH YORKS   Map 7
P R CHESWOLD LODGE
Tel: 01302 533 000
Follow the Racecourse signs, then the Leisure Park signs. Close to Junction 3 of the M18, on the A638.

This Brewers Fayre establishment is one of the more modern of its type, and the first thing that children will notice is the Charlie Chalk Funfair to the left of the main entrance. This is a large open-air complex containing many different rides: there is a train, battery-operated cars, a bouncy castle and sundry other rides, climbing frames and slides.

The interior of this modern building has been designed to resemble something from the Victorian era, with Welsh dressers and cast-iron stoves adding to the atmosphere. The main dining area (non-smoking) is a long open room with honey-pine farmhouse chairs and tables which can seat around a hundred people. The décor here is plain and simple, with floral print wallpaper and floral pictures on the wall.

At one end of this room you will find the Charlie Chalk Fun Factory, a huge hangar-like room where the adventure cage spans three storeys, complete with the usual ball swamp, slides and other activities. There is a separate ball pit and play area for the very young, a nursery area in another corner complete with suitable toys and play equipment, and, adjacent to this, there is a bumper-car area with electric cars. There is plenty of plastic garden furniture for adults to use whilst supervising their children. Children's meals can be ordered and served in this area.

At the rear of the building, the main bar has seating for over two hundred people on platformed sections surrounding the bar. The décor here is slightly more subdued but along the same lines as the main restaurant, and smoking is permitted. There is a large stone-flagged terrace to the rear of the building which contains parasoled wooden picnic tables, and a shop selling ice-creams and sweets for children.

There are two baby-changing facilities on the premises and plenty of high chairs.

✗ (11.30am to 10pm) £2–8: oriental prawns, Teviotdale pie, turkey fillet, fried scampi, vegetable moussaka

Children: own menu, half portions
ℂ Ale: Boddington's, Castle Eden and guests
ℙ Lots

DOWLISH WAKE, nr ILMINSTER, SOMERSET   Map 2
ℙ NEW INN
Tel: 01460 52413
The village is south-east of Ilminster. Head for Kingstone and it is nearby.

This very appealing village has many fine stone buildings and a lovely church, but is probably most notable as the home of Perry cider: the mill is well worth a visit.

The New Inn is a well-proportioned stone building with a very pleasant and quite spacious bar: the beams are decorated with hops, and there is good wooden furniture, including some old settles, and a large inglenook fireplace with a seat in it alongside the iron stove.

The family room is at the back of the pub and has wide windows which look out to the lawned garden stretching back alongside the skittle alley. There are plenty of bench tables on the grass, and for the children a wooden climbing frame and a slide.

✕ (12pm to 2pm and 6.30pm to 9.15pm) £2–11: soft roes on toast, Bellew sausage & rosti, fish of the day, nut roast, braised duck
    Children: own menu, smaller portions
◎ Ale: Butcombe, Wadworth's and guests
℗ Own car park

DROITWICH, WORCS   Map 4
℗ℝ THE CASTLE, **Worcester Road**
Tel: 01904 770 128
On the A38 in the centre of town.

....

This splendid brick house, in the heart of the celebrated spa town, has been converted with sympathy and style to make a delightful family pub and restaurant, which is now open throughout the day. Food is available at lunchtime and in the evening (all day on Sunday) and, apart from the normal menu, there is a good choice of freshly cooked dishes of the day.

The pub has a series of well-proportioned rooms which have been smartly furnished and decorated in rich colours. The dining room has bay windows and doors on to the garden, which has a lawn with bench tables and a very large play area with a great variety of equipment – a delight for children.

The lengthy bar faces an open-plan lounge and there are various rooms and alcoves where the customers can settle (children must confine themselves to the dining room). For example, there is a lovely wood-panelled room at one end of the bar and a wonderful circular room at the other. It has a high ceiling with a glass dome and the effect is heightened by the lavish wallpaper. Several comfortable easy chairs are scattered about.

High chairs are made available and there are baby-changing facilities. It's a very smart and welcoming family pub, and has a good choice of real ale, too.

....

✕ (12pm to 2pm and 6pm to 9pm; Sun 12pm to 6pm) £1–8:

dim sum, broccoli & hazelnut bake, steaks, boozy beef pie, Thai
spiced lasagne
Children: own menu
◐ Ale: Greenall's, Tetley
Ⓟ Own car park

Nr DUDLEY, WEST MIDLANDS   Map 4
ⓅⓇ HIMLEY HOUSE, Himley
Tel: 01902 892 468
Just off the A449 to the west of Dudley, at Himley.

The substantial and stately 18th-century manor house has pillars at
the front entrance, and the façade is invigorated by masses of greenery
and flowers.

The ground floor is given over to the bar and the restaurant and is
sensibly divided into smaller units. Some of the walls are panelled in
wood, and screens of wood and glass are used to create alcoves. The
high ceilings and tall Georgian windows give a nice feeling of space
and grandeur to the place.

Away from the bar there is a pleasant brick-walled room with a
wooden ceiling, and alongside, another appealing dining area with a
wood-burning stove. A no-smoking family dining area has been set up
on a dais, and it is next to the Funky Forest, a play area for young
children.

From there you can look out to the terrace or enjoy the beautiful
garden with its immaculate lawns and magnificent trees. There are
plenty of bench tables with parasols, and a play unit. Himley House
has lots of high chairs and a nappy-changing facility. There is a
twenty-four-bedroom hotel attached to the pub.

� (12pm to 2.30pm and 5pm to 10pm; weekends 12pm to 10pm)
£2–9: moules marinières, chilli con carne, mixed grill, haddock &
chips, lemon chicken
Children: own menu

⊙ Ale: Courage, John Smith's, Webster's
ℙ Ample

Nr DUNSTABLE, BEDS   **Map 5**
ℙℝ OLD RED LION, **Houghton Regis**
Tel: 01582 867 439
On the A5120 at Houghton Regis.

....

This family pub and restaurant is close both to Junction 12 of the M1 and to the A5. It is a handsome old pub, built from timber and brick, and has a massive and steep tiled roof with tall chimneys.

If you have been belting along the motorway, the Old Red Lion would be a pleasant place to pause and refresh yourself. If it's sunny, look no further than the delightful stretch of lawned garden, which has several trees and plenty of bench tables. A bouncy castle is set up for the children.

The bar is in the original part of the pub and is easy on the eye, with its old panelling blackened with age. The lounge area has padded settles and an open fireplace.

The spacious restaurant is housed in an extension with a high wooden ceiling. Wide windows overlook the garden and it's a pleasant spot to have some food, which is available throughout the day. High chairs are available, and so are nappy-changing facilities.

....

✗ (11.30am to 10pm) £2–8: hot mushrooms, haddock & chips, steak & kidney pie, vegetable crumble, chicken Balti
   Children: own menu
⊙ Ale: Boddington's, Flowers, Greene King
ℙ Own car park

DURHAM, CO DURHAM
Ⓡ **Undercroft Restaurant**
Tel: 0191 386 3721
In the cathedral, through the cloisters.

Map 9

The restaurant is actually part of the cathedral itself – located through the cloisters next to the bookshop and opposite the cathedral treasury. As you might expect, parking is not too easy around here, particularly in summer, and it is best to use the multi-storey which is well signposted on the approach to the city from the motorway. It's only a short walk and Durham is a nice place to browse.

The restaurant has light pine furniture with fine stone walls. Food is available here all day with a number of daily specials for lunch and always a vegetarian dish.

The facilities for mothers and babies have been improved with the provision of a shelf, a chair and paper towels in the Ladies, and a baby can be changed there. And a further improvement is that the restaurant is now wholly a non-smoking one.

There's no garden here as such and the lawns in the middle of the cloisters are out of bounds, but there are several places where you can sit and relax and enjoy the surroundings. And the Cathedral is a majestic sight.

✕ (10am to 5pm; Sun from 11am) £2–5: soup, quiche, daily specials, cold buffet
Children: half portions
No credit cards accepted
Ⓟ Public car parks

DYMCHURCH, KENT   Map 3
Ⓗ CHANTRY HOTEL, 21 Sycamore Gardens
Tel: 01303 873 137
Close to the centre of the village

The hotel has a wonderful position overlooking a long, sandy beach and the wide-open sea. Some of the rooms have the advantage of delightful views and a veranda also faces seawards. To get to the beach you cross a little bridge and a traffic-free promenade; it is very safe since the sea is shallow and you can wade out a long way. The hotel has a boat for the use of guests. The garden offers plenty of space and there are swings on the lawn, plus a paddling pool and boules.

The building dates from the 19th century, is half-timbered with weatherboarding over the brick, and has some dormer windows. Most of its rooms are suitable for families and the suites have bunk beds for children in a separate bedroom.

It is a friendly and comfortable hotel which is well organized to look after families and does not cost the earth.

Nearby: Apart from the beaches which stretch along this part of the coast there is an array of things to do and see. Golfers have many fine courses within reach, including those at Deal and Sandwich; wildlife enthusiasts can head for Port Lympne and Howletts zoo parks; there are castles to see at Dover, Deal and Walmer; and railway buffs can travel on the Romney, Hythe and Dymchurch and the Kent and East Sussex railways. Canterbury, with its famous cathedral, is not too far away.

✗ Dinner (6.30pm to 8pm) £12: mushrooms in garlic, salmon with asparagus, pudding and cheese
Children: own menu, half portions
£ Low

✓ Best Bargain Break: £52 per person, 2 nights – dinner, b&b
Children: free in the low season; variable rates otherwise
Facilities: 2 cots and 2 high chairs; baby-listening system
6 rooms, 2 family, 3 suites
Open all year

P Own car park

EAST ILSLEY, BERKS Map 5
P **CROWN & HORNS**
Tel: 01635 281 205
Off the A34.

This agreeable 18th-century pub is well worth a short detour; it's off the busy A34 not far north of Junction 13 of the M4. The village is in 'horsy' territory and the sport of kings motif is prevalent in the pub, with lots of prints of famous jockeys on the walls, horse brasses on the beams, and so on. Some of the customers arrive by horse and there are stables alongside the pub.

There are two rooms where children may go: a small one facing the main bar and a larger one to the side, and both are well provided with wooden tables and chairs. There is also a small dining room.

The old stable yard with its paved floor and chestnut trees has a colourful array of umbrellas over the tables and, during the summer, a cold table is set up and barbecues are prepared.

X (11am to 2pm and 6pm to 10pm) £2–10: cottage pie, lemon sole, sirloin steak, chicken Kiev, vegetable lasagne
Children: half portions
D Ale: Wadworth's, Morland's, Fuller's, Bass, Theakston's
P Own car park

EAST PORTLEMOUTH, nr SALCOMBE, DEVON Map 1
H **GARA ROCK HOTEL**
Tel: 01548 842 342
Take the road to the coast from the A379 at Frogmore.

The hotel was originally a row of coastguards' cottages and there are glorious views of the cliffs, the sea and the surrounding National Trust land. You can see a sandy cove down below which can be reached via a footpath. Gara Rock provides the flexibility families need: there are twenty-two self-contained suites which accommodate up to six people (some have bunk bedrooms), and the Balcony Suite, with its spectacular views, up to nine. The hotel also has a few twin-bedded, double and single rooms. Guests can therefore choose to prepare their own meals or use the hotel's catering facilities – bar snacks and dinner are available every evening.

Great care is taken here to make life as easy as possible for parents, with plenty of cots and high chairs and a baby-listening system. There is a lot for the children to do – apart from the beach, there are acres of grassy garden in which there is a heated outdoor swimming pool and paddling pool, a hard tennis court and an exceptionally good adventure playground; skittles can also be played. There are swings and a roundabout for tiny children. Inside is a games room with table tennis and table football, and the hotel organizes various entertainments like the weekly Magic Show and children's party. A playgroup is organized for two hours a day on five days of the week for under sixes (run by a trained nanny), and there is a 'Fit Kids Club' for older children. There is a sauna, sun bed and gymnasium, and a room for teenagers, aptly called the Wreck Room.

All the family can enjoy the superb walks in this beautiful part of Devon, even though there is so much to do at the hotel that you need never leave its grounds. On a sunny summer day you can have a relaxing lunch on the lawns, and the barbecue is usually in full swing. Children's suppers are available at 5.45pm.

This hotel manages to care for families extremely well and offers outstanding value for money. All sorts of extra activities are organized: swimming galas, magic shows, children's parties, and quiz nights; and a clown is in attendance at Saturday lunchtimes.

Nearby: If you fancy some sightseeing, there is much to choose from within easy reach. The children will enjoy the National Shire Horse Centre and the Dartmoor Wildlife Centre; enthusiasts will head for the Dart Valley Railway; while the Dartington Cider Press Centre has an array of craft shops and a couple of restaurants. Buckfast Abbey, the

Torbay Aircraft Museum, and Compton Castle are all nearby, as is the busy resort of Torquay.

....

� Bar snacks (12pm to 2pm and 6.30pm to 8.30pm) £2–8: a range of hot and cold dishes;
Dinner (6.30pm to 8.30pm) £8–10: carvery, plus an *à la carte* menu
Children: own menu
£ Medium (the suites vary from £139 to £999 per week)
✓ Best Bargain Break: £88 per person, 3 nights – b&b
Facilities: 20 cots and 15 high chairs
Open Easter to Oct
◻ Ale: Palmer's
ℙ Own car park

EAST PRESTON, WEST SUSSEX   Map 3
ℝ **OLD FORGE RESTAURANT, The Street**
Tel: 01903 782 040
Off the A259 and in the centre of the village.

....

This very appealing brick and flint building, its walls festooned with ivy, is of 17th-century vintage and was once a forge. Inside you will find a very attractive and comfortable restaurant; its array of oak beams and gnarled pillars testifies to its long history, and the brass and copper *objets d'art* enhance the appeal of the place. There is a remarkable collection of Toby jugs and miniature bottles of spirits.

The emphasis is very much on fresh food, and especially fish; you will often have a choice of locally caught lobsters, scallops and crab. We think the three-course lunch offers particularly good value.

The Ladies is spacious and a baby can be changed in comfort on the table; there is a chair and a good supply of paper towels. Several high chairs are made available.

....

✕ Lunch (12pm to 2pm) £10: moules marinières, braised steak in red wine, pudding or cheese;
Dinner (7pm to 10pm) £15: baked avocado pear with Stilton, roast pheasant, pudding or cheese
Children: half portions
Closed Sun dinner/all day Mon
Ⓟ Own car park

EAST STOKE, nr WAREHAM, DORSET   Map 2
Ⓗ **KEMPS COUNTRY HOUSE HOTEL**
Tel: 01929 462 563
On the A352 west of Wareham.

Facing south to the Purbeck Hills, this Victorian rectory, built, according to a stone plaque on the façade, in 1874, is marked at the entrance by some towering pine trees.

The interior is handsome, with well-proportioned rooms, which are stylishly decorated. The restaurant, with its bright flowered wallpaper, is particularly attractive, as is the conservatory, which opens out to a terrace and lawned garden with a pond. There is a well-proportioned and comfortable lounge, a welcoming bar with stained-glass panels above the serving area, and a second lounge with several sofas and armchairs.

In the main building we looked at a nicely decorated family room (with a double and single bed) which has wide windows giving excellent views of the Dorset countryside. A new block of rooms has been built in the garden and these are very spacious and bright with furniture and decorations of excellent quality. They could all accommodate a cot or an extra bed without any strain.

Nearby: The coast is not far away, and the best sandy beaches are at Swanage and Studland. Railway buffs could take in a ride on the Swanage Railway, and Durlston Country Park also lies in that direction. There are many other attractions within reach: Corfe Castle, the Tank Museum, the Tutankhamun Exhibition and the Sea Life Centre at

Weymouth. Local amenities include a leisure centre, squash and tennis courts, fishing, riding and water sports.

✕ Bar snacks (12pm to 1.30pm) £2–6: smoked chicken & asparagus terrine, steak pudding, roulade of pork, savoury pancake, beef casserole;
Lunch (12pm to 1.30pm) £9: whitebait, grilled local plaice, pudding or cheese;
Dinner (7pm to 9.30pm) £19: Poole Bay mussels, soup, rack of lamb, pudding or cheese
Children: own menu, half portions
£ Medium
✓ Best Bargain Break: £90 per person, 2 nights – dinner, b&b
Children: free up to 7 years; £5 from 7 to 12
Facilities: 2 cots and 1 high chair; baby-listening to every room
15 rooms, 4 family
Ⓟ Own car park

EASTBOURNE, EAST SUSSEX   Map 3
ⓅⓇ THE BEACHY HEAD, Beachy Head
Tel: 01323 728 060
Take the Beachy Head road east out of Eastbourne and head for the Point.

Set high atop the Sussex Downs on the famous landmark, this Brewers Fayre pub/restaurant affords the most spectacular views of the sea and the surrounding countryside. Apart from the coastguard station, it is the only building in sight. Look for a large brick and clapboard barn-style complex with ample car parking.

The internal layout is semi-circular in style with the bar and serving areas as its focal point. The dining areas split the building, with smoking and non-smoking areas to either side. The decorative features reflect either the agricultural nature of the surrounding countryside or the nautical history of the promontory after which it is named.

There is an enclosed children's play area containing a wooden fort and jungle trail complete with underground tunnels and a 'commando'-style rope and tyre slide. Parents can sit at wooden picnic tables and supervise their children.

Immediately to the left of the family entrance is the Charlie Chalk Fun Factory, where children can play either on video game consoles or in the jungle gym for the price of 50p; soft drinks, toys and snacks can also be purchased here. Children are not permitted in the main bar area, but can enjoy a drink with adults at tables nearby. With baby-changing facilities, many high chairs, and food available all day and every day, this is very much a family pub.

....

✕ (11.30am to 10pm; Sun from 12pm) £2–8: steak & kidney pie, tagliatelle carbonara, chicken masala, sirloin steak, fish pie
Children: own menu
♌ Ale: Flowers, Boddington's and guests
🅿 Ample

EASTLEIGH, HANTS   Map 3
🅿🆁 THE HUT, Chandlers Ford
Tel: 01703 266 626
On the Bournemouth Road at Chandlers Ford, close to Junction 13 of the M3.

....

This large, 1950s-style pub was built from brick and has black and white cladding on the upper storey. The spacious bar area is comfortably furnished and its wood panelling gives it an agreeable atmosphere.

The restaurant is sizeable and wooden stairs lead from one level to another. A mill-wheel, sacks of grain and rough wooden panelling reinforce the restaurant's theme, and there are alcoves with tables here and there.

Very much aimed at the family market, there are many high chairs available, baby-changing facilities in the Ladies, and baby food is provided free of charge.

There are two stretches of garden: one at the side with a play area, and another at the rear with bench tables and a bouncy castle.

....

✗ (12pm to 2.30pm; Sat 12pm to 11pm; Sun 12pm to 10.30pm) £3–11: prawn sundae, seafood tagliatelle, rump steak, gammon steak, burger
  Children: own menu
◖ Ale: Boddington's, Flowers and guests
🅿 Own car park

ELSTED, nr MIDHURST, WEST SUSSEX   **Map 3**
🅿 **ELSTED INN**
Tel: 01730 813 662
Off the A272 three miles west of Midhurst.

....

The pub has changed its name on occasions. It used to be The Ballards, and long before that the Railway Inn. If you consult your dictionary you will discover that a ballard is a bald-headed man or an ancient musical instrument rather like a large xylophone.

Whatever the merits of the various names, real ale enthusiasts will certainly be interested in this pub, which always has some interesting guest beers. The owner has maintained the Victorian character of the place with small grates, sash windows, etc. There is certainly a homely and pleasant atmosphere, and an excellent family room. It is a cosy one with partly panelled walls, a fitted carpet, its own toilet facilities and its own entrance to the garden.

The garden is a long, enclosed grassy one with fruit trees and plenty of bench tables. There is a boule pitch and a barbecue, and a separate area for young children is sensibly kept free of dogs.

The menu changes each day and everything is cooked on the spot from local ingredients.

....

✗ (12pm to 2pm and 7pm to 10pm) £2–10: mussels in garlic, beef in beer, local trout, salmon fillets, spatchcock in lemon & ginger
  Children: own menu, half portions
☐ Ale: Ballard's, Fuller's and guests
☐ Own car park

ELY, CAMBS   **Map 6**
Ⓡ **OLD FIRE ENGINE HOUSE, 25 St Mary's Street**
Tel: 01353 662 582
In the town centre – on the A10.

....

Hard by the superb cathedral, you will find this handsome 18th-century building which, at the turn of the century, really did house the town's fire engine, and was originally built as a farmhouse.

The Old Fire Engine House, Ely

Its attractive rooms now house an art gallery on the upper floors as well as a restaurant, and the dining room, a pleasant, well-proportioned room with a tiled floor and good oak tables, looks out to a delightful walled garden, with a smooth lawn and several shady apple trees. On summery days, this is a delightful place to have a meal, and the restaurant also serves morning coffee and afternoon tea.

The cooking is English in emphasis and local ingredients are used whenever possible. If you need to change or feed a baby, there is a shelf in one of the bathrooms.

....

✘ Lunch (12.30pm to 2pm) £18: local asparagus, roast leg of lamb, apple pie & cream;
Dinner (7.30pm to 9pm) £18: pickled herrings, beef braised in Guinness & port, syllabub
Children: half portions
Open 10.30am to 9pm; closed public holidays, 2 weeks from 24 Dec, Sunday evenings
◖ Ale: Adnams
℗ At side and on street

ESHER, SURREY   **Map 3**
℗ℝ **THE MOORE PLACE, Portsmouth Road**
Tel: 01372 463 532
On the west side of Esher, on the A307.

....

This imposing building is a hybrid of 17th- and 18th-century architecture and has an interesting past. The wife of the great poet, Lord Byron ('mad, bad and dangerous to know', as Lady Caroline Lamb described him), lived here from 1841 and it became a hotel in the 1920s.

Now a part of the Beefeater chain, it is worth the cost of a slap-up meal just to sit at a table in the library. It's a wonderful oak-panelled room with an ornate plaster ceiling, tapestries on the walls and a minstrel's gallery. Wide windows look over the garden and there is a conservatory room and two other rooms where you can dine.

There are excellent facilities for families. A huge garden runs at the back of the building and it overlooks a public golf course. From the bench tables the adults can supervise their young charges as they tackle the commando assault course or enjoy the swings and the play unit. There are plenty of high chairs and baby-changing facilities.

✕ (12pm to 2.30pm and 5pm to 10.30pm; all day at weekends) £2–11: pork satay, steaks, ocean bake, fried haddock, three-bean feast
Children: own menu
◖ Ale: Boddington's, Flowers and guests
ℙ Own car park

EVESHAM, HEREFORD & WORCS   **Map 4**
Ⓗ EVESHAM HOTEL, Coopers Lane
Tel: 01386 765 566 (Freephone reservations: 01800 716 969)
Just off the A44 by the river, and close to the town centre.

The building was modernized early in the 19th century but its origins lie back in the 16th century. A modern wing was added behind the original building a few years ago and as you approach the entrance it is difficult to believe that there are forty bedrooms here. We looked at several of them and were most impressed by the amount of space which is provided and at the high degree of comfort. Not only are the decorations and the furniture of a high quality but it is indicative of the concern for guests' comfort that easy chairs are provided in each room. There is ample space, too, for a cot or an extra bed.

In the original building we looked at a marvellous family suite under the rafters, which are still in place. There is a double bedroom with a bathroom and up a few steps is a little sitting area. On the other side, and up some more steps, there is a twin-bedded room. It is an excellent, practical and most attractive set of rooms for a family.

Many of the bedrooms look out to the gardens, over two acres of lawns with bright flowers and many mature trees, including several ancient mulberry trees and a venerable cedar. You can laze around on the terrace or try your hand at croquet or putting, and there is play equipment for children, including a slide, a swing, a climbing frame and a trampoline. If the weather is unkind there is an indoor play area with toys, a slide and many board games. Above all, you can take some exercise in the indoor swimming pool, where the provision of toys, floating mats and water pistols ensures plenty of fun; table tennis and table football are also provided.

Great care is taken at this hotel to welcome guests of any age; families are cared for in the same way as everyone else. Parents are given a baby box in case they've forgotten anything. There is a vast range of drinks to sample in the bar. It is an extremely comfortable and friendly place; any hotelier who leaves copies of the *Dandy* and *Beano* in the lavatories gets our vote every time.

Nearby: Beautiful countryside and all the interesting places in the Cotswolds lie close to hand: Sudeley Castle, Cotswold Farm Park, Sezincote, Snowshill Manor, Cotswold Wildlife Park, Ragley Hall and Coughton Court. The famous towns and villages are within easy reach: Stratford-upon-Avon, Broadway, Stow-on-the-Wold, Winchcombe, Bourton-on-the-Water and Chipping Campden.

✗ Lunch (12.30pm to 2pm) £14: crab cocotte, Tangier chicken, pudding or cheese (or a buffet lunch for under £7);

Dinner (7pm to 9.30pm) £18: Somerset salad, roast rack of lamb, sticky toffee pudding

Children: own menu, half portions

£ High

✓ Best Bargain Break: £45 per person per night – dinner, b&b

Children: £3 for each year (ie £3 for a one-year-old, £6 for a two-year-old, etc)

Facilities: 5 cots and 3 high chairs; baby-listening system

40 rooms, 1 family

Ⓟ Own car park

Nr EXETER, DEVON   **Map 1**

ⓅⓇ St George & Dragon, Clyst St George

Tel: 01392 876 121

On the A376 south-east of Exeter at Clyst St George. Near Junction 30 of the M5.

The St George & Dragon has very much the look of a traditional inn, long and low with a half-timbered façade and bay windows. The lounge bar maintains that traditional air; it is a sizeable wood-panelled room with wooden furniture and a couple of quiet alcoves.

The restaurant is housed in a relatively new extension. It is a congenial room with brick walls and a bank of tall windows which make it bright and airy. Timber pillars and a central fireplace refer back to the inn's origins, and there is a central food servery. Three high chairs are made available, and there is space in the disabled toilet area when you need to attend to a baby.

A pleasant lawned garden is at the rear of the pub. There are several bench tables, some pretty trees, and a slide and some swings for the children. Food is served throughout the day on Sundays, and the special menus, two courses at £8.95 or three at £11.25, offer good value.

✕ (12pm to 2pm and 6pm to 10.30pm; Sun 12pm to 10pm) £2–11: garlic prawns, mixed grill, steaks, fish & chips, courgette crumble

Children: own menu
℗ Ale: Bass
Ⓟ Ample

FALMOUTH, CORNWALL   Map 1
Ⓗ ROYAL DUCHY HOTEL, Cliff Road
Tel: 01326 313 042
Near the town centre and overlooking the bay.

The hotel, which celebrated its centenary in 1993, is in a superb situation overlooking the broad sweep of Falmouth Bay. Recently renovated, it is in pristine order with very appealing public rooms. The spacious L-shaped bar looks over the terrace and the gardens and has the great bonus of views out to sea, as does the elegant dining room.

We looked at several family bedrooms and were impressed by the amount of space provided. Many of the rooms have panoramic views over the bay.

The facilities at the Royal Duchy are first class. The well-designed leisure centre (for the use only of guests) has a sizeable pool, a paddling pool and a whirlpool; alongside there is a games room with table tennis, snooker and a few amusement machines.

Nearby: Leisure facilities are readily available in the locality and include golf, tennis, squash, fishing, horse riding and every type of water sport. There are many safe and sandy beaches within easy reach. The attractions are many and varied and include Trelissick Garden, Pendennis Castle, the Seal Sanctuary, Goonhilly Earth Station, Flambards Theme Park, Godolphin House and St Michael's Mount.

✕ Bar snacks (12pm to 2pm) £2–7: beef Stroganoff, chicken tikka, mixed grill, lasagne, lamb & apricot pie;
Lunch (12.30pm to 2pm) £9: salmon & prawn terrine, braised calves liver with bacon, pudding;

Dinner (7pm to 9pm) £16: stuffed roast quail, soup, roast leg of lamb, pudding or cheese

Children: own menu, half portions

£ High

✓ Best Bargain Break: £98–135 per person, 2 nights – dinner, b&b

Children: free under 2 years; £5 from 2 to 5; £25 from 6 to 11; £35 thereafter (including meals)

Facilities: 6 cots and 6 high chairs; baby-listening system

43 rooms, 6 family

Open all year

Ⓟ Ample

FAR SAWREY, CUMBRIA   Map 8
Ⓗ THE SAWREY HOTEL
Tel: 015394 43425
On the B5285, one mile from the west side of the Windermere car ferry.

The hotel is situated close to the famous lake, and the ferry runs every twenty minutes during the summer and is always busy. The core of the building is of 18th-century origin, and various additions have been made over the years; for example, the stables were made into a bar, called the Claife Crier, and for parents who fancy a sustaining glass of Theakston's it is useful to know that there are various alcoves, away from the bar, where they and their children can settle down. There is a good range of bar snacks available here at lunchtimes.

There is another bar in the main part of the hotel and a large lounge with plenty of easy chairs. The family rooms, functional and comfortable, provide adequate space. One of the hotel's bonuses is its lovely lawned garden, partly enclosed by hedges; it's a fine place to sit in the sun.

This hotel offers excellent value to families, especially if you take advantage of their four-day or weekly terms in the off-peak periods.

Nearby: The village of Near Sawrey is famous as the home of Beatrix

Potter, and a pilgrimage to her house, Hill Top, will no doubt be on the programme. In the heart of the Lakes, you will hardly be short of holiday diversions, even on the simplest level of walking through the lovely countryside, or enjoying the water sports which are available on the lakes. Within easy reach are Fell Foot Park; Grizedale Forest with its wildlife centre and various nature trails; the Steamboat Museum at Windermere; John Ruskin's house, Brantwood, which you can also see from the deck of the steam yacht *Gondola*, which cruises on Coniston Water; the Lakeside and Haverthwaite Railway; and so on.

✕ Bar snacks (11.30am to 2.30pm) £2–7: rollmop herring, Cumberland sausage, local smoked trout, sirloin steak;
Dinner (7pm to 8.45pm) £14: 5 courses, changed each day (eg, Stilton vol-au-vents, poached salmon, fresh fruit salad, cheese)
Children: own menu, half portions
£ Medium

✓ Best Bargain Break: £58 per person, 2 nights – dinner, b&b
Children: cots £5; half price to age 13
Facilities: 4 cots and 2 high chairs; baby-listening to each room
22 rooms, 3 family, 1 set interconnecting
Open all year except second half of Dec

Ale: Black Sheep, Theakston's, Jennings

P Own car park

FARNBOROUGH, SURREY **Map 3**

P R MONKEY PUZZLE

Tel: 01252 546 654

On the A327, south of Junction 4A of the M3.

The original brick pub has been painted light yellow and the Monkey Puzzle has been radically expanded to form a spacious family pub and restaurant.

The whole building is encircled by lawns and terraces (with plenty of bench tables) and there is a particularly pleasing stretch of lawn, with an array of shrubs and trees, to the rear of the pub. A play unit has been set up here for the children and, in the summer months, a bouncy castle adds to their fun.

The bar area, very busy with local business people when we visited at lunchtime, leads out to the patio. It's a congenial spot, with wood-panelled walls, wide windows, padded settles and a large brick fireplace.

Alongside, there is a dining area in a similar style, and the family restaurant is a capacious open-plan room but divided by screens and a central fireplace into smaller units. One of these is an almost circular room, panelled entirely in wood, with a high pointed ceiling. It all hangs together very well and there is a play zone here for the smaller children. High chairs are plentiful and there is a nappy-changing facility.

....

✖ (11.30am to 10pm) £2–8: hot mushrooms, Teviotdale pie, vegetable crumble, lasagne verdi, sirloin steak
　Children: own menu
◻ Ale: Boddington's, Flowers and guests
Ⓟ Ample

FELIXSTOWE, SUFFOLK　　　　　　　　　　　　　　**Map 6**
Ⓟ **FERRYBOAT INN, Felixstowe Ferry**
Tel: 01394 284 203
Follow the A14 through the town as far as you can go.

....

Over an open fireplace which separates the bar from the family room is a sign: 'This Aged Hostelry Serving Sailors and Fishermen since c.1800'. It is an appropriate message from an inn which is low-beamed, ancient and very much of the Suffolk coast. There is a whiff of Peter Grimes in this area, a rustic and nautical attraction. To drive beyond the inn is to drive into the sea, or at least into a boatyard, and the place has a sense of mystery and history.

The pub is open from 11am until 11pm, and bar food is always available. There are family benches in the garden beside the inn and in front, and a large expanse of grass and the sea and beach beckon beyond.

It should be said that the family room, a recent extension, is the main restaurant, and the refurbishment has maintained the character of the inn.

....

✕ (12pm to 2.30pm and 6pm to 9.30pm) £2–7: chicken curry, plaice & chips, mixed nut risotto, lasagne, steak & kidney pie
   Children: own menu, half portions
◷ Ale: Adnams, Bass, Flowers, Tetley
ℙ Own car park

FEOCK, nr TRURO, CORNWALL   Map 1
ℙ Punch Bowl & Ladle Inn
Tel: 01872 862 237
On the B3289 south of Truro.
....

A marvellous job has been done in renovating this fine old pub, which looks so smart and appealing with its white-painted walls under a thatched roof. There is masses of space inside, and it is nicely arranged in various rooms and alcoves. The wooden beams, pillars and wood panelling are very much in character and there are good wooden tables and extremely comfortable armchairs and sofas scattered about.

Families are welcome to use three alcove rooms, which are all well away from the bar. They are very attractive, with their full complements of low black beams and thick plaster walls, and all are comfortably furnished with padded bench seats and easy chairs. Outside there is a terrace with a few tables and chairs.

It's a most attractive pub which also offers a good selection of food, and, during summer, it is open throughout the day.

....

✕ (11.30am to 2.30pm and 6.30pm to 10pm) £2–7: smoked salmon, halibut, lamb chops, pie of the day, steak teriyaki
   Children: own menu, half portions

Ale: Bass, Boddington's, Flowers, Tetley's and guests
Ample

FOLKESTONE, KENT   Map 3
P R **THE BRICKFIELD**
Tel: 01303 273 620
Close to Junction 13 of the M20. Take the Folkestone road.

There is a children's play area with climbing frames, bridges, tunnels and slides outside the family entrance to The Brickfield, an impressive new public house which stands where once there was a pond. Inside the building, children are greeted by the Charlie Chalk Fun Factory, which has its own young people's bar and offers a Magic Roundabout and a host of other delights.

The interior of the pub has an emphasis on brick, as befits its name, and it is cool, low-beamed and welcoming, with a variety of alcoves for diners and drinkers. Children are allowed anywhere in the pub save the area immediately near the bar. There is a separate baby-changing room, and fifteen high chairs are available. Food is served at all times.

The decoration is tasteful, with floral pictures and reproductions dominating. The Brickfield is, of course, less than a mile from the Channel Tunnel, five minutes from the Folkestone to Boulogne crossing and only a ten-minute drive from Dover. It is also within easy reach of all the delights that Kent has to offer.

The pub is attached to a Travel Inn which has forty rooms, all with *en suite* bathrooms; the eighteen rooms on the ground floor are family rooms. The remaining rooms are double rooms which can be converted for family use. Prices range from £34 to £50.

✕ (11.30am to 10pm) £2–8: oriental prawns, fish pie, chicken masala, turkey fillet, tagliatelle carbonara
Children: own menu

146

🍺 Ale: Boddington's, Flowers, Marston's and guests
🅿 Lots

FORDWICH, nr CANTERBURY, KENT Map 3
🅿 FORDWICH ARMS
Tel: 01227 710 444
In the centre of the village opposite the town hall.

....

This very popular pub is in a most attractive village a couple of miles north-east of Canterbury. It is a large and attractive mock-Tudor inn, which was built in the thirties, and is opposite the ancient town hall. It is smartly furnished, with lots of oak panelling in evidence and an open fire in the bar.

The large and sedate family room (which becomes a restaurant in the evening) also has its quota of wood panelling and is similarly well furnished with plenty of tables and chairs. It overlooks a terrace and a large lawned garden, which runs down to the River Stour where lots of boats can be seen. Centuries ago, seagoing ships used to come this far up the river. It is now safely fenced off to protect the children and there are plenty of tables and benches scattered about. There is a flagged terrace as well where you can sit.

....

✖ (12pm to 2.30pm and 6pm to 10pm, Mon to Sat) £2–8: paprika beef & rice, bacon & onion pudding, lasagne, salmon & prawn bake, beef curry
Children: half portions
🍺 Ale: Boddington's, Fremlins and guests
🅿 Own car park

FOWNHOPE, HEREFORD & WORCS Map 4
⊞ℙ GREEN MAN INN
Tel: 01432 860 243
In the centre of the village on the B4224.

We were delighted to find this handsome pub some years ago. It is situated in beautiful countryside, very close to the lovely River Wye. It is a classic 15th-century inn with most of the essential attributes: a black-and-white part-timbered façade, a low-beamed bar, and above all a friendly atmosphere. One of its most celebrated landlords would not have had any trouble with drunken customers – he was Tom Spring, bare-knuckle heavyweight champion of England.

You will always find food on the go here, and the dining room, housed in an old barn, is a lovely sight – very spacious, with black beams and pillars, and an outlook on one side to a very large grassy garden with lots of trees and flowers. There are swings and a climbing frame for children.

The bedrooms are well furnished and very comfortable: indeed, their style and ambience put many a three-star hotel to shame. Of the three family rooms, two have a double and single bed and the other a double and two singles. The pub has the great advantage, too, of having a separate room off the main bar where children can sit with their parents. It is the Buttery, a comfortable and spacious room with plenty of wooden settles and tables. The adults have a good selection of real ales to sample, including Marston's.

Nearby: The pub is close to Hereford with its famous cathedral, and the delightful Wye Valley meanders in crazy loops south to Ross-on-Wye and beyond. Guests can fish the Wye since the landlord has rights to a mile of river. There are many castles to see on the borders, including the famous triangle of the Skenfrith, Grosmont and White castles. The Falconry Centre at Newent will certainly be on the children's visiting list, as will the Wye Valley Centre with its maze, butterfly house and bird centre.

....

✗ Bar food (12pm to 2pm and 6pm to 10pm) £2–8: plaice & chips, grilled trout, Tom Spring's steak sandwich, lasagne verdi, chicken curry;
Dinner (7.15pm to 9pm) £15: seafood St Jacques, beef Stroganoff, pudding or cheese
Children: own menu, half portions
£ Medium
✓ Best Bargain Break: £73 per person, 2 nights – dinner, b&b
Children: £2.50 under 5 years; £7.50 from 5 to 12 years
Facilities: 3 cots and 3 high chairs; 3 baby-listening lines
19 rooms, 4 family
Open all year
⌓ Ale: Hook Norton, Marston's, Sam Smith's
Ⓟ Ample

FRENSHAM, SURREY   **Map 3**
Ⓟ **MARINERS HOTEL, Mill Bridge**
Tel: 01252 792 050
On the A287 south of Farnham, and close to Frensham Ponds.

....

You cannot miss this large Victorian building, painted in its smart trim of cream and white, on the main road south. The name of the pub suggests definite nautical connections, and the story is that the original house, which burnt down in the last century, was used as a depot for smugglers en route between the south coast and London.

It is a very spacious and cheerful place with a large bar area. Off to one side is a room with a vaulted ceiling and plenty of wooden tables, and families are welcome to park themselves here. There are several high chairs available. The Mariners is open all day and every day, and food is always available.

There are two large patios on each side of the pub and a small lawned area with bench tables.

....

✗ (12pm to 2pm and 6pm to 10pm) £2–12: canelloni, plaice & chips, vegetarian pizzas, fillet steak, local trout
  Children: own menu
◑ Ale: Courage, Gale's, Marston's and guests
Ⓟ Own car park

FYFIELD, nr ABINGDON, OXON   **Map 5**
Ⓟ **WHITE HART**
Tel: 01865 390 585
Off the A420, seven miles from Abingdon.
....

It would be difficult to nominate a better pub than the White Hart, with its delightful atmosphere and wide choice of real ale and excellent food. It is impossible to name a better family pub.

There are no fewer than four rooms in which children are welcome with their adults: a pretty gallery, which overlooks the main bar; a spacious, well-furnished room down some stairs; and yet another room on the ground floor with tables, a large open fireplace and wood-panelled walls. On Sunday lunchtimes, a fourth area, a lovely room with wooden beams and pillars, which is normally the restaurant, is also pressed into service. The pleasant lawned garden is ringed by trees and the children's playground has swings, a slide and a climbing frame.

The pub, built in the 15th century as a chantry house, is actually

owned by St John's College, Oxford, and any academic would feel
at home in the bar with its high, handsome vaulted ceiling – and a
handsome selection of real ales too.

You will find an imaginative and wide-ranging selection of food on
tap as well. It's home-made, and even the bread is baked on the premises.
There is a table and chair in the Ladies to help with changing or feeding
of babies, and there are two high chairs.

The White Hart is an exceptional pub in every way, where the whole
family is made welcome.

....

✕ (12pm to 2pm and 7pm to 10pm) £2–9: spinach & feta strudel,
   steaks, moussaka, chicken Strasbourg, local trout, venison casserole
   Children: own menu, half portions
Ѻ Ale: Boddington's, Hook Norton, Theakston's, Wadworth's and
   guests
Ⓟ Own car park

GARGRAVE, nr SKIPTON, NORTH YORKS   Map 9
ⓅⓇ ANCHOR INN
Tel: 01756 749 666
On the A65 just west of Gargrave.

....

When we listed this pub a decade ago in the first edition of the *Guide*
we called it 'a handsome stone roadside pub, which dates back to the
16th century'.

It still has its handsome stone façade but the interior has been totally
changed and the pub is very much devoted to the family market. It
is open all day and dispenses food for most of its opening hours, has
plenty of high chairs, a children's menu and a nappy-changing facility. In
addition, there is a little play area indoors for the under-5s and two
substantial playgrounds in the large garden at the rear.

The very spacious interior has been made into a series of interlocking
rooms and alcoves, on various levels and divided by wood and glass
screens. There is wood panelling here and there, low ceilings, padded

benches, the occasional sofa and sizeable no-smoking areas (in particular the family dining room). It all adds up to an agreeable atmosphere with food at reasonable prices and a good selection of real ales.

✗ (11.30am to 10pm; Sun from 12pm) £2–8: prawn cocktail, steak & kidney pie, plaice & chips, sirloin steak, chicken Alexandra
Children: own menu
◑ Ale: Boddington's, Jennings, Whitbread
🅿 Lots

GERRARDS CROSS, BUCKS   Map 5
🅿🆁 **THE APPLE TREE**
Tel: 01753 887 335
On the A40 on the outskirts of the town.

Smart in its coat of white paint, there is the welcoming look of a village inn to The Apple Tree, which is on the fringe of this commuter town. The well-maintained garden, mostly lawned and with plenty of bench tables, some of which have been placed under shady trees, is an added bonus. There is a children's play unit with slides on a safe bark surface.

The original part of the pub houses the cosy bar, with its low ceiling and long padded benches; there are prints and copper warming-pans on the walls.

Families are well catered for here, since several high chairs are provided and there are baby-changing facilities in the Ladies. The restaurant is spacious and agreeably designed: it has a high sloping ceiling, plush wallpaper above wood panelling, a brick fireplace and screens of wood and coloured glass between the tables.

The pub is open throughout the day (and bar meals are available at all times), whereas the restaurant is open during the hours listed below.

....

✕ (12pm to 2.30pm and 5pm to 10.30pm; weekends 12pm to 10.30pm) £2–13: prawn sundae, seafood tagliatelle, Normandy pork, sirloin steak, three-bean feast
Children: own menu
◖ Ale: Boddington's, Flowers and guests
ℙ Own car park

GLEN PARVA, nr LEICESTER, LEICESTERSHIRE   Map 7
ℙℝ THE COUNTY ARMS
Tel: 0116 277 1093
South of Leicester on the A426, between Glen Parva and Blaby.

....

When you see a large 1930s-style red-brick building by the roadside at a set of traffic lights, you have found the County Arms, a pub and restaurant with excellent facilities for families. A sloping driveway from the car park brings you up to an enclosed garden area, partly flagstoned and partly grass, with a wood-chipped area at one end upon which there is a small adventure play unit. There is a small gate at the rear of the garden which leads directly on to the tow path of the Grand Union Canal (a favourite fishing spot). Care should be taken with young children as the banks are unguarded and open.

The main entrance to the restaurant and bar is situated at the front of the building, inside a small walled forecourt. At the top of a canopied stairway the first sign that greets you is the one indicating a baby-changing facility, which is situated in the entranceway to the Ladies. A lot of effort has gone into the interior décor, where there is much bric-à-brac, mainly associated with farming and canal work: hand-painted barge decorations are much in evidence.

In the main restaurant there is a stone-walled area with farmhouse chairs and tables to seat around twenty people. Then the restaurant opens out into several separate sections and up to a platformed area at the rear where a very large bay window overlooks the garden and play area.

To the left of the entrance is the main bar, where pub food is served throughout the day. Fully carpeted throughout, there are many separate seated areas both surrounding the bar and on a raised area which looks out over the surrounding fields. Once again, the decorations hark back to the age of barge transportation. The rural nature of this building is further enhanced by the plentiful use of weathered wooden beams, wall struts and ceiling panelling.

✕ (11am to 10.30pm; Sun from 12pm) £2–13: prawn sundae, half rack of ribs, seafood tagliatelle, burgers, fried scampi
  Children: own menu, half portions
🍺 Ale: Everard's, Morland's and guests
🅿 Own car park

GLOUCESTER, GLOS
Map 4
P R LONGFORD INN, Longford
Tel: 01452 523 519
On the A38, just south (the Gloucester side) of its junction with the A40.

....

The original building, stately and painted cream, has been extended to make a very spacious family pub and restaurant. A Travel Inn has been built alongside.

In the gardens surrounding the Longford Inn there are two children's play areas; and the pub contains all the necessary facilities for families, including several high chairs and a nappy-changing unit. Bar snacks are available all day and the restaurant times are shown below. The pub has a children's certificate.

The extensive bar area has large windows, including a handsome bay window beneath which sit several tables. The restaurant is designed on different levels under a high ceiling. Separate halves of a small boat have been used to create booths in one area, and the stern of the good ship *Longford* (registered in Gloucester) forms another booth in the middle of the room. The decorations are colourful, with many prints on the walls. A second dining room is very attractive, too, with its expanse of wide windows.

....

✕ (12pm to 2.30pm and 5pm to 10.30pm; weekends all day) £2–13: pork satay, Indonesian chicken, pasta Lucana, fried scampi, fillet steak
Children: own menu
Ale: Boddington's, Flowers and guests
P Ample

Nr GLOUCESTER, GLOS   **Map 4**
ⓅⓇ Cʀᴏss Hᴀɴᴅs, **Brockworth**
Tel: 01452 863 441
At Brockworth, on the roundabout where the A417 crosses the A46.

....

This agreeable pub is built of stone, its façade partly pebbledashed
and enlivened by hanging baskets of flowers. It has been extended to
encompass a very large family pub and restaurant with loads of high
chairs, nappy-changing facilities, a Fun Factory, and a play unit on one
side of the pub (where a bouncy castle also makes an appearance during
the summer).

A comfortable semicircular bar occupies one end of the pub and
overlooks a lawned garden. Alongside, there is a wood-panelled restaurant with French windows on to a terrace. Beyond you will find
a large area with stone walls and wide windows. The main restaurant
has a high ceiling, wood-panelled walls and padded settles. It is a bright
and cheerful spot and has one dining area on a dais. The family dining
room comes next, where the Fun Factory is positioned. Doors lead out
to the garden with its play area.

....

✕ (11.30am to 10pm) £2–8: hot mushrooms, fish pie, sirloin steak,
   vegetable crumble, lasagne verdi
   Children: own menu
Ⓓ Ale: Boddington's, Flowers, Marston's and guests
Ⓟ Own car park

Nr GLOUCESTER, GLOS   **Map 4**
ⓅⓇ Tʜᴇ Dᴏɢ, **Over**
Tel: 01452 521 191
On the A40, just west of its junction with the A417.

....

The core of this building dates from the 17th century, although it has
been much extended over the years. It was once a bakehouse and one
of the old ovens still sits in a wall near the bar. It is a very attractive

bar, with its brick walls, and an extension is very much in keeping; a vaulted ceiling is held in place by heavy wooden beams and there are many windows of pleasant proportions.

Another bar, on a lower level, has a low beamed ceiling, a fireplace with a wood-panelled surround, and displays of china and pottery.

The large wood-panelled restaurant is a relaxing place, and sports a number of bookshelves. A handsome conservatory, with a tall and pointed ceiling and brick walls and pillars, has been added. Diners can look out to little gardens on both sides.

There is a big grassy garden at the back of the pub, and a terrace with a few tables and chairs, and a small play unit has been installed on a safe bark surface. High chairs and baby-changing facilities are made available.

....

✕ (12pm to 2.30pm and 5.30pm to 10.30pm; Sun 12pm to 10pm)
   £2–11: cod smokey, fish & chips, mushroom strudel, mixed grill, sesame chicken
   Children: own menu
◑ Ale: Bass
ℙ Own car park

Nr GLOUCESTER, GLOS   Map 4
ℙℝ TWELVE BELLS, Witcombe
Tel: 01452 862 521
On the A417 south-east of Gloucester, at Witcombe.

....

This nice old stone pub sits below a wooded hillside and offers an excellent range of facilities for families. For a start, a large lawned garden stretches on two sides of the building, and there is a Travel Inn attached to the pub. There are plenty of high chairs and a nappy-changing unit, and food is available throughout opening hours (bar snacks when the restaurant is closed).

The interior is very much in the traditional style. The bar is an attractive place, the ceiling beams hung with pewter tankards and with a stone-flagged floor in one area where there is a dartboard. The lounge section has brick pillars and a brick fireplace, old timber panelling and windows of good proportions.

The sizeable restaurant occupies one side of the building. More wooden beams are hung with copper pots and pans, and china jugs. As in the bar areas there are brick pillars and walls, and wooden panelling. A high wooden ceiling graces one end of the restaurant, which is decorated as a grain store and has the appropriate artefacts on display: rakes, forks and sacks of grain.

....

✗ (12pm to 2.30pm and 5pm to 10.30pm; weekends all day) £2–13: prawn sundae, salmon fillet, beef & Boddington's pie, chicken tikka masala, Normandy pork
Children: own menu
◗ Ale: Boddington's, Marston's, Wadworth's
Ⓟ Own car park

GRASMERE, CUMBRIA   **Map 8**
Ⓟ **TRAVELLER'S REST**
Tel: 015394 35604
On the A591 north of the village.

....

This long white pub is reputed to be the oldest building in Grasmere. Flanked by spectacular views of the Langdale Pikes, Helvellyn and the Fairfield Horseshoe, it provides a handy resting place for walkers and tourists.

There is lots of space to eat outside, either in the beer garden or on the tables at the front of the pub. The smart and traditional interior has a very agreeable lounge, with padded benches ranged along the plastered stone walls, and families have their own room up a few stairs at one end of the pub. There is plenty of space here and there is a pool table. An alternative for families is the large dining room at the other end of the building.

Two high chairs are available and there are baby-changing facilities:

just ask the helpful staff. It is a useful pub for families to know since it is open throughout the day (Monday to Saturday) and has a limited menu during the afternoon period.

Its sister pub, the King's Head, is four miles away on the same road, and also has excellent facilities for families.

....

✳ (12pm to 3pm and 6pm to 10pm) £2–11: chicken Kiev, vegetable lasagne, lamb brochette, sirloin steak, Cumberland sausage
   Children: own menu, half portions
🍺 Ale: Jennings
🅿 Own car park

GREASBY, MERSEYSIDE   Map 8
🅿🆁 THE TWELFTH MAN
Tel: 0151 677 5445
On the B5139, close to Junctions 2 and 3 of the M53.

....

This very substantial roadhouse-style pub and restaurant also encompasses a hotel with rooms at a reasonable price. It is near the northern tip of the Wirral and very close to the great golf links at Hoylake.

The bar is very spacious and there are lounge areas at each end. They are smartly decorated and have padded settles running along the walls; one of them has a skylight of coloured glass.

The pub is open throughout the day, as is the restaurant, which is housed in a large L-shaped room with wide windows, some of which overlook a patch of garden. It is a pleasant spot, nicely decorated and furnished, and with lots of prints on the walls and some corner cupboards with displays of china. High chairs are available and there is a children's menu. The 'Specials Table' offers three- and four-course meals at bargain prices from £6.99 to £11.99.

....

✳ (11.30am to 10.30pm; Sun 12pm to 10pm) £2–12: broccoli tempura, spiced lamb, grilled halibut, Mexican bake, peppered steak
   Children: own menu

⍭ Ale: Boddington's
ℙ Own car park

Nr GUILDFORD, SURREY   Map 3
ℙℝ **WORPLESDON PLACE HOTEL, Worplesdon**
Tel: 01483 232 407
On the A322 north of Guildford at Worplesdon.

....

The imposing old house has towering trees at the front, and the main garden, at the side, is a superb spot to sit on a summer day. There is a great expanse of lawn, with many mature trees, and it leads down to a lake where there is an abundance of birds. The children will enjoy the pets' corner by the lake and they also have an adventure playground and a bouncy castle.

The rooms in the Worplesdon Place are on the grand scale and the two main dining rooms are splendid. A huge bay window in the first overlooks the terrace and the gardens and there are murals, potted plants and lots of framed prints. The adjoining room has a rich wallpaper above the wood panelling and another huge bay window. Nearby there is yet another dining room: panelled in wood and with a series of Spy cartoons on the walls.

The large bar area has been designed on various levels, and the same style has been maintained – wood panelling, with prints and posters on the walls.

It's an interesting place and has excellent facilities for families, including high chairs and a nappy-changing facility.

....

✕ (12pm to 2.30pm and 5pm to 10.30pm; weekends 12pm to 10.30pm) £2–11: pork satay, steaks, Louisiana chicken, ocean bake, three-bean feast
   Children: own menu
◔ Ale: Boddington's, Brakspear's, Flowers, Wadworth's
ℙ Own car park

HAIL WESTON, CAMBS   Map 6
ℙ THE ROYAL OAK
Tel: 01480 472 527
Off the A45 north of St Neots.

....

This fine 17th-century pub is always in pristine order, inside and out. Situated in a small village, it is painted white, with dormer windows set in a steeply pitched thatched roof; and cheerful window boxes and baskets of flowers adorn the walls. The inside is very much in keeping, with oak pillars, splendid beams and a huge inglenook fireplace – a smart and agreeable bar.

Families are welcome in their own room off the bar; it has several tables and bar billiards. Two high chairs are provided. There is also a restaurant which is open in the evenings and at Sunday lunchtimes.

The garden is safely enclosed and the large lawn has plenty of tables and chairs with sun umbrellas. Behind a row of firs, the play area has swings, a slide, a climbing frame and a seesaw. There is also a patio area with several tables. The sensible landlord prohibits dogs from the garden.

....

✕ (12pm to 2.30pm and 7pm to 10pm; not Sun pm and Mon

pm) £2–5: scampi, plaice & chips, vegetable curry & rice, turkey Kiev, burgers
Children: own menu
ⅅ Ale: Adnams, Wells and guests
ℙ Own car park

HARDINGTON MANDEVILLE, SOMERSET　　　　Map 2
ℙ **MANDEVILLE ARMS**
Tel: 01935 862 418
Off the A30 between Crewkerne and Yeovil.

....

This pub was enlarged some years back and is very smart and comfortable. The spacious open-plan bar still has its low ceilings, old wooden beams and pillars, good wooden tables and brick walls, as well as a good-quality carpet.

The family room, at one end of the pub, is done in the same style and doubles as a restaurant. The licensees make the valid point that parents should stay with their children and not leave them to their own devices while they prop up the bar.

There is a delightful garden at the front of the pub. It is surrounded by a small stone wall and looks very cheerful with its collection of sun umbrellas and colourful flowers.

Food is served every day from a wide-ranging and enterprising bar menu, and in the winter, a three-course Sunday lunch is available for around £7.

....

✘ (12pm to 1.45pm and 7.30pm to 10pm) £1–11: fresh vegetable pancake, seafood au gratin, steaks, spicy pork in ginger, moussaka
Children: own menu, half portions
ⅅ Ale: Boddington's, Flowers, Marston's and guests
ℙ Own car park

HARROGATE, NORTH YORKS   Map 9
🄡 BETTYS CAFE TEAROOMS, 1 Parliament Street
Tel: 01423 502 746
Off the A61 near the town centre and opposite Montpelier Gardens.

....

This is certainly not a place to be missed if you have children and
are visiting this attractive town. It is a rare opportunity for parents of
young children to relax in a stylish tearoom, where the high standards
never waver. It is a bustling place with wide windows on to Montpelier
Gardens, and the décor of marble-topped tables, Art Nouveau mirrors
and 1920s-style prints is most appealing. There are real flowers on your
table, real tea or coffee in your cup, and an excellent range of snacks,
hot or cold meals, cakes and pastries. Live piano music is played during
the evenings.

In addition, Bettys gives a proper welcome to families; apart from
charming service and an interesting children's menu, it offers first-class
facilities: changing mats, playpen, potties, bibs and beakers are all
made available, plus many high chairs; and most of the restaurant is
non-smoking. The kitchen will also provide baby foods.

....

✗ (9am to 9pm) £1–7: scrambled eggs with smoked salmon, cheese
& herb pâté, Masham sausages with red cabbage, rarebits, rosti
with bacon
Children: own menu, half portions
🄿 Street parking

Nr HARROGATE, NORTH YORKS   Map 9
🄿🄡 NELSON INN
Tel: 01423 500 340
Two miles west of Harrogate on the A59 to Skipton.

....

This old stone pub has long been a familiar sight to motorists on the
Skipton road and has now been greatly extended to accommodate
a wealth of facilities for families. Food is available throughout the

day, high chairs are provided in generous quantity and there is a nappy-changing facility. If you add to that a large indoor amusement area for children (Treasure Island with a ball pool and many other items) and a play unit in the enclosed garden, you can see that this is very much a family-orientated operation.

Not that the adults will feel unloved, because the interior is designed in an agreeable way, with Laura Ashley-style wallpaper amongst the stone walls, wooden panelling, glass screens and painted skylights. It is comfortable and welcoming, the food is reasonably priced and there is a choice of real ales.

....

✕ (11.30am to 10pm; Sun from 12pm) £2–8: oriental prawns, chicken escalopes, steak & kidney pie, vegetable crumble, marinated lamb
   Children: own menu
�'ꞏ Ale: Boddington's, Castle Eden
Ⓟ Own car park

HARTLEY WINTNEY, HANTS   **Map 3**
Ⓟ Ⓡ **THE HARTFORD BRIDGE**
Tel: 01252 842 037
On the A30 on the east side of the village.

....

This substantial brick building, now painted a shade of lemon, is alongside the A30 and has recently been converted to a sizeable family pub and restaurant.

At one side there is a terrace with several bench tables and, alongside, a children's play unit. Glass doors lead into the family dining room, which is a no-smoking area. A Fun Factory for younger children has been placed here and there are all kinds of playthings, including a ball swamp and a magic roundabout. The children also have their own snack and soft drinks bar. Plenty of high chairs are available, and there are nappy-changing facilities.

The comfortable bar has a choice of real ales and there are two pleasant dining areas here. They're nicely decorated with wood panelling and there is a small and intimate room, with only two tables, alongside. From here you enter a delightful high-ceilinged room with three large windows and double doors to the terrace.

It's a welcoming and well-designed place with excellent facilities for families.

....

✕ (11.30am to 10pm) £2–8: oriental prawns, haddock & chips, turkey fillet, tagliatelle carbonara, vegetable moussaka
Children: own menu
◑ Ale: Boddington's, Flowers
Ⓟ Lots

HARWICH, ESSEX   Map 6
Ⓡ THE PIER AT HARWICH, The Quay
Tel: 01255 241 212
On the quayside, in the town centre.

....

This stately listed building on the quayside dates from 1874, and contains a small hotel on the upper floors and two excellent restaurants. If you are catching a ferry, make sure that you have time to sample some fine and fresh fish at The Pier.

On the ground floor, you will find the bar, with plenty of comfortable seats; the Ha'penny Pier restaurant is alongside and is very well suited to the family budget since a main course of fish and chips costs just over £5 and the children's menu of soup, fish and chips and ice-cream costs just over £4 and is splendid value for money.

Both these rooms have bold and cheerful murals and so has a part of the upstairs restaurant, which is divided into two areas; the second room has smart pine tables and some wonderful original travel posters. Both rooms have wonderful views out to sea.

....

✕ Ha'penny Pier (12pm to 2pm and 6pm to 9.30pm) £2–7: Pier haddie, cod, haddock or plaice & chips, broccoli and cream cheese bake, supreme of chicken;

Dinner £17: marinated herring fillets, grilled sea bass, sherry trifle
Children: own menu, half portions
Open all year
🍺 Ale: Adnams
🅿 Own car park

HASTINGS, EAST SUSSEX   Map 3
Ⓗ **BEAUPORT PARK HOTEL, Battle Road**
Tel: 01424 851 222
On the A2100 between Battle and Hastings.

The regular lines and warm red brick of this splendid Georgian mansion make a most appealing sight, especially when you take in the pillared main entrance and the dormer windows in the steep roof. It is a wonderful setting for this elegant hotel and was once the home of Sir James Murray, who was second in command to General Wolfe at Quebec. It has a lovely setting in about thirty acres of parkland, which includes a formal Italian garden with superb trees, and a tranquil sunken garden, partly enclosed by an old stone wall.

The smooth lawn at the front contains a putting green, and beyond there is a hard tennis court and a grass badminton court. At the back of the hotel is a giant chess board, a boule pitch and a croquet lawn. Above all, there is an outdoor heated swimming pool, surrounded by pleasant lawns on which to loll. Next door, there is a riding school and six squash courts; and golfers should be in their element since there is both a 9-hole and an 18-hole golf course, plus a golf driving range.

Nearby: Hastings Castle and Battle Abbey, which is actually built on the land where William the Conqueror defeated Harold. Parents will perhaps favour a visit to the Carr Taylor vineyards; and within a reasonable radius you can visit Rudyard Kipling's home, Bateman's, Herstmonceux Castle and Drusillas, with its zoo, miniature railway, large adventure playground, restaurant and pub.

✗ Bar snacks (10am to 10pm) £1–5: soup, pâté, vegetarian pancake, coquille fruits de mer, ploughman's;
Lunch (12.30pm to 2pm) £15: hors d'oeuvres, roast loin of pork, pudding or cheese
Dinner (7pm to 9.30pm) £18: chicken liver pâté, grilled Scotch salmon, pudding or cheese
Children: own menu, half portions
£ High
✓ Best Bargain Break: £100 per person, 2 nights – dinner, b&b
Children free up to 16 years
Facilities: 4 cots and 2 high chairs; baby-listening service on three lines
23 rooms, 1 family
Open all year
Ⓟ Own car park

Nr HASTINGS, EAST SUSSEX   Map 3
ⓅⓇ THE WHITE HART, Guestling
Tel: 01424 813 187
On the A259 north-east of Hastings at Guestling.

The White Hart is an old coach house which stands on the road which links the south coast resorts. It is just beyond the limits of Hastings, a bubbling seaside town which offers a Sea Life Centre, a Smuggler's Adventure and an historic castle.

The White Hart itself stands at the top of the long climb which leads out of Hastings, and from its garden one looks down on the whole of East Sussex. It is a beautiful and breathtaking sight. The garden is behind the inn. It is large and offers a variety of amusements for children, as well as family benches and a barbecue area. There are slides, climbs, swings, a bouncy castle, a seesaw and a springy duck, and beyond the garden there is land belonging to the inn. This is a charming area in which to stroll, to play or simply to feast one's eyes on the marvellous view.

167

The interior of the pub has retained much of the old coach house tradition, and the fireplace is built upon the old wishing well, which is still visible. There is a play area for children, who are allowed anywhere except in the lower bar, and they will be fascinated by the décor, which has a fairy-tale quality, a distinct flavour of Hansel and Gretel, as well as a rural motif.

The dining area of the pub is in several parts, and on several levels, and there are small wooden 'houses' which add to the fairy-tale quality. They are named The Ringel, The Potting Shed, The Wood Shed, etc., and offer secluded dining areas for families or parties. Food from the bar is available at all times, and the restaurant is open all day at weekends. The pub is open from 11am until 11pm.

Children are offered their own menu, and there are bibs, play packs, booster seats and eighteen high chairs. Special baby-changing facilities are available, and there are plans for a refurbishment which, while retaining the present popular style, will provide a 'children's discovery room'.

✖ (12pm to 2.30pm and 5pm to 10.30pm; weekends all day) £2–13: pork satay, salmon fillet, ocean bake, peppered steak, haddock & chips
Children: own menu

◐ Ale: Boddington's, Flowers, Wadworth's
Ⓟ Ample

Nr HEATHFIELD, EAST SUSSEX   Map 3
Ⓗ WEST STREET FARMHOUSE, Maynards Green
Tel: 01435 812 516
On the B2203 just south of Heathfield in the village of Maynards Green.

This is a delightful brick farmhouse, built in an L-shape, parts of which date back to the 17th century. It is surrounded by nearly four acres of grounds, a large part of which comprise smooth lawns: a lovely spot for the children to play (there are some swings) and for the adults to relax. The views of the surrounding countryside are superb.

The two bedrooms, one with a double and the other with twin beds, are most attractive with their low-beamed ceilings and they overlook the garden. A bathroom is shared between them and they can both accommodate a cot.

Down below, there is a pleasant and cosy lounge with a television and a wood-burning stove, and the compact dining room is next door. A family could rent both bedrooms and have their own very peaceful self-contained unit.

Nearby: This is a delightful part of England, with glorious countryside all around and with the coastline from Brighton eastwards within easy reach. Nature lovers will head for Drusillas Park, the Seven Sisters Country Park and the Bentley Wildfowl Trust (there is also a motor museum here). Bateman's, where Rudyard Kipling wrote many of his books, is nearby, as is Herstmonceux Castle, Michelham Priory and the Bluebell Railway.

✖ Dinner (7pm) £9 (by prior arrangement)
   Children: half portions
   £ Low
   Children: no charge up to 3 years; half price from 3 to 10

Facilities: 1 cot and 1 high chair; baby-listening by arrangement
2 rooms
Open all year
No credit cards accepted
Unlicensed
P Own car park

HELTON, nr PENRITH, CUMBRIA   Map 8
Ⓗ **BECKFOOT HOUSE HOTEL**
Tel: 01931 713 241
Off the A6 south of Penrith.

The house is actually about a mile south of the village of Helton, which has a pub and is itself six miles or so from Penrith. It is quite a stately house, built of stone in the late 19th century, with a large and immaculate lawn at the front with a charming sundial and a great fir tree. It is surrounded by a variety of fine trees and at the back of the house the ground slopes up to a small paddock which is also encircled by trees. There is plenty of room for children to play, and they have an adventure playground. There is easy access to the fells with many delightful walks and masses of wildlife to spot.

The rooms are beautifully proportioned and contain several fine marble and oak fireplaces; the spacious sitting room is furnished with a variety of comfortable easy chairs. You have splendid views of the gardens and the countryside beyond, and an open fire for cooler evenings. Board games and children's toys are available. Like the lounge, the dining room has nice wood panelling and wide windows overlooking the garden.

This is very much a house where families are made welcome, and there are cots and high chairs as well as three family rooms. As you would expect of this handsome and spacious place, they are of a generous size and very well furnished and decorated: one has a double and two single beds, and the others each have a double and a single bed. All the bedrooms here have their own *en suite* facilities and television sets.

Nearby: There is much to do and see in this part of Cumbria, especially if you like walking, riding or water sports. Ullswater is a few miles away, as is Haweswater Nature Reserve. Up the road is the pretty village of Askham which lies next to the huge Lowther Park with its deer park and nature trails. It also has an adventure playground and a miniature railway. A sprint down the motorway will take you close to all the other tourist attractions of the Lakes – Grasmere, Ambleside, Coniston, Windermere and so on.

✕ Dinner (7pm)
  Children: half portions
  £ Medium
✓ Best Bargain Break: 99 per person, 3 days – dinner, b&b
  Children: free up to 7 years; half price from 8 to 16
  Facilities: 1 cot and 1 high chair
  6 rooms, 3 family
  Open Mar to Nov
  No credit cards accepted
Ⓟ Ample

HEREFORD, HEREFORDSHIRE   Map 4
ⓅⓇ STARTING GATE, Holmer
Tel: 01432 274 853
On the A49 at Holmer, alongside the racecourse.

Hereford is an interesting city and has a celebrated and ancient cathedral, as well as a racecourse, next to which stands the appropriately named Starting Gate. It was originally a gracious and well-proportioned 18th-century building which has been extended to provide a range of facilities needed by a family pub and restaurant. For example, high chairs are available, as are nappy-changing facilities.

The interior retains its charm and has an agreeable lounge at the front of the building. It has the benefit of stately Georgian windows, and a brick fireplace. There is another sitting area alongside and, incongruously, a golf putting game has been installed there. The immediate bar area has a low wooden ceiling, brick walls and padded settles.

The restaurant is a series of alcoves: one with wood-panelled walls, another with painted brick walls larded with prints, and another with pictures of famous racehorses. Upstairs, there are more dining areas, including a lovely conservatory room with a high vaulted ceiling.

On a warm day you might sit at one of the bench tables on the terrace.

....

✕ (12pm to 10.30pm; Fri and Sat till 11pm) £2–13: Greek dip, three-bean feast, sirloin Oscar, Louisiana chicken, fried scampi
   Children: own menu
◑ Ale: Boddington's, Flowers, Fremlin's
🅿 Ample

HESSENFORD, CORNWALL   **Map 1**
🅿 **COPLEY ARMS**
Tel: 01503 240 209
On the A387.
....

You will find this smart-looking pub at a point midway between St Germans and Looe. The old stones of the facade are covered in creeper and roses, with many tubs of bright flowers adding to the fun.

The River Seaton runs through the grounds of the pub and you can sit on the bench tables alongside the water. Alongside there is a sizeable play area with swings, a seesaw, a slide and some climbing frames.

The long and spacious lounge bar has plenty of tables and chairs, and booths with wooden settles. There are prints on the walls and an iron stove. The family room is comfortable and opens on to the patio area at the side of the pub. We noticed a couple of high chairs in the family room, and a buffet is also set up in there.

....

✕ (12pm to 2pm and 7pm to 9.30pm) £2–8: fisherman's pie, moussaka, Mexican chicken, cod & chips, curry
   Children: own menu
◑ Ale: Hicks
ℙ Own car park

HEVINGHAM, NORFOLK   Map 6
ⒽⓅ Marsham Arms Hotel, Holt Road
Tel: 01603 754 268
On the B1149 north of Norwich.

....

This appealing inn, smartly decorated under its tiled roof, stands in the countryside about seven miles from Norwich and was originally a hostel for farm labourers, built in the 19th century. The wooden beams and large open fireplace survive from the original design.

The building has been extended over the years especially to provide better facilities for families, who are welcome to use a spacious and nicely furnished room away from the bar. It is a no-smoking area. There is an excellent range of food on offer, and a good choice of real ales.

There is a terrace with tables and chairs and wooden benches – a pleasant place to sit in the sun with a meal or a drink. Alongside there is a children's play area, which is surrounded by trees.

Eight comfortable rooms are situated in a smart single-storey block

173

alongside the pub. These are spacious rooms, equipped with either twin or double beds and sofa beds. They can accommodate a family of four without any strain and offer very good value for money.

The Marsham Arms, out in the countryside but so close to Norwich, provides excellent all-round facilities for families.

Nearby: The Broads are quite close and it is not too long a drive to reach the coast, where two quiet and sandy beaches can be recommended – at Sea Palling and Happisburgh. This stretch of coast is, mercifully, undeveloped. There are many tourist attractions within reach: Norfolk Wildlife Park, Thrigby Hall wildlife gardens, Blickling Hall, and on the north Norfolk coast, Felbrigg Hall, the Norfolk Shire Horse Centre and the North Norfolk railway.

....

✕ Bar Snacks (11am to 2.30pm and 6pm to 10pm) £1–12: lasagne, fried scampi, steaks, whole lemon sole, smoked chicken;
Dinner (7pm to 10pm) £15: smoked mackerel, chicken supreme, pudding or cheese
Children: own menu, half portions
£ Medium
Children: free up to 5 years; £8 from 5 to 14 years
Facilities: 2 cots and 3 high chairs; 2 lines for baby-listening
8 rooms, all family
Open all year
◖ Ale: Adnams, Bass, Greene King
Ⓟ Own car park

Nr HEXHAM, NORTHUMBERLAND   **Map 9**
Ⓗ **Rye Hill Farm, Slaley**
Tel: 01434 673 259
Off the B6306 south of Hexham.

....

This is a delightful 17th-century stone farmhouse which has been converted with taste and provides excellent facilities for visitors. The building forms an open courtyard with the farmhouse at one end and the guests' bedrooms situated in the central part.

The agreeable dining room has some pine panelling and pine tables and the adjoining comfortable lounge includes a toys and games cupboard. We looked at several bedrooms, all of which have their own bathrooms, and were most impressed by the high standards of the furniture and decorations. There is a very spacious family room (with a double bed and two bunk beds for children) at one end of the building and it has superb views of the countryside from one of its windows (another window looks into a large barn).

A larger party should consider renting the Old Byre, which can accommodate up to nine people. There is a twin-bedded room, a double, and a bunk bedroom for children, plus a substantial living area with a kitchen. On a self-catering basis the cost ranges from £350 to £600.

There are thirty acres of grounds including a good stretch of garden and a patio, and there are fine views of Slaley Forest and the undulating farmland. There is loads of room for children to play and they will find a swing, a slide and a climbing frame in the grounds. Indoors, there is an excellent games room with a pool table, and plenty of games and easy chairs.

Nearby: Northumberland has sometimes been called the 'forgotten county', and if you want glorious, unspoiled countryside, and an area crammed with history – in short a place to enjoy without hustle and bustle – this is the place to be. Hadrian's Wall runs just to the north of Hexham and you can follow the line of forts from the Roman Army Museum near Haltwhistle east to the Roman site of Corbridge. A bit further afield is Kielder Forest and Kielder Water, and the interesting city of Durham.

✕ Dinner (7.30pm) £10
Children: own menu, half portions
£ Low
Children: free up to 2 years; half price up to 12
Facilities: 1 cot and 1 high chair

6 rooms, 2 family
Open all year
No credit cards accepted
Ⓟ Own car park

HIGHER BURWARDSLEY, CHESHIRE
Ⓟ PHEASANT INN
Tel: 01829 70434
Off the A534 or A41 west of Nantwich.

Map 8

This lovely old pub, built in the 17th century, has a marvellous location about ten miles from Chester in the Peckforton Hills, with splendid views across Cheshire to Wales. The Pheasant has outstanding facilities for all its customers and especially for families, who are welcome to use the spacious conservatory, a most agreeable room with its smart furniture and wonderful views.

In addition there is a sizeable lounge bar where the beamed ceiling is complemented by wooden pews and tables, and plush benches and chairs. It is also notable for the huge fireplace, open on two sides and

176

believed to be one of the biggest in the country. There is also a very pleasant restaurant, the Highland Room.

On summer days you can sit on the stone terrace at the front of the pub and enjoy the view, and families can enjoy the grassy garden where there is a play area with swings, a slide and a climbing frame, and plenty of bench tables for the adults.

This is an excellent family pub in delightful surroundings.

✕ (12pm to 2pm and 7pm to 9.30pm) £2–9: liver & onions, Lancashire hotpot, smoked salmon, sirloin steak, rack of lamb
   Children: own menu, half portions

◗ Ale: Bass and guests

▣ Own car park

HOLNE, DEVON   Map 1
Ⓡ OLD FORGE
Tel: 01364 631 351
Holne is well signposted off the A38 near Ashburton. The Old Forge is by the church.

You will find this attractive café sitting in front of the village church. The walls of the Old Forge are painted a crisp white and complement the black beams on the ceiling. The bellows and anvil which were used by the last smith, Fred Pearse, are still here.

If you drop in on a cool day you will be able to sit by the roaring fire. Families receive a friendly welcome here and food is available throughout the day. It's almost all home-made too, and children have a good range of snacks from which to choose.

The Old Forge now opens on Friday evenings (by popular local demand) when customers can take their own wine with them – and there is no corkage charge.

At the front of the Old Forge in the courtyard are some bench tables and some of these are under a pretty wooden canopy which is hung with flowers.

The café also sells some locally made craft goods and foods.

....

✗ (10am to 5.30pm daily) £1–4: full breakfast, quiche & salad, cottage
pie, curries, cream tea
Unlicensed
No credit cards accepted
Closed Nov to Feb
P Own car park

HOPE COVE, nr KINGSBRIDGE, DEVON   **Map 1**
H THE COTTAGE HOTEL
Tel: 01548 561 555
Look for Hope Cove off the A381 and take Inner Hope Road.

....

A comfortable family hotel which has an idyllic position overlooking
two safe beaches, which are protected by a grassy headland on one side.
From the terrace and the two acres of sloping garden you look out to
Thurlestone across Bigbury Bay. There are swings in the garden and a
good-sized playroom upstairs with table tennis, space invaders, a piano
and a wide window overlooking the sea.

We have had several reports about this hotel praising the helpful and
hard-working staff, who clearly understand how to look after families.
The bedrooms are very comfortable and many of them have balconies
overlooking the sea.

Nearby: This is one of the loveliest parts of Devon and not the least of the
attractions are the many sandy beaches; at Hope Cove itself, Salcombe,
Bantham Bay and Thurlestone, for instance. The South Devon Coast
Path runs through Hope Cove. The children will certainly enjoy a visit
to the National Shire Horse Centre and the Dartmoor Wildlife Park; while
Buckfast Abbey, the Dart Valley Railway, the Torbay Aircraft Museum
and Compton Castle are all within reach. Golfers can take advantage of
the special rates available to guests at Bigbury Golf Club.

....

✕ Bar snacks (12pm to 1.30pm) £1–9: sirloin steak, tortellini au gratin, plaice & chips, lobster salad;
Dinner (7.30pm to 8.30pm) £17: avocado with prawns, soup, roast duckling, pudding and cheese
Children: own menu, half portions
£ Medium

✓ Best Bargain Break: £42 per person per night – dinner, b&b
Children: £2 under one year; £6 from 1 to 3 years; £10 from 4 to 8 years; £13.50 from 9 to 12 years (includes meals)
Facilities: 6 cots and 6 high chairs; baby-listening system
35 rooms, 5 family
No credit cards accepted
Closed Jan

Ⓟ Own car park

HORNDEAN, nr PORTSMOUTH, HANTS   Map 3
Ⓟ Ⓡ **RED LION**
Tel: 01705 593 202
Just off the A3(M) north of Portsmouth.

If you are on your way to catch a ferry and have time to spare, pop into Horndean which is minutes away from the A3.

In the village square with its war memorial, and not far from Gale's Brewery (which has a shop), you will find this rambling and charming pub, with its steep roofs and dormer windows.

The restaurant is housed in the old part of the listed building and is very appealing by dint of its low wooden-beamed ceiling, alcoves and cottage-style windows. The restaurant extends into another room on a different level and there is a spacious bar.

Outside you will find an enclosed garden with bench tables, and a bouncy castle was in position when we visited.

The Red Lion serves food throughout the day; there are high chairs and a baby-changing facility.

✗ (11.30am to 10pm; Sun from 12pm) £2–8: fish dippers, chicken escalopes, tagliatelle carbonara, turkey fillet, vegetable moussaka
Children: own menu
◐ Ale: Boddington's, Flowers and guests

HORRINGER, SUFFOLK   Map 6
P BEEHIVE
Tel: 01284 735 260
On the A143, just south of Bury St Edmunds.

....

The simple flintstone front of this 18th-century pub gives no clue to the roominess of the interior. There are several rooms, well proportioned and pleasantly intimate under the low ceilings, gathered around a central bar area; they include two delightful small rooms at one side, with wood panelling and excellent oak and pine furniture, and families with children are welcome there.

There is a wide range of interesting food at the Beehive, and new dishes appear on the menu (and on the blackboard of daily specials) at regular intervals. There is an enterprising wine list as well. If the weather is warm you might enjoy the food on the smartly furnished terrace, or in the immaculate garden. These areas are floodlit in the evenings. There is a small farm next door and children are welcome to visit the various animals: sheep, geese, horses, chickens and ducks.

....

✗ (12pm to 2pm and 7pm to 9.45pm) £2–9: scrambled eggs with smoked haddock, taramasalata with pitta bread, steak sandwich, fresh salmon fishcake, shredded lamb stir-fry
Children: half portions
◐ Ale: Greene King
P Own car park

HUCKNALL, nr NOTTINGHAM　　　　　　　　Map 7
P **MALT SHOVEL**
Tel: 0115 963 0144
On the B683 north of Nottingham.

Look for a cream-painted building with wooden lapboards on the side of the road. There are car parks situated to the rear and to the side of the building where you will also find the main entrance to the restaurant. At the front of the pub is a raised grassed area where there are several picnic bench tables; there are plans to install children's play equipment next year.

It is a very open and spacious building which is basically split into three parts: the restaurant (where families are currently permitted to sit and dine); the lounge bar; and the public bar. The restaurant has, as its central feature, a large stone log- and coal-burning fireplace, and there are a number of glass cabinets dotted around containing chinaware, padded settles throughout, wooden farmhouse tables and chairs, and padded stools. It is light and airy, and a quiet place to dine.

✕ (12pm to 2pm and 6pm to 9.30pm; not Sun lunchtime) £2–10: garlic mushrooms, mushroom Stroganoff, fillet steak, oriental chicken, cassoulet of duck
　Children: own menu, half portions
◔ Ale: Shipton's, Tetley's, Greenall's and guests
P Own car park

Nr HUDDERSFIELD, WEST YORKS　　　　　　Map 9
P R **THE SHIP, Mirfield**
Tel: 01924 493 364
Close to junction 25 of the M62. Take the A644 east to Mirfield.

You must turn past The Swan and cross the bridge, and then you will see The Ship, a white-painted stone building. Towards the rear of the car park there is a garden and a patio area and it has a play area at the centre containing several large climbing frames and slides. At one end of this area is a miniature grand prix racing circuit (with electric cars) and an area for a bouncy castle (both safely enclosed).

If you enter the pub from the patio there is a long dining room, part of which is balustraded and raised. Beyond, there is a two-storey fun centre containing a ball swamp, slides and ropes. Further into the pub, you will find several lounge areas, and the open-plan main bar has a raised gallery at the far end. The decoration is mainly pine, brass and chintz and there is a magnificent Victorian wood and brick fireplace in the corner off the bar. The atmosphere is pleasant and welcoming and all the facilities a family needs are in place: high chairs, nappy-changing units, plenty of space, and the availability of food throughout the day.

The Calder Canal runs alongside the pub.

....

✗ (11.30am to 10pm) £2–8: onion bhajis, haddock & chips, chicken escalopes, tagliatelle carbonara, steak & kidney pie
　Children: own menu, half portions
◖ Ale: Boddington's and guests
ℙ Ample

Nr HUNTINGDON, CAMBS　　　　　　　　Map 6
ℙ THE OLDE MILL, Brampton
Tel: 01480 459 758
Between Huntingdon and Brampton off the A141 in Bornholme Lane, which is signposted.

....

Listed in the Domesday Book, The Olde Mill stands on an island in the River Ouse. It was once a saw mill, and the gentle sound of running water from the mill wheel, visible in the centre of the inn, is one of the soothing comforts of this delightful place. To add to its interest, The Olde Mill is said to be haunted.

The setting is idyllic, by the river bank which is decked with trees and flowers. There is a small garden with a springy frog and a see-saw horse, a lovely patio and a barbecue facility. The other building on the island has recently been acquired, and there are plans to enlarge the garden and to open an indoor children's play area. Farmland and boats give further beauty to the scene, and free mooring is provided for those travelling by boat who might like to linger a while. This offer is extended to those who would like to moor overnight.

The pub has a children's licence, and the bar stands to one side of the entrance while the restaurant is on several levels beyond the mill wheel. Baby-changing facilities are centred in the Ladies' toilet, and there are five high chairs, bibs, children's cutlery and special children's packs. It is advisable to book a table in advance if you wish to dine on a summer evening.

There is a children's menu and a variety of other options for young people. The public house is open from 11 in the morning until 11 at night, and bar food may be had at any time during these hours.

....

✕ (12pm to 2pm and 5pm to 10.30pm; weekends 12pm to 10.30pm)
£2–11: pork satay, three-bean feast, steaks, ocean bake, mushroom mornay chicken
Children: own menu

◌ Ale: Boddington's, Flowers, Castle Eden, Wethered's and guests

🅿 Ample

HUTTON, nr WESTON-SUPER-MARE, AVON   Map 2
Ⓗ MOORLANDS
Tel: 01934 812 283
In the village, which is south of Weston-super-Mare and can be reached from the A371 or A370.

This is a most attractive Georgian house in a village which sits at the foot of the Mendip Hills. The garden spreads over two secluded acres with lawns, trees, rockeries, a lovely display of flowers, a kitchen garden and a paddock where pony rides are arranged. It is relaxing and safe for children to play; there is a slide, a climbing frame and a garden badminton set. Both the dining room and the comfortable lounge look over the gardens and beyond to the wooded hills.

The outlook of Mr and Mrs Holt is stated in their brochure: that they receive visitors into their own home as guests and try to make them feel at home. That certainly includes children, since there are five rooms which can accommodate two adults and a child. Two of them have a double and two single beds.

There is a vegetable garden and the owners use as much of their own, and local, produce as possible.

Nearby: If you like an active holiday you could hardly be in a better spot: golf, fishing and a dry ski slope are available in the locality. The traditional seaside resort of Weston-super-Mare is quite close and it has an excellent leisure centre. Glastonbury and Wells are nearby; as are Cheddar Gorge, the Wookey Hole caves, Ebbor Gorge and the East Somerset railway. A bit further afield, nature lovers can head for Chew Valley Lake and Cricket St Thomas Wildlife Park.

✕ Dinner (6.30pm) £10: home-made soup, beef Italien, pudding and cheese
£ Low
Children: 25% up to 2 years; half price thereafter
Facilities: 4 cots and 3 high chairs; baby-listening system
7 rooms, 5 family
Open Jan to Oct inclusive

P Own car park

Nr HYDE, GREATER MANCHESTER   Map 8
P R GUN INN, Hollingworth
Tel: 01457 762 388
Where the A57 and A628 meet at Hollingworth.

The Gun Inn stands at a very busy junction, its stone walls somewhat sombre. It was built in the 18th century and has an agreeable L-shaped bar with a low beamed ceiling and open fireplaces. There are two lounge areas to the side, where families might settle; one has some shelves filled with books and the other a display of old bottles and a wood-burning stove.

The restaurant is housed in an old barn with a high ceiling. All sorts of artefacts relating to milling hang from the rafters, and prints and beer tankards decorate the walls. It's great fun, and there is another smaller room up a few stairs. High chairs are made available and food is served throughout the day.

X (12pm to 10pm; Sat until 8pm) £2–13: Bury black pudding, giant Yorkshire puddings, Barnsley chop, venison casserole, seafood pancakes
   Children: half portions
O Ale: Boddington's, Castle Eden
P Own car park

ICKHAM, KENT   Map 3
P DUKE WILLIAM
Tel: 01227 721 308
Off the A257 about five miles east of Canterbury.

Set in a pleasant village, this roomy and attractive 17th-century pub has a cheerful air. The style is set by the ebullient and friendly landlord who was a professional chef for twenty years or so and who produces a very wide choice of freshly cooked dishes, both at the bar and in the spacious restaurant. The set menu is very good value at under £14 and high chairs are available.

Families can take advantage of a room at the back of the pub, which leads out to a delightful lawned garden, crowded with plants and flowers, or of the conservatory which was built recently and is a no-smoking area. To one side is a patio and some swings; there is more patio with goldfish ponds at the back – all this is lit up on summer evenings. From here you look out on rolling farmland.

....

✕ (12pm to 2pm and 6.30pm to 10pm, not Sun pm or Mon am, except bank hols) £2–10: Duke William brunch, plaice & chips, spaghetti carbonara, sausages & mash, pizzas
   Children: own menu, small portions
◯ Ale: Adnams, Fuller's, Shepherd Neame, Young's
🅿 Ample street parking

ILFRACOMBE, DEVON   Map 1
Ⓗ SOUTHCLIFFE HOTEL, Torrs Park
Tel: 01271 862 958
Near the centre of the town.

....

Once a Victorian gentleman's residence, this large building retains its attractive stained-glass windows and original marble fireplaces. The owners, Mr and Mrs Anderson, have attacked the family market with great resolve and everything here is geared up for parents with young children.

Apart from the many cots and high chairs, there is a children's playroom with all sorts of toys, a Wendy House and a small model railway. Board games can also be made available, and cartoons are shown on the video in the playroom. There are loads of books around the hotel, plus a games room for older children with a pool table and darts. Just as useful for parents is a kitchen where food can be prepared for small children; and there is also a washing machine, a spin drier, an iron, etc on the premises.

The attractive rear garden has a lawn on two levels, a fine display of flowers and a couple of copper beech trees. You can sit happily in the sun and there is room for the children to play. They have a swing and the owners provide various garden games. The lounge, with its comfortable chairs and sofas, overlooks the garden, as does the dining room.

You can be assured that the food will be of good quality here, because the owners used to run an excellent wholefood restaurant in Shrewsbury – the Good Life, which is still recommended in the *Family Welcome Guide*.

Nearby: Ilfracombe is a popular holiday resort with many attractions and if you fancy a change from the beaches there is a good indoor swimming pool. The children will no doubt enjoy a visit to Watermouth Castle, Exmoor Bird Gardens and Combe Martin Wildlife Park; while the adults will perhaps argue the case for Braunton Burrows nature reserve, Arlington Court and Dunster Castle. The beauty of Exmoor is on the doorstep, too.

✗ Dinner (6.30pm): melon & orange salad, diced pork in cider, pudding and cheese
Children: own menu, half portions
£ Low
✓ Best Bargain Break: £160 per person per week – dinner, b&b
Children: first child free up to 5 years (before mid-July and after the end of August); one third of full rate up to 2 years; half from 2 to 11; three quarters from 12 to 14
Facilities: plenty of cots and high chairs; baby-listening system
14 rooms, 4 family, 4 sets interconnecting
Open Easter to Sept
No credit cards accepted
🅿 Own car park

ILKLEY, WEST YORKS   Map 9
® BETTYS CAFE TEAROOMS, 34 The Grove
Tel: 01943 608 029
In the town centre.

....

This busy and cheerful tearoom, like the other Bettys (qv Harrogate, Northallerton and York), is immediately appealing, with its marble-topped tables, basket-weave chairs, pot plants and delightful collection of teapots on shelves around the walls. There are real flowers on the tables and the tea is also made from real tea leaves; there is a wide selection, as there is of coffee.

The long room has windows down one side which makes it a bright and airy place; and those adjectives might also apply to the staff, who cope with the demands of a busy café with great charm.

Above all, the Ilkley tearooms welcome families, providing an interesting children's menu and superb mother and baby facilities, with a playpen, changing mat and chair in the Ladies and eight high chairs in the restaurant. Most of the café is no-smoking.

....

✗ (9am to 6pm) £1–7: rarebits, raclette & ham florentine, cheese & herb pâté, haddock & chips, bacon muffins
   Children: own menu, half portions
   Open every day except Christmas Day and Boxing Day
P Public car park at rear

Nr IPSWICH, SUFFOLK   Map 6
P OSTRICH INN, Wherstead
Tel: 01473 601 994
On the A137 south of Ipswich at Bourne End.

....

This inn was once known as The Dock Arms, for a public house has stood here since 1612, and the Ostrich Inn is close to the West Terminal of Ipswich Docks. It retains much of its 17th-century flavour in its interior and boasts a charming garden with swings, slides, family benches and a dovecote. There is a pleasant patio with a goldfish pond.

A high chair is available on request, there is a children's menu, and half portions are also provided. All major credit cards are accepted, and children are welcome anywhere in the dining area.

There are plans to offer accommodation in the near future, and the inn is within easy access of some lovely countryside, boating facilities and the centre of Ipswich, an historic town with a splendid new theatre.

The Ostrich Inn opens from 11am to 2.30pm, and from 6.30pm until 11pm. Food is available for most of that time.

....

✕ (12pm to 2pm and 7pm to 10pm) £2–11: devilled whitebait, plaice & chips, sirloin steak, scampi, chestnut casserole
   Children: own menu, half portions
◻ Ale: Flowers, Tetley
P Own car park

Nr IPSWICH, SUFFOLK   Map 6
P THE SWAN, Westerfield
Tel: 01473 251 447
Just north of Ipswich on the B1077 at Westerfield.

....

A light, welcoming and comfortable public house on the outskirts of Ipswich, The Swan is situated in a pleasant village, and it is argued that an inn has stood here since the early 17th century, although it is believed that it was once on the opposite side of the road. This is a quiet house much valued by the locals, and it has a small, well-tended garden with flowers, trees, family tables with umbrellas for shade, and a slide.

The pub is open from 11am until 2.30pm, and from 5.30 until 11pm, and food is available for most of that time, with provision for children and two high chairs available.

Two steps lead up from the bar to the restaurant, which is light and airy and opens on to the garden. The agricultural decoration reflects the surrounding area, but the dominant character is one of quiet comfort and welcoming care. Home-cooked bar food supplements the standard menu. Children are always welcome in the restaurant, which is very much a family dining area.

....

✕ (12pm to 1.45pm and 7pm to 10pm) £2–10: nut risotto, plaice & chips, sirloin steak, lasagne, chicken Balti
   Children: own menu, half portions
◑ Ale: Tetley, Tolly and guests
ℙ Own car park

KEIGHLEY, WEST YORKS   Map 9
ℙℝ THE BEECHES TOBY HOTEL
Tel: 01535 510 611
Just to the east of Keighley on the A650.

....

The Beeches occupies a modern stone building with an agreeable look, due to its irregularly shaped roofline, wide windows and conservatory. Alongside the upper car park there are grass verges and a stone-flagged terrace with wooden picnic benches and parasols; here the children will find a fully enclosed play area containing a wooden assault course on a safe bark surface.

Families are encouraged to use the restaurant entrance and the first impression one gets is of having walked into a Victorian cottage. There is plenty of dark wood panelling, a stone fireplace with velvet wing-backed armchairs at either side, and much bric-à-brac on shelves and in cabinets all around. This small lobby area is linked via an archway to the lounge and it is in these two areas that families may enjoy a snack and a drink.

The main restaurant is split into several distinct areas by the use of wooden balustrades or glass cabinets. The furniture is predominantly dark wood to match the panelling. However, a conservatory built on the front of the building is furnished in light pine with bamboo roof blinds and rattan furniture, which gives it a colonial look.

At the opposite end of the building is the main bar which is done as a stylized coaching inn; once again dark wood panelling abounds, and there are padded settles, wooden and wrought-iron tables, and bosun chairs. High chairs are provided, too.

....

✕ (12pm to 2pm and 5.30pm to 10pm; Sun all day) £2–13: garlic prawns, wild mushroom steak, sesame chicken, cashew nut paella, lemon sole

Children: own menu, half portions

◖ Ale: Bass, Stones

ℙ Own car park

Nr KESWICK, CUMBRIA   **Map 8**
Ⓗ **MARY MOUNT HOTEL**
Tel: 017687 77223
On the B5289 south of Keswick.

....

The hotel has a wonderful location on the shores of Lake Derwentwater, amid the relaxing surroundings of water, mountains and woodland. It is an excellent base for exploring this part of the Lake District.

The Mary Mount is housed in an imposing 1930s slate-fronted building with dormer windows, and the public rooms are spacious and bright. They include a comfortable lounge, a very welcoming wood-panelled bar and a sizeable dining room with wide windows which overlook the gardens. These are extensive, with sloping lawns, lots of fine trees and a stream. It is a delightful place in which to sit and enjoy the peace and quiet.

We looked at several of the bedrooms and were impressed by the amount of space provided and by the excellent standards of the furnishings and decorations. This was especially so in a very large family room which has four single beds and plenty of room for some easy chairs; with three windows looking out to the lovely surroundings, it is a very bright and welcoming room. Six rooms are contained in an adjoining bungalow and these rooms are very quiet and secluded; two large double rooms can easily accommodate an extra bed or a cot.

The Mary Mount is a very congenial family hotel in a beautiful location and the rooms are reasonably priced.

Nearby: All the outdoor pursuits of the Lakes are here to be enjoyed – walking and climbing, water sports, fishing, horse riding and golf. The many attractions of the Lakes are all within reach, including Lowther Park, Grasmere, Townend, Belle Isle, Brantwood, the Grizedale Forest Centre, Fell Foot Park and the Ravenglass and Eskdale Railway.

....

✖ Bar snacks (12pm to 2pm) £1–6: pâté, smoked trout, plaice & chips, Cumberland sausage;
Dinner (6.30pm to 9pm) £13: prawn platter, lamb chops, pudding or cheese
Children: own menu
£ Medium
Children: £5 up to 4 years; half price thereafter
Facilities: 2 cots and a high chair
14 rooms, 5 family
Open all year
🅿 Own car park

KETTERING, NORTHANTS
Map 7
Ⓗ **KETTERING PARK HOTEL**
Tel: 01536 416 666
Just south of Kettering, close to the new link road (A14) between the M1 and A1.

....

This is one of several new hotels built by the enterprising Shire Inns Group. Aimed at the business market during the week, its location and excellent range of facilities make the Kettering Park Hotel an appealing place for families to visit at weekends.

It is a handsome modern structure, built of brick, with a steeply pitched roof with a double line of dormer windows. The interior is very smart indeed; the reception areas have deep sofas and armchairs, wood panelling, oil paintings and the occasional tapestry on the walls, and the theme is continued in the comfortable bar and the attractive restaurant.

The emphasis is on comfort and especially so in the spacious family rooms. We looked at several and were impressed by the high standard of decoration and furnishings. The rooms have plenty of space for a double bed, two extra beds for children and a cot or two. Some rooms interconnect and can be used as family suites.

The Leisure Club has superb facilities, including a sizeable swimming pool (13 × 9 metres), two glass-backed squash courts and a gym with some serious equipment. All the facilities are properly supervised and include a children's pool, a whirlpool, sauna, solarium and steam room. In addition there is a snooker room with two full-size tables. There is also a pleasant garden with a rockery and a pond.

Family activity weekends are a special feature of this hotel and we recommend it as a smart and modern establishment with splendid facilities.

Nearby: The hotel has special concessions for guests at the Kettering Leisure Village and at Wicksteed Park. If you are in the mood for sightseeing, you can head for Boughton House, Lamport Hall, Lilford Park, Althorp, Rockingham Castle, Southwick Hall, or Canons Ashby. Billing Aquadrome is another attraction, along with the Waterways Museum and Grafham Water.

....

✗ Bar snacks (12pm to 2pm, Mon to Sat) £2–5: buffet, mushroom & courgette casserole, beef casserole;
Lunch (12.30pm to 2pm) £13: seafood fettucine, brochette of lamb, pudding or cheese;
Dinner (7pm to 9pm) £22: duck liver parfait, poached salmon, pudding or cheese
Children: own menu, half portions
£ High

✓ Best Bargain Break: £62 per person per night – dinner, b&b
Children: free up to 16 years
Facilities: 4 cots and 6 high chairs; baby-listening

88 rooms, 16 family, 4 sets interconnecting
Open all year
◑ Ale: Thwaites
🄿 Ample

KETTERING, NORTHANTS   Map 7
🄿🅁 TELFORD LODGE
Tel: 01536 310 082
One mile south-west of Kettering, on the A43 close to the junction with the A14. Follow signs to Telford Way Industrial Estate.

If you are haring along the A14 and you and your family need a break, the Telford Lodge, a new purpose-built and very spacious pub and restaurant, might be the right place for you. It's a well-designed and functional building which is open all day and every day and provides food, including children's menus, from 11.30 in the morning until 10 o'clock at night. And, if you want to break your journey overnight, there is a Travel Inn alongside – one of Whitbread's hotels with reasonably priced rooms.

The restaurant is large and bright, broken up by brick pillars here and there and with wide windows on to a terrace. There is a raised dining area at one end. Plenty of high chairs are provided and there are, in these politically correct times, both mother and baby and father and baby rooms.

Alongside the restaurant there is a huge indoor play area (Charlie Chalk's Fun Factory) which contains an amazing array of playthings – heaven for children, who must be supervised by their adults. Up above there is an adventure playground (£1 entry fee) with a multitude of rope swings, scramble nets and other things on which to climb, jump and swing.

In addition to the restaurant, there is an equally spacious bar area, comfortably furnished, bright and appealing. Laid out on two levels, the screens and the wooden panelling make it a congenial place to settle; it has the atmosphere of a busy brasserie.

If it's a pleasant day, you can sit on the paved terrace at the front of the pub. There is an enclosed play unit for children and it has a safe surface.

✗ (11.30am to 10pm) £2–8: onion bhajis, fillet of plaice, chicken escalopes, Teviotdale pie, tagliatelle carbonara
Children: own menu
Ale: Boddington's, Flowers, Marston's and guests
P Loads

KIDDERMINSTER, HEREFORD & WORCS **Map 4**
P R MARE & COLT
Tel: 01562 824 116
On the A449 just south of Kidderminster.

This is an unremarkable roadside pub with a railway line running behind it, but it has the virtue of possessing a huge lawned and enclosed garden, with a scattering of trees, a children's play park, swings and a slide. It's a good spot to settle on a warm day while the children let off steam.

High chairs are made available in the restaurant, which is a large L-shaped room with brick walls, enlivened by prints, farming artefacts, bookshelves (with books), and a selection of copper pans and china plates above the food service area.

The sizeable bar is in much the same style, with a low beamed ceiling, curved padded benches and small cottage-style windows. With a nod to the Mare & Colt's past as a traditional pub, there is a dartboard at one end of the bar. The pub is open all day and serves bar food, and the restaurant hours are shown below.

✗ (12pm to 2.30pm and 6pm to 10.30pm; Sun 12pm to 10.30pm) £2–13: Cajun prawns, sirloin Oscar, ocean bake, three-bean feast, Louisiana chicken
Children: own menu

Ⓓ Ale: Boddington's, Flowers and guests
Ⓟ Own car park

KINGS LANGLEY, HERTS   **Map 5**
ⓅⓇ **LANGLEYS, Hempstead Road**
Tel: 01923 263 150
In King's Langley (on A41).

....

This very substantial three-storeyed house, with bay windows and dormers, was a family home until a couple of decades ago. It is now a very large pub and restaurant with excellent facilities for families, and there is a Lodge Inn with forty bedrooms alongside.

You approach the pub through a pleasant front garden with stately trees and you will notice the veranda with its railings and some white wrought-iron furniture. A patio at the front has some bench tables.

The sizeable family dining area (no-smoking) is in two main sections and is attractively laid out with wooden furniture, smart wallpaper and lively prints on the walls (one of a cockatoo catches the eye, for instance). The second room is up a few steps and has a good cast-iron fireplace with the original tiles, and a large bay window. There is a baby-changing room here and a large play area with a ball swamp and other playthings. The pub has several high chairs and booster seats.

The other dining areas are attractively done and some of the tables are laid out in booths with padded settles. The bar has plenty of comfortable seats and there is another nice brick fireplace here.

At the back of the pub there is another stretch of lawn with tall trees, and a paved terrace with plenty of bench tables. The big play area has a safe surface and a bouncy castle is provided during the summer months.

....

✕ (12pm to 10pm; Sun until 9pm; breakfasts are served from 7am)
£2–9: prawn platter, Cumberland sausage, Cajun chicken, peppered
steak, lasagne
Children: own menu

🍺 Ale: Theakston's

🅿 Own car park

KINGSCOTE, GLOS
Map 4

🅷🅿 **HUNTER'S HALL**
Tel: 01453 860 393
On the A4153 west of the junction with the A46.

This impressive old coaching inn, built of mellow stone, stands alone
opposite the turning to Kingscote Village. It is very much a pub
which welcomes families and has plenty of space to cope with the
large number of people who gather to eat and drink here. There
is a good-sized bar and a large dining room on the other side of
the pub.

Upstairs, there is a lot more space, including a room specifically
designed for families. It is a pleasant spot, nicely decorated and well
furnished with pine tables. At very busy times you can overflow into
a beamed function room alongside.

The garden is really delightful: it is huge with an immaculate lawn
and is beautifully laid out with bushes and small trees. There are lots
of tables; and a play area with swings, a mini assault course, and a fort.
Barbecues are held here at weekends.

The various bedrooms are in the converted stable block and blacksmith's shop alongside the inn and the one family room is ideal for a
family of four, since it has two bedrooms, a small dining area and a
small kitchen.

Nearby: This is a delightful part of the world with some interesting
towns in which to browse – Tetbury and Malmesbury, for example. You
can easily reach the Wildfowl Trust at Slimbridge, and Berkeley Castle,

with its remarkable history, is quite close, as is the famous Westonbirt Arboretum.

....

✘ Bar snacks (12pm to 2pm and 7pm to 9.45pm) £3–9: seafood tagliatelle, whole grilled plaice, lamb & red wine casserole, steak & kidney pie, vegetarian chilli;
Dinner (7pm to 9.45pm) £16: fresh asparagus, whole roast poussin, pudding or cheese
Children: own menu
Facilities: 1 cot and 4 high chairs
£ Medium

✓ Best Bargain Break: £49 per person, 2 days – b&b
Children: cot free; extra bed £5
12 rooms, 1 family
Open all year

◻ Ale: Bass, Hook Norton, Uley, Wadworth's

ℙ Own car park

KINGSTEIGNTON, nr NEWTON ABBOT, DEVON   Map 1
ℙ **OLD RYDON INN, Rydon Road**
Tel: 01626 54626
Just north of Newton Abbot. Follow the Kingsteignton signs from the A380. At top of a hill turn right and Rydon Road is at the bottom of the hill on the right.

....

Once a farmhouse, this is a handsome building, parts of which date back to the 13th century. A steeply pitched roof overhangs the building at the back, and the front is beautifully proportioned, white-painted, and with wisteria clinging to it.

Inside are a series of small rooms with hugely thick walls and black ceiling beams. Up some stairs above the bar is a room where families are welcome to go: it was once the hayloft, and is a lovely room with plenty of tables at which to park yourselves. On Sundays and Mondays and at lunchtimes families have alternative places to go: the restaurant and dining room are also available, and are very pleasant and cosy rooms. In the restaurant, there is a table with a glass centre and below it you can see an old well which should interest the children.

In addition there is an attractive conservatory alongside the terrace and a pretty lawned garden with a swing.

A wide range of original food is always available and all of it is freshly prepared and cooked; and there is a high chair. Close to the south-west end of the M5, and only a short detour off the A38, this is a pub which is well worth seeking out.

✕ (12pm to 2pm and 7pm to 10pm) £1–6: egg & smoked salmon mayonnaise, seafood casserole, beef & mushroom pie, butterbean & vegetable gratinée, Tandoori chicken
Children: own menu

Ale: Bass, Wadworth's and guests

P Own car park

KINGSTON, nr LEWES, EAST SUSSEX **Map 3**
P THE JUGGS, The Street
Tel: 01273 472 523
South of Lewes and signposted off the A27.

This delightful pub, with a half-tiled façade, dates from the 15th century and has a splendid bar with a low beamed ceiling and a big open fireplace; there are prints on the walls, an array of wooden tables and padded benches. The owners emphasize that they try to cater for a wide spectrum of customers, and their facilities for families are first-class.

The sizeable family room (a no-smoking area) is particularly attractive, with brick floor and walls, lots of wood in view and wide windows to a patio. Alongside there is another agreeable room with a low ceiling, an old pew against one wall and a collection of brass pans and china jugs.

On the other side of the pub there is a charming little eating area, which used to be the kitchen (and was once a stable) and has a slanting beamed roof, whitewashed walls and smart furniture. Families are very welcome here, too, and it can be reserved in advance. The rest of the bar can also be used for casual eating. An enterprising range of food is on offer here and the landlord takes great pains to offer a wide range of non-alcoholic drinks, which include fruit juices.

A long, brick-floored terrace runs outside the pub. There is a fine display of flowers and plenty of bench tables. A further patio area is enclosed by a hedge on one side and a wall on the other and children can have fun on the sturdy timber climbing frame. With a little patch of lawn as well, this is a lovely spot to have a drink or an alfresco meal.

X (12pm to 2pm and 6pm to 9.30pm) £2–9: haddock & chips, vegetable savoury, fillet steak, salt beef sandwich, chicken tikka
Children: own menu
☐ Ale: Harvey's, King & Barnes
P Own car park

KNARESBOROUGH, NORTH YORKS
Map 9
H THE DOWER HOUSE
Tel: 01423 863 302
On the A59 at the foot of Knaresborough High Street.

This is an archetypal English country house hotel. Built in the 17th century, its well-proportioned brick walls are covered in ivy. It is located in a delightful part of Yorkshire and the town has the remains of a famous castle.

The entrance hall of the hotel leads into the lounge bar, a congenial spot with wooden beams, seats upholstered in red velvet and an inglenook fireplace built from stone and brick. This is turn leads to the dining room, which has an enclosed veranda overlooking the gardens at the rear. This dining area is a large and airy modern extension to the building with plain brick walls and dark wooden furniture.

The garden comprises a grassed and terraced area which stretches right around the side of the building and contains evergreens and summer flowers. Another area, beyond a stone wall, has a small stone-flagged terrace on either side of which are two rose gardens. Here, there are wrought-iron tables and chairs with parasols. An interesting feature of these gardens is an 18th-century detached stone building which has been converted into a double bedroom.

The hotel has a leisure club which includes a 12-metre swimming pool, a whirlpool spa and a fully equipped fitness room complete with aerobic machines, machine weights and dumbbell weights. Along a small corridor leading from this area there is a solarium and a steam room. Guests have free use of all the facilities except the solarium.

The bedrooms are well appointed and comfortable; some are in the original 18th-century building, and other modern rooms are in the extensions to the hotel.

Nearby: There is a host of things to do and see in the vicinity, beginning with the adjoining cities of York and Harrogate, while the Dales and the North York Moors can be reached easily. Castle Howard, Fountains Abbey, Newby Hall and Gardens, Flamingo Land, Harewood House and many other attractions are close at hand.

✖ Bar snacks (12pm to 2pm, Mon to Fri) £2–6: lasagne, jacket potatoes, sandwiches;
   Dinner (7pm to 9.30pm) £19: smoked mackerel timbale, soup, braised oxtails, pudding
   Children: own menu
   £ High
✓ Best Bargain Break: £48–55 per person per night – dinner, b&b
   32 rooms, 14 family
   Children: free of charge
   Facilities: 2 cots and 3 high chairs; baby-listening
   Open all year
🄿 Own car park

KNOWLE, WARWICKS   Map 4
🄿🅁 **WILSON ARMS**
Tel: 01564 772 559
On the A4141 at Knowle.

....

This stately pub, several centuries old, suits the pleasant town of Knowle very well. Smartly painted white, the two original buildings are connected by a single-storey brick extension to form a very large pub and restaurant. There is a small terrace at the front of the pub and a patch of garden with a few bench tables.

The large bar, its walls panelled in wood, is housed in the main building, and was very busy when we visited during a lunchtime; it has the bustling atmosphere of an authentic pub.

The restaurant covers a lot of space and has been skilfully designed. The lounge area has brick walls, wooden beams and a handsome fireplace; the bay window gives plenty of light. The restaurant is a splendid long room under a high ceiling with ancient wooden pillars and sturdy beams. Again, the bay windows give lots of daylight and create a welcoming atmosphere. It's a very agreeable place to have a meal. Several high chairs are provided and babies can be changed in the disabled toilet area. The menu is extensive and the Sunday lunch is good value at under £9 for two courses.

....

✕ (12pm to 2pm and 6pm to 10pm; Sun 12pm to 10 pm) £2–11: chicken tikka, scampi, mushroom strudel, steaks, minted lamb cutlets
Children: own menu
⌂ Ale: Bass
Ⓟ Own car park

Nr KNOWLE, WARWICKS   Map 4
Ⓟ Ⓡ ORANGE TREE
Tel: 01564 782 458
South of Knowle on the A4141 at Chadwick End.

....

This agreeable old village inn has been greatly extended but its character retained. The bar area still has its low ceiling held in place by wooden beams and the small diamond-paned windows are true to the origins of the building. Alcoves with sofas and padded benches have been placed to the side of the bar and it's an inviting place to sit with a glass of real ale, of which there is a good choice.

The restaurant has been constructed on two levels and is divided into a series of small rooms and alcoves. The wide windows make the area bright and cheerful. High chairs are provided and there is a nappy-changing facility in the Ladies. The family dining room is a no-smoking area, and it contains a play area for toddlers.

The gardens are extensive and include a grassy area at the front of the pub with several bench tables. At the back there is a very large stretch of lawn with several mature trees and a children's play unit. Unusually for a pub, crazy golf has been installed, and in summer a bouncy castle is set up for the children.

....

✕ (11.30am to 10pm) £2–8: fish dippers, Teviotdale pie, vegetable moussaka, gammon steak, plaice & chips

203

Children: own menu
ⅅ Ale: Boddington's, Castle Eden, Flowers
Ⓟ Own car park

KNUTSFORD, CHESHIRE   Map 8
Ⓡ DAVID'S PLACE, 44 King Street
Tel: 01565 633 356
In the centre of the town.

....

This restaurant has been in the *Guide* since its first edition over ten years
ago and its standards have never wavered. It is located in a smart and
interesting street and those words apply also to David's Place, which
is housed in what was once a general store and bakery. Reports have
commended the quality of the food ('excellent') and its presentation
('superb'), and the welcoming staff.

Beyond the agreeable bar area there is a very attractive dining room,
spacious and bright, and alongside there is another connecting room. A
little balcony holds two tables. The furniture includes some nice wicker
chairs and large pots contain trailing plants.

Children can have smaller portions of the various dishes, and the
lunch menu offers excellent value. A series of regional menus are offered
in addition to other choices; when we visited, tarte Alsacienne and poulet
au Riesling caught the eye. A glass of wine is included in the price of
£15.50 for two courses.

....

✗ Lunch (12.30pm to 2pm) £19: fresh asparagus, herbed liver
  dumplings, pudding or cheese;
  Dinner (7pm to 10pm) £24: smoked salmon & dill pâté, roast loin
  of venison, pudding or cheese
  Children: small portions
  Closed Sun and bank holidays
Ⓟ Public car park or street parking

LANGHAM, LEICS   Map 7
P NOEL ARMS
Tel: 01572 722 931
Off the A606 in the centre of the village.

This pub is only a stone's throw from the famous Ruddles brewery. It is an attractive and spacious pub with a small patio by the front entrance.

You enter a long, low-ceilinged bar furnished with good wooden furniture: an oak chest, settles and nice tables. Families are welcome to occupy one end of this room, where they are well away from the bar area. But there is also a pleasant and spacious coffee room on the other side of the pub. There was a very enticing cold buffet on display when we last visited. A traditional Sunday lunch is served for around £10.

The pub is open from 11am to 11pm from Monday to Saturday, and also offers breakfasts from 10 o'clock onwards – so it is a useful pub for families. The accommodation comprises three bedrooms.

✗ (11.30am to 3pm and 6pm to 10pm) £2–9: devilled whitebait, smoked salmon, plaice & chips, venison pie, moussaka
     Children: half portions
P Ale: Marston's, Banks's
P Own car park

LANTEGLOS, nr CAMELFORD, CORNWALL   Map 1
H HOTEL LANTEGLOS
Tel: 01840 213 551
A mile off the A39 at Helstone (near Camelford).

This hotel is run for families by a family who have taken the utmost care to provide everything necessary for parents and children to have a good holiday.

It's a lovely stone country house set in fifteen acres of delightful garden, sheltered by mature trees, and with its own stream. It was built as a rectory for the local church by the famous architect, Augustus Pugin. There are splendid facilities – plenty of indoor and outdoor play areas, a woodland fort, and a spacious heated swimming pool and paddling pool in the lawned gardens.

A splendid conservatory has been built alongside the bar and its great advantage is that it looks over a play area. So the adults can sit there in peace and still keep an eye on their offspring. There is a hard tennis court, a squash court and a badminton court. Bowood Park golf course is next door to the hotel: guests have direct access, priority tee times and reduced green fees, and the hotel has concessionary rates at ten other golf courses. There is a children's entertainer at peak times.

There are a number of self-catering lodges and the rents vary from £110 to £525 a week.

Nearby: If you should wish to venture forth for other entertainment, there are safe and sandy beaches close at hand: Daymer Bay and Trebarwith Strand, for example. The famous Bodmin Moor is a few miles south, and nature lovers will perhaps head for the Tamar Otter Park. Wesley's Cottage, Pencarrow, Lanhydrock and the Farm Park near Launceston are other nearby attractions.

....

✘ Bar snacks (12pm to 2pm and 6pm to 10pm) £2–7: steak & mushroom pie, Cornish fish bake, chicken curry, scampi, sirloin steaks;
Dinner (7.30pm to 9.30pm) £15: ham & asparagus roulade, roast poussin, pudding or cheese
Children: high teas
£ Medium

✓ Best Bargain Break: £33 per person per night – dinner, b&b
Children: first child under 5 is free, and the second one at certain times; thereafter, children are charged on a sliding scale from £12 to £20 a day
Facilities: over 20 cots and over 20 high chairs; baby-listening system
17 rooms, 13 family
Closed Dec to Feb

Ⓓ Ale: Tinners
Ⓟ Own car park

LAVENHAM, SUFFOLK   Map 6
ⒽⓇ **THE GREAT HOUSE, Market Place**
Tel: 01787 247 431
In the centre of town.

The town has many beautifully preserved medieval buildings; over 300 are listed as being of historic significance. The Great House was built in the 14th and 15th centuries, and acquired a new front when it was renovated in the 18th century. Its other claim to fame is that it was the home of the writer Stephen Spender in the 1950s.

It is now a delightful hotel and restaurant, which has been decorated and furnished with great style and taste. As the manager told us, the rooms have 'cheerfully out of kilter floors and well-worn antiques'. The four rooms justify their description as suites, since they all have sitting areas. Two of them have separate and spacious sitting rooms, and the newest suite has two double bedrooms and a lounge.

You are offered excellent value for money here, and that goes for the food as well as the accommodation. The menu has an enterprising choice of dishes, and you can have a snack for as little as £2. The three-course Sunday lunch costs around £15 (£9 for children). The whole family, from babies to grandmothers, is welcomed here, in the French tradition: which is not surprising since the management is French. We were not surprised to learn that the hotel won a 'value for money' award a couple of years ago.

At the back of the hotel there is a paved terrace, with plenty of space. It is surrounded by flowers and greenery and can be left open to the weather or completely covered, at the top and the sides, with canvas. This is a good solution to the problems of the English climate but plans are afoot to install a conservatory here.

Below the terrace there is a walled garden which has the merit of being a sun trap. It is in two sections, both lawned; at one end there is a barbecue, and at the other some swings for the children.

Nearby: The town is a splendid place in which to browse, as are the neighbouring ones of Long Melford and Sudbury. The children will enjoy Clare Castle Country Park and the adults will enjoy Cavendish Manor Vineyards. You can also reach Ickworth, Gainsborough's House in Sudbury, Blakenham Woodlands Garden and the Colne Valley Railway with ease.

....

✗ Bar snacks (12pm to 2.30pm) £4–9: moules marinières, lamb casserole, onion & bacon quiche, brochette of pork, bouillabaisse; Dinner (7pm to 10.30pm, Tues to Sat) £17: rabbit pâté, brandade of cod, pudding or cheese
Children: half portions
£ High

✓ Best Bargain Break: £49 per person per night – dinner, b&b
Children: free up to 3 years; £10 from 4 to 12 years; £15 thereafter
Facilities: 1 cot and 3 high chairs; baby-listening system
4 rooms, 3 family
Open all year, except Jan

Ⅰ Ale: Greene King
Ⅰ At front

LEDBURY, HEREFORD & WORCS Map 4
Ⓗ **WALL HILLS COUNTRY GUEST HOUSE, Hereford Road**
Tel: 01531 632 833
Off the A438 west of Ledbury.

This handsome and spacious red-brick Georgian house stands on the side of a hill which overlooks the pleasant town of Ledbury, and beyond you have superb views of the Malvern Hills. The front entrance is bright and welcoming with a porch full of pot plants and hanging baskets of flowers. The large walled garden is an ideal spot for guests to relax in, and mostly consists of lawns, but with well-established shrubs and flower beds. The several acres of grounds include a 15th-century cruck barn, and there is an Iron Age fort on a neighbour's land.

You will receive a very friendly and enthusiastic welcome from Mr and Mrs Slaughter, who have plenty of space for their guests: the sitting room is large and comfortable and has French windows looking out to the walled garden. The dining room is similarly spacious and attractive, and contains a well-stocked bar. All the bedrooms are large and can take an extra bed or cot and have views of the surrounding countryside. The family room has loads of space and includes a double bed, a single bed and a sofa bed, and has its own bathroom.

The cooking, in the hands of David Slaughter, has prompted much favourable comment from the guests. Most of the vegetables are home-grown and organic and some unusual varieties are often on the menu, which changes every day and always includes a vegetarian and a fish dish.

Nearby: Ledbury is excellently placed for holidaymakers to take advantage of the lovely countryside all around, and the many attractive towns such as Hereford, Gloucester, Malvern and Cheltenham. The Wye Valley is close by and there are many other attractions, such as the castles at Eastnor and Goodrich, the Falconry Centre at Newent, the Nature Reserve at Knapp, the Malvern Hills Animal and Bird Gardens, and the Birtsmorton Waterfowl Sanctuary.

....

✘ Dinner (7.30pm to 9pm) £16: baked avocado au gratin, breast of pheasant, fresh fruit tartlets
   Children: high teas, small portions
   £ Medium

✓ Best Bargain Break: £74 per person, 2 nights – dinner, b&b
   Children: £5 to £15, depending on age (includes breakfast)
   Facilities: 2 cots and 1 high chair; baby-listening by arrangement
   3 rooms, 1 family
   Open all year except Christmas and New Year

Ⓟ Ample

LEDSHAM, MERSEYSIDE   Map 8
P R Tudor Rose
Tel: 0151 339 2399
At the junction of the A540 and A550.

....

This substantial hotel and restaurant stands near a busy crossroads, and is a mock-Tudor building with good facilities for families, including no fewer than eight high chairs and a nappy-changing unit in the disabled toilets.

There are several bench tables on the lawn at the front of the Tudor Rose, but it's a bit noisy here. A better bet would be the enclosed garden at the side where there is also a sizeable play area.

The large bar has three open-plan lounges with wide windows, and a pleasant alcove room with wooden panelling, an iron range and copper pots and pans. The extensive restaurant maintains the mock-Tudor style, with its wooden panelling and diamond-paned windows. There is also a conservatory room with a domed wooden ceiling.

There is loads of space here and it has the advantage of serving food throughout the day. The special menus are good value at £6.99 or £9.99 for three courses.

....

✕ (12pm to 10.30pm) £2–12: Thai chicken, steak Diane, spiced lamb, grilled plaice, Mexican bake
Children: own menu
◒ Ale: Boddington's, Cain's, Flowers
P Lots

Nr LEIGHTON BUZZARD, BEDS   Map 5
P R White Hart, Hockcliffe
Tel: 01525 210 637
At the junction of the A5 and A4012 at Hockcliffe.

....

If you are travelling north or south on the A5, or on the nearby M1, the White Hart would be a convenient place to stop for a rest and some refreshment. All the facilities needed for families are in place, including high chairs and baby-changing facilities.

The garden is particularly pleasant. It is enclosed and has a well-tended lawn and several bench tables with parasols. There is an enchanted castle on which the children can play.

The pub itself is a substantial two-storeyed building, with a heavy overhanging roof and pillars on the ground floor. Smartly painted white, the façade is enlivened by lots of greenery and flowers in hanging baskets.

The large bar area has been decorated in the 'Olde English' style; it has a wood and plaster ceiling, an open fireplace and wood-panelled walls, and there are copper artefacts here and there. It's pleasant enough and the restaurant is housed in two large conservatory rooms which overlook the garden.

....

✕ (12pm to 2.30pm and 5pm to 10.30pm; weekends 12pm to 10.30pm) £2–11: pork satay, three-bean feast, steaks, ocean bake, Indonesian chicken

    Children: own menu

◫ Ale: Boddington's, Flowers and guests

ℙ Own car park

Nr LINGFIELD, SURREY   **Map 3**
ℙℝ RED BARN, **Blindley Heath**
Tel: 01342 834 272
On the B2029 near Lingfield.

....

An old farmhouse, a lovely brick building with a tile-hung upper storey, and a splendid old barn have been used as the core of this substantial pub, which has excellent facilities for families.

The large family dining room is a fine sight with its wooden beams and pillars, and one end sits under a vaulted wooden ceiling and has a large brick fireplace. There is a little play area with a slide, an amusement machine, Lego, etc. This is a no-smoking area and there are plenty of high chairs available, plus a nappy-changing facility.

The main part of the pub comprises a long bar with many comfortable chairs and benches. The barn has been turned into a huge dining area and has a remarkable interior with old wooden pillars and cross-hatched beams under its vaulted roof; there are farm implements and horse brasses on the walls, colourful prints, stags' heads and sets of antlers, wooden pews and dressers and a large fireplace.

The garden is delightful, with fine displays of flowers and an enclosed lawned area with bench tables and a large adventure playground for the children.

The pub is open throughout the day and food is available at all times.

....

✕ (11.30am to 10pm; Sun from 12pm) £2–8: fish dippers, sirloin steak, fried scampi, vegetable crumble, chicken Balti
   Children: own menu
◯ Ale: Boddington's, Flowers
ℙ Own car park

LITTLE BOLLINGTON, CHESHIRE   Map 8
ℙℝ NAGS HEAD
Tel: 01565 380 486
Very close to Junction 7 of the M56. Take the A556 towards Knutsford.

....

This pub and restaurant seems to be encircled by busy roads and is an excellent place to pause for some relaxation if you are on the move with your family. It is a traditional-looking old pub with bay windows and a pebble-dashed façade which is painted cream, and has lots of flowers in baskets to enliven it.

There is loads of space inside and the family dining areas are particularly pleasant. One of them has brick walls and a high wooden ceiling, wood panelling here and there, a splendid fireplace with a wood-burner, and padded benches. The conservatory restaurant has pale wooden beams and pillars and overlooks the garden, which has a paved terrace and a lawn where a play unit has been positioned.

The bar is also very congenial, with its low ceiling and brick walls. It includes a couple of comfortable lounge areas, one of which benefits from the building's bay windows. Two stone fireplaces add considerably to the charm.

High chairs and baby-changing facilities are provided, and food is served throughout the day.

....

✕ (11.30am to 10pm) £2–8: onion bhajis, haddock & chips, Teviotdale pie, tagliatelle carbonara, chicken escalopes
   Children: own menu
◑ Ale: Boddington's, Castle Eden, Flowers, Marston's
Ⓟ Ample

Nr LITTLEHAMPTON, EAST SUSSEX   Map 3
Ⓟⓡ ROUNDSTONE, **East Preston**
Tel: 01903 785 423
On the A259 at East Preston.

....

The pleasing brick building has its ground storey smartly painted in cream and there is a large enclosed grassy garden with bench tables at one side. A play unit is there to amuse the children and a bouncy castle comes into use during the summer.

Inside, the large conservatory room overlooks the garden and is an inviting place to settle on a summer day. Beyond the conservatory, the restaurant is split up into alcoves and smaller areas by screens – so there is no feeling of being adrift in a large space. Plenty of prints adorn the walls and there are even some flying ducks.

The bar is just as welcoming. It has a wooden ceiling with cross-beams, a nice fireplace and plenty of wood panelling.

Several high chairs are made available, and nappy-changing facilities also. Food is served throughout the day.

....

✗ (11.30am to 10pm) £2–8: hot mushrooms, chicken Balti, steak & mushroom pudding, vegetable crumble, fish pie
Children: own menu
○ Ale: Boddington's, Flowers
ℙ Plenty

Nr LIVERPOOL, MERSEYSIDE   Map 8
ℙℝ CHAPEL BROOK
Tel: 0151 480 9614
Close to the junction of the M57 and M62. On the A5080 towards Liverpool.

....

If you are speeding along the motorways and feel like a break you will find all the facilities a family needs at Chapel Brook: high chairs, baby-changing units, food available at all times, and a great deal of space in pleasant surroundings.

The building, a massive, purpose-built affair, would not win any prizes for aesthetic appeal but is much more inviting than the average motorway service station. The interior has an open-plan design and there are wide windows all round. Brick walls with some wood panelling, brick and timber pillars and colourful lights and lampshades are the main features, and prints and china plates decorate the walls.

A huge Fun Factory has been made and children have an array of playthings on which to swing, jump, slide and bounce. They have their own snack and soft drinks bar here. There is also an outdoor play area beside a paved terrace with several bench tables.

....

✗ (11.30am to 10pm) £2–8: fish dippers, steak & mushroom pudding, lasagne verdi, gammon steak, turkey fillet
Children: own menu
○ Ale: Boddington's, Flowers and guests
ℙ Lots

LONGHORSLEY, nr MORPETH, NORTHUMBERLAND

Map 9

P LINDEN PUB

Tel: 01670 516 611

On the A697 north of Morpeth.

At the end of a long driveway you will find the Linden Hall Hotel, a glorious Georgian mansion built from local stone in 1812 for a local bigwig and set in three hundred acres of splendid parkland.

Behind the hotel is the delightful Linden Pub, a converted granary which is built of the same stone as the hotel. Inside, the stone walls, decorated with old advertising signs, have been retained, along with the exposed beams, and there is an open fire.

The large family room has been made under the rafters, and the terrace outside has plenty of tables and chairs and a giant draughts board. An excellent range of food is served, including a children's menu and half portions.

It is an excellent family pub.

✗ (12pm to 2pm and 6.30pm to 9pm) £2–7: kipper pâté, leek & pasta crumble, fillet of sole, grilled lamb cutlets
Children: own menu, half portions

◖ Ale: Boddington's, Theakston's, McEwan's

P Own car park

LOWER HARDRES, KENT

Map 3

P THE THREE HORSESHOES

Tel: 01227 700 810

Off the B2068 south of Canterbury.

This lovely old coaching inn with its flat-brick front was built some time around 1700. The friendly landlord has deeds which date back to that time. He displays his sense of tradition further in the wide range of beers he makes available straight from the barrel. He reckons to have served over 300 different brews in the last ten years.

It's a charming and relaxed 'pubby' pub; as the landlord stresses, a real pub – 'untrendy, with no space invader or cigarette machines'. Children, who must be supervised, are welcome in a pleasant room overlooking the large garden which, in its turn, overlooks mile after mile of open country.

Bar food is served at lunchtimes only, at markedly low prices, and mention must be made of the fine selection of English cheeses which is always available. Barbecues are held regularly and jazz is occasionally played.

You should note that the pub is closed on Mondays, except for bank holidays.

....

✗ (12pm to 3pm, Tues to Sat) £2–5: ploughman's, Spanish omelette, smoked mackerel & salad, terrine, hot dish of the day
◑ Ale: Young's and guest
ℙ Own car park and street parking

_____

LOWESTOFT, SUFFOLK   Map 6
ℙℝ The Foxburrow, Yarmouth Road
Tel: 01502 572 441
On the A12 about two miles north of Lowestoft.

....

The motif that runs throughout the decoration of this inn, built on a site which has long housed a wayside tavern, is that of fishing and the sea. The restaurant is on various levels and offers several secluded alcoves. The reception desk is in the shape of the bow of a ship, and the sides of boats offer backing for some of the diners.

The bar is the front of the house, and behind it is the restaurant area. Food is served for most of the time that the pub is open, and twelve high chairs are available. There are baby-changing facilities, and children are well catered for.

There is a pleasant garden with picnic tables and a play area for children containing slides and climbing frames. A Travel Inn is being built alongside the inn, and will offer accommodation early in 1996.

....

✕ (12pm to 10.30pm) £2–13: Greek dip, Normandy pork, Indonesian chicken, pasta Lucana, ocean bake
Children: own menu
🍺 Ale: Adnams, Boddington's, Flowers
🅿 Plenty

LOWESWATER, CUMBRIA   **Map 8**
🅿 **KIRKSTILE INN**
Tel: 01900 85219
Off the B5289 south of Cockermouth.
....

This 16th-century inn has an idyllic situation close to Crummock Water, and from the bar you can see the brooding outline of Melbreak Fell in the background. It is very peaceful here, made more so by the splendid old church which is opposite the pub – these two focal points of village society, preaching and pints, are often found to be close neighbours.

Families will find this a very useful pub, since food is available (including breakfast from 8am and afternoon teas) during most of the day, and they can use either a small lounge at the side of the bar, or a room in an adjacent barn, which has a pool table, jukebox, etc. On warmer days you can enjoy a drink and a meal on the terrace or the lawn which runs along the front of the pub.

....

✗ (12pm to 2.30pm and 6pm to 9pm) £2–9: omelettes, Cumberland sausage, haddock & chips, sirloin steak, bean & tomato casserole Children: own menu

� Ale: Jennings

Ⓟ Own car park

LULWORTH COVE, DORSET   Map 2
Ⓗ MILL HOUSE HOTEL AND BISHOP'S COTTAGE HOTEL, West Lulworth
Tel: 01929 400 404
At Lulworth Cove.

....

Lulworth Cove is a very popular tourist spot and these two related hotels are in the heart of it, on the one and only main street, which is traffic free.

The two hotels are situated side by side and share their various facilities. Bishop's Cottage was once the home of Bishop Wordsworth of Salisbury, and is an appealing small hotel which sits comfortably in the shelter of Bindon Hill. The nice little bar and the spacious dining room both look out to the small enclosed garden, and down some steps is the sister hotel.

The Mill House is a pleasant old stone building; it seems to have grown in higgledy-piggledy fashion and that is part of its charm. There is a café/restaurant on the ground floor, and the residents' lounge and dining room are on the first floor, along with some of the bedrooms. The latter have a cottagey feel with their sloping walls and dormer windows. The attractive terraced gardens are well sheltered by the surrounding hills and, at the far end, there is an excellent swimming pool, surrounded by grass on which to loll. There are wonderful views of the famous cove from here.

The kitchen produces fresh food for the hotel and the café: local fresh shellfish is a speciality and vegetarian meals are also available. Meals can be taken either in the Bishop's Cottage restaurant or the Mill House restaurant, which has an extensive menu, so the whole environment is very flexible for families.

Nearby: This is a splendid holiday area with lots of interesting coastline to see and particularly good sandy beaches at Swanage, Weymouth and Studland. The Dorset coastal path runs past Swanage and there is a nature reserve at Studland. Inland, there is superb countryside to explore, as well as the Sea Life Centre at Weymouth and Durlston Country Park. Other places to visit include Corfe Castle, the Swanage Railway, the Tutankhamun Exhibition, Thomas Hardy's cottage, the prehistoric Maiden Castle and Athelhampton.

....

✕ Bar meals (12pm to 2.30pm and 6pm to 9.30pm) £2–11: lasagne, crab & lobster salad, fresh fish, homemade pies;
Dinner (7pm to 9.30pm Mill House) £12: four-course set menu;
(6pm to 10pm Bishop's Cottage) £12: crab cocktail, baked bream, dessert
Children: own menu, half portions
£ Medium

✓ Best Bargain Break: from £65 per person, 2 nights – dinner, b&b
Children: free up to 3 years; £8 from 3 to 7 years; £10 from 8 to 11 years
Facilities: 6 cots and 4 high chairs; baby-listening system
26 rooms, 5 family, 2 sets interconnecting
Open all year

🅿 Limited, but public car park nearby

LUSTLEIGH, DEVON

Map 1

P **Cleave**

Tel: 01647 277 233

Just off the A382 north of Bovey Tracey. Watch for the sign.

The village is largely composed of lovely thatched, granite cottages and is famous for its May Day festival. The 15th-century pub, thatched like most of its neighbours, suits the village perfectly. You can sit at peace in the lawned garden at the front of the pub. It is a secluded spot, sheltered by trees and with a fine array of greenery and flowers all around. There are two sizeable bars inside and an attractive dining room, and families are made welcome in a pleasant wood-panelled room at the back of the pub. There are several tables, some padded chairs and a high chair, and only one amusement machine; it is a no-smoking area.

It is useful to know that the Cleave is open all day (Monday to Saturday) during the summer months, and there is a very good choice of food available.

✗ (12pm to 2pm and 7pm to 9pm) £2–11: whole lemon sole, steak & kidney & Guinness pie, rump steak, chilli con carne, lasagne
   Children: own menu

◑ Ale: Bass, Castle Eden, Flowers

P On street

LYDLINCH, nr STURMINSTER NEWTON, DORSET   Map 2
Ⓗ HOLEBROOK FARM
Tel: 01258 817 348
Just off the A357 two miles west of Sturminster Newton.

You will find this very attractive Georgian farmhouse, built of light-coloured stone, in a quiet setting and surrounded by the green fields of the family-run farm.

One of the benefits of staying at Holebrook Farm is that you can elect to use the rooms on either a bed-and-breakfast or a self-catering basis, since they all have well-equipped kitchens and plenty of space. The accommodation, contained within converted stables and the old dairy, is furnished to a high standard and many of the original features have been used to good effect: the wooden beams and the stall partitions, for instance.

Two of the rooms in the stables can interconnect, if desired, to form a suite for a family of four; another larger unit contains two twin-bedded rooms and a sizeable sitting-cum-dining room with an integral kitchen.

The dairy has been converted in fine style to give four cottages, each with a sitting room and kitchen and a bedroom made even more attractive by the sloping ceiling. These cottages are suitable for two adults and a baby only.

The flexibility inherent in the accommodation will suit many families and so will the excellent facilities and all the freedom which the gardens and the surrounding open spaces allow, especially to the children. At one side of the house there is a sizeable and well-maintained lawn bordered by hedges and shrubs, and in another part of the garden, there is a small swimming pool. There are other activities laid on for guests: clay pigeon shooting, with tuition, can be arranged, for example; one of the outbuildings has been converted into a games room with a pool table, table tennis and other games. There are also two exercise machines.

Nearby: Sherborne Abbey and the neighbouring ruined castle are close, as are the butterfly gardens at Compton House. Montacute House, Ham Hill Country Park, the Fleet Air Arm Museum and Hambleden Hill can

222

all be reached with ease. A little further away in various directions you can reach Cricket St Thomas Wildlife Park and Longleat, Stourhead and Kingston Lacy, and the Rare Breeds Centre near Gillingham.

....

✗ Dinner (7pm) £12
  Children: half portions
  £ Medium
  Children: half price
  Facilities: 3 cots and 3 high chairs
  6 rooms, 1 family, 1 set interconnecting
  Open all year
P Plenty

LYNMOUTH, DEVON   Map 1
Ⓗ TORS HOTEL
Tel: 01598 753 236
On the A39.

....

The hotel stands prominently over the pretty seaside town of Lynmouth, and from the terrace and the various public rooms and most of the bedrooms you have splendid views of the sea and the harbour.

The hotel has been refurbished and the bars and the restaurant are very smartly and comfortably decked out. There is a table tennis room at one end of the hotel and a pool table in another games room. Outside, the hotel has several acres of woodland in which to relax, and a heated swimming pool.

Nearby: You can swim at many of the nearby beaches, and fishing, tennis and golf are all available locally. You are on the outskirts of Exmoor and the Park Centre is not too far away near Dulverton. Children will perhaps relish a visit to Watermouth Castle or the Exmoor Bird Gardens, while Arlington Court and Dunster Castle can easily be reached.

....

✖ Bar snacks (12.30pm to 1.45pm) £2–5: grilled king prawns, leeky pies, venison sausages, tagliatelle;
Dinner (7pm to 8.45pm) £17: smoked mackerel salad, soup, roast turkey, pudding or cheese
Children: own menu, half portions
£ High

✓ Best Bargain Break £38 per person per night – dinner, b&b
Children: free up to 14 years
Facilities: several cots and high chairs; 4 baby-listening lines and 2 baby alarms
35 rooms, 5 family, 2 interconnecting
Closed 2 Jan to 1 Mar

P Own car park

LYTCHETT MINSTER, nr POOLE, DORSET   Map 2
P R **BAKERS ARMS**
Tel: 01202 622 900
On the A35 at the roundabout where it meets the A351 west of Poole.

The Bakers Arms was listed in several early editions of the *Guide* and has now become a part of the Brewers Fayre chain.

It offers considerable facilities for families within its spacious rooms: there is an indoor play area with lots of equipment, nappy-changing facilities, plenty of high chairs and a large outdoor adventure playground, which is safely enclosed and has a bark surface.

The pub is open throughout the day and food is available for most of the time. The family dining area is spacious and is of course a no-smoking room. The interior is welcoming and is sensibly divided up into a number of small rooms and alcoves, with wooden tables and pews, padded chairs and benches. The brick walls, glass screens and wooden pillars add to the agreeable atmosphere.

✖ (11.30am to 10pm; Sun from noon) £2–8: onion bhajis, sirloin steak, fish pie, vegetable crumble, steak & kidney pie

Children: own menu
ⓓ Ale: Boddington's, Wadworth's
ⓟ Own car park

Nr MACCLESFIELD, CHESHIRE   **Map 8**
ⓟⓡ BLACKSMITH ARMS, Henbury
Tel: 01625 424 312
On the A537 west of Macclesfield.

....

This is an inviting traditional roadside pub, the façade painted white and enlivened by an array of flowers in baskets and pots. The interior has been revamped and extended to make a spacious pub and restaurant with excellent facilities for families, including high chairs and a nappy-changing unit. The garden at the back, overlooked by a terrace, is delightful; the tables on the lawn were very popular when we visited on a warm June day and the children were enjoying the play unit, which is safely enclosed.

The bar area is L-shaped, and it has a comfortable lounge with a bay window. The brick fireplace has horse brasses and beer tankards above, and there are black-and-white photographs on the walls. The restaurant occupies two rooms, decorated with cheerful wallpaper; there is some wood panelling and a coloured glass skylight above the main dining room which has windows on three sides, some of which overlook the terrace and garden. It is a bright and welcoming pub which is open all day and provides food at all times.

....

✖ (11.30am to 10pm; Sun 12pm to 9.30pm) £2–8: barbecued ribs, haddock & chips, Cajun chicken, mixed grill, spicy vegetable salsa Children: own menu
ⓓ Ale: Boddington's, Castle Eden and guests
ⓟ Own car park

Nr MAIDENHEAD, BERKS

Map 5

P **SHIRE HORSE**, Bath Road
Tel: 01628 825 335
West of Maidenhead on the A4.

As the name suggests, this pub is next door to the Shire Horse Centre, which is so popular with families. It is a rambling brick building with bay windows and one of its attractions is the huge garden. There is a wide stretch of grass in front with some bench tables and a very extensive garden at the side. Here there are plenty of mature trees to give shade on a summer day and lots of bench tables. The children will enjoy the grassy spaces and there are swings and a Wendy House.

There is plenty of room inside the pub too. The low-ceilinged bar has a few sofas and easy chairs and there is a pleasant lounge with comfortable chairs alongside a brick fireplace with a wood-burning stove.

The restaurant is at one end of the pub and leads out to the garden. Part of it has a tiled floor, and the upper level is carpeted and has wooden bookshelves (and books). Some high chairs are available and the pub is open all day.

✘ (12pm to 2pm and 6pm to 9pm) £2–9: gammon steak, lasagne, ham & eggs, sirloin steak, scampi
   Children: own menu
○ Ale: Courage
P Own car park

Nr MAIDSTONE, KENT

Map 3

P R **THE MALTA INN**, Sandling
Tel: 01622 717 251
Close to Junction 6 of the M20 on the Aylesford road. The Malta Inn is next to the Museum of Kent Life.

In the 18th century, the only access to the inn which stood on the site now occupied by The Malta Inn was from the River Medway. Times have changed, but much of the original building remains, and is listed. The Medway is still a great attraction, and there are pleasure boat trips along the river from close to the inn, and a service which will take you by boat to the centre of Maidstone. There is the added attraction that the inn stands next door to the Museum of Kent Life in beautiful countryside.

The Malta Inn has many charms of its own to offer. There is a riverside patio with family tables and umbrellas, and two children's play areas with a maze, climbing frames, bouncing tyres, seesaw, climbs, slides and bridges.

The interior maintains the river theme, with boats, oars and pictures forming part of the decoration, and a lower bar appropriately named 'The Smuggler's Cave'. The ground floor has a vast bar area, and a children's licence has been applied for, but the upper levels house the restaurant, and children may go anywhere in this area. There are special baby-changing facilities, and fifteen high chairs are available. The pub opens from 10.30am until 11.00pm, and bar food is always available.

The restaurant itself is a fascinating labyrinth of alcoves on various levels. There are many 'cottages' within this area which offer seclusion for couples or families, and many tables have views of the river. It is a delightful blend of intimacy and family welcome.

✕ (12pm to 2.30pm and 5pm to 10.30pm) £2–13: pork satay,

pasta Lucana, ocean bake, beef & Boddington's pie, peppered steak

Children: own menu

◖ Ale: Boddington's, Flowers and guests

⯁ Lots

MALMESBURY, WILTS   **Map 2**

Ⓗ Ⓡ OLD BELL HOTEL, Abbey Row

Tel: 01666 822 344

In the town centre.

....

The Old Bell was recommended in the first edition of the *Guide* in 1984 and we are delighted to welcome back this delightful and historic hotel. It has new owners, Nigel Chapman, who also runs the distinguished Woolley Grange (see the entry under Bradford-on-Avon), and Nicholas Dickinson, formerly managing director of Le Manoir aux Quat'Saisons. A great deal of refurbishment has been done over the last year or two, and one of the laudable aims is to offer good facilities for families.

Malmesbury is a charming town and one of the oldest in England (its charter dates back to 930). The hotel stands in the shadow of the famous Norman abbey and was originally built as a hostelry in 1220 by the Abbot, Walter Loring. The mellow stone of the façade is a delight and the interior of the building is spacious and has an ageless charm. For example, the Great Hall still has its 12th-century fireplace, sturdy wooden pillars and heavy ceiling beams, and the effect is complemented by the old wooden settles and tables. Bar meals are served in these wonderful surroundings, and the dishes on offer are not only imaginative but also very good value. That goes for Sunday lunch, too, which is a real bargain at £12.50 for three courses.

Adjoining the Great Hall, there is a splendid lounge with large and inviting sofas (and a piano), and residents can use a more secluded room or the library. The dining room, built at the turn of the century specifically as such, is imposing. A huge bay window at one end, and other windows opposite, give ample light.

The Edwardian chandeliers and oil paintings complete the overall effect.

We looked at several bedrooms, all appointed with style and comfort foremost in mind. Many of them at the front of the hotel, including a family suite, have views across the roofs to the countryside beyond.

Young children are well provided for. The Den is their play room – great fun with its murals of animals and of Mowgli, and with plenty of toys and a blackboard. The owners intend also to make an outdoor play area on a lawn below the car park. The main garden, its lawn and flower beds well sheltered, looks down to the River Avon, and there is a gazebo at one corner.

The Old Bell is an inviting hotel which offers a warm welcome to families.

Nearby: The town itself has great charm and the Cotswold villages are all within easy reach. Westonbirt Arboretum is very close, as are Sheldon Manor, Corsham Court, Bowood House and Lacock Abbey. Bath, Stonehenge and the prehistoric stone circles at Avebury, and Longleat are not too far away.

....

✗ Bar snacks (10am to 3pm and 6pm to 10pm) £3–7: Welsh rarebit with ham, black pudding with fried onions, duck liver parfait, marinated salmon, smoked chicken & avocado salad;
Dinner (7.30 to 9.30pm) £19–24: tartare of salmon, venison faggots, pudding or cheese
Children: own menu
£ High
Children: babies free; nominal charge thereafter for breakfast
Facilities: 6 cots and 6 high chairs; baby-listening system
34 rooms, 4 family
Open all year
🅿 Own car park

MARLBOROUGH, WILTS   Map 2
Ⓡ **POLLY TEA ROOMS, High Street**
Tel: 01672 512 146
In the main street opposite the Castle and Ball Hotel.

....

This is a delightful town, full of Georgian buildings (and antique shops) and with a couple of fine churches. The Polly Tea Rooms suits it well. It is a traditional English tea shop which really looks the part, with an abundance of beams holding up the ceilings, old photographs and prints on the walls and always a good display of cakes and scones, large vats of jam and so on – and friendly, helpful staff. You can pile into a full, heart-stopper breakfast until 11.30 in the morning and then lunch takes over until about 3 o'clock, and in between times there are snacks, gâteaux and ice-creams.

If you need to change a baby there is ample room in the Ladies, plus a table and a chair.

....

✕ (8.30am to 6pm; weekends until 7pm) £2–6: salade Niçoise, chicken Mexico, locally smoked trout, plaice & chips, fried scampi
   Children: small portions
Ⓟ In the main street

MATLOCK, DERBYSHIRE   Map 7
Ⓡ **STRAND RESTAURANT, 43 Dale Road**
Tel: 01629 584 444
Near the town centre, and on the A6.

....

This nicely decorated restaurant has echoes both of a teashop and a brasserie, with its tiled floor, pot plants and wooden tables and chairs. It is on two levels, with a gallery running round the edges of the high-ceilinged room.

All the food here is freshly cooked by the owners, who offer an enterprising choice of dishes which change on a daily basis according to the produce available at the markets. Youngsters are very welcome at lunchtimes, and also during the early evening, but must not outstay that welcome at night. Pizzas and pasta dishes are on the menu on Monday and Wednesday evenings.

You could just about manage to change a baby in the Ladies.

Live music is played at times during the week: there is jazz on Thursday evenings, for example, and a piano on Friday.

✗ Lunch (12pm to 2pm) £2–9: broccoli & mushroom crumble, cottage pie, sirloin steak, Brooklyn tuna bake, lambs kidneys & bacon;
Dinner (7pm to 10pm) £16: asparagus & Parma ham, crispy roast duck, pudding or cheese
Children: own menu, half portions
Open Tues to Sat; open on Mon during summer
◗ Ale: Tetley
⊞ Own car park

MAWGAN PORTH, CORNWALL   Map 1
Ⓗ BEDRUTHAN STEPS HOTEL
Tel: 01637 860 555
On the B3276 – the main coast road from Newquay to Padstow.

....

The hotel takes its name from the array of huge rocks by the beach said to be the stepping stones of the legendary giant Bedruthan. It is a modern and spacious hotel which is totally geared to the holiday needs of families; there are masses of cots and high chairs, and almost all the rooms are family rooms. The facilities for adults are excellent, including two squash courts, indoor and outdoor heated swimming pools, a short tennis and full-size tennis court, snooker, table tennis, carpet bowls, giant chess and skittles. Other activities include archery, fencing, and crazy golf, and there is a new gym and an aerobics centre. Golfers can take advantage of a concessionary rate at St Mellion.

The facilities for children are outstanding: as well as the swimming pools there are various play areas (including adventure playgrounds, swings and an area for football), children's films, etc. The 'jungle tumble' play area has a ball pool, tube slide, rope ladders and biff bags; it is indoors and is supervised and has a special toddlers' area. To take the younger children off your hands there is a playgroup every morning except Sundays. The children's entertainment programme is extensive and includes treasure hunts, craft workshops, cookery classes and painting.

The hotel has a farm and a large market garden, so it is not surprising that most of the vegetables and quite a lot of the fruit used are home-grown. The fish is caught locally, and the bread is made on the spot too. As at its sister hotel, the Trevelgue near Newquay (qv), there are some excellent wines at remarkably good prices and a good selection of vegetarian dishes. The hotel provides a range of home-made puréed foods for babies. All round you get astonishing value for money.

Nearby: You need never leave the hotel, but there is no shortage of outside attractions. Mawgan Porth beach, right in front of the hotel, is safe and sandy, and there are several excellent beaches at Newquay, a busy resort about six miles away. It has an excellent zoo. The Lappa

Valley Railway will appeal to many families, as will the Dairyland Farm
Park and Trerice, a superb Elizabethan manor house. Bedruthan Steps
itself, a National Trust beauty spot, is only a short walk away.

✕ Lunch (12pm to 2.30pm) £2–9: buffet;
   Dinner (7.45pm to 9.30pm) £13: crab cakes, soup, loin of pork,
   pudding or cheese
   £ Medium
✓ Best Bargain Break: £75 per family (4 people) per day – dinner,
   b&b
   Children: a quarter to three quarters of the adult rate; free of charge
   in some off-peak periods
   Facilities: 60 cots and 45 high chairs; baby-listening system in
   every room
   75 rooms, 70 family, 13 sets interconnecting
   Closed Nov to March
◖ Ale: Bass
Ⓟ Own car park

MAWGAN PORTH, CORNWALL   Map 1
Ⓟ THE MERRYMOOR
Tel: 01637 860 258
B3276 from Padstow to Newquay, just past Bedruthan Steps.

Set in an idyllic spot right on the bay of Mawgan Porth is a big
cream-painted building alongside the river that feeds into the sea.
The pub itself is large and airy with picture windows providing a
panoramic view of the bay and the famous Bedruthan Steps. Leading
off from the main bar are four separate areas suitable for use by
families; one is no-smoking and another has a counter for serving
food and non-alcoholic drinks. The bar and eating areas have white
artex walls, dark wood beams, bench-style seating and 'mate's' and
'captain's' chairs.

The extensive bar snack menu changes daily and makes the best use of local fish and vegetable produce. High chairs are available and there are baby-changing facilities.

In front of the pub is a small grassed and enclosed beer garden which seats sixty people at wooden picnic tables. The view from this area is unrivalled and food can be taken from the pub for alfresco gatherings. There are some children's swings at one end.

Above the pub there are seven en suite bedrooms, two of which are for families, but cots can be placed in the other double rooms (all have television and tea/coffee-making facilities). All the rooms are light and airy and four have views over the bay. There is an intercom service available for monitoring babies, if parents are in the main bar and eating areas. There is a separate lounge (again with a sea view) and dining area for residents.

....

✕ (12pm to 2pm and 6pm to 9pm) £2–7: seafood platter & chips, potato, leek & cheese bake, cashew nut risotto, pizza
Children: own menu and half portions
℗ Ale: Worthington, Wadworth's, Hardy's and guests
Ⓟ Ample

MAWGAN PORTH, CORNWALL   Map 1
ⓅⓇ Travellers Rest, Trevarrian
Tel: 01637 860 245
Signposted off the B3276 Newquay to Padstow road.

....

This white-painted pub is a conversion of two cottages high up on the hillside overlooking Bedruthan Steps. It is a great place at which to break a journey, or to make your 'local' if staying in the area. The food is excellent and the welcome is extremely friendly.

The main bar area has two stone-built fireplaces, one of which is inglenook in style and has a clay bread oven. The other has a working log and coal fire. Part of the room is stone-flagged and the rest is carpeted throughout and leads through to the family room. There is a pool table here and it is the home of the colourful family parrot, which is adored by all children who visit this pub. At the other end of the pub there is a restaurant which can seat up to forty people and where an extensive menu is available.

At the rear there is a small stone-flagged area with picnic benches and a play slide for children. The Travellers Rest is an agreeable pub and is enlivened by the landlord's dog, which jumps eight feet to ring time on a brass bell suspended behind the bar.

✕ (11am to 11pm) £2–12: calamari, crevettes in garlic, vegetable Mexicana, rump steak, marinated rack of pork
Children: own menu, half portions
Ale: Hicks, Tinners
Ⓟ Own car park

MAWNAN SMITH, CORNWALL **Map 1**
Ⓗ **Budock Vean Hotel**
Tel: 01326 250 288
Follow the road south through Mawnan Smith.

A blaze of flowers marks the entrance to Budock Vean, which has a lovely façade of mellow stone, with a tiled upper storey. The estate has an interesting history, though little of the original buildings remains; even the mansion built in the 18th century was mostly demolished. It has been a hotel since the 1920s and is now under the enterprising management of the Francis family.

The hotel sits amid sixty-five acres of gardens and is encircled by rolling countryside and wooded hillsides. The grounds extend to the Helford River where the manager moors a boat and runs occasional trips on the water.

The leisure facilities are first-rate and include a pretty and interesting golf course, laid out over nine holes but with different tees coming into play for the front and the back halves. The golf course has its own clubhouse with a bar and a snooker table. The sizeable swimming pool is housed in an attractive building with a domed wooden roof. Sliding glass doors lead to a terrace which overlooks the garden and part of the golf course. In addition, there are two all-weather tennis courts.

The hotel has a comfortable and relaxed air, aided in no small way by the friendly and efficient staff. The bar area gives on to a conservatory and a paved veranda with the gardens beyond. There are a couple of lounges and a high-ceilinged dining room whose windows overlook the golf course.

Families are made very welcome at Budock Vean and, apart from the established leisure facilities, children can participate in many activities during the summer months: sailing, diving, swimming, clay pigeon shooting and horse riding. There is a Minis Club which organizes nature trails, treasure hunts, face painting and so on.

This is a splendid hotel in a delightful holiday area.

Nearby: There are excellent beaches and all the water sports are available, as well as several fine golf courses (as well as Budock Vean itself). Local attractions include Pendennis Castle, Glendurgan Garden, the Seal Sanctuary at Gweek, Goonhilly Earth Station, Flambards Theme Park and the Poldark Mine.

✕ Bar snacks (12pm to 2.15pm) £2–7: omelettes, club sandwich, chicken curry, spaghetti Bolognese;

Dinner (7.30pm to 9pm) £19: seafood salad, roast Cornish pheasant, pudding & cheese
Children: own menu, half portions
£ High
✓ Best Bargain Break: £49–79 per person per day – dinner, b&b
Children: free up to 14 years
Facilities: 8 cots and 6 high chairs; baby-listening system
58 rooms, 2 suites (many other rooms can accommodate extra beds and cots)
Open all year
Ⓟ Own car park

MAWNAN SMITH, CORNWALL   Map 1
Ⓟ RED LION
Tel: 01326 250 026
In the centre of the village.

In an earlier edition of the *Guide* we described the Red Lion as an archetypal village pub. The assessment is still sound as we welcome it back to our pages. The pub stands at the angle of two roads, a splendid 15th-century building with a thatched roof supported by stone walls which are smartly painted white.

The main bar has the ambience of a village pub, comfortable and informal, with all sorts of objects on the wood-panelled walls: prints, china plates, a mirror, a clock. The bar itself is wedge-shaped and a series of rooms encircle it under low ceilings. The style is maintained throughout, with an eclectic selection of decorations on the walls. The whole place has a relaxed and pubby atmosphere.

Close to the bar there is a high-ceilinged dining room, with a fine display of china on the walls. At the far end of the pub there is a very cosy, low-ceilinged family room with nice little windows. A high chair is made available and there is an excellent choice of food (including fresh fish every day) in this very attractive and welcoming village inn.

� (12pm to 2pm and 7pm to 9.30pm) £2–12: oriental king prawns, fillet of pork Calvados, seafood tagliatelle, fish of the day, beans & celery & coriander chilli
Children: own menu, half portions
Ⓓ Ale: Bass
Ⓟ Own car park

MAYFIELD, EAST SUSSEX   **Map 3**
Ⓟ **MIDDLE HOUSE, High Street**
Tel: 01435 782 146
On the A267 south of Tunbridge Wells.

The village of Mayfield can trace its history back to well before the Norman Conquest. It was once a home for the archbishops of Canterbury, and in the 16th century, the manor became the property of Sir Thomas Gresham, keeper of the Privy Purse to Elizabeth I and founder of the London Stock Exchange. Middle House was built for Sir Thomas, and it is one of 40 buildings in Mayfield listed as being of special historical interest. It is a Grade I listed building, 'one of the finest examples of a timber-framed building in Sussex'. It has priest holes and tunnels, which date from the 18th century when Mayfield was a centre for smugglers.

Middle House was a private residence until the late 1920s, but it is now a pub and a restaurant and provides accommodation with eight bedrooms, one of which is a family room. The bedrooms have *en suite* bathrooms, and the Elizabethan room has a four-poster bed. All of the bedrooms are heavily beamed and are individual in character.

The pub is open from 11am until 11pm, and bar food is always available. Children are allowed anywhere, but there is a separate family lounge. A high chair is available in the dining room.

Among the features of the interior of Middle House are an inglenook fireplace that provides a weekly spit roast, and a large ornate wooden carved fireplace in the entrance hall. This fireplace is the work of

Grinling Gibbons and was once in the house of the Royal College of Physicians in London.

The village is as lively as it is lovely, but there is a restful, beautifully planted garden at the rear of Middle House. There are family benches and picnic tables with umbrellas, and a log house for children. The garden slopes and offers a beautiful view of the Vale of Heathfield.

....

✗ (12pm to 2pm and 7pm to 9.30pm; not Sun pm) £2–10: open sandwiches, steak & kidney pie, roast duck, pasta with salmon & prawns
Children: half portions
◪ Ale: Greene King, Harvey's, Wadworth's and guests
ⵑ At the side

MELMERBY, CUMBRIA   Map 8
ⱴ **VILLAGE BAKERY**
Tel: 01768 881 515
On the A686 ten miles east of Penrith (Junction 40 of the M6).

....

This is a most enterprising and picturesque restaurant. Housed in an 18th-century converted barn, it is set in some spectacular Cumbrian countryside where you will find some marvellous views.

The restaurant has stone walls, a stone-flagged floor, good wooden tables and chairs, and a Welsh dresser against one wall. There is a small and elegant conservatory on the front of the building. Upstairs under the wooden rafters the craft gallery has an excellent range of products and there are several tables here too.

The food is baked in the restaurant's own wood-fired brick oven and the bread, pie and pizzas use wholemeal flour ground at a local water mill. Many of the vegetables are grown organically on a smallholding at the back of the restaurant. The menu is comprehensive: you can enjoy breakfasts (the full breakfast, traditional or vegetarian, will set you up for the day), lunches, savoury snacks, and cream teas, all at very reasonable prices. The restaurant has won many awards, including a *Sunday Times* one for organic food at the Royal Show.

Mothers with babies can feed and change them in the Ladies, where there is a pull-down shelf and a changing mat.

The Village Bakery is in a lovely location right by the village green, which stretches away from the front door.

....

✗ (8.30am to 5pm; Sun 9.30am to 5pm) £1–7: Inverawe kippers, courgette & tomato bake, Lakeland char, Chester pie, baker's lunch
Children: half portions
Closes at 2.30pm in Jan and Feb; closed at Christmas

Ⓟ Own car park

MICKLEOVER, DERBYSHIRE Map 7
ⓅⓇ Nags Head
Tel: 01332 513 104
Off the A38 at Mickleover.
....

In the centre of the town you will encounter a mini-roundabout and on the left you will see a large black-and-white-beamed Tudor-style building, which is the Nags Head.

Like all the Scottish and Newcastle Homespreads pubs there is a sign which will lead you to the family entrance, on the right-hand side and to the rear, off the main car park. Also to the rear there is an enclosed wood-chipped play area with an elaborate wooden climbing frame, slides and other play equipment. Immediately outside and behind this is a grassed area containing picnic benches where the adults may eat and drink alfresco whilst their children play.

After passing through the family entrance you will find the baby-changing facility, which has a pull-down changing table and a nappy dispenser.

In the main body of the pub you will encounter a large stairway which leads up to a converted ballroom where the theme is the circus

Big Top. The owners have gone to great lengths to make the best and most decorative use of all the available space within the building. There are numerous alcoves, balconies and split-level seating areas from which to choose. The circus/toy room theme has been enhanced by the effective use of a myriad of bric-à-brac. The children will enjoy it.

Children under 14 are not permitted in the main bar area. Beyond it is a no-smoking dining area, a long room, split-levelled and alcoved to provide four separate sections. At the far end is the Funky Forest room, containing a ball pit and soft toys for younger children.

....

✕ (12pm to 2.30pm and 5.30pm to 10pm; Sun 12pm to 10pm) £2–9: moules marinières, mixed grill, seafood pie, lemon chicken, lasagne
   Children: own menu
◯ Ale: Theakston's
Ⓟ Own car park

MILTON, CAMBS   **Map 6**
Ⓟ **WHITE HORSE**
Tel: 01223 860 327
North of Cambridge, off the A10 or A14.

....

This is a genuine local public house where all visitors are made welcome. An inn has long stood on this site, and although the frontage is less than attractive, the interior and the rear of the pub offer much. There is a large open fire which warms two bars, and a newly built family room which opens on to the garden where there are family benches, a barbecue for summer evenings, and a children's play area with swings, climbs, slides and a rocking horse.

There are baby-changing facilities in the ladies' toilet, and provision for the disabled. The agricultural implements that decorate the bar add to the ambience, and the pub serves home-cooked food throughout the day. There is a children's menu and a high chair is available.

....

✕ (11am to 9.30pm) £2–10: chilli con carne, gammon, chicken curry, broccoli bake, steak & kidney pie
   Children: own menu, half portions
◗ Ale: Ind Coope Burton, Tetley, Tolly and guests
🅿 At rear

MILTON KEYNES, BUCKS   Map 5
🅿🆁 **WOLVERTON HOUSE**
Tel: 01908 261 570
Just off the A5 near its junction with the A422. Follow the signs for Wolverton/Wolverton Mill.

Wolverton House is a gracious 18th-century stone country house, set in ten acres of lovely parkland. Magnificent old trees, firs and copper beeches among them, stand sentinel at the front of the building.

The main entrance takes you into a courtyard formed by the old stable blocks; dozens of people were taking full advantage of the sunshine when we visited in June. It was a pleasant scene.

The bar area is extensive, with wide windows, and beyond there is a series of dining areas. A small no-smoking room is quiet and intimate under a low ceiling; the walls, which bear various farming artefacts, are partly wood-panelled. Up a few stairs there is another attractive room with an old iron cooking range and a wide window. Alongside you will find a stately dining room with a big window on to the park, and there are three more well-proportioned dining areas, one of which has a play area for young children. High chairs are available in quantity and there are nappy-changing facilities.

The huge lawned garden is ringed by trees and plenty of bench tables are set out. An outside bar has now been put in place and the children have the use of an extensive play area and a bouncy castle.

It is a splendid and welcoming place – well worth a detour from the A5 or the M1.

✕ (11.30am to 10pm) £2–8: onion bhajis, fish pie, tagliatelle carbonara, vegetable crumble, chicken Alexandra
Children: own menu
Ⓟ Ale: Boddington's, Flowers and guests
Ⓟ Lots

MILTON STREET, nr ALFRISTON, EAST SUSSEX   Map 3
Ⓟ SUSSEX OX
Tel: 01323 870 840
Watch out as it's easy to miss: take the road to Alfriston off the A27, turn left on the road to Litlington and left again to Milton Street.

The Sussex Ox has been in the *Guide* since the first edition and is one of our favourites, a secluded and traditional country pub set in lovely Sussex countryside near the pretty village of Alfriston.

There are excellent facilities for families. The 'sty', at the back of the pub, is the family room and has a brick floor, nice pine tables and settles, and doors on to the garden. It is a pleasant and airy room (and two high chairs are available) and an alternative for families is the spacious Harness Room, an appealing room on two levels with a beamed ceiling, a dresser and oak pillars.

There are some bench tables set out at the front of the pub, but the huge, safely enclosed garden at the rear is an instant attraction on summery days. You can sit at your ease and enjoy the views of gentle Sussex hills, while the children play on the large wooden climbing frame, Wendy House, slide and seesaw. It is a delightful spot, maintained in pristine condition.

A good range of freshly cooked food is available every day and the menu changes to suit the seasons; but there is always fresh fish and seafood available. Barbecues are held on summer weekends and during the winter there are special dining evenings (Thai, seafood, Indian, etc.).

This is an outstanding family pub where everyone, from the youngest to the oldest, will be welcome.

✗ (12pm to 2.15pm and 6.30pm to 9.30pm) £2–10: cheesy cottage pie, whole plaice, nut loaf, steak & ale pie, ham & eggs
Children: own menu, half portions
◖ Ale: Greene King Abbot, Harvey's and guests
🅿 Own car park

MINCHINHAMPTON, nr STROUD, GLOS   Map 4
Ⓗ **BURLEIGH COURT HOTEL**
Tel: 01453 883 804
Off the A419 east of Stroud. The hotel brochure has a good map.

Burleigh Court is a handsome Cotswold-stone manor house, its façade covered in Virginia creeper. It sits in five acres of immaculate gardens on the side of Golden Valley and you have wonderful views of the surrounding countryside.

The emphasis at the hotel is placed firmly on comfort and style: from the attractive furnishings of the lounge areas and the dining room to the charming and spacious bedrooms, which have each been decorated and furnished in their own individual ways. Ten of the bedrooms can easily accommodate a cot or an extra bed for a child, and there are also two suites. We looked at the ground-floor suite, an ideal design for a small family: there is a sitting room as you enter, with a double bed behind a screen, and a separate bedroom with bunks for younger children. It has the great bonus of looking straight out to the garden and the swimming pool.

The gardens are a delight, the smooth lawns at the back divided here and there by stone walls, and the swimming pool is a genuine Victorian plunge pool – a fine sight. At the front, a huge expanse of lawn, ringed by mature trees, slopes away from the hotel. A little fountain plays in a corner and there is a play area for the children, with swings, a climbing frame, a rope ladder and a tree house. On the other side there is a large and very smooth putting green and a practice net.

This is a delightful hotel where all the family will receive a warm welcome.

Nearby: The hotel is on the fringe of Minchinhampton Common, where you can play golf, go riding or walking or just browse in the sun. Within a reasonable radius you can reach Berkeley Castle and Sudeley Castle, Westonbirt Arboretum, the Cotswold Water Park, the Wildfowl Trust at Slimbridge, the Cotswold Wildlife Park near Burford, and the various attractions at Bourton-on-the-Water. All the charms of the Cotswolds lie in one direction and of the lovely city of Bath in the other.

....

✕ Bar snacks (12pm to 2pm and 7pm to 9pm) £3–6: hot and cold buffet, bangers & mash, samosas, seafood bake;
Dinner (7pm to 8.45pm) £20: crabmeat crêpes, braised chicken breasts, pudding or cheese
Children: high teas, flexible portions
£ High

✓ Best Bargain Break: £54 per night – dinner, b&b
Facilities: 2 cots and 2 high chairs; baby-listening to each room
17 rooms, 2 suites, 3 sets interconnecting
Open all year

🅿 Own car park

MOONFLEET, nr WEYMOUTH, DORSET   Map 2
Ⓗ **MOONFLEET MANOR HOTEL**
Tel: 01305 786 948
Off the B3157 north-west of Weymouth.

....

The owners rightly describe Moonfleet Manor as an hotel and sports resort, since the sporting facilities are exceptional. Many of them are housed in the Ball Park which has a squash court, table tennis, a full-sized indoor bowling green, a snooker table, two automated 9-pin bowling lanes and two bars. There is a pool table, table football and amusement machines. It is a wonderful place, with lots of space, and you could spend all day there.

There are many other facilities too: two hard tennis courts, an indoor swimming pool with a children's pool, a short tennis court, and a sandpit, adventure playground and indoor play areas for the children.

The core of the hotel is a very handsome Georgian manor house which was restored near the end of the 19th century. It sits right by Chesil Beach in a beautiful location and has its own pleasant lawned gardens.

One of the many virtues of the hotel is the amount of space put at the guests' disposal: a large lounge and bar with nice cane furniture and sofas, and a sizeable dining room with a conservatory where children have their suppers at 6 o'clock.

The bedrooms are similarly generous in size, especially the family rooms: three of them are suites with interconnecting double and twin bedrooms and some have double beds with bunk beds for children. All of them have enchanting views. There are also three cottages which can be rented on a self-catering basis.

This is a really splendid family hotel with exceptional facilities where everyone, from grandparents to grandchildren, will find much to enjoy.

Nearby: The huge expanse of Chesil Beach is shingle, but nearby Weymouth has a sandy beach and a Sea Life Centre, which will attract the children. In the other direction lies Abbotsbury, with its ruined abbey and famous gardens and swannery. If you go inland, the lovely town of Dorchester is quite close and Thomas Hardy's cottage and the Tutankhamun Exhibition can be seen. If you are in the mood for sightseeing you can visit the country house of Athelhampton, the tank museum at Bovington Camp and Clouds Hill, the memorial to T. E. Lawrence.

....

✕ Coffee shop (12pm to 2.30pm and 6pm to 10pm) £2–6: salads, ploughman's, lentil crumble, lasagne;
   Dinner (7pm to 9pm) £14: smoked mackerel, medallions of beef, pudding or cheese

Children: own menu, half portions
£ High
✓ Best Bargain Break: £84 per person, 2 nights – dinner, b&b
Children: from 15% to 80% of the adult rate, depending on age
Facilities: 8 cots and 6 high chairs; baby-listening system
39 rooms, 6 family, 4 sets interconnecting
Open all year
◯ Ale: Hall & Woodhouse
P Own car park

MOTCOMBE, nr SHAFTESBURY, DORSET   Map 2
H P COPPLERIDGE INN & COUNTRY HOTEL
Tel: 01747 851 980
At the north end of Motcombe village.

This converted ancient manor farm has dazzling views of the Dorset countryside and was owned by the Marquis of Westminster in the early 19th century.

The main building, the old farmhouse, is set at one end of a quadrangle around which are the beautifully converted barns and stables. The bar area, like most of the rooms in the building, retains its farmhouse atmosphere with pine chairs and tables, and there are farm implements dotted around the walls. At one end of the room there is a balcony area where families can sit and enjoy a drink or a meal from the extensive bar menu. Beneath this is an entrance to the comfortably furnished conservatory which, in turn, leads on to a patio area with white garden seating; it's a real sun-trap in the summer. Alongside there is a lawned area with picnic bench seating and a children's play area with swings, slides, climbing frames and a wooden fort.

In addition to the main restaurant, there is a no-smoking eating area. A small and pleasant room, it has a log-burning stove, and fishing prints and artefacts adorn the walls.

In contrast, the theme of the restaurant itself, a light and airy room with pine beams, is game. There are hunting dog prints, some flintlock

247

rifles, and stuffed fish and animals on the walls. A charming lounge is situated alongside the restaurant and families also congregate here to eat. Its stone-flagged floor, pine settles and large fireplace make it a very cosy spot.

The accommodation has been built around a partly grassed courtyard with two appealing fountains and ornate lamps. You can enjoy an alfresco drink or a snack on the wrought-iron benches. The rooms are generous in size, especially the family rooms, and furnished to high standards of comfort.

The Coppleridge has two tennis courts and a cricket pitch, and facilities in the village include clay pigeon shooting, an equestrian centre and a sports centre. This hotel offers excellent facilities and very good value to families.

Nearby: There is a wide choice of places to see, including Kingston Lacy, Hambledon Hill, the Fleet Air Arm Museum at Yeovilton, Montacute House, the Wookey Hole Caves, Stourhead and Longleat. The fine cities of Bath and Salisbury are within easy reach.

....

✗ Bar snacks (11am to 2.30pm and 6pm to 10.30pm) £2–12: smoked trout terrine, fish pie, Somerset pork, cauliflower & ham mornay, lamb tikka;
Dinner (7pm to 9.30pm) £15: salmon & prawn pancake, rack of lamb, home-made ice-cream (bistro menu at £10 also available)
Children: own menu, half portions
£ Medium

✓ Best Bargain Break: £75 per person, 2 nights – dinner, b&b
Facilities: 2 cots and 3 high chairs; baby-listening
10 rooms, 2 family

◖ Ale: Butcombe, Hook Norton, Spitfire

ℙ Ample

MOUNTNESSING, nr BRENTWOOD, ESSEX **Map 6**

[P][R] THE GEORGE AND DRAGON, Roman Road

Tel: 01277 352461

On the B1002, three miles from Ingatestone, five miles from Brentwood, close to junctions with the A12 and A1023.

The Roman Road on which the George and Dragon stands was once the main road from London to Chelmsford. A tavern here is mentioned in the Domesday Book, and an area close to the pub provided a burial ground in the Great Plague. Mountnessing is proud of its history, and there is a magnificently restored windmill within easy walk of the George and Dragon; the old stocks are preserved on the common. Contemporary pride is shown in the pub's sponsorship of the local football team which fields sides at many age levels.

As is appropriate for a one-time coaching inn, a large bar confronts you as you enter. The wooden beams maintain the sense of history, and there are some fascinating photographs and historical costumes, including that of a jester. Children are welcome throughout the restaurant which is vast, with room for 130 diners. They can be seated on different levels, in both large areas and intimate alcoves.

The garden is picturesque and well tended, with a spacious eating area, where there are barbecues on summer evenings. There is a play area with a slide growing from the shoe in which the old woman lived, and a bouncy castle is also erected on occasion.

There are changing facilities within the Ladies' toilet, and as well as a dozen high chairs, booster seats are available for small children.

The restaurant is open for lunch and reopens at 5pm, but bar meals are served throughout the day.

✕ (12pm to 2.30pm and 5pm to 10.30pm) £2–13: pork satay, minted lamb steak, salmon fillet, haddock & chips, vegetable mornay
Children: own menu

Ale: Boddington's, Brakspear's, Flowers, Wethered's and guests

[P] Ample

MULLION, CORNWALL   **Map 1**
Ⓗ **Polurrian Hotel, Polurrian Cove**
Tel: 01326 240 421

Follow your nose through Mullion, past the cricket ground – you may have to ask, although there is a hotel sign.

....

This excellent hotel underwent considerable refurbishment during 1993. New facilities include two-bedroomed family suites and, most useful for families, a resident nanny and a crèche. From the expansive gardens of the Edwardian building you will have some breathtaking views down to the sea. If it is action rather than contemplation that you require, there is plenty to divert you: a putting green, hard tennis court, squash court and a superbly equipped grassy play area with a slide, trampoline, sandpit and swings – all enclosed for parents' peace of mind. Down below is a sandy cove where you can do some surfing.

The indoor games area has snooker, bar billiards and table tennis, and the leisure club has an indoor swimming pool with a paddling pool and a mini-gym, plus a sauna and a solarium. There is also an outdoor heated swimming pool.

There is a warm and relaxing atmosphere at this hotel, which has everything necessary for a happy family holiday, including children's outings to local attractions. Self-catering accommodation is also available.

Nearby: Most of the surrounding land is owned by the National Trust, and there are delightful walks to take. Mullion golf course is just a couple of miles away, and there are many attractions within reach: Goonhilly Earth Station, the Flambards Theme Park, Poldark Mine, the Seal Sanctuary at Gweek and St Michael's Mount.

....

✖ Buffet lunch (12pm to 2pm) £2–8: chicken & chips, cold buffet, scampi, fisherman's pie, moussaka;
Dinner (7pm to 8.45pm) £18: quenelle of sole, soup, roast leg of pork, pudding or cheese
Children: own menu, half portions
£ High

✓ Best Bargain Break: £105–200 per person, 3 nights – dinner, b&b
Children: free up to 14 years
Facilities: 12 cots and 10 high chairs; baby-listening system
40 rooms, 6 family
Open Mar to Jan
P Own car park

MUNGRISDALE, nr PENRITH, CUMBRIA   Map 8
H NEAR HOWE FARM HOTEL
Tel: 01768 779 678
Off the A66 between Penrith and Keswick.

Idyllic is the only word which adequately describes Near Howe, a lovely double-fronted farmhouse built of the traditional dark-hued stone of this part of the country. After you have driven up a long and bumpy road you can look back at the moorland which dips and rolls beneath. This is the Mungrisdale Valley over which John Peel and his companions used to hunt.

You will certainly find peace and tranquillity here, not least in the garden which fronts the house. It has an immaculate lawn, is safely enclosed and ringed with trees, and all around is the glorious countryside. It is a wonderful base for a holiday in an area which has so much to offer: fishing, golf, water sports, walking, or just plain relaxing.

There is a spacious and comfortable residents' lounge and a games room with a pool table, toys and records. The attractive dining room was built in the old dairy and through an arch is the bar. The views from the well-furnished bedrooms are wonderful and there is an excellent family room, with a double and single bed, at one end of the building.

Four cottages can be rented on a self-catering basis and they also have enticing views over the fells. The rents vary from £160 to £450 a week.

Nearby: If you fancy seeing the sights you are only a short drive away from the popular parts of the Lakes: Grasmere, Windermere, Coniston

Water and so on. Much nearer to hand are Ullswater and Derwent Water, and Lowther Park with its nature trails, adventure playground and miniature railway.

....

✕ Dinner (7pm) £9
   Children: own menu, half portions
   £ Low
   Children: half price under 12 years
   Facilities: 2 cots and 2 high chairs
   7 rooms, 1 family
   Open Mar to Nov
   No credit cards accepted
◗ Ale: Mitchell's
Ⓟ Loads

NAILSEA, AVON   **Map 2**
Ⓟ THE OLD FARMHOUSE
Tel: 01275 851 889
Off the B3130 at Nailsea.

....

Situated in the middle of a modern housing estate, this welcoming inn is a real oasis. Here the modern conversion of a 17th-century farm and barn has been accomplished with some respect for the finer points of the original building.

You pass into the bar areas through a heavy wooden door. The main bar has excellent wooden furniture: high-backed chairs, stools and round tables. Families should head for the converted stone barn with its wooden beams. There are no fewer than seven separate seating areas, divided by balustraded partitions. Farm implements and saddlery decorate the walls, and an outstanding feature is the huge stone fireplace with a stag's head above.

In addition, families are welcome to use a very comfortable annexe off a second bar which is located in the old farmhouse. With its inglenook fireplace, padded chairs and benches, this is a welcoming spot for a family group. The extensive menu includes a carvery (two sizes, depending on your appetite) and a cold buffet.

There is a large patio area surrounding the barn, on which there are wooden bench tables and a play area with swings, a Wendy House and other children's playthings.

This is an excellent family pub which has the added advantage of being open all day from Monday to Saturday.

....

✘ (12pm to 2.15pm and 6pm to 10pm; Sun until 2pm and 7pm to 9 pm) £2–10: chicken tikka, lasagne, garlic steak, whiting & chips, leek & potato bake

    Children: own menu, half portions

◖ Ale: Badger, Wadworth's

▣ Ample

NAILSWORTH, GLOS   Map 4
▣ WEIGHBRIDGE INN, Avening Road
Tel: 01453 832 520
On the Avening/Tetbury road, B4014, and not far from Amberley and Minchinhampton Common.

....

We have fond memories of this pub – the first we entered with our baby daughter of a few weeks. We were directed to their excellent family room – and naively thought that there were thousands of pubs like this where families are welcome.

It is a delightful white-painted building with an interior of rough stone walls and good wooden furniture. Families are well catered for with two rooms where children are welcome; a small one off the bar with a large open fireplace, oak tables and a settle; and upstairs a superb high-ceilinged beamed room with an array of polished oak tables and chairs. It leads out to a grassy sloping garden and a patio with several bench tables and sun umbrellas.

There is an excellent choice of food at reasonable prices, and the owners do not fry any food at all. Neither is there music in the pub nor any of those obnoxious 'amusement' machines. What a wonderful haven for all the family.

....

✗ (12pm to 2pm and 7pm to 9pm) £2–6: two-in-one pie (steak & mushroom pie with cauliflower cheese), turkey & sweetcorn pie, lasagne, vegetable & lentil crumble
Children: half portions
☕ Ale: Wadworth's, Usher's, Smiles and guests
🅿 Own car park

NANCENOY, nr HELSTON, CORNWALL   Map 1
🅿🆁 TRENGILLY WARTHA INN
Tel: 01326 40332
Between Constantine and Gweek.

....

The inn is situated down the narrow country lanes east of Helston and not far from the Helford River where it cuts deep into the Cornish landscape. There are signs here and there which point the way to the place and, eventually, you will find a long cream-painted building with a conservatory at the front. The latter room, a no-smoking area, is where families are welcome to settle if they have young children in tow; the adjoining entrance hall contains a pool table. Behind this is a pleasant and spacious bar and real ale enthusiasts will be pleased to hear that there is always a wide choice of beers available and that the choice is rotated on a regular basis.

At the back of the bar there is a comfortable and pleasantly furnished lounge with an open fire; and the restaurant is a very pretty and relaxing place. The cooking is excellent and always includes a good selection of fish.

On summer days, you can take advantage of the covered patio and the very pretty garden with its array of flowers and bushes. The gardens have recently been extended and now include a lake. It's a quiet and peaceful spot with a view across the lush valley of a distant village church.

The pub has six agreeable bedrooms, some of which can accommodate two parents and a child – but there are no larger family rooms.

....

✗ Bar snacks (12pm to 2.15pm and 6.30pm to 9.30pm) £2–7: Provence fish soup, smoked venison, Trengilly cassoulet, seafood strudel, steak & kidney pudding;
Dinner (7.30pm to 9.30pm) £18: grilled goat's cheese, guinea fowl, pudding
Children: own menu, half portions

◖ Ale: a varying choice

℗ Own car park

Nr NANTWICH, CHESHIRE   Map 8
℗ⓡ BARBRIDGE INN
Tel: 01270 528 443
Just off the A51 on the south-east side of Nantwich. The pub is signposted.

....

This pleasant pub has a traditional appearance and boxes and baskets of flowers brighten the façade. It has a wonderful location alongside the Shropshire Union Canal and it was a great treat to sit in the very large garden, under a shady tree, and gaze at the water and the occasional passing boat or barge. As well as its lovely lawned garden, the pub has a terrace, and there is a sizeable children's play area, which is safely enclosed.

Inside, the open-plan bar has padded benches around the walls, colourful wallpaper and prints on the walls and corner cupboards with displays of china. A conservatory room looks out to the garden and a large dining area faces the canal. It's a delightful spot and the pub is open all day through the summer months (Easter to September).

Families are made very welcome here and high chairs are available, as are nappy-changing facilities.

....

✗ (12pm to 2.30pm and 6pm to 9pm; Sun 12pm to 9pm) £2–8:

mushroom & cheddar bake, Cumberland sausage, lasagne verdi, beef Madras, Pembrokeshire lamb

Children: own menu

◲ Ale: Boddington's, Cain's

ℙ Own car park

NEEDINGWORTH, nr ST IVES, CAMBS   Map 6
ℙℝ **Pike and Eel Hotel**
Tel: 01480 463336
Go into the village and look for the sign to the pub on the main street.

....

This is a delightful place for a family outing. There are acres of space around the pub, which is right on the banks of the River Ouse. It is a big and attractive stone building, partly Tudor, once owned by Ramsey Abbey, and was the site of an old chain ferry. Long lawns sweep down to the river's edge with lovely trees all around, and there is a good array of small boats, moored at the pub's marina.

Inside there is a spacious bar and two rooms which children can use. Both are heavily beamed and low-ceilinged in the original Tudor part of the inn, and are very comfortably furnished. A large garden room restaurant has been attached to the front of the pub, and families are welcome to eat here. It is nicely laid out and is very bright and cheerful, with rows of windows looking out to the garden and the river. Several high chairs are provided. The pub is open all day.

....

✕ (12pm to 2pm and 7pm to 10pm) £2–12: pickled seafood, roast of the day, carrot & almond loaf, trout, steaks
Children: small portions

◲ Ale: Bass, Greene King, Fuller's, Ruddles

ℙ Plenty

NEWBURY, BERKS — Map 5
Ⓟ Ⓡ ROBIN HOOD, **London Road**
Tel: 01635 40636
On the A4 where it joins the A34 (on the east side of Newbury).

This is a well-proportioned brick building with an iron balustrade at ground level. The bar is welcoming and spacious with wood-panelled walls (there are some assegais on one of them), comfortable benches, and a few armchairs in a bay window. A pool table takes up one corner.

The restaurant is housed in an extension and there is a pleasant bar area here. The dining area is very appealing, a long room with a high vaulted roof of wood and glass above brick walls with some wooden panelling. It's bright and attractive and the garden room effect is heightened by the many potted plants. High chairs are provided but no specific nappy-changing facilities. There is a small garden with a few bench tables.

Strangely for a Bass pub, there is no real ale on offer here.

✗ (12pm to 2pm and 6pm to 10pm; Sun all day) £2–13: chicken tikka, steaks, fish & chips, cream Brie & courgette crumble, steak pie
   Children: own menu
Ⓟ Own car park

NEWBY BRIDGE, nr ULVERSTON, CUMBRIA — Map 8
Ⓗ SWAN HOTEL
Tel: 015395 31681
On the A590.

The core of this hotel is a 17th-century coaching inn. It has a wonderful position by the River Leven at the end of Lake Windermere and its 300 yards of lake frontage has moorings for boats. You can fish here or, even better, sit quietly on the terrace behind a screen of roses.

There is loads of space in the garden which runs at the rear of the hotel and there is a croquet lawn and a golf practice net. An adjoining field is often the take-off point for hot air balloons, and there is a helipad here too. The indoor facilities include table tennis, darts, a small snooker table and a good selection of board games.

The various public rooms are very agreeable and include a stately, high-ceilinged cocktail bar and another spacious bar; the Tithe Barn, with its stone walls and wooden rafters; and, below, the Mailcoach Wine Bar, which offers a good range of bar meals in an informal atmosphere. It is good to report that there is a nappy-changing facility nearby.

The bedrooms are furnished and decorated to a very high standard and the family rooms are light and bright and have plenty of space. Two of the family suites have separate bunk bedrooms for children.

The Swan is a top-class family hotel in a delightful location.

Nearby: You are in the heart of the Lake District and an active holiday can start with all the water sports which are easily available, plus walking, fishing, golf and riding. The Lakeside and Haverthwaite Railway is on the doorstep, as is Fell Foot Park, with its own water sport facilities, picnic areas and adventure playground. Holker Hall, Sizergh Castle, Levens Hall, the Grizedale Forest Centre, Brantwood, Belle Isle and the Steamboat Museum at Windermere are all within easy reach.

⋯⋯⋯⋯⋯⋯⋯⋯⋯⋯⋯⋯⋯⋯⋯⋯⋯⋯⋯⋯⋯⋯⋯⋯⋯⋯⋯⋯⋯⋯⋯⋯⋯

✖ The Mailcoach (11.45am to 2.45pm and 6.30pm to 9.45pm) £2–7: Mailcoach pie, steak baguette, fillets of plaice, vegetable lasagne; Dinner (7pm to 9pm) £18: hors d'oeuvres, fillet of beef Wellington, pudding or cheese
Children: own menu, half portions
£ High

✓ Best Bargain Break: £57 per person per night – dinner, b&b
Children: cots £4; £18 extra bed (including breakfast)
Facilities: 4 cots and 3 high chairs; baby-listening system
36 rooms, 3 family
Open all year

🄳 Ale: Boddington's and guests

🅿 Own car park

Nr NEWCASTLE-UNDER-LYME, STAFFS   Map 4
PR SWAN WITH TWO NECKS, Blackbrook
Tel: 01782 680 343
East of Market Drayton where the A53 meets the A51 at Blackbrook.

The main part of the building – mellow brick, nicely proportioned and with a gable at one end – looks as though it has always been a pub. But it was once a garage and has now metamorphosed to a sizeable family pub and restaurant. And very cheery it looks, with ivy on the façade and masses of flowers in hanging baskets.

The terrace and lawn have several bench tables and look towards low wooded hills. There is a children's play unit and in summer a bouncy castle.

The bar has an inviting alcove to one side, with a fireplace, nice chairs and padded benches. The restaurant, on a higher level, is in the same style and has windows along one wall, colourful light fittings and prints on the walls. The large family restaurant is split into several areas, with the same bright décor. One room overlooks the terrace and the garden and there is a separate little alcove with a table set for eight people – a suitable place for a family meal.

Plenty of high chairs are provided and there is a nappy-changing facility. The children will be in their element in the Fun Factory with all its toys and play equipment, and there is a soft drinks bar.

✗ (11.30am to 10pm) £2–8: hot mushrooms, fish pie, marinated lamb steak, vegetable crumble, steak & kidney pie
Children: own menu
◖ Ale: Boddington's, Flowers, Marston's
P Own car park

NEWNHAM, nr SITTINGBOURNE, KENT Map 3
P **GEORGE INN, 44 The Street**
Tel: 01795 890 237
South-west of Faversham off the A2.

....

This really is the garden of England. Newnham is a beautiful village, complete with cricket club, with the church and the pub in the centre of the dwellings. The George was built in 1540 as part of the estate of Thomas Hart, but it did not become an inn until 1718, when it took its name from the reigning monarch. It later became a celebrated coaching inn.

The George is noted for its excellent home-made food. It does not offer a children's menu or half portions, but the suggestion is that children share a meal. Credit cards are not accepted.

There is a delightful big garden which is backed by rolling farmland, and the garden offers family benches and much space for play. The inn is very popular, with many customers travelling far to dine here, and there is a lunchtime menu and a larger evening menu.

....

✗ (12pm to 2pm and 7pm to 10pm; not Sun and Mon pm) £2–12: moules marinières, cottage pie, chilli con carne, fillets of sole, rack of lamb
D Ale: Shepherd Neame and guests
P Ample

NEWPORT, ISLE OF WIGHT Map 3
R **GOD'S PROVIDENCE HOUSE**
Tel: 01983 522 085
In the middle of the town, by St Thomas's church.

....

The unusual name, so the story goes, refers to the luck of its inhabitants in escaping the ravages of the Plague. Some parts of the building date back before 1665, although it is a charming mixture of styles, with Georgian windows, for example.

Three rooms make up the restaurant, all nicely furnished with oak tables and wheelback chairs; one room looks out on to the pretty square, with its church and small shops.

The staff are friendly and welcoming and there are four high chairs available. You can change a baby in the Ladies, where there is a wide shelf, and a chair can be put in there, too.

....

✗ (9am to 5pm; not Sun) £1–5: roast of the day, steak pie, wholemeal quiche, roast chicken
   Children: half portions
Ⓟ On the street

NEWQUAY, CORNWALL   Map 1
Ⓗ **THE BRISTOL**
Tel: 01637 875 181
On the west side of Newquay.

....

The large bay windows and turrets give a pronounced Edwardian look to this substantial seaside hotel, which was founded by the Young family in the 1920s. On the outskirts of the town, the building has a splendid position high above the sands of Tolcarne Beach, where the amenities include a surfing school, beach huts and a café. Guests can stroll down to the sand in minutes, and there is plenty of choice of beaches in the Newquay area.

The Bristol has excellent facilities if the weather is variable. There is an indoor swimming pool, and you have a choice of table tennis, snooker or pool. A sauna and a solarium will perk you up, too.

Comfortable lounges overlook the sea, and the dining room is a splendid and rather stately room with windows which give diners a view over Newquay Bay. We looked at several bedrooms, which all had the great merit of providing plenty of space – an essential on a family holiday. There are four family suites (three of which have delightful views of the sea), and these comprise a large bedroom with a double and a single bed and an adjoining twin-bedded room suitable

261

for children. Many other rooms contain a double and a single bed and also have ample space for a cot.

The Bristol is an impressive seaside hotel with excellent facilities for families, the whole enterprise underpinned by the experience of the Young family.

Nearby: All the amenities of a thriving coastal resort are available – wind surfing, sailing, swimming and fishing, as well as golf and tennis, and the hotel can arrange such activities as clay pigeon shooting. There are many superb sandy beaches and, from the north of the town, you can walk the coastal path. Nearby attractions include Trerice, the Lappa Valley Railway and the Dairyland Farm Park.

....

✕ Bar snacks (12pm to 2pm) £2–8: varied choice of hot and cold dishes;
Dinner (7.15pm to 8.45pm) £17: Scotch salmon mayonnaise, soup, beef olives au vin, pudding & cheese
Children: own menu, half portions
£ High
✓ Best Bargain Break: 20% discount for two or more nights
Children: free up to 16 years
Facilities: plenty of cots and high chairs; baby-listening to every room
74 rooms, 15 family, 4 suites
Open all year
Ⓟ Own car park at rear

NEWQUAY, CORNWALL   Map 1
Ⓗ TREVELGUE HOTEL
Tel: 01637 872 864
On the B3276 Newquay–Padstow road.

....

The brochure for this hotel proclaims it a 'parents' haven – children's paradise' and that is an apt description, since it is a hotel dedicated to family holidays and everything is provided to ensure every member of a family is properly looked after. It is a modern, purpose-built hotel with very spacious rooms: the majority of them are suites with a separate twin-bedded room for children. The views over the bay are delightful.

Even if it is pouring with rain the superb indoor facilities will keep anyone amused: they include a snooker room, a swimming pool with separate children's pool, table tennis, pool, games machines and lots of space where children can play. There is a play room and a hobby club and an indoor jungle trail for young children. For the older children, there is a special disco. Nearby in Newquay itself is the Fun Factory, which is an indoor play area for under-12s. Playgroups are organized every day by the childcare staff, who also run other entertainments; and the hotel will hire buggies, pushchairs, baby walkers and so on to guests.

When the sun shines, there is another excellent swimming pool in its own grassy garden, a hard tennis court, a paddle tennis court and squash court, a boule pitch, giant chess, a badminton court, a golf net and practice hole and mini-football pitches. There's an adventure playground, a sandpit and a pirate ship, all within easy viewing and shouting distance of the terrace, upon which you can enjoy your drinks with an easy mind. There are nine acres of grounds in which the children can roam and three acres of garden. A barbecue area has now been added to the facilities and families can cook their own food here. The latest attraction is a BMX cycle trail.

Below the hotel are some lovely sandy beaches. Under-6s can be abandoned to the playgroup each morning from Monday to Friday and over-6s are taken on various outings and offered Punch and Judy shows, parties, galas, games and magic shows, etc. Parents will be interested in the wine list, which has some real bargains.

Entertainments are put on every evening, so it is just the place for an active, gregarious holiday for families with young children. The food, by the way, is bound to be fresh – the hotel has its own market garden, makes its own bread and pasta, etc. When we visited recently our dinner was first-class.

The Trevelgue offers tremendous value for money. It has won several awards, including one in 1994 as the most parent-friendly hotel in the UK.

Nearby: The busy resort of Newquay is just down the road and has safe, sandy beaches. It is one of the main surfing centres in Britain. The children may want to visit the zoo, the Dairyland Farm Park and the World in Miniature; the Lappa Valley Railway and the lovely Elizabethan house at Trerice are within easy reach.

....

✕ Bar lunch (12pm to 2pm) £1–4: burgers, baked potatoes, pizzas, salad;
Dinner (7.30pm to 9pm) £10: potted crab, chicken bonne femme, pudding or cheese
Children: own menu
£ Medium

✓ Best Bargain Break: £34 per person per night – dinner, b&b
Children: varies from free to 20% discount
Facilities: 70 cots and 70 high chairs; baby-listening
70 rooms, 60 family
Closed Nov to Mar

🅿 Own car park

Nr NEWQUAY, CORNWALL   **Map 1**
🅿 **QUINTRELL INN, Quintrell Downs**
Tel: 01637 874 427
On the A392 at the junction with the A3058.

....

This is a very large and thriving pub which becomes extremely busy at holiday times. All the facilities needed are in place and include a large lawned garden above the car park; it has plenty of bench tables and an excellent adventure playground. Close to the pub and adjoining the barbecue bar (and barbecues are held every evening at 5 o'clock), there is a delightful lawn, overhung by scores of trees which give shade to the picnic tables.

The Quintrell Inn is a spacious and rambling pub, the various rooms highly congenial under their low wooden ceilings. All the walls are panelled in wood and display a great variety of prints, mugs, jugs and bottles. At one end there is a cosy family room which has several easy chairs. Part of the bar area has windows on to the garden and the other side is more of a lounge: there is plenty of space here.

The appealing restaurant has wide, floor-length windows on one side, and there is a snug alcove with a table for eight diners. A dining room on an upper level has a variety of equine artefacts – horse brasses, saddles, collars, bridles and so on.

It's an interesting pub which is clearly very popular.

✗ Bar food (12pm to 2.15pm) £2–10: calamari, plaice & chips, Cornish pasty, scampi, steaks;
Restaurant (7pm to 10pm) £2–13: garlic mushrooms, steak au poivre, chicken Malai, Mediterranean lamb, vegetable lasagne
Children: own menu
◑ Ale: Boddington's, Flowers and guests
ℙ Lots

NEWTHORPE, nr LEEDS, NORTH YORKS   Map 9
ℙℝ NEW INN
Tel: 01977 682 325
On the B1222 and close to the A1 at South Milford.

This is a gigantic family pub which has the added attraction for children of a Fun Factory housed in a separate building at the back of the pub. This has all sorts of amusements – a ball pool, slides, tunnels, toys and games – and is always supervised by a member of staff. In addition, there are children's rides on the terrace, a playground on a safe bark surface and a bouncy castle.

If the children are catered for, so is everyone else, since the pub serves food throughout the day and for most of the evening. There is a children's menu, high chairs and a nappy-changing facility.

The interior of the New Inn may be large but it is not overwhelming since it is designed on various levels; for example, one of the two large bars is downstairs and the pub is divided into manageable eating areas (several of which are no-smoking) by the use of wooden pillars and glass screens. It is comfortable and welcoming and has food on offer at decent prices.

✗ (11.30am to 10pm; Sun from 12pm) £2–8: fish dippers, sirloin steak, chicken masala, fillet of salmon, tagliatelle carbonara
Children: own menu
◖ Ale: Boddington's, Whitbread
ℙ Own car park

NEWTON, LINCS   **Map 7**
ℙ RED LION
Tel: 01529 497 256
In the village, off the A52 east of Grantham.

This delightful pub, long and low and built of stone, is a real find in a county which is very short of places we can recommend.

Children are welcome in three rooms in the pub: in the food bar, notable for its penny farthing in one corner; in a very smartly furnished family room with a nautical theme and big open fireplace; and in another lovely room at the garden end of the pub. It is furnished with padded wooden settles, a little dresser and plenty of wooden tables.

The garden itself is enclosed and immaculate, with a long, smooth lawn, a swing and a slide, a small paved patio with white furniture, and lots of bright flowers.

The food is based on a comprehensive cold buffet: lots of fresh salads, prawns, pies and an array of meats. The landlord serves small, normal or large portions and to tackle the large plate you would have to be in the gargantuan class. On Saturday evening and Sunday lunchtime a carvery of hot roasts is also available.

An unusual feature of the pub is the presence of a squash club with two courts, and visitors can play here if they book in advance.

✖ (12pm to 2pm and 7pm to 10pm) £1–9: soup, pâté, cold buffet
Children: own menu, half portions
◔ Ale: Bass, Bateman's
🄿 Own car park

Nr NEWTON ABBOT, DEVON   Map 1
🄿🄡 COOMBE CELLARS, Combeinteignhead
Tel: 01626 872 423
West of Newton Abbot off the A380.

This substantial old pub, smartly painted white and with its façade splashed bright with pots and baskets of flowers, has a memorable location at the edge of the Teign estuary. From the pub's wide windows and its terraces you can view the water and the abundance of bird life.

It is a pleasure to welcome Coombe Cellars back to the *Guide* after a gap of several years, during which the interior has been remodelled. The bar area has a low ceiling of wooden beams and a number of padded wall-benches, where you can sit and admire the view. A lounge area has some easy chairs placed by a sizeable fireplace with a wood-burning stove.

The restaurant extends around the seaward side of the building. There is wood panelling in evidence, padded settles and a central brick fireplace. The decorations have a nautical theme: ropes, anchors, lifebelts, fishing nets, parts of boats and many prints. Near the family dining area you will find a small indoor play area with a ball swamp.

On a sunny day you have your pick of three terraces: a paved one in front of the car park, one which overhangs the water on the other side of the pub, or the enclosed lawned garden which has plenty of bench tables. A play area has been established here on a safe bark surface and its focal point is a wooden pirate ship; in summer there is also a bouncy castle.

It is a splendid pub with excellent facilities for families, including high chairs and a nappy-changing unit.

✗ (11.30am to 10pm) £2–8: fish dippers, tagliatelle carbonara, chicken
Balti, steak & kidney pie, haddock & chips
Children: own menu
◐ Ale: Boddington's, Flowers and guests
P Lots

NORTH BOVEY, DEVON   Map 1
P **RING OF BELLS**
Tel: 01647 440 375
Off the A382 south of Moretonhampstead.

The pub itself is part of a conversion of a thatched lodging house in
the centre of the village. The main entrance is at the rear of a paved
courtyard, formed by the main building and an old stable. After the
portico entrance, you turn left along the passageway and enter the
main bar via a lounge area with a large wood-burning stove at one
end. This room is set aside for families. Beyond the main bar, through
a low-ceilinged passageway, is the stable bar where children are also
welcome if they are eating with accompanying adults.

On the other side of the building you will find the main restaurant
and dining area, where an extensive menu is available to the hungry
traveller. Wooden settles, wheelwright chairs and benches abound
throughout, and each area is variously carpeted and flagstoned. The
effect is enhanced by white-painted rough stone walls and black wooden
beams.

When the weather is fine you may sit out at picnic tables in the
courtyard and nearby there is a small grassed area with a swing.
There is no music in this pub, in keeping with its character as a
good, old-fashioned country hostelry.

Up two spiral staircases from the pub are three family bedrooms (£15
to £30 per adult per night), and three cots are available as required.

✗ Bar snacks (12pm to 2pm and 6.30pm to 9pm) £3–14: snails in
garlic, fillet of salmon, local pheasant, steaks, supreme of chicken

Children: small portions
℗ Ale: Dartmoor, Wadworth's, Burton and guests
Ⓟ On street

NORTH CURRY, SOMERSET   Map 2
Ⓟ THE RISING SUN, Knapp
Tel: 01823 490 436
Between the A361 and the A378 east of Taunton. Look for the North Curry sign.

It is well worth the effort to seek out this 15th-century inn, which was once licensed for cider only. If you head for North Curry, you will find some well-placed signs just outside the village to point you to the pub.

It has been renovated and expanded, and very smart it looks in its coat of white paint, with baskets of bright flowers and honeysuckle adorning the front walls. There is a little terrace at the front and another one at the back of the pub.

The bar is a most attractive room with ancient wooden beams which form a square pattern in the ceiling; wooden pillars make an open screen to the dining room. Very smart and comfortable chairs and banquettes furnish the bar, where there is a huge open fireplace with an iron stove.

The family room, with its stone walls and old oak panelling, is a delight. There are padded settles and several tables and another huge walk-in fireplace with an iron cooking range.

Although you have a wide choice of food (and we had an enjoyable lunch at The Rising Sun a summer or two ago) the owner specializes in fish. There are some unusual varieties here; talapia, black bream, Indian Ocean bass and gurnard, as well as plaice, Dover sole, brill and monkfish. The three-course Sunday lunch is great value at under £8. There are two double rooms for rent, at under £40 each per night.

Seek out The Rising Sun: it is only a very short drive from Junction 25 of the M5.

✗ (12pm to 2pm) £1–8: cauliflower au gratin, Welsh rarebit, grilled plaice, spicy pork sausages, grilled rib eye steak;
Dinner (7pm to 9.30pm) £8–18: bouillabaisse, whole Brixham plaice, hot spiced crab, beef Stroganoff, supreme of chicken aioli
Children: half portions

◻ Ale: Bass, Boddington's, Exmoor

Ⓟ Own car park

NORTH LANCING, WEST SUSSEX   Map 3
ⓅⓇ **Sussex Potter**
Tel: 01903 753 210
Just off the A27 at North Lancing.

An archetypal 1930s pub, spacious, with high gables and steep roofs, the Sussex Potter has assumed many roles for its customers before becoming a part of the Beefeater chain.

It is a smart and appealing place and has a good local bar trade, partly because of its range of real ales – and they even serve mild, which is rare in this neck of the woods.

At the rear of the pub there is a very pretty garden, with a lawn, some mature trees and a lively display of flowers and shrubs. Several bench tables are scattered about and the children's play area has swings and a slide. A very pleasant room, with a wooden roof and a skylight of coloured glass, overlooks the garden.

Further inside, the bar has brick walls and comfortable padded benches. Upstairs there is an inviting lounge; it has timber and plaster walls, a low ceiling and a nice collection of plates and prints as decoration. The restaurant comprises three rooms on different levels – all busy when we visited – and includes one with a huge bay window. It's very well organized, bright and bustling.

For families there are excellent facilities, including high chairs and nappy-changing facilities in the Ladies.

✕ (12.30pm to 2.30pm and 5pm to 10.30pm; weekends all day)
£2–13: Cajun prawns, minted lamb steak, pasta Lucana, ocean bake, steaks
Children: own menu
🍺 Ale: Boddington's, Flowers, Castle Eden, Whitbread
🅿 Own car park

NORTH WEALD, ESSEX   Map 6
🅿 **The Talbot, 275 High Road, Tylers Green**
Tel: 01992 523966
Exit 7 on the M11. Take the A414 to Chelmsford, the Talbot roundabout on which the pub stands is approximately a mile from Exit 7.

An inn has stood on the spot where The Talbot now stands for nearly a hundred years and, dominating the roundabout junction which bears its name, the pub is a familiar landmark. The interior has many reminders of a famous period during the pub's history. There are flying jackets, a model aeroplane, a propeller and photographs from the years between 1942 and 1945 when the Tylers Green Airfield at North Weald played such a significant part in the defence of the

United Kingdom. Although no longer used by the Royal Air Force, the nearby aerodrome is still home to a flying club, and it is also the site for huge car boot sales, miniature car races and celebrations of all kinds.

The Talbot has a large garden with an attractive play area of slides and climbs for children. On sunny days, there is also a bouncy castle. Children may eat anywhere in the restaurant, but two special areas, one in the entrance space and another in an elevated open room close to the entrance to the garden, are set aside for parents and children who are not dining.

The pub is open from 11 in the morning until 11 at night, and food is served from 12.00 until 10.30. Two high chairs are available, and it is planned to increase this number, and half portions are provided as well as a children's menu. Changing facilities for babies are to be found in the Ladies.

....

✗ (12pm to 10.30pm) £2–13: pork satay, steaks, ocean bake, seafood tagliatelle, beef & Boddington's pie
  Children: own menu, half portions and other options
◗ Ale: Boddington's, Flowers, Adnams, Wadworth's
🅿 Spacious

NORTHALLERTON, NORTH YORKS   Map 9
🅁 BETTYS CAFE TEAROOMS, 188 High Street
Tel: 01609 775 154
On the main street.

....

On the town's main thoroughfare you will find this civilized and charming café, the smallest of the celebrated chain of Bettys. The long room is pleasingly decorated and has prints on the walls and a display of teapots on high shelves. The standards are extremely high and the welcome for families is wholehearted.

There are changing facilities in the Ladies (and a playpen) upstairs and, as well as several high chairs, nappies, bibs and beakers will

1

Aust

Malmesbury

Tormarton

M5

M4

M4

Pewsham

Swindon

Avebury

Weston-
super-
Mare

Nailsea

Bristol

A38

A46

A4

Bathford

Bath

Bradford-
on-Avon

Marlborough

A4

Hutton

Compton
Martin

Norton St Philip

West
Huntspill

Cannington

A39

Withypool

A39

Wells

A36

Bishop's Lydeard

A396

Ashcott

Batcombe

M5

North Curry

A38

Taunton

Trent

Motcombe

A30

Salisbury

A36

Dowlish Wake

A30

Lydlinch

A354

Hardington
Mandeville

A356

Ansty

A35

Seatown

Sydling St
Nicholas

Plush

Lytchett Minster

East Stoke

Christchurch

West
Bexington

Dorchester

A35

Studland

Bournemouth

Moonfleet
Weymouth

A352

Lulworth
Cove

2

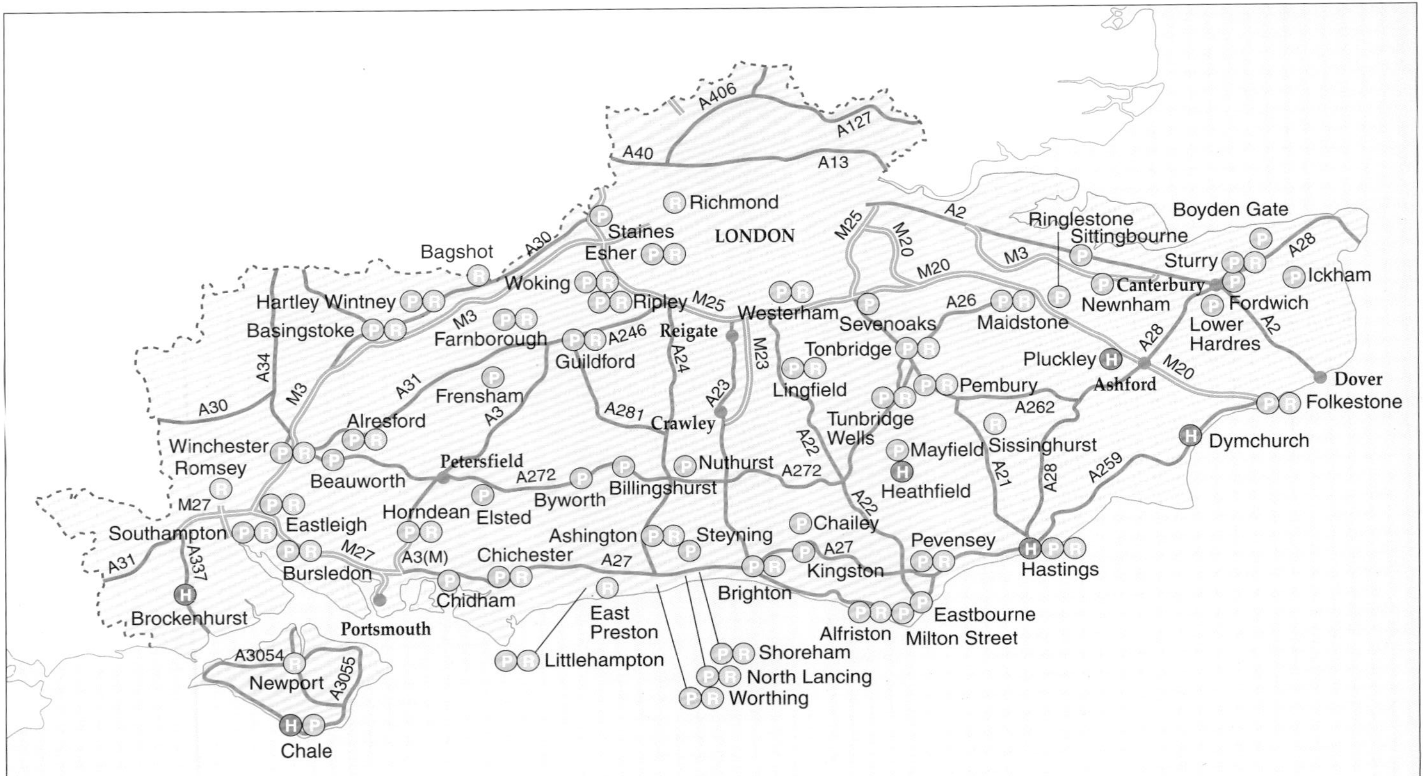
LONDON
Richmond
Staines
Esher
Bagshot
Woking
Ripley
Hartley Wintney
Basingstoke
Farnborough
Guildford
Reigate
Westerham
Sevenoaks
Maidstone
Ringlestone
Sittingbourne
Boyden Gate
Sturry
Canterbury
Ickham
Newnham
Fordwich
Lower Hardres
Dover
Folkestone
Pluckley
Ashford
Tonbridge
Lingfield
Pembury
Tunbridge Wells
Mayfield
Sissinghurst
Heathfield
Dymchurch
Frensham
Alresford
Winchester
Romsey
Beauworth
Petersfield
Nuthurst
Crawley
Billingshurst
Byworth
Elsted
Horndean
Eastleigh
Southampton
Bursledon
Chichester
Chidham
Portsmouth
Brockenhurst
Ashington
Steyning
Chailey
Kingston
Pevensey
Hastings
Brighton
Eastbourne
Alfriston
Milton Street
East Preston
Littlehampton
Shoreham
North Lancing
Worthing
Newport
Chale
A406
A127
A40
A13
A2
M25
M20
M3
A28
A30
A34
A26
A246
A24
M23
A31
A3
A281
A23
A22
A262
A272
A21
A259
M27
A337
A3(M)
A27
A3054
A3055

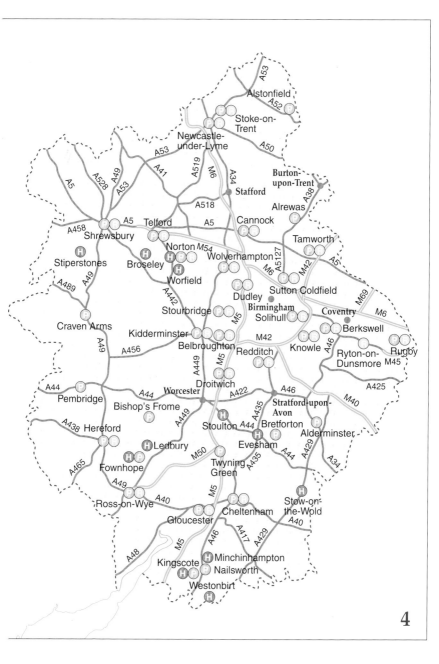

4

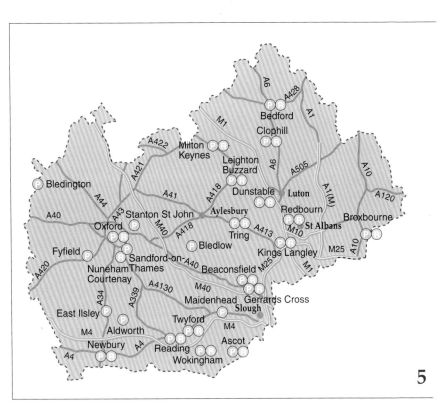

5

Blakeney
West Runton
Cromer
A149
A148
A148
A140
A149
Snettisham
A149
A1065
Hevingham
A47
Norwich
A47
King's Lynn
Castle Acre
A11
Great
Yarmouth
Stow
A134
Swainsthorpe
Bardolph
A140
A143
A15
A47
A47
Peterborough
A10
Lowestoft
A1
A1065
A12
Ely
Thetford
A143
Needingworth
A134
A143
Huntingdon
A10
Bury St Edmunds
A1120
A1
Milton
Stonham
A12
A428
Horringer
Aspal
Aldeburgh
Hail Weston
Cambridge
Nowton
A14
Woodbridge
A604
Barrington
A134
Lavenham
Ipswich
A14
A12
Saffron
Dedham
Felixstowe
Walden
Wix
Harwich
M11
A120
A120
Colchester
A12
Peldon
Clacton-on-Sea
North Weald
A131
Woodham
Chigwell Row
A414
Walter
Chelmsford
Chingford
Mountnessing
Southend-on-Sea
A127
Shoeburyness
M25

6

7

8

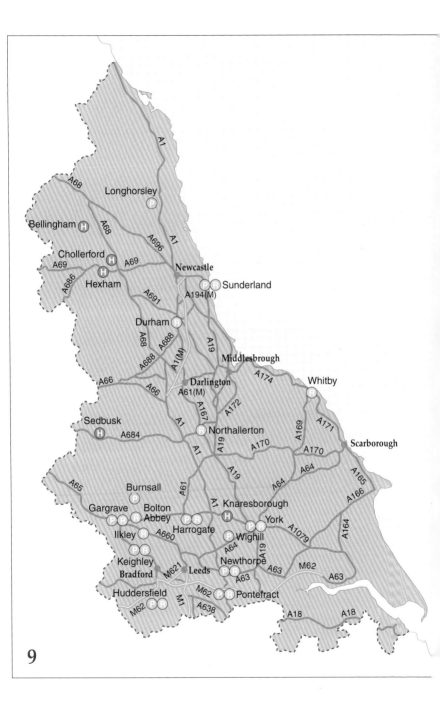

9

10

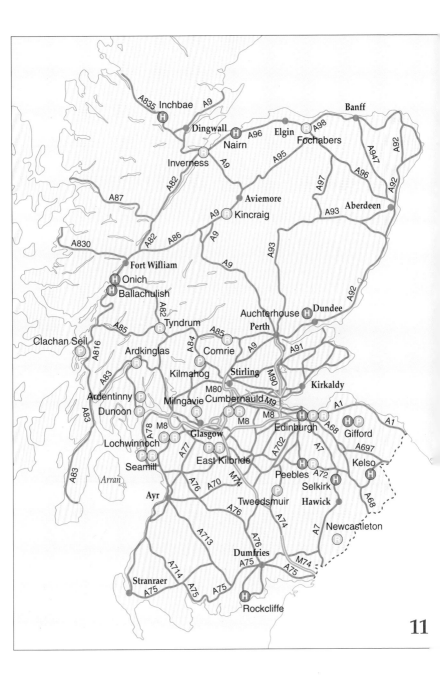

11

be provided. The infants' and children's menu shows real flair and imagination.

The home-made cakes are hard to resist and there is also a wide range of savouries, grills and sandwiches, as well as an excellent range of tea and unusual blends of coffee.

✗ (9am to 5.30pm; Sun 10am to 5.30pm) £1–7: rarebits, haddock & prawn croustades, omelettes, cheese & herb pâté, scrambled egg with smoked salmon
Children: own menu, half portions

P On street and car park nearby

Nr NORTHAMPTON, NORTHANTS **Map 7**

P R MIDWAY HOTEL, Wootton

Tel: 01604 769 676

On the A508 just south of Northampton and close to Junction 15 of the M1.

If you are belting along the M1 and need a break, the Midway is a mere minute or two from the motorway. It is a large purpose-built hotel, pub and restaurant with excellent facilities for families.

The restaurant, which has several high chairs available, has wide windows on to the terrace and the garden. It's a pleasant room, with brick pillars, and the décor and furniture give it something of a Twenties look. Alongside there is a small lounge bar, with comfortable padded benches.

The bar, which is open throughout the day and serves bar snacks at all times, is spacious. A central fireplace is a focal point and there is a sitting area under a vaulted roof at one side. In addition a room with windows on three sides is a congenial place to sit in comfort.

The hotel has thirty bedrooms and the prices are reasonable, especially at the weekend.

✗ (12pm to 2.30pm and 6pm to 10.30pm; Sun all day) £2–11:

chicken tikka, mixed grill, steaks, fish & chips, Brie & courgette crumble
Children: Own menu
⌷ Ale: Bass
Ⓟ Lots

Nr NORTHAMPTON, NORTHANTS   Map 7
ⓅⓇ THE TURNPIKE, Harpole
Tel: 01604 832 340
On the A45 west of Northampton and close to Junction 16 of the M1.

This is a huge, rambling pub and restaurant with excellent facilities for families: several high chairs, baby-changing facilities, and a sizeable children's play area in the garden. The Turnpike is open all day throughout the week and serves food from midday until 10.30pm. It's a useful stopping point if you are travelling on the M1.

The garden is large and grassy and there are lots of bench tables and space for the children to play. When you go inside you will find a large bar area with a central fireplace. There is another comfortable sitting area on an upper level.

The restaurant seems to have been conceived as a vast stable. It is designed on several levels and broken up into a number of small areas and alcoves. There is a liberal use of wood – panels, pillars and ceilings – and the walls are primarily brick, and hung with prints. It all hangs together reasonably well and the designer has even included a wishing well.

....

✕ (12pm to 10.30pm; weekends until 11pm) £2–13: Greek dip, gammon steak, seafood tagliatelle, beef & Boddington's pie, rump steak
  Children: own menu
☐ Ale: Boddington's, Flowers, Marston's and guests
Ⓟ Ample

Nr NORTHAMPTON, NORTHANTS   Map 7
ⓅⓇ WORLDS END, Ecton
Tel: 01604 414 521
On the A4500 at Ecton.

....

The pub is housed in a delightful three-storey 17th-century building of mellow stone. We were told that during the Civil War, soldiers who were near death found their final resting-place here – hence the name.

There are three main areas to the pub. The dining room has flowered wallpaper and the many windows ensure a bright and welcoming ambience. Some of the tables are situated on a dais and there is a pleasant bar here.

The bar is on the first floor. Comfortable sofas are separated into booths by screens of wood and coloured glass. It's a nice place to have a quiet drink and another room contains more sofas and a pool table.

On the ground floor you will find the family room, which leads out to the garden, the terrace and the children's play area. A bouncy castle is in place during the summer months. The family room includes a play room for younger children and there are baby-changing facilities in the Ladies.

The pub serves food all day and plenty of high chairs are available.

✕ (11.30am to 10pm) £2–8: fish dippers, vegetable moussaka, turkey fillet, sirloin steak, lasagne verdi
  Children: own menu
◑ Ale: Boddington's, Marston's and guests
ℙ Ample

NORTHWICH, CHESHIRE   **Map 8**
ℙℝ Winnington Lodge
Tel: 01606 74217
On the A533.

The very smart black-and-white building has an impressive porticoed entrance and masses of space. The high ceilings have a number of skylights with coloured glass, fans and chandeliers. In the bar, there are several pleasant lounge areas with comfortable padded settles; prints on the walls and cupboards with china and pewter on display add to the cheerful ambience. Two of the areas have wood panelling, open fireplaces and jazzy coverings on the furniture.

The Winnington Lodge is aimed at the family market, and several high chairs are available in the restaurant, which is divided into three agreeable rooms, wood panelled and with huge bay windows overlooking the garden. You can sit in the sun on one of the two terraces at the back or in the lawned garden where there is a play unit. The children can also enjoy all the equipment in Adventure Island, a very large indoor play area.

This is an excellent pub with all the facilities which a family might require, and it is open throughout the day and serves food from midday to 9pm.

✕ (12pm to 9pm; Sat until 10pm) £2–8: mushroom & cheddar bake, seafood crêpes, steaks, lasagne, Cumberland sausage
  Children: own menu

Ⓓ Ale: Boddington's, Castle Eden and guests
Ⓟ Own car park

NORTON, SHROPSHIRE   Map 4
🅷🅿🆁 **Hundred House Hotel**
Tel: 01952 730 353
On the A442 between Bridgnorth and Telford.

This hotel and pub has been renovated and adapted with great style by the Phillips family. You enter a bright and airy reception area, with a tiled floor, exposed brick walls, doors with stained-glass panels, and bunches of dried flowers and herbs hanging from the ceiling.

The style is continued in the various rooms which make up the bar and restaurant areas. There is a lovely high-ceilinged room with a Colebrookdale cast-iron range, and families can sit here together. There are windows on to the sizeable garden, shaded by trees. The two donkeys, Gerrard and Susan, are still on hand to crop the lawns.

The large bar has cast-iron cooking pots and other utensils hanging from the beamed ceilings – a suitable reminder of the old industries of this region, where nearby Ironbridge is regarded as one of the cradles of the Industrial Revolution. The museums there are well worth a visit.

The bar is on two levels, and families can relax at the tables in the eating area, which is notable for a huge fireplace. There is a great emphasis on food here, and the menu certainly looks enticing. Some of the produce will come from the hotel's own vegetable garden: mangetout and asparagus, perhaps, as well as the herbs.

Food is available every day and the three-course Sunday lunch is good value at around £11.

The bedrooms are furnished and decorated with great style, and they include a high proportion of family rooms. The hotel also has two cottages in Ironbridge which are let on a self-catering basis.

Nearby: There is no shortage of entertainment in this part of the world. The beautiful countryside of south Shropshire can easily be reached and a trip through Ludlow to Stokesay Castle and Clun and back through the Carding Mill Valley is recommended. The famous Ironbridge Gorge Museum is close at hand, as is the Midland Motor Museum and the Aerospace Museum at Cosford. The Severn Valley Railway runs from Bridgnorth.

....

✕ Bar snacks (12pm to 2.30pm and 6pm to 10pm) £3–11: savoury pancakes, avocado & crab gratin, sirloin steak, salmon fishcakes, lasagne:
  Dinner (6pm to 10pm) £18: salmon & sole terrine, roast rack of lamb, pudding or cheese
  Children: own menu, half portions
  £ High
✓ Best Bargain Break: £95 per person, 2 nights – dinner, b&b
  Children: free up to 16 years
  Facilities: 3 cots and 5 high chairs: baby-listening system
  10 rooms, 5 family
  Open all year
🍺 Ale: Brain's, Phillips, Flowers and guests
🅿 Own car park

NORTON ST PHILIP, SOMERSET Map 2
Ⓟ GEORGE INN
Tel: 01373 834 224
On the A366.

....

A magnificent and classic old inn dating from the 13th century and possibly even earlier, where little has been done to spoil an oak-beamed and wood-panelled interior with its old tables and wooden settles. The landlord, thank goodness, has no music in the pub nor any of those ghastly games machines with their hideous electronic noises.

Children are welcome in one of the lounges, which is large and very much in character, with a good array of tables and chairs and a huge stone fireplace. Another children's room comes into play at the weekend when the Dungeon Bar, which held a group of the rebel Duke of Monmouth's men prisoner in 1685, is open. Take a look at the splendid wooden ceiling. The Monmouth Room is also available at times for families.

On sunny days you can sit in a small courtyard, with a part-paved, part-cobbled floor, and surrounded by thick stone walls and heavy roofs. Alternatively there is a pretty lawned garden with several apple trees, and from there you look out across playing fields to the local church.

There is a good choice of hot and cold food available throughout the day, both at the bar and in the restaurant, and a traditional three-course lunch is served on Sundays for around £8. There are two high chairs available.

....

✗ (10am to 2pm and 6.30pm to 10.30pm) £2–12: vegetarian lasagne, baked potato with ham & cheese, guinea fowl, mixed grill, steaks
  Children: small portions
Ⓓ Ale: Bass, Wadworth's
Ⓟ Own car park

NORWICH, NORFOLK   Map 6
PR THE RACECOURSE, Rackheath
Tel: 01603 720421

Half a mile off the Norwich ring road, the A47, just outside the village of Rackheath. The Racecourse is two and a half miles from Norwich city centre.

Driving into the vast car park at the front of The Racecourse, one feels one is approaching a famous country house, for all is style and elegance. The inn is fronted by family tables with parasols sheltering drinkers from the sun. The site is also home to the local pigeon fanciers, and in the very large garden one can watch petanque, the Provençal version of boule. This garden has something for all. There is a patio, family benches, a barbecue area, trees, flowers, and even rabbits to be seen scuttling in and out of the hedge border. For children, there is a 'house' in which to climb, swings and slides, and, at night, all can be floodlit.

This is one of two gardens that the inn offers, for, at the rear of the building, there is an enclosed area with climbs and slides, and this is reached from the Charlie Chalk Fun Factory. This is a vast space in the inn which has been a conference room and a night club, and which is now full of games and delights; a play zone even boasts a Magic Roundabout. It is a most impressive area for young people, and, with the garden as one entrance, and the family dining room as the other, it offers a seclusion and safety where children may indulge themselves.

There are changing facilities in the Ladies, and eight high chairs, as well as booster seats, are available in the restaurant.

Although The Racecourse has a family licence, children are not encouraged in the bar area, and those who seek privacy and quiet will be able to find it in one of the many nooks and crannies in the vast dining space. The recent fire at Norwich City Library has destroyed the records relating to the building, but it is known that it stood in the grounds of the racecourse which existed here in the 18th century. The decoration reflects this link with the past, and the pub, low-beamed and welcoming, can boast one magnificent fireplace said to have come originally from a noble house in the city.

The inn has been fully developed, but there is a possibility that some of the splendid rooms on the first floor could be used to offer accommodation to guests in the future. Opening hours are 11am to 11pm, and food is available at all times.

....

✕ (11.30am to 10pm) £2–8: onion bhajis, fillet of salmon, chicken escalopes, sirloin steak, vegetable crumble
  Children: own menu
◑ Ale: Boddington's, Flowers and guests
𝗣 Ample

Nr NORWICH, NORFOLK   Map 6
𝗣𝗥 Village Inn, Little Melton
Tel: 01603 810 210
Off the B1108 west of Norwich.

....

This very large pub and restaurant is fully equipped to deal with families, and one of its great advantages is that food is available all day and every day right through to 10 o'clock at night.

The huge bar and restaurant area does not overwhelm you with its size because it is broken up by alcoves and wooden screens; and the wooden tables, padded settles and colourful carpet give a very smart and welcoming appearance to the interior.

The family room is also sizeable and has plenty of tables and chairs and a fine array of play equipment for the children: slides, a Lego table, a rocking horse and a blackboard and balloons for very small children. Outside there is an excellent play unit, and a changing table is provided in the Ladies' toilet area.

When a fine selection of real ales and reasonably priced wines and an uncomplicated menu are added to the comprehensive facilities, this adds up to an excellent (and very popular) family pub.

....

✕ (11.30am to 10pm, Sun from 12pm) £2–8: onion bhajis, fish pie, sirloin steak, vegetable crumble, chicken Balti
  Children: own menu

🍺 Ale: Boddington's, Flowers and guests (eg Wadworth's, Woodforde's, Marston's)

🅿 Lots

Nr NOTTINGHAM, NOTTS Map 7
🅿🄁 Wheelhouse, **Wollaton**
Tel: 0115 928 3520
A few miles east of Nottingham city centre. Follow the signs to Wollaton Park.

It is worth taking a little trouble to find the Wheelhouse, since it is a pleasant place for a family to eat and drink. If the exterior of this stone building looks plain, the inside is a children's paradise. It is very close to Wollaton Hall and its park, a magnificent Elizabethan building that is ornate enough to have been built by the Victorians. Wollaton Hall also houses a natural history and an industrial museum.

The family entrance is situated next to a small stone-flagged terrace with picnic benches, and a bouncy castle. It is from this point onwards that it is plain to see that the brewery has gone to great lengths to provide amenities to entertain the children. Immediately opposite a covered entrance is another set of doors, leading to a play area containing a wooden adventure fort, slides and various other play equipment. When you enter the main building there is a no-smoking family sitting area specifically set aside for parents with young children. Alongside is the Funky Forest Room with a ball swamp, a TV showing cartoons and various small play machines.

The main bar area curves its way round to the opposite end of the building, and there is another area for families. The main restaurant comprises three rooms divided by wooden partitions and glass windows. What is remarkable about this establishment is the amount of effort that has gone into making a plain building an interesting place to visit, especially for children. The place abounds with whirling clowns and toy aeroplanes – as well as the usual antique memorabilia which festoon the adult sections.

There are no fewer than twenty high chairs and around ten booster seats, and nappy-changing units are provided.

....

✗ (12pm to 3pm and 5.30pm to 10pm; weekends all day) £2–9: moules marinières, Cajun chicken, Cumberland sausage, plaice & chips, gammon steak
Children: own menu
◻ Ale: Home's, Theakston's
Ⓟ Ample

NOWTON, nr BURY ST EDMUNDS, SUFFOLK   Map 6
Ⓗ **HIGH GREEN HOUSE**
Tel: 01284 386 293
Off the A134 south of Bury St Edmunds; the brochure has a clear map.

....

The original part of this remarkably interesting house was built early in the 16th century, and the spacious sitting room displays many of the characteristics of Tudor building: wood and plaster walls, a beamed ceiling and a huge brick fireplace. It is a delightful room and is well

283

matched by the dining room alongside. The other half of the house was added in Victorian times.

All the bedrooms have their own bathrooms and the one on the ground floor has been redesigned to make a small family suite. There are two more attractive twin-bedded rooms on the upper floor, both with low ceilings and old wooden doors, and the views across the rolling Suffolk countryside will soothe the mind. Finally, there is a magnificent room with ancient wooden pillars and beams and a fine four-poster bed. You walk through a narrow corridor to a spacious bathroom which has the upper part of the Tudor chimney still in place.

The house is surrounded by a large lawned garden. There is an old covered well in the front garden, and apple trees to one side. The lawns are walled or fenced, but there is a pond at the side, so the children must be careful. But there is masses of space to play, and the house is surrounded by open countryside, where there are pleasant walks.

If you want some peace and quiet in unusual surroundings you should head for High Green House; the prices are very reasonable too.

Nearby: This is good fishing country, and if you are in the mood for sightseeing, Ickworth Mansion is nearby; as is Norton Tropical Bird Gardens, and West Stow Anglo-Saxon Village. The delightful old towns of Lavenham and Long Melford, Cavendish Manor Vineyards and Clare Castle Country Park are a short drive away.

....

✗ Dinner (7.30pm to 9pm) £13 (must book ahead)
   Children: high teas
   £ Low
✓ Best Bargain Break: £80 per person, 3 nights – dinner, b&b
   Children: babies free; half price from 2 to 5 years; 20% discount from 5 to 12
   Facilities: 2 cots and 1 high chair; baby-listening
   4 rooms, 2 family
   No credit cards accepted
   Open all year

P Ample

NUNEHAM COURTENAY, OXON   Map 5
R **NOTCUTTS GARDEN CENTRE**
Tel: 01865 343 454
At the junction of the A423 and the B4015, south of Oxford.

This is a large, well-organized and smart garden centre, and its restaurant
mirrors the very high standards which are clearly maintained. It is clean
and bright and airy, with good solid tables and chairs, and large windows
look over a most attractive lawned garden with avenues of trees. There is
a spacious terrace where you can sit and have a snack or a meal when
the weather is kind.

The self-service restaurant offers an excellent range of food, which is
nicely displayed and generously served by polite and helpful staff.

If you have a baby in tow, high chairs are made available, and there
is a baby-changing unit installed in the disabled toilet area.

X (9.30am to 5pm) £2–5: lasagne, lamb casserole, cauliflower cheese,
  roast of the day, steak & mushroom pie
  Children: half portions
  Unlicensed
P Own car park

NUTHURST, WEST SUSSEX   Map 3
P **BLACK HORSE**
Tel: 01403 891 272
On a minor road off the A281 south-east of Horsham.

This is a very appealing village pub, housed in what was once part of a row
of cottages and is now a long, low, red-brick building. Inside, the rooms

are delightful, with low-beamed ceilings, an abundance of good wooden furniture, and paved stone floors, with a big open fire in one bar and a substantial wood-burning stove in the other. There are two other rooms in the same style and children are welcome in the one furthest from the bar. It's very well furnished and you can see the structure of the old walls.

This is a busy pub but when we visited, the food, which is available every day, was served up with commendable efficiency.

There is a patio at both the front and the rear of the pub, with plenty of bench seats, and a pretty lawned garden, well shaded by tall trees and with a cheerful stream swooping through it.

....

✗ (12pm to 2.30pm and 7pm to 10pm) £2–8: steak & kidney pie, ploughman's, mixed grill, stuffed trout, vegetable crumble
  Children: own menu
◐ Ale: Eldridge Pope, King & Barnes, Wadworth's and guests
ℙ Own car park

OTTERY ST MARY, DEVON   **Map 1**
Ⓗ **FLUXTON FARM HOTEL**
Tel: 01404 812 818
On the Tipton St John Road, which runs south of Ottery St Mary.

....

This is a handsome 16th-century Devon longhouse situated in the Otter valley, and most of the rooms have splendid views to friendly wooded hills across the valley. Although it is no longer a farm, the owners keep some ducks and chickens and several cats.

The delightful gardens spread across a couple of acres, with a stream running through, and are partly enclosed by an old stone wall. Adults can take their ease on the wide lawns, shaded perhaps by one of the many stately trees. The owner has a miniature train on which he occasionally runs round the grounds; there is a putting green and a trout pond and a licence can be bought for fishing on the Otter.

There are two charming and comfortable lounges; the one in the older part of the house has a low ceiling and splendid crooked windows. The dining room has a fine open fireplace and a beamed ceiling, and there is a small bar.

We looked at several bedrooms, nicely proportioned with lovely views. The two family rooms (both with a double and two single beds) have plenty of space, and one has a single room alongside and can be used as a family suite.

Nearby: This is an attractive area for holiday makers, with pretty countryside, and the coast is very close with an excellent choice of clean, sandy beaches. Children will be interested in nearby Bicton Park, the Donkey Sanctuary and Farway Countryside Park. The amazing building, A la Ronde, near Exmouth is also well worth a visit, as are the Maritime Museum in Exeter and Killerton House. On the other side of the Exe Estuary, you can visit the Dawlish Warren Nature Reserve.

....

✗ Dinner (6.45pm) £7
   Children: own menu, half portions
   £ Medium
   Children: babies free; one third of full rate up to 5 years; half price thereafter
   Facilities: 2 cots and 1 high chair; baby-listening by arrangement
   12 rooms, 2 family
   Open all year

No credit cards accepted
🅿 Own car park

OXFORD, OXON   **Map 5**
🆁 BROWNS, 5–11 Woodstock Road
Tel: 01865 511 995
*On the A34 close to its junction with the A423 and just north of the city
centre (near St Giles).*

....

This big, bustling restaurant has a simple and effective décor of
bentwood chairs and wooden tables, and lots of plants and mirrors.
The ambience is that of a cheerful and relaxed brasserie. A large skylight
gives a spacious effect to the place, and in summer the entire frontage
of the restaurant can be opened.

The menu concentrates on salads, pasta and grills, and offers plenty of
things to appeal to a young palate. There are lots of high chairs available;
and there are even two mother and baby rooms with changing tables
and chairs. The staff make a real effort to welcome parents with young
children; indeed people of all ages find a warm welcome.

You can eat breakfast until noon, and the special lunchtime dishes,
posted on blackboards, are generally a little cheaper than the usual menu;
they generally sell out by 3 o'clock.

The restaurant is very spacious and over half is no-smoking.

....

✗ (Mon to Sat 11am to 11.30pm; Sun from 12pm) £2–11: pasta
with various sauces, fisherman's pie, roast poussin, burgers, steak
& mushroom & Guinness pie
Children: own menu, small portions
Closed at Christmas
🅿 On street

Nr OXFORD, OXON

Map 5

PR THE EVENLODE

Tel: 01865 881 215

On the A40 between Oxford and Witney.

This pub has ever been a familiar sight to people travelling along the A40. It stands four square at the top of a rise and is covered in Virginia creeper. The extensive lawned garden is a tempting (if noisy) place to settle on a warm day, and there are plenty of trees to provide shade. The garden is enclosed by a picket fence and there is a good-sized play area and a bouncy castle.

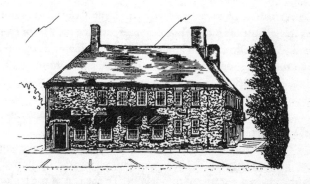

The Evenlode is aimed at the family market and food is available throughout the day. There are plenty of high chairs, a nappy-changing facility and a children's menu.

There is loads of space inside, and the bar is a pleasing room with its beamed ceiling and comfortable padded settles. The lounge area at one end has a stone fireplace and a settee and easy chairs. The restaurant rambles around the pub with a variety of rooms at the customers' disposal. The beamed ceilings are complemented by a variety of wooden furniture, prints and black-and-white photographs on the walls, displays of china and old bottles, and other artefacts.

✕ (12pm to 10.30pm; weekends until 11pm) £2–13: pork satay, ocean bake, beef & Boddington's pie, seafood tagliatelle, steaks
Children: own menu

Ⓓ Ale: Boddington's, Flowers and guests

Ⓟ Own car park

PADSTOW, CORNWALL Map 1
Ⓗ THE OLD CUSTOM HOUSE
Tel: 01841 532 359
By the quayside, centre of Padstow.

....

The combination of a classy hotel in a classic Cornish environment makes this a must for those who wish to experience the best of Cornish hospitality. The Old Custom House is a combination of three buildings built in the 1800s, one of which was the original Customs and Excise building. The hotel sits right next to and overlooks the fully operational fishing harbour in the centre of the town. From the hotel rooms there are views right across the bay to St Enodoc and its surrounding dunes and the countryside.

You can enter the hotel via the public house, which was the Custom House. This is a long oak-beamed room with a balustraded balcony; pine tables and chairs are scattered throughout. To the rear of the building is an area where families can sit together and it is comfortably furnished with padded benches and pine furniture. It contains a stone-built coal-burning fireplace, games machines and a pool table. Leading off from this area is a glass conservatory which contains padded cane furniture and semi-tropical plants (this is a no-smoking area).

The family bedrooms are comfortably furnished and well appointed with some fantastic sea views. All rooms are *en suite* and have the facilities expected in a hotel of this calibre.

The restaurant is housed in an adjacent building and seats nearly a hundred people in congenial surroundings. It has a cocktail lounge at the far end and in one corner a carvery is being constructed and is due to open for the 1996 season.

290

From its position on the quayside this hotel, bar and restaurant offers excellent facilities in an inviting setting.

Nearby: There are many excellent sandy beaches and you can explore the coastline along the Cornwall coastal path. All the usual leisure pursuits are readily available and there are splendid golf courses at Trevose and St Enodoc, in whose churchyard John Betjeman is buried. The delights of Bodmin Moor are close and sightseers can head for Trerice, Pencarrow and Lanhydrock.

✕ Bar snacks (12pm to 2pm and 6.30pm to 9pm) £2–8: Caribbean chicken, ratatouille with garlic bread, haddock & chips, grilled gammon;
Dinner (7pm to 9pm) £17: crab & prawns au gratin, sirloin steak, pudding or cheese
Children: own menu, half portions
£ High
Children: free to 3 years; half price from 3 to 12
Facilities: 3 cots and 4 high chairs
27 rooms, 8 family
Open all year
Ⓟ Own car park

PELDON, nr COLCHESTER, ESSEX   **Map 6**
Ⓟ **THE ROSE**
Tel: 01206 735 248
South of Colchester on the B1025.

The original house was built in the 14th century, and some of the ancient oak beams bear testimony to the age of the building. There has been an inn on this site for more than two hundred years. The public house is open throughout the day and food is available at any time, but the afternoon speciality is the cream teas. The restaurant is open at lunchtime and in the evening, and four high chairs are available.

There is a children's menu, and half portions are also provided. Children are not allowed in the bar area, but are welcome elsewhere.

This is a beautiful place, and the developments that have been made, such as the light and relaxing conservatory, blend well and tastefully with the original structure, whose character is preserved.

The house stands in lovely countryside and is close to National Trust land, a wildlife nature reserve and the boating attractions of Mersea. The garden is a delight, with a large area for children containing a swing, and ponds on which moorhens glide and water voles scutter.

....

✕ (12pm to 2pm and 7pm to 10pm) £2–13: Dover sole, sirloin steak, mushroom & cashew Stroganoff, coq au vin, steak & kidney pudding
　Children: own menu, half portions
◻ Ale: Boddington's, Flowers and guests
▣ Ample

PEMBRIDGE, HEREFORD & WORCS　　　　Map 4
▣ NEW INN
Tel: 01544 388 427
On the A44 between Kington and Leominster.

....

This is a quiet and delightful village in lovely surroundings, and this marvellous black-and-white 14th-century inn, which was once a courthouse, suits it admirably. Considering its proximity to the Welsh border it is perhaps surprising that it survived all the violent mayhem which afflicted this part of England centuries ago.

Inside is a marvellous public bar, which looks as though it hasn't changed since the inn first traded, with a flagstoned floor, huge open fireplace, black beams and a curved wooden settle. The lounge where children may be taken is large and comfortable, with inviting armchairs and sofas and some nice wooden tables. There's no garden – just a couple of picnic tables outside on the cobbled front.

You will find some interesting bar snacks here, plus a Sunday lunch for around £6; and there is a high chair on the premises. Some friends of ours who usually stop here on their way to and from Hereford races have given us enthusiastic reports of the food.

....

✕ (12pm to 2pm and 7pm to 9.30pm) £2–7: mussels in lemon butter, poached salmon, crispy duck salad, fillet of pork in cider apple & cream, steak sandwich
  Children: half portions
🍺 Ale: Courage
🅿 Own car park

PEMBURY, nr TUNBRIDGE WELLS, KENT   Map 3
🅿🆁 **The Camden Arms, High Street**
Tel: 01892 822 012
The village is just east of Tunbridge Wells off the A21. The pub is opposite the village green.

....

The Camden Arms is on the site of an old coaching inn, and the interior design does much to reflect that period. There are some fascinating railway station signs as well as the 18th- and 19th-century pictures and antiques. The car park is on one side of the inn as you approach from the main road, while the secluded, safe garden stands on the far side.

The garden boasts a bouncy castle, swings, a climb and slide, family benches and a barbecue area. It is pleasantly set out and attractively sheltered by trees.

Children are welcome in the restaurant and have their own menu, junior selections and other options. Baby food is provided free, and there are changing facilities in the ladies' toilet. There are four high chairs, and booster seats are also available. The inn is open all day and bar snacks are always available. The restaurant hours are shown below.

✕ (12pm to 2.30pm and 5pm to 10.30pm; weekends all day) £2–13: Greek dip, beef & Boddington's pie, pasta Lucana, sirloin Oscar, fried scampi
Children: own menu
◑ Ale: Boddington's, Flowers, Wadworth's and guests
ℙ Lots

PENDOGGETT, CORNWALL   Map 1
ℙ **CORNISH ARMS**
Tel: 01208 880 263
On the B3314 north of Wadebridge.

This attractive 16th-century pub has an exterior partly covered by slate and the floors inside are of the same material, probably from the local Delabole quarries.

As you enter there are three low-ceilinged rooms adjoining each other, all comfortably and attractively furnished. The smallest of them has a padded settle curving around the walls; the Coffee Room is a delightful and cosy room, with padded benches around its walls. There are leaded windows and pictures of the inn in former years on the walls.

Families with children are welcome to use the Coffee Room at lunchtimes and the restaurant is also available to them in the evenings. When the sun shines, the pleasant garden, with views across the fields towards Port Isaac, is the place to enjoy a drink and some food. There are plenty of bench tables and it is safe for children.

For the unencumbered adult drinker the spacious back bar, with more padded settles and a good array of wooden tables, is the place to be. There's a good, friendly atmosphere here in which to sup a couple of glasses of the strong Pendoggett Special.

The pub is open all day from Monday to Saturday.

....

✗ (12.30pm to 2pm and 6.30pm to 9.30pm) £2–12: lemon sole, beef & ale casserole, salmon fishcakes, rack of lamb, liver & bacon
Children: own menu, half portions

◖ Ale: Bass, Flowers, Pendoggett Special, Sharp's

ℙ Own car park

PENRITH, CUMBRIA   Map 8
Ⓗ North Lakes Hotel
Tel: 01768 868 111
Just off Exit 40 of the M6.

....

This hotel was built only a few years ago, and presents a fairly functional face to the multitude of traffic which passes its location close to Junction 40 of the M6. But the interior belies these first impressions, and the high vaulted ceilings with wooden beams, stone fireplaces and excellent furnishings give a smart and spacious tone to the hotel. There is quite a large garden at the back of the hotel.

The leisure club, unlike many others which lay claim to the description, offers proper facilities and has plenty of space. The pool is sizeable and superbly done under a vaulted pine roof and includes a children's pool; there are two excellent glass-backed squash courts; and an exercise room well equipped with bikes and other good-quality equipment. There is also a snooker room.

The hotel has six family rooms. Apart from two parents, they can accommodate up to three children, with bunk beds and a convertible sofa. Since children under 16 stay free, these rooms, charged at the standard rate, represent very good value if you are on the move with several youngsters. Parents will be grateful that, at weekends, the Action

Pack will take the children off their hands and involve them in a host of games and competitions.

Unusually for a hotel of this size, proper draught ale is served – a perfect way to round off a busy day in the Lake District or a couple of hours in the leisure club.

Nearby: Penrith itself is an interesting town, as is Appleby just down the A66. Beautiful Ullswater is on the doorstep while the southern Lakes with all their attractions are not far away: Grasmere, Belle Isle, Lake Windermere. The children will enjoy a visit to Hill Top, the home of Beatrix Potter. Nearer to hand for the hotel is Lowther Park with its nature trails and adventure playground.

X Bar meals (12pm to 2pm) £2–5: chicken curry, beef & mushroom pie, vegetable stir-fry, filled jacket potatoes;
Lunch (12.30pm to 2pm; not Sat) £10: salmon mousse, roast leg of pork, pudding or cheese;
Dinner (7pm to 9.30pm) £18: savoury mushrooms, honey-baked ham, pudding or cheese
Children: own menu, half portions
£ High
✓ Best Bargain Break: £69 per person per night – dinner, b&b
Children: free up to 16 years
Facilities: 6 cots and 5 high chairs; baby-listening system for every room
84 rooms, 6 family, 6 sets interconnecting
Open all year
⫐ Ale: Thwaites
℗ Own car park

PETERBOROUGH, CAMBS

Map 6

Ⓡ **Notcutts Garden Centre, Orton Waterville**

Tel: 01733 234 600

South-west of Peterborough, on the A605 at Orton Waterville.

This is one of the excellent chain of Notcutts Garden Centres, and has recently been refurbished and extended; there is, for example, a new glasshouse here.

The range of garden products is just as extensive as in the other Notcutts centres (qv Bagshot, Nuneham Courtenay and Solihull), and in between browsing you can have a drink or a meal in the attractive restaurant. It is a spacious place, with comfortable furniture of high quality. Quality is also the hallmark of the food; there is an enterprising selection of dishes, generously served and reasonably priced.

✕ (9.30am to 5pm) £2–5: lasagne, lamb casserole, cauliflower cheese, roast of the day, steak & mushroom pie
Children: half portions
Unlicensed

Ⓟ Own car park

PEVENSEY, EAST SUSSEX

Map 3

ⓅⓇ **Coopers, Stone Cross**

Tel: 01323 763 212

On the B2104 between Hailsham and Eastbourne.

The Coopers is just a few miles from Pevensey, near which William the Conqueror landed in 1066. His half-brother, Robert of Mortain, built the castle there.

If you have been sightseeing, pause and refresh yourself at the Coopers, a neat, two-storey building with a white-painted façade and a tile roof. There is a patio and a cheerful stretch of garden by the entrance.

Inside you will find an agreeable bar with plush padded settles (and a good selection of real ales), and a sizeable restaurant; it's comfortably furnished and coloured lampshades adorn the low ceiling. The family area comprises two rooms, one of which has a play area for small children (there's a ball swamp, for example). There are prints of Donald Duck and scenes from Alice in Wonderland on the walls.

The facilities for families are excellent: several high chairs, baby-changing facilities, and a good-sized children's play area with a safe surface in the enclosed garden. There are bench tables here and a bouncy castle is installed during the summer. There is another patio and a garden in a more secluded spot on the other side of the pub, which is open throughout the day.

....

✕ (11.30am to 10pm) £2–8: onion bhajis, fish pie, sirloin steak, vegetable moussaka, tagliatelle carbonara
  Children: own menu
◑ Ale: Boddington's, Flowers, Harvey's and guests
ℙ Own car park

PEWSHAM, nr CHIPPENHAM, WILTS   Map 2
ℙ **LYSLEY ARMS**
Tel: 01249 652 864
A couple of miles east of Chippenham, on the A4 at the junction with the A342.

....

This very large and busy roadside inn is smoothly painted white under its steep roof with dormer windows. The façade is bright with flowers, some of them in tubs, and bench tables are placed between them.

A long bar greets you as you enter and on the other side of a large fireplace there is a very comfortable sitting room. It also has an open fireplace, some attractive wooden furniture, and a display of teapots and other china.

At the other end of the pub you will find the dining areas. There is a fine old carved oak settle against one wall, and the wood-panelled room is a congenial spot with its wide windows. It sports a grandfather clock and an array of china plates on shelves. Beyond is the Garden Room, which is another dining area, and this leads out to a secluded lawned garden, enclosed by hedges, and with several bench tables.

On the other side of the hedge another large garden, which is immaculately maintained, skirts the car park. There is a fun trail here: an array of equipment which includes slides, swings, climbing frames, balancing beams and a sandpit.

This pub has excellent facilities and families are made particularly welcome by the licensees, Roy and Hilma Skinner.

....

✕ (12pm to 2.15pm and 7pm to 9.30pm; Fri and Sat 6.30pm to
   10.30pm) £2–12: melon & ham parcels, Lysley chicken, steaks,
   boozy beef pie, oriental pork
   Children: own menu, half portions
◑ Ale: Bass, Boddington's, Eldridge Pope, Whitbread
℗ Own car park

PLUCKLEY, nr ASHFORD, KENT   **Map 3**
Ⓗ **ELVEY FARM, Pluckley**
Tel: 01233 840 442
Off the A20 west of Ashford.
....

At the end of a quiet country lane you will find the splendid Elvey farmhouse, which was built in 1430. The adjoining stables and an oast house have been converted with great skill and sympathy, the abiding aim being to preserve the existing features of the building.

The two communal rooms are delightful. The restaurant is housed in an old barn and the ancient black beams are decorated with old farm implements; long wooden tables complete the picture. Alongside, there is a very comfortable lounge with brick walls and a beamed ceiling, plenty of easy chairs, a good selection of books, a bar and french windows leading out to the garden.

The various rooms offer a great deal of flexibility for family accommodation, since most of them are equipped with kitchens and can therefore be rented as self-catering apartments. For example, the five units made from the stables fall into this category, and another comprises a double bedroom and a twin-bedded room which could accommodate two children. All the rooms are furnished to the highest standards and the wood panelling ensures a warm and appealing ambience.

The oast house offers the same flexibility, since it contains a sitting room, kitchen and three separate bedrooms, two of which are contained in the roundel. The house could be rented as a self-contained unit by a family and we have rarely seen a more interesting and attractive building.

Elvey Farm (and it is still a working farm, by the way) is an absolute delight, and its setting amid rolling countryside ensures guests peace and seclusion.

There is plenty of space for children to play, a sun terrace and a spacious lawn; and the stable apartments have their own little verandas. Guests are welcome to explore the farm, and in H. E. Bates country they should see plenty of darling buds. There are many pubs and restaurants within reach and the nearest one, the Rose and Crown, at the bottom of the lane, has an excellent reputation for its food.

Elvey Farm offers outstanding value, stylish accommodation, and the flexibility to suit the needs of any family, who can use the place as an hotel or on a self-catering basis, or as a mixture of both.

Nearby: This is an excellent base from which to enjoy the many attractions of this part of the country. Wildlife enthusiasts will head for Port Lympne Zoo Park or Howletts, and railway buffs can enjoy both the Kent and East Sussex and the Romney, Hythe and Dymchurch railways. Sissinghurst Castle Gardens, Scotney Castle Gardens, Bedgebury Pinetum, Leeds Castle and the historic town of Canterbury are all within easy reach.

....

£ Medium
Children: cot £5; £15 from 3 to 16 years
Facilities: 2 cots and 2 high chairs; baby-listening
10 rooms, 6 family
Open all year
P Ample

PLUSH, DORSET   **Map 2**
P **Brace of Pheasants, Piddletrenthide**
Tel: 0130 04 357
Signposted from the B3143 near Piddletrenthide.

....

This is a super pub in every way and well worth a short drive along country lanes. In fact you can reach it very easily from Cerne Abbas if you turn into Piddle Lane and go straight across country.

It is a most attractive building, made by amalgamating two cottages and the village forge, and now sits under its thatched roof. The bar takes up one side of the pub, and is a long room with a beamed ceiling and an open brick fireplace at one end.

The family room, the old kitchen, is to one side of the bar and is a bright and cheerful place, with polished wooden tables.

To add to the pleasure of a visit here, the garden is really lovely, with a sloping lawn against a backcloth of trees, a rockery and an iron seat encircling a large tree. A children's play area has also been installed with a climbing frame, etc.

The food (available every day) is enterprising and there is a very good choice of real ales which are rotated at regular intervals.

It's a lovely spot – but please note the opening hours: in the evening, especially in winter, it is often not open until 7pm.

....

✕ (12pm to 1.45pm and 7pm to 9.45pm) £2–13: crab savoury, bouillabaisse, liver with bacon & onions, rosettes of lamb, fish pie
Children: own menu, half portions

☐ Ale: Bass, Greene King, Smiles, Tetley, Wadworth's and guests

☐ Own car park

POLGOOTH, nr ST AUSTELL, CORNWALL   Map 1
☐ POLGOOTH INN
Tel: 01726 74089
On the A390, south-west of St Austell.

Polgooth is a small village situated in a picturesque valley which was once the site of the richest tin mine in Cornwall. On the outskirts of the village overlooking the valley you will find this cream-and-black-painted building.

The main bar was once the miners' counting house and is a large L-shaped room with stone walls, wood panelling and massive black roof beams. To the right and left at each end of the room are two large stone fireplaces. There are padded benches lining the window areas with several wooden tables surrounded by large and small farmer's chairs. To the left of the main bar is the family room, which is similar in style to the main bar area. A door leads out from this on to a small grassed terrace where there are several picnic benches.

To the right of the main bar is the restaurant area; it resembles a barn with its open roof beams and has a plethora of farming and mining equipment on display (look also for the massive buffalo horns above the doorway). This room can seat upwards of thirty people and shares the main fireplace that links through to the bar.

There is a children's play area at the side of the pub with climbing frames, slides and swings.

✕ (12pm to 2pm and 6.30pm to 10.30pm) £2–10: garlic mushrooms, venison, vegetable chilli, poached salmon, steaks
Children: own menu, half portions

🍺 Ale: Tinners, Wilson's
🅿 Own car park

Nr PONTEFRACT, WEST YORKS   Map 9
🅿🆁 **DARRINGTON HOTEL, Darrington**
Tel: 01977 791 458
Off the A1, south of Pontefract, at Darrington.

This substantial brick building, partly painted white, has a strategic location close to the Great North Road and was once a popular coaching inn. It has been developed to make a spacious family pub and restaurant with all the necessary facilities: food is available all day, and there are numbers of high chairs, plus a baby-changing unit.

The family entrance leads into the main dining area, which is split into several smaller areas with padded bench seating and farmhouse-style tables and chairs. The central feature of this area is an old-fashioned mechanical railway with a model of a castle at its centre. Alongside, there is a dining area set aside for the younger clientele, and it has a Funky Forest play area containing a ball pit, sundry other equipment and television cartoons.

In the main body of the pub the bar area has a number of smaller alcoves and rooms in which families may dine and which lend a cottagey feel to the building. The decoration of each room rings the changes but the effect is relaxing and comfortable: wooden furniture, Welsh dressers and wall cabinets, prints and photographs. It hangs together well and the Darrington is an ideal place in which to break a journey between the south and the north of Britain, especially if you are travelling with your family.

Alongside and attached to the pub is a small hotel which has twenty-six bedrooms.

✗ (12pm to 10pm) £2–9: prawn platter, chicken tikka masala, vegetable lasagne, haddock & chips, peppered steak
Children: own menu, half portions

Ⓓ Ale: Home's, Theakston's, Younger's and guests
Ⓟ Own car park

POULTON LE FYLDE, LANCS   **Map 8**
ⓅⓇ MILLERS ARMS, Singleton
Tel: 01253 882 668
In the village of Singleton, on the B5269.

This is a stone's throw from the M55 and not far from Blackpool. The Millers Arms is a nice old building, painted cream, and with a colourful display of flowers at the front.

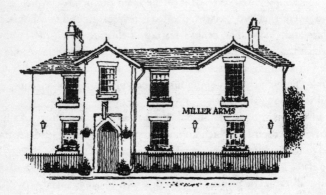

The L-shaped bar retains the comfortable atmosphere of a village pub, created by the brick pillars, beamed ceiling, occasional wood panelling and padded settles. A small conservatory has a play area for tiny children.

An extension at the rear houses quite a large restaurant, which is a no-smoking area. The room is split into a series of alcoves, whose main features are wooden beams and ceilings, and brick pillars. There is a central fireplace and an eclectic display of decorations: prints and black-and-white photographs, and a coracle suspended from one of the ceilings. Another dining area is enclosed by a glass roof.

The family market is firmly in mind with the provision of high chairs and a nappy-changing facility; and there is a sizeable play area to one side of the building.

....

✘ (12pm to 2.30pm and 5pm to 10.30pm; weekends 12pm to 10.30pm) £2–13: Greek dip, peppered steak, chicken Oscar, three-bean feast, ocean bake
   Children: own menu
◑ Ale: Boddington's and guests
Ⓟ Own car park

Nr PRESTON, LANCS   **Map 8**
ⓅⓇ BELL & BOTTLE, Newton-with-Scales
Tel: 01772 684 288
On the A583, east of Kirkham.

....

This is a massive and rambling roadhouse between Blackpool and Preston, and it has been equipped with all the accoutrements of a family pub and restaurant, including plenty of high chairs, baby-changing facilities and play areas; food is served throughout the day.

The bar has a traditional look by dint of its low ceiling, and there is comfortable seating and floral wallpaper. The restaurant is decorated in a similar style and is divided into several different areas. One has a bay window, in which sits a table for eight people and another dining room also has the benefit of a bay window. A very pleasant conservatory room runs along two sides of the building and overlooks the play area.

There is also an indoor play area for toddlers in the family dining room, and a Fun Factory has lots of equipment for children, plus a soft drinks bar.

In addition, there is a very large bar room for adults at one end of the building. It has a good pubby atmosphere and includes a pool table.

....

✕ (11.30am to 10pm) £2–8: hot mushrooms, fried scampi, chicken Balti, gammon steak, vegetable moussaka
Children: own menu
◐ Ale: Boddington's, Castle Eden, Flowers
Ⓟ Own car park

Nr PRESTON, LANCS   Map 8
ⓅⓇ Lea Gate
Tel: 01772 720 476
West of Preston on the A583, close to the junction with the A584.

A pub and restaurant built in the substantial style of a typical roadhouse, the Lea Gate has a sizeable bar area with wide windows and a brick fireplace. Down a few stairs there is a pleasant lounge bar with a couple of comfortable alcoves and a low ceiling. A Travel Inn has been built at the back of the pub.

A number of themes have been employed in the decoration of the restaurant. At first you notice a hot-air balloon and a wooden biplane – so it's aviation. Then the main restaurant has a number of tables under little tiled roofs and there is a waterfall – so it's what? In addition, there is a wood-panelled dining room with a table for eight people, and an upper eating area has a sporting theme: tennis rackets on the panelled walls, cricket bats and pads, golf clubs and prints of sportsmen (the Honourable F. S. Jackson, for example).

High chairs and baby-changing facilities are provided and food is available throughout the day.

✕ (12pm to 10.30pm) £2–13: pork satay, seafood tagliatelle, rump steak, ocean bake, fried scampi
Children: own menu
◐ Ale: Boddington's, Flowers and guests
Ⓟ Own car park

Nr PRESTON, LANCS Map 8
🅿🆁 Poachers Tavern, Bamber Bridge
Tel: 01772 324 100
On the A6 at Bamber Bridge.

....

This large family pub and restaurant was opened in 1993 and is alongside
a retail park (Sainsbury's et alia) and very close to Junctions 29 and
30 of the M6. It includes a Lodge Inn, which offers accommodation
at reasonable prices. Liberal use has been made of timber and brick in
the construction of the place, and it has a tiled roof.

It is a rambling place and made very agreeable by the further use of
plenty of wood: on the ceilings, and on the walls in the form of panelling.
It has a bright décor, with smart Laura Ashley-style wallpaper and china
plates and copper pans on the walls. The family dining area is split up
by wooden screens and lots of toys have been placed on high shelves.

The upstairs dining room has been done amusingly as a library –
the wallpaper is printed with the spines of thousands of books – and
a cartoon figure hangs from a library ladder. Below is the bar. It's
good fun.

The bar itself is very smart with its wooden panelling painted dark
green, its wooden screens and its many prints.

A terrace at the back of the pub looks over a play area, enclosed
and with a safe bark surface. High chairs are provided, as is a
nappy-changing facility.

....

✗ (11am to 10pm) £2–9: moules marinières, Cumberland sausage, fish
& spicy pepper pot, sirloin steak, vegetable lasagne
Children: own menu
◑ Ale: Theakston's and guests
🅿 Lots

PROBUS, nr TRURO, CORNWALL   **Map 1**
P HAWKINS ARMS
Tel: 01726 882 208
On the A390 east of Truro.

....

The infamous slave-trader, Sir Christopher Hawkins, owned this coaching inn in the 18th century, and the stone building sits hard against a bend in Probus.

The main bar is quite small, its walls lined with upholstered benches; there are a few wooden tables and chairs, and brass artefacts, plates and paintings decorate the walls.

Families are welcome to use a cosy little room at the rear of the pub. On sunny days, they might head for the garden with its picnic tables; there are climbing frames for the children. From here there is an excellent view of the spire of the church of St Probus and St Grace, built in the 15th century and one of the tallest spires in Cornwall.

....

✗ (12.30pm to 2.30pm and 5.30pm to 8.30pm) £2–9: scampi & chips, steaks, burgers, omelettes
   Children: own menu, half portions
◖ Ale: Hicks, Tinners
P Own car park

Nr RADCLIFFE ON TRENT, NOTTS   **Map 7**
P R SHEPHERDS, **Stragglethorpe**
Tel: 0115 933 3337
Just outside the villages of Cotgrave and Stragglethorpe, approximately one mile south of the A52 Nottingham to Grantham road.

....

Painted white and with a thatched roof, this building houses an extensive pub and restaurant which is firmly aimed at the family market. On entering you are confronted by the long main bar which runs the entire length of the building. Furnished in pine throughout, it is a bright and welcoming place to sit and drink or dine. Families are welcome throughout the pub, which has been granted a children's certificate (except for a small area containing game machines and a pool table). Opposite the main bar and separated by a stone-flagged floor are two large raised dining areas which each seat around forty customers. Next to the entrance is a smaller dining area with padded settles and tables, and cosy alcoves for smaller parties.

At the far end of the main bar is the designated family room, a no-smoking area. It is a congenial spot, the tables placed in nooks and crannies separated by balustraded divisions. Beyond this room there is a stone-flagged patio with wrought-iron tables and chairs. It sits by a separate building which houses a Charlie Chalk Fun Factory, with its array of play machines and its own soft drinks bar. The activity area has enough slides, ropes, swings, climbing frames and ball swamps to keep any number of children happy.

In addition there is an adventure playground outside, plus a miniature racing track and hovercraft vehicles for the children to drive.

All in all, this is very much a family outlet, and practical amenities such as high chairs and nappy-changing units are provided. Food is served throughout the day.

....

✕ (11.30am to 10pm) £2–8: hot mushrooms, vegetable crumble, steak & kidney pie, lasagne verdi, chicken Balti
   Children: own menu
◑ Ale: Boddington's, Marston's and guests
ℙ Ample

RAINHILL, MERSEYSIDE   Map 8
ℙℝ SHIP INN
Tel: 0151 426 4165
East of Liverpool on the A57 and close to Junction 7 of the M62.

....

Recently renovated, the Ship occupies a substantial brick building which has a traditional look. When we visited, a new lodge with thirty-four bedrooms was being completed alongside.

The inviting bar has padded benches and some nice wicker chairs, and there are two large lounge areas, both with an interesting selection of prints of ships and sailing boats, horses and sportsmen.

The restaurant has a cheerful décor, aided in part by the various skylights of coloured glass. The main dining room has several alcoves and glass-panelled walls, and a table for six diners occupies the space beside one of the bay windows. In addition there is a splendid conservatory room with a tiled floor and a wooden ceiling which soars up to a dome.

High chairs are provided here and food is served throughout the day.

....

✕ (11.30am to 10.30pm; Sun 12pm to 10pm) £2–12: broccoli tempura, Thai chicken, spiced lamb, grilled halibut, steak & kidney pie
Children: own menu
◖ Ale: Boddington's, Higson's
ℙ Own car park

RAVENSHEAD, nr NOTTINGHAM, NOTTS　　　　**Map 7**
ℙℝ **THE HUTT**
Tel: 01623 792 325
Just off the A60 north of Hucknall.

....

Now is the time to 'hit the Hutt', but not just for pizzas. Look for a series of red-bricked cottage buildings on the side of the road, at the front of which, and leading from the main car park, is the family entrance.

The building has a chequered history. Originally attached to the local priory, it was used as almshouses; it was a vicarage in the 18th century; and then a coaching inn. Scottish and Newcastle, as with all the Homespreads establishments, have made an excellent conversion into a place where families are very welcome.

The main bar is like a miniature baronial hall, with dark wood panels embellished with crests, high-pitched beam ceilings, hung tapestries and hunting trophies. Children under 14 are not permitted in this area.

The main dining room is Victorian in style, with elaborate friezes on the ceiling and walls, Doric-style pillars at all entrances and a large and ornate marble log-burning fireplace at one end of the room. Here one can enjoy a range of well-prepared food in a luxurious setting. Alternatively there is a separate no-smoking room at the opposite end of the main bar, where the theme is based on the Sheriff of Nottingham and Sherwood Forest; there are bows, arrows and lances in abundance. In the corner of this room is the toilet for the disabled where there are baby-changing facilities consisting of a pull-down tray with a nappy dispenser, sink, hand drier and toilet. Many high chairs are made available.

At this end of the pub there is a door leading out to the Funky Forest Room, which contains a large range of play equipment where children can enjoy their fun and fantasy. At the rear of the pub there is an outdoor play area with picnic bench tables and parasols at one side.

....

✕ (12pm to 2.30pm and 5.30pm to 10pm; weekends all day) £2–9: prawn platter, chicken Kiev, vegetable lasagne, sirloin steak, haddock & chips
Children: own menu
◑ Ale: Morlands, Theakston's and guests
Ⓟ Lots

Nr READING, BERKS   **Map 5**
ⓅⓇ Fox Inn, Cane End
Tel: 01734 723 116
On the A4074 north of Reading.

....

A few miles from Reading and minutes away from Mapledurham House, this large pub, plainly built of brick with a tiled upper storey, has been converted into a Brewers Fayre outlet and has very good facilities for family groups. For a start, there is plenty of space inside; high chairs are provided; and there is a nappy-changing unit in the Ladies.

The terrace at the side of the pub has several bench tables, and the large lawned garden has a play unit and a bouncy castle, which was proving very popular with some young children on the summer day when we visited.

Inside there is a little play area for toddlers and a Fun Factory where children can amuse themselves. It is adjacent to the family dining area (no-smoking), a comfortable room on two levels. Windows overlook the garden. There is another restaurant by the bar and a pleasing lounge, with padded benches and a nice fireplace, beyond.

....

✖ (11.30am to 10pm) £2–8: fish dippers, chicken Alexandra, steak & kidney pie, tagliatelle carbonara, gammon steak
  Children: own menu
◖ Ale: Gale's
ℙ Own car park

Nr READING, BERKS   **Map 5**
ℙℝ THE ROUNDABOUT, Tilehurst
Tel: 01734 418 922
On the A329 at Tilehurst, north-west of Reading.

....

This expansive red-brick pub is located on a busy roundabout on the outskirts of Reading, and was transformed over a decade ago into a family pub and restaurant (part of the Beefeater chain).

The restaurant has been 'themed', though not outlandishly; as you might guess, it takes the form of a roundabout or carousel. It's a bit of fun, especially for children, and there are funfair signs scattered about: Punch and Judy, Roll-a-Ball-a-Ball, and so on. The restaurant is spread over a couple of floors, with plenty of nooks and crannies with just a few tables. The tables under the eaves are cosy.

There is an extensive bar area, which is split into three separate areas. Brick walls, wooden pillars, a large brick fireplace and nice curved settles give it a pleasant atmosphere.

The garden at the rear is mostly well-trimmed lawn, and it includes a children's play area. A few bench tables are set out.

Families are made welcome and there are plenty of high chairs and booster seats, as well as baby-changing facilities. The Sunday lunches are good value.

✕ (12pm to 2.30pm and 5pm to 10.30pm; weekends 12pm to 10.30pm) £2–13: pork satay, ocean bake, king prawn salad, steaks, marinated chicken
Children: own menu

Ale: Boddington's, Brakspear's, Flowers

P Lots

REDBOURN, HERTS **Map 5**

P R **Chequers Inn**

Tel: 01582 792 359

On the A5 just south of Redbourn.

This pleasant thatched pub sits at the roadside on Watling Street and one would not guess, at first glance, just how much space is available.

The first clue might be the size of the car park, and a long stretch

of lawn forms one of its boundaries. High hedges provide some shade and there are plenty of bench tables. On the other side another lawn, with more bench tables, is enclosed by a fence, and there is a good-sized and well-equipped play unit, with a safe bark surface.

The Chequers has its eye on the family market, and high chairs and baby-changing facilities are made available. The smart restaurant area has a beamed ceiling, a brick fireplace, stylish Sanderson-type wallpaper and cottagey windows. The tables stretch right along the front of the pub, and the style is maintained with wooden beams and pillars and brick fireplaces.

The appealing bar has a lounge area, nicely turned out with its comfortable furniture and screens of wood and glass. The pub is open throughout the day.

....

✗ (12pm to 2.30pm and 6pm to 10pm; Sun 12pm to 10pm) £2–9: barbecued chicken wings, seafood pie, peppered steak, mixed grill, vegetable lasagne

Children: own menu

⬭ Ale: Courage, John Smith

ℙ Lots

REDDITCH, HEREFORD & WORCS Map 4
ℙℝ NEVILL ARMS, Astwood Bank
Tel: 01527 892 603
On the A441, south of Redditch, at the junction with the B4090.

....

This handsome brick-walled pub has been expanded to form a very large family pub and restaurant. Although there is loads of space, the interior has been skilfully divided into a series of smaller, interconnected rooms and alcoves, some on slightly different levels to others. The wide windows, cheerful decorations, wooden screens, coloured lights, and prints on the walls combine to make it an attractive pub.

The facilities for families are outstanding and include a no-smoking family dining room with a play area which has a ball swamp and other amusements. There are several high chairs, a nappy-changing facility and a children's menu; and food is available throughout the day. The garden includes an enclosed adventure playground for the children.

✕ (11.30am to 10pm; Sun from 12pm) £2–8: prawn cocktail, sirloin steak, vegetable crumble, chicken masala, haddock & chips
  Children: own menu
◐ Ale: Boddington's, Castle Eden, Flowers
ℙ Own car park

REDMILE, NOTTS   Map 7
Ⓗ Peacock Farm
Tel: 01949 842 475
Off the A52 west of Grantham. Follow the signs to Belvoir Castle.

This farmhouse was built early in the 18th century, and is no longer part of a working farm. Instead it offers most of the facilities necessary for an enjoyable family break or holiday. As you enter the property you will see a lovely lawned garden, with several apple trees, swings, a climbing frame and a see-saw. There is a small covered swimming pool, a summer house, a play room with table tennis and a pool table, and ten bikes for guests to use.

A bar area sits alongside the partly wood-panelled dining room, and there is a small patio where you can enjoy a drink on summer days. The guests' sitting room, with windows on two sides, is bright and comfortably furnished with sofas and easy chairs.

A great advantage of Peacock Farm is the presence of five family-sized rooms, and the rooms on the top floor, with sloping ceilings under the rafters, are especially attractive. A family room on the first floor (with a double and a single bed) shares a bathroom with a small single room and could be used as a family suite. The ground floor rooms, with French windows on to the lawn, are sizeable and include a family room. The Coach House, which

315

has two single beds and two bunk beds and a bathroom, is a self-contained family suite, and there is another separate family room by the patio.

The cooking is based on fresh local produce, and the fruit, vegetables and herbs will mostly come from the garden. Real ale fans will be pleased to hear that the bar serves Ruddles bitter.

Nearby: The famous Belvoir Castle is just up the road, and indeed can be seen from several of the rooms in the farmhouse. The interesting town of Grantham is just a short drive away, with Belton House and Woolsthorpe Manor, where Sir Isaac Newton was born, not very far away. Grimsthorpe Castle is a short drive away and west towards Nottingham you will find Colwick Country Park, with its water sports, fishing and a nature reserve, Green's Mill, and the Holme Pierrepoint water sports centre.

....

✗ Bar snacks (12pm to 9pm) £2–6: pasta carbonara, steaks, fresh Grimsby cod, vegetable casserole;
Dinner (7pm to 9pm) £14: mushrooms with Stilton, stuffed breast of chicken, raspberry & almond torte
Children: own menu, half portions
£ Low
Children: cot £5; two thirds of the adult rate from 3 to 10 years
Facilities: 3 cots and 2 high chairs; baby-listening and a patrol
10 rooms, 3 family suites
Open all year
◯ Ale: Ruddles
ℙ Own car park

Nr REDRUTH, CORNWALL

Map 1

Ⓟ FOX AND HOUNDS, Comford

Tel: 01209 820 251

On the A393 Falmouth Road, two miles out of Redruth.

This 17th-century inn is very appealing, its long, low, white-painted façade bright with displays of flowers.

The main bar is furnished in agreeable cottage style, with brasses and coaching memorabilia, and has a large inglenook fireplace. Alongside a low-ceilinged room, there is a small family room and the restaurant leads off it. It can seat around fifty people and is comfortably furnished with padded bench seats and wooden tables and chairs.

At the rear of the restaurant a door leads to a grassed patio area with picnic benches, local stone benches, swings and a climbing frame.

✗ (Mon to Fri 11am to 3pm and 6pm to 11pm; Sat all day)
£2–12: avocado corn bake, cashew nut paella, rainbow trout and daily specials
Children: own menu, half portions
Ⓓ Ale: Hicks, Bass, Tinners
Ⓟ Own car park

RICHMOND, SURREY

Map 3

Ⓡ REFECTORY, 6 Church Walk

Tel: 0181 940 6264

Park either in the Paradise Road multi-storey or in Sheen Road. Street parking is easy on a Sunday.

The restaurant is in a quiet corner by the parish church and you can sit in the paved courtyard by the entrance if the weather is kind. The charming dining room has a bay window and is agreeably furnished with pine tables. With its open fireplace and the watercolours of local scenes on the walls, it is a relaxing place to be.

The restaurant has always been a favourite of ours since it is one of the

317

few in London which offers a genuine welcome to all the family: apart from the high chairs, the owners provide a changing table in the Ladies, and no one looks askance at breast-feeding mothers. But this is also a real restaurant with freshly cooked English food and splendid vegetables and puddings, generously served. Above all, the prices continue to be sensible: a rare thing in the London area. There is an unusual wine list, too, with English and Australian wines.

This is a popular restaurant and booking ahead is advisable; it is also open for coffee from 10am to noon and for afternoon teas from 2pm to 5pm, Tuesday to Saturday.

....

✕ Lunch (Tues to Sun 12pm to 2pm) £10: crab mousse, paprika pork casserole, rhubarb & orange fool
Children: smaller portions
Closed Mondays, Christmas and New Year, and 2 weeks in August
◻ Ale: Young's
ℙ Street or public car park

RINGLESTONE, KENT   **Map 3**
ℙ RINGLESTONE INN
Tel: 01622 859 900
Not far from Junction 8 of the M20. Turn on to the B2163 and follow signs to the village, via Hollingbourne and Doddington.

....

Built in 1533, the Ringlestone was originally used as a hospice for monks, but it became an ale house around 1615. The inn has changed little since then and has its original brick and flint walls, oak beams and inglenooks. Even the later addition of the dining room has tables which were specially made from the timbers of an 18th-century Thames barge.

There is an English oak sideboard which has an inscription, carved in 1632, 'A Ryghte Joyouse and welcome greetynge to ye all'. This is as appropriate today as it was three hundred years ago. A right warm welcome is always available between the hours of 12 and 3pm, and 6 and 11pm.

To complement the historic inn there is a beautiful garden, two acres of landscaped lawns, shrubs, trees and rockeries. A water garden has four charming ponds linked by cascading waterfalls culminating in a delightful fountain. The patio outside the restaurant enables diners and drinkers to enjoy the pleasures of this aspect of the garden, while closer to the farmland is a hopscotch area which is very popular with children.

In the words of the landlord, 'children welcome in an adults' playground'. There is a children's licence so that they may go anywhere in the inn, and a high chair is available as well as changing facilities in the ladies' toilet.

The inn is immensely popular with visitors from the continent as well as with people from Kent and the rest of the south-east, for this really is a place of rare beauty steeped in history. There are only three buildings in Ringlestone, of which the inn is one, and there are plans that the inn should acquire an empty adjacent house for use as bed and breakfast accommodation.

Lunches in the inn are buffet lunches with a wide selection of hot and cold foods; evening meals are served in the restaurant with candles as the only form of lighting. There are delights in food, beer and wines, with home-made pies like lamb and Stilton a speciality. There is also a strong belief in François Maximilien Misson's dictum, 'Blessed be he that invented pudding'.

....

✖ (12pm to 2.15pm and 6.30pm to 10pm) £2–10: mussels provençale, garlic chicken, beef goulash, chicken & bacon pie, lasagne
Children: half portions
◑ Ale: wide selection, e.g. Marston's, Morland's, Theakston's, Shepherd Neame, Ind Coope Burton, etc.
ℙ Ample

RIPLEY, SURREY   **Map 3**
ℙℝ Jovial Sailor, **Portsmouth Road**
Tel: 01483 224 360
On the B2215, which runs parallel to the A3.

··

This pub, which stands on the original London to Portsmouth road, has a traditional air, built of brick with a tiled upper storey and bay windows.

The interior is in traditional style, too, with wooden furniture, horse brasses and prints on the walls, and brass lamps. You can settle down to eat in various different areas in the spacious interior; brick pillars and screens have been used to provide a number of interconnecting rooms. The bar extends around the front of the pub and there is a pleasing lounge section at one end, with timber pillars and a large inglenook fireplace with armchairs alongside.

A paved terrace at the back of the pub sits beside an extensive lawn with bench tables. A children's play area, with a safe surface, has been placed here and there are some swings. In addition, there is an indoor play area with a ball swamp and other equipment, and some amusement machines.

Other facilities for families include high chairs, a nappy-changing unit and a children's menu. The pub is open throughout the day and food is served at all times.

··

✕ (12pm to 10pm) £2–9: spicy prawns, Cajun chicken, plaice & chips, sirloin steak, lasagne
   Children: own menu
◑ Ale: Courage, John Smith's, Theakston's
ℙ Own car park

Nr ROCHDALE, LANCS   **Map 8**
🄿🅁 THE MANOR, Norden
Tel: 01706 50027
On the A680, north-west of Rochdale.

....

This certainly is a manor house, built from mellow stone and with steep roofs and elegant pointed windows. It sits high above the industrial sprawl of Rochdale and, after being the family home of a director of the Hudson Bay Company, was a hospital before being converted to a pub and restaurant.

The stately, high-ceilinged rooms provide acres of space, for example in the bar area where there are settees scattered along the walls. A dining room at one side has a fine wooden fireplace and a large bay window, and the walls are covered in an appropriately stylish wallpaper.

A lovely conservatory room has windows on four sides and a high wooden roof, and there is a family dining room alongside with brick walls. A very large Fun Factory has been installed on one side of the building with a lounge alongside. The amenities any family needs are present: high chairs, baby-changing units, and two outdoor play areas on the lawns. The Manor serves food throughout the day.

It is a splendid building and is well worth a visit.

....

✗ (11.30am to 10pm) £2–8: hot mushrooms, fried scampi, sirloin steak, plaice & chips, tagliatelle carbonara
    Children: own menu
◖ Ale: Boddington's, Castle Eden and guests
🄿 Ample

Nr ROCHDALE, LANCS   Map 8
P R STUBLEY OLD HALL, **Littleborough**
Tel: 01706 377 921
North-east of Rochdale on the A58.

This is an extraordinary place to find on the outskirts of an industrial town. It was built by a wealthy businessman in 1855 but resembles a manor house of a much earlier century. Built of lovely soft-hued stone, it has mullioned windows and a heavy stone roof.

The bar is a delight, with its stone walls and a huge fireplace; a pool table is concealed in an alcove but still seems incongruous in such a setting. The gracious entrance hall has a wealth of old wooden beams and solid timber pillars, and there are settees here and there.

You take a grand wooden staircase to the restaurant, and the first room has a vaulted roof with vast cross beams. The main room can only be described as baronial, with yet another huge stone fireplace, and coats of arms incorporated in the leaded windows. Alongside there is a smaller dining room, and it has a splendid fireplace too.

Stubley Old Hall is a remarkable and interesting building and well worth a look. It has all the facilities a family needs, including high chairs, a mother and baby room, and the availability of food throughout the day. There is a lovely lawned garden at the side, bright with flowers, and it incorporates a children's play area.

✗ (12pm to 10pm) £2–12: vintage mushrooms, salmon fillet, sirloin steak, seafood pancakes, venison casserole
   Children: own menu
◯ Ale: Boddington's
P Own car park

ROCHE, CORNWALL
Map 1

P **Victoria Inn**
Tel: 01726 890 207
On the A30 Liskeard to Redruth.

....

Just outside the small town of Roche, this roadside inn, once a staging post for the London to Penzance mail coach, is a small white building with a car park at the front and a garden with a children's play area at the back.

To the left, as you enter the pub, is a small and cosy family room. The main bar has wood-panelled walls and an assortment of copper ornaments and bric-à-brac (including rifles). This area is fully carpeted and has a coal-burning stove set in a fireplace whose blazing warmth would be a comfort on cold days. There are chalkboard menus here which list a great variety of home-made dishes.

There is another small family room where you can settle for a meal or a drink, and you may notice that the bar is constructed from old cognac kegs. Alongside is the restaurant, which can seat up to thirty people in a nicely decorated room which also contains bric-à-brac and has a small stone fireplace set in oak panelling at one end.

....

✗ (12pm to 2pm and 6.30pm to 9pm) £2–10: whitebait, Cajun chicken, vegetarian chilli, plaice & chips, steaks
  Children: own menu
◖ Ale: Wilson's, Tinners, Hicks
P Own car park

ROMSEY, HANTS
Map 3

R **Cobweb Tea Rooms, 49 The Hundred**
Tel: 01794 516 434
Close to the centre of the town and opposite the entrance to Broadlands.

....

The Cobweb Tea Rooms are housed in a building which is 500 years old in parts, although it has an 18th-century front. The façade is freshly painted and is cheerfully decorated with an abundance of bright flowers which grow in tubs and hanging baskets. Inside you will find an archetypal English tea shop, immaculately laid out and in pristine order. The old wooden beams and pillars testify to the age of the building and are nicely offset by the cream-painted plaster walls, the brick fireplace and the wide window on to the street.

At the back there is a walled patio with a flagged floor, full of bright flowers and the cheerful sounds of birds.

The owner is happy to welcome families and makes her private accommodation available to mothers who need to attend to babies. A toy box is provided, as are babies' feeding cups.

You can have snacks throughout the day, and light lunch dishes from noon; all the food is home-made.

....

✕ (Tues to Sat 10am to 5.30pm) £1–4: soup, toasted sandwiches, chicken curry, goulash, beans on toast
  Children: half portions
  No credit cards accepted
P Public parking 100 yards away

ROSS-ON-WYE, HEREFORDSHIRE   **Map 4**
P R TRAVELLERS REST
Tel: 01989 563 861
On the roundabout at Junction 4 of the M50.

This is a very large and recently built family pub and restaurant which, nevertheless, is about to be extended; and a Travel Inn is being built alongside, which will have forty-two bedrooms.

The Travellers Rest, built of stone and with wooden cladding, looks like a huge bungalow and is located in a very busy spot off the M50. The long bar has large windows and is a comfortable spot with its array of padded settles.

The restaurant seats just under a hundred diners but will soon be extended to take another forty covers. It has a traditional appearance, with brick walls, a central brick fireplace, colourful lights, wooden screens, prints, copper pots and pans, and tapestries here and there on the walls.

The pub is open all day and serves food at all times. High chairs and baby-changing facilities are provided. There is an enclosed garden with lots of bench tables and two children's play areas.

✗ (12pm to 10.30pm; Fri and Sat till 11pm) £2–13: prawn sundae, peppered steak, ocean bake, fried scampi, Indonesian chicken
  Children: own menu

325

⬭ Ale: Boddington's, Marston's and guests

🅿 Lots

ROTHERHAM, SOUTH YORKS   Map 7
🅿🆁 **The Brecks**
Tel: 01709 531 516
On the A631 near Wickersley, between Junction 1 of the M18 and Junction 33 of the M1.

This is a sizeable building of red brick, with a green tiled roof, which is located close to a roundabout. There are some wooden picnic tables at the front.

Alongside the large car park at the rear is an enclosed wood-chipped area containing a small climbing frame and other equipment.

At the front of the main bar there is an enclosed and covered veranda where families can drink and enjoy the delicious bar snacks on offer (including a chalk board selection of Breck Specials). The whole bar is comfortably appointed, with carpeted floors, wooden and padded settles, dark wood farmhouse tables and chairs; and with prints on the walls and various china and copper artefacts on the shelves.

The restaurant area is extremely spacious and divided into a number of smaller rooms and alcoves: behind the veranda is a room which will seat approximately thirty people, for example, and a small alcove room with three tables. Up a short flight of stairs is a small balcony area with tables for four around the outside and a table in the round, suitable for large families, at its centre. There is also an upper balcony area containing seating for up to twenty people.

....

✗ (12pm to 10.30 pm) £2–13: Greek dip, seafood tagliatelle, salmon fillet, burgers, gammon steak
Children: own menu, half portions
🍺 Ale: Boddington's, Flowers
🅿 Own car park

ROWARTH, CHESHIRE   **Map 8**
🅿 **LITTLE MILL INN**
Tel: 01663 746 305
Off the A626 Marple–Glossop road. There is a turning on the south-west side of the village of Charleworth and then you will find signs to Rowarth and the Little Inn.

....

The pub is situated in marvellous rolling countryside – the drive to it across the hills is a delight, and we were lucky enough to do it on a sunny autumn day. The original building was an 18th-century mill, and photographs inside show how the mill wheel was swept away by a flood in 1930. Chris Barnes, the licensee, has recently installed a new wheel, 36 feet in diameter, and it is in full working order.

The family room is off the bar and is charmingly furnished with seats and tables from a railway dining car and has a good collection of train pictures, including the Flying Scotsman. The carriage itself, at the back of the pub, now houses three bedrooms and is called the Derbyshire Belle Motel. The bar is most attractive with its stone pillars, wooden beams and padded settles, and there is a lovely old fireplace too. There is a small pool room off the bar.

The children will be delighted with the garden because it has four swings, a climbing frame and a tree house with a slide which takes you right across the mill stream to the other side. Great fun. The adults can watch from the terrace at the front of the pub.

The pub is open all day and you will find food on offer throughout opening hours. There is a high chair on the premises.

....

✖ (11am to 11pm) £1–5: Bury black pudding, grilled trout, curries, salads, plaice & chips
   Children: own menu, half portions
Ⓓ Ale: Banks, Marston's, Hanson's and guests
Ⓟ Own car park

ROWSLEY, nr MATLOCK, DERBYSHIRE   Map 7
Ⓡ CAUDWELL'S COUNTRY PARLOUR
Tel: 01629 733 185
Signposted off the A6 between Matlock and Buxton.

....

This is a wonderful place to bring the family for an afternoon out with a difference. The small but immaculate café is part of the Caudwell's Mill Craft Centre complex. This features a working 19th-century flour mill, driven by a water wheel, and five craft workshops open to the public where glassblowers, wood-turners and potters keep alive dying traditions.

The food is almost entirely vegetarian, with all the flour used having been ground at the mill, and everything is prepared freshly every day. No additives are used in the food and every effort is made to use environmentally friendly products: recycled paper, etc. Their policies are to be applauded and encouraged.

The complex is surrounded by lawns and a mill stream idles its way past. It is a peaceful haven away from the commercialism that has blighted so much of beautiful Derbyshire.

You can change a baby in the disabled toilet, where there is a pull-down shelf.

....

✕ £2–4: tuna & anchovy tart, crofters pie, spinach & mushroom bake, lasagne
Children: half portions, own menu on request
Open 10pm to 6pm, winter until 4.30pm; closed Christmas Day, Boxing Day and weekends in Jan/Feb
No credit cards accepted
Unlicensed
🅿 Own car park

RUDDINGTON, NOTTS — Map 7
🅿🆁 THE NOTTINGHAM KNIGHT
Tel: 0115 921 1171
South of Nottingham, on the A60/A52 junction near Ruddington.

Hard by the roundabout you will find this building of red brick with a tiled roof.

The main bar is a large area occupying one side of the building. Tiled and carpeted floors, comfortable padded chairs and wooden tables throughout, and a stone fireplace create an agreeable atmosphere. To the left of the bar is the entrance to the main restaurant, where the first thing of interest to children is the Funky Forest – a play room with a ball swamp and lots of other equipment.

To the left of the Funky Forest a small family dining area seats about thirty people. Beyond it is the main dining room, a long room fancifully decorated rather like a doll's house. French windows give access to a semi-circular grassed patio with plenty of bench tables at which to drink or eat. Alongside there is an enclosed children's play park, with a safe surface – it has enough climbing frames and slides to occupy the most boisterous of children; and a bouncy castle is erected during the summer.

The Nottingham Knight is very much in the family market and provides several high chairs and baby-changing facilities. It has a Lodge Inn alongside, where the bedrooms are let at very reasonable prices.

✳ (11am to 11pm; Sun from 12pm) £2–9: spicy prawns, steak & kidney pudding, lemon chicken, chilli con carne, sirloin steak
Children: own menu
◻ Ale: Home's, Theakston's
ℙ Own car park

RUGBY, WARWICKS   Map 4
ℙℝ **Bell and Barge**
Tel: 01788 569 466
Close to Junction 1 of the M6, on the A426.

....

Recently built, the Bell and Barge at first glance resembles a light industrial building, but it is presentable enough – built from brick and with wide windows. It is surrounded by landscaped lawns and there is a pleasant shrubbery by the entrance.

The spacious open-plan interior is light and airy by virtue of the big bay windows, and there are comfortable sofas here and there. The menus offer a good choice of dishes and the Sunday lunch is good value. Several high chairs are provided, but there are no baby-changing facilities – parents must cope in the toilets.

At the rear of the pub, there is a pretty little garden by a stretch of water (the Oxford Canal).

....

✳ (12pm to 2pm and 6pm to 10pm) £2–11: tiger prawns, cashew nut paella, mixed grill, steaks, fish & chips
Children: own menu
◻ Ale: Bass
ℙ Lots

RYTON-ON-DUNSMORE, WARWICKS   **Map 4**
Ⓡ **RYTON ORGANIC GARDENS**
Tel: 01203 303 517
*On the B4029 east of Coventry. It is signposted from the A45 and
the A428.*

....

The restaurant has been expanded and now comprises an attractive
open-plan area with a tiled floor and a wall of windows on to a terrace
and the gardens beyond.

It is part of the National Centre for Organic Gardening and all the
food is freshly cooked from ingredients grown on the spot. No additives
are ever used.

The Centre has twenty acres of gardens, which include a rose garden,
a herb garden, a wild flower meadow, a picnic area and a children's
play area with a wooden climbing frame and some swings. There is a
table and chair and paper towels in the Ladies, if a baby needs to be
changed.

The menu changes on a daily basis and is reasonably priced. You
can also sample a comprehensive choice of organic wines from France,
Germany, Italy and England, and organic beers and lagers.

Events and exhibitions are held throughout the year; for example,
the National Organic Food & Wine Fair.

....

✗ (9am to 5.30pm; Sat 7pm to 9.30pm) £1–4: broccoli quiche,
  Hungarian pancakes, mushroom homity pie, celery & walnut
  casserole, pork & prune pie
  Children: small portions
  Open all year
Ⓟ Own car park

Nr SAFFRON WALDEN, ESSEX   Map 6
℗ THE BELL, Wendens Ambo
Tel: 01799 540382

The village is on the B1039, two miles from Saffron Walden and just west of Audley End. The pub is within walking distance of Audley End station which is in the village of Wendens Ambo.

There were once two villages, Wendens Parva and Wendens Magna, but when the two parishes joined, the name became Wendens Ambo, *ambo* being Latin for 'both'. In 1576, the house which is now The Bell was part of a 40-acre farm, and six pilasters on each face of the chimney stack are a fine testimony to Elizabethan workmanship.

It was in 1806 that The Bell first became a pub. It belonged to Bishop Stortford's Brewery and later to Benskins, but in 1902 it became a free house, which it remains to this day. It is a small, neat, clean, welcoming house with alcoves and low beams. There is a small dining room which is an extension and which acts as a family room.

There is a garden of the utmost charm. It is delightfully set out with flowers, some in unusual containers, and has family tables with umbrellas and a well-used barbecue area. There is a wooden Wendy House for the children, who can also find pleasure in the seesaw, the swings, the climbs and the tricycle. All is shaded by trees, and a goat is one of the garden's occupants. At the bottom of the garden is a nature walk, for The Bell is set in the prettiest of countryside.

The village itself is beautiful, with thatched houses and a cricket ground with more than an air of romance about it. The magnificent Audley End is close by, as is the attractive and historic town of Saffron Walden and some of the lovely countryside of north Essex.

✗ (12pm to 2pm and 7pm to 9pm; not Mon pm) £2–9: moussaka, beef & ale pie, mixed grill, Cajun chicken, chilli con carne
    Children: own menu

◑ Ale: Adnams, Ansell's, Hardy's and guests

℗ Ample

ST AUSTELL, CORNWALL
Map 1
H CARLYON BAY HOTEL
Tel: 01726 812 304
Off the A390 east of St Austell.

The hotel was built in 1930 and has a marvellous location in 250 acres of grounds, which include an excellent golf course of 6500 yards, and a well-established nine-hole short course. The extensive landscaped gardens are a delight, due in no small part to the excellent climate of the Cornish Riviera, and have marvellous views of the bay. The coastal path and Crinnis Woods, part of the hotel grounds, are lovely spots to explore.

The facilities here are superb. As well as the golf courses, there are two hard tennis courts and an outdoor heated swimming pool. Children are catered for with an adventure paddock which has a tree house, a slide and a trampoline. If the weather is unkind you can enjoy the splendid indoor leisure centre which has an excellent swimming pool, a children's pool, sauna, solarium and spa bath. There are two snooker tables, table tennis and a children's play room.

This excellent hotel offers a high standard of service and comfort to give a relaxing and agreeable family holiday. It is good to report that there is an extensive and healthy menu for children and a good choice of vegetarian dishes, all served in the refurbished Bay View Restaurant.

Nearby: The coastline is dotted with lovely sandy bays, including one below the golf course. If you fancy seeing the sights, Charlestown, an 18th-century port, is on the doorstep and has a visitor centre; Mevagissey has a folk museum. There are many other attractions within an easy drive: the ruined Restormel Castle, Lanhydrock, the farm park at Bodmin, Dobwalls Theme Park, Trelissick Garden, the Dairyland Farm Park, Trerice and the Newquay Zoo.

X Lunch (12.30pm to 2pm) £11: duck liver pâté, medallions of venison, pudding;
Dinner (7pm to 9pm) £23: mille-feuille of crab & prawns, smoked salmon & scrambled eggs, roast pheasant, pudding & cheese

Children: own menu
£ High
✓ Best Bargain Break: £142–174 per person, 2 nights – dinner, b&b
Children: from £3 a day to 70% of the adult rate
Facilities: 6 cots and 6 high chairs; baby-listening system
73 rooms, 3 family, 15 sets interconnecting
Open all year
Ⓟ Own car park

Nr ST AUSTELL, CORNWALL   Map 1
Ⓟ Holmbush Inn, Holmbush
Tel: 01726 68691
Off the A390 from St Austell to Lostwithiel.

....

This pub is a white-and-green-painted building with a prominent stone chimney stack. The main bar occupies a large low-ceilinged room. On the right-hand side as you enter is the food servery and you may either order from this counter or ask for waitress service at any table throughout the pub.

The building has been recently refurbished, and the designer has made wood panelling a major feature. There is generous seating throughout, with several alcoves. A games room has pool and various electronic machines for children over 14 years of age, and the main family room is adjacent to this at the front of the pub; it is decorated in the style of a Victorian dining room (with lamps and paintings around the walls). Leading off is a large glass conservatory with a tiled floor, where you can eat or drink and enjoy the sunshine. At the front of the pub is a large cobbled area with white wrought-iron tables and chairs which is enclosed by a low stone wall.

This pub is quiet and comfortably appointed and when we visited was clearly a popular place for lunch. It's certainly a place to visit if staying in the St Austell area or when travelling to the South Cornish coast.

....

✗ (12pm to 2pm and 6.30pm to 9pm) £2–7: butterfly chicken,

prawn fritters, steak & Guinness pie, cauliflower & broccoli bake

Children: own menu, half portions

🍺 Ale: Tinners

🅿 Own car park

ST HELENS, MERSEYSIDE   Map 8
🅿 **BOTTLE & GLASS, Rainford**
Tel: 01744 882 712
Off the A570 at Rainford, just south of Junction 3 of the M58.

The Bottle & Glass is an attractive traditional pub built of sandstone and with bay windows at the front. Virginia creeper has been grown over the façade and many baskets and window boxes of bright flowers made a vivid display when we visited it during last summer.

The interior has a markedly traditional appearance, too. The spacious L-shaped bar has wood-panelled walls and a high degree of comfort by dint of the padded settles and other easy chairs.

Several bench tables are set out at the front of the pub, and there is a play area at the side, with swings and a climbing frame on a safe bark surface.

The pub closes during the afternoon, except on Sunday when it is open throughout the day.

🍴 (12pm to 2pm and 6pm to 9pm; Sun all day) £2–10: oriental spring rolls, beef goulash, pasta Florentine, mushroom & nut fettucine, steaks

Children: own menu

🍺 Ale: Greenall's and guests

🅿 Own car park

ST HILARY, nr PENZANCE, CORNWALL   Map 1
Ⓗ ENNYS
Tel: 01736 740 262
Off the A30 or A394 east of Penzance.

You must traverse a few hundred yards of a narrow lane, its banks loaded in spring with bluebells, before you arrive at Ennys, a beautiful Cornish manor house which was built in 1688. Its stone walls, covered in wisteria and Virginia creeper, look over a peaceful sunken garden. It is a delightful spot and you walk through to an open-air heated swimming pool with encircling terrace. Alongside there is an excellent grass tennis court, and a further stretch of garden; part of it is a herb garden, and there is also a children's swing on the grass.

The house itself has beautifully proportioned rooms, including a wood-panelled dining room and a comfortable lounge with an open fireplace. The three bedrooms in the main house are stylishly decorated and furnished and have their own bathrooms and lovely views.

A barn alongside the house has been converted to provide two attractive suites, each with a double bedroom, twin-bedded room and bathroom. They are ideal for family occupation.

Ennys is a small working farm, and guests are welcome to walk the fields which stretch down to the River Hayle.

336

This is a delightful base for a family holiday, in a lovely rural setting, but with beaches and towns within easy reach. The food is mostly cooked from home-grown ingredients, with fresh fish and shellfish often available – even the bread is baked daily on the premises. The children have their high teas at 5.30pm, so that the adults can relax over their candlelit dinner.

Nearby: There are numbers of excellent beaches within easy reach – Prussia Cove, Whitesand Bay, Praa Sands, etc. – and St Michael's Mount and Land's End are a short drive away. You can easily reach Paradise Park, Poldark Mine, the Flambards Theme Park, Godolphin House and the Seal Sanctuary near Helston. Fishing, pony trekking and golf can all be arranged, and there is a wind-surfing school nearby at Marazion. The Minack open-air theatre stages plays in Porthcurno.

✕ Dinner (7pm) £15: avocado mousseline with prawns, supreme of chicken, iced nut cake
  Children: own menu
  £ Medium
✓ Best Bargain Break: £90 per person, 2 nights – dinner, b&b
  Children: two thirds of adult rate up to 10 years
  Facilities: 2 cots and 2 high chairs; baby-listening
  5 rooms, 2 family suites
  Open all year
  No credit cards accepted
Ⓟ Own car park

ST MAWGAN, CORNWALL · Map 1
Ⓟ **THE FALCON**
Tel: 01637 860 225
Off the B3276 out of Newquay.

This charming 16th-century pub, its walls covered with wisteria, suits its village well. It's a picturesque spot, protected within a deep wooded valley about two miles from the sea. The church of St Mawgan was largely built in the 13th century and there is a Carmelite convent in the village.

The Falcon has recently undergone considerable refurbishment. The main bar is welcoming, with its log fire, pine settles and many coaching prints on the walls. The dining area, at the rear of the bar, also has pine furniture and paintings by local artists on its walls – and they are for sale.

A cobbled courtyard at the back of the pub has plenty of stone tables and there is a large enclosed grassy area with picnic tables and a covered barbecue. The children's playground has climbing frames and slides. The many trees and shrubs make it a particularly agreeable place to enjoy a meal or a drink.

....

✗ (12pm to 2pm and 6.30pm to 9pm) £2–10: lamb and cranberry casserole, Indian platter, vegetable and hazelnut crumble, seafood provençale, sirloin steak
Children: half portions

◑ Ale: St Austell

Ⓟ Own car park

ST MERRYN, NORTH CORNWALL   Map 1
Ⓟ **Farmers Arms**
Tel: 01841 520 303
On the B3276 Padstow to Newquay and near the village crossroads.

....

The long cream-and-red-painted brick building is near the centre of the small village. At the back of the pub there is a large terrace with wrought-iron tables and chairs to seat around seventy people. From this area you pass through stained-glass doors into a large hallway filled with equine and farming bric-à-brac. On the right of this hallway is a games room containing electronic machines.

The main bar is an attractive room with its old stone walls, stone-flagged floor, and a lovely wrought-iron cooking range, complemented by the wooden furniture. An interesting feature of the room is the old well.

Food is served in the carpeted lounge, half of which is a no-smoking area. The Stable Room leads off the lounge and is the main family room, a spacious and pleasantly appointed area which can seat about sixty people. Stained-glass doors open out to the terrace at the rear.

This pleasant and welcoming family pub has accommodation available in the form of two double and two family rooms; light, airy and well decorated and all with their own bathrooms.

✕ (12pm to 2pm and 7pm to 9pm; all day in summer) £2–10: smoked mackerel, vegetable crumble, steaks, ham & eggs, grilled lemon sole
  Children: own menu, half portions
🍺 Ale: Hicks, Tinners
🅿 Own car park

Nr SALISBURY, WILTS   **Map 2**
🅿 **BARFORD INN, Barford St Martin**
Tel: 01722 742 242
On the A30, west of Salisbury and just beyond Wilton.

This old coaching inn was refurbished in splendid style a few years back. There is loads of space in the pub and the interior is comfortable and welcoming.

Families are welcome to use the area to the left as you enter; it is well away from the bar. Stone, brick and wooden pillars, half-walls made from old brick and ancient wooden beams have been used to excellent effect, and there is a good selection of pewter, copper and brass artefacts on the walls.

An alternative for families is a no-smoking lounge on the other side of the pub. This is a delightful room with a beamed ceiling, an open fireplace and horse brasses on the walls. Alongside, the lounge bar is just as smart, with wooden pillars, plush bench seating, wood-panelled walls and another huge open fireplace.

Outside, you can sit in a nice sunny courtyard. There are plenty of bench tables and the scene is enlivened by baskets and tubs of bright flowers.

....

✖ (12pm to 2pm and 7pm to 9.30pm) £2–11: locally smoked salmon, spinach & mushroom lasagne, chicken tikka masala, noisettes of lamb, lamb's liver & onions
  Children: half portions
🍺 Ale: Hall & Woodhouse
🅿 Own car park

Nr SALISBURY, WILTS   **Map 2**
🅿🆁 PHEASANT HOTEL, **Winterslow**
Tel: 01980 862 374
Six miles north-east of Salisbury on the A30 at Winterslow.

....

Any regular traveller along the A30 will have seen the Pheasant Hotel; it is a prominent building, very smart in its coat of cream paint with a wooden-clad façade and an array of flowers in window boxes and hanging baskets. It looks like a 1920s roadhouse and is now a very large family pub/restaurant.

Open all day and every day, with food available most of the time, it is a very useful place for families, especially if they want to break a journey.

When we visited there was a children's party in full swing at the family end of the pub. There is a children's play area here with a ball swamp, toys and a Lego table. Parents of small children will find a nappy-changing facility and plenty of high chairs, and in the pleasant lawned garden (safely enclosed) there is an excellent wooden play unit.

The interior of the pub is nicely designed with wood panelling and beams much in evidence and comfortable padded benches and seats. It is split into a series of interconnected rooms and one of them, with a wooden floor, a brick fireplace and a bar billiards table, resembles an old-style snug.

It all adds up to a very agreeable family pub with excellent facilities.

....

�֍ (11.30am to 10pm; Sun from 12pm) £2–8: oriental prawns, gammon steak, fillet of salmon, vegetable crumble, tagliatelle carbonara
Children: own menu
◗ Ale: Boddington's, Flowers, Wadworth's
Ⓟ Lots

SANDFORD-ON-THAMES, OXON   Map 5
Ⓟ KINGS ARMS, Church Road
Tel: 01865 777 095
Just off the A4074 south of Oxford. There is a sign to the pub.

....

The pub has a wonderful location by a lock on the Thames and its garden runs for about fifty yards alongside the water. That is the great attraction of the Kings Arms, and the terrace and garden were packed with lunchtime customers when we visited on a hot June day. A huge tree provides some shade and there is a children's play area and some slides.

There is an indoor play area too for young children (with a ball swamp, etc), and high chairs are provided; there is also a baby-changing facility.

It is a really spacious pub with low beamed ceilings, brick pillars and floors which are partly paved and partly tiled. There are two big brick fireplaces at either end of the pub and plenty of colourful prints on the walls. A line of windows overlooks the water. It's a very congenial place to have a meal and a drink, and has comprehensive facilities for a family.

....

✖ (12pm to 3pm and 6pm to 10pm; weekends 12pm to 9pm) £2–11: barbecued chicken wings, seafood pie, sirloin steak, Cajun chicken, lasagne
Children: own menu

⟠ Ale: Courage, John Smith's, Theakston's
🄿 Lots

SAUNTON, nr BARNSTAPLE, DEVON   Map 1
🄷 SAUNTON SANDS HOTEL
Tel: 01271 890 212
On the B3231.

This large and impressive hotel, prominently situated above the rolling
expanse of Saunton Sands, has an excellent range of facilities for families
and succeeds in looking after them well.

There is an indoor swimming pool, with a paddling pool for the
children, and a sauna; there is a squash court, a mini-cinema, a pool
table and table tennis. The sizeable outdoor pool also has a paddling
area for children and sublime views over the sands and the sea; there
is a putting green, a hard tennis court, swings and a children's play
area and a path down to a long stretch of sandy beach. Horse riding,
sailing, wind-surfing and fishing can all be arranged by the hotel staff;
just down the road is Saunton Golf Club, a splendid links course which
offers a stern test for any golfer.

One of the great bonuses of this hotel is the presence of a nanny,
who is in attendance from 10am to 5pm every day and until 3pm on
Sunday. There are plenty of toys here and lots of organized activities.

The bedrooms are comfortable and well appointed, some with little
terraces or balconies and many with enchanting views over the bay.
There are also seventeen self-catering apartments, many of which look
out over the dunes and the estuary.

Nearby: Saunton Sands spreads below the hotel and there are many other
fine beaches including Woolacombe and Croyde Bay. Nature lovers should
see Braunton Burrows, one of the largest nature reserves in Britain, and the
children will enjoy a visit to Exmoor Bird Gardens. They will have fun, too,
at Watermouth Castle, and Arlington Court is well worth a visit.

✖ Lunch (12.30pm to 2pm) £9: soup, roast turkey, fresh fruit salad;
  Dinner (7.30pm to 9pm) £18: melon & Parma ham, brochette of
  monkfish & scampi, pot roast pheasant, pudding or cheese
  Children: own menu, half portions
  £ High

✓ Best Bargain Break £124–168 per person, 2 nights – dinner, b&b
  Children: free up to 2 years; 60% discount from 2 to 5; 40%
  discount from 6 to 11 years
  Facilities: 15 cots and 15 high chairs; baby-listening line for
  every room
  94 rooms, 19 family, 12 suites
  Open all year

Ⓟ Own car park

SEATOWN, nr CHIDEOCK, DORSET   Map 2
Ⓟ ANCHOR

Tel: 01297 489 215

*Turn off the A35 in the middle of Chideock, opposite the Church and
Castle Inn; follow the road for three-quarters of a mile to Seatown.*

A large encrusted anchor from a ship wrecked on the infamous Chesil
beach in 1748 and raised by fishermen in 1985 appropriately sprawls
across the lawn of this well-situated 17th-century whitewashed pub. It
stands with a cluster of other cottages on the edge of the beach in a
valley between Golden Gap and Doghouse Hill. The wide expanse of the
coastal scenery can be enjoyed from the tables on the terrace of the small,
square family room, which is across the corridor from the main bar.

The sloping lawned garden is to one side of the pub, and the famous
anchor and a rowing boat provide unusual play equipment for the
children. Another stretch of garden goes down to the beach, and there
is a boule pitch and a sandpit.

During the summer months (Whitsun to September) the pub is open
all day and food is available at all times.

✕ (summer 12pm to 9.30pm, winter 12pm to 2pm and 6.30pm to 9.30pm) £2–9: steak & mushroom pie, seafood platter, curry & rice, whole local plaice, rump steak
Children: own menu, half portions

◻ Ale: Palmer's and guests

℗ Space for 20 cars

SEDBUSK, nr HAWES, NORTH YORKS   **Map 9**
Ⓗ **THE STONE HOUSE HOTEL**
Tel: 01969 667 571
Off the A684 near Hawes.

This delightful country hotel is situated amid glorious scenery on the edge of the Yorkshire Dales. It has been highly recommended for many years in the *Family Welcome Guide*, not only for the outstanding value it represents but also for the warm and friendly welcome which Mr and Mrs Taplin offer.

The house, a listed building, was converted less than a decade ago, and enormous care was taken to preserve its character. An old broom cupboard houses the serving hatch to the tiny bar, and the old library has been retained. There are plenty of books there, and a snooker table and an interesting collection of vintage slot machines. The hotel is encircled by a lawned garden, which includes a grass tennis court.

The food is cooked from fresh produce, and even the sausages are made on the spot. Children can have high teas, and although lunches are not served, the owners will supply packed lunches, if requested.

The hotel also has a niche in literary history. That wonderful writer, P. G. Wodehouse, found a name for his famous butler after meeting the original owner of Stone House, Hugh Crallan, whose own butler was called Jeeves.

Nearby: You may fancy a packed lunch because this is wonderful walking country, or you can vary this with some horse riding and fishing. It's a marvellous part of the world for touring around to see the sights: the Dales Folk Museum, Bolton Castle, Jervaulx Abbey and Richmond Castle are all within easy reach; and further away to the south you can visit Malham Cove, Stump Cross Caverns, and Bolton Abbey. Fishing, golf and sailing are all readily available in the locality.

✗ Dinner (7pm to 8pm) £16: Morecambe Bay shrimps, tenderloin of pork, double chocolate mousse, cheese
Children: half portions, high teas
£ Medium
✓ Best Bargain Break: £35 per person per night – dinner, b&b
Children: £6–12 (including breakfast)
Facilities: 3 cots and 3 high chairs; baby-listening system
18 rooms, 3 family
Closed Jan
ℙ Own car park

Nr SEVENOAKS, KENT　　　　　　　　　　　　　　　**Map 3**
ℙℝ **BADGER'S MOUNT, London Road, Halstead**
Tel: 01959 534 777
Close to Junction 4 of the M24. Take the A21 towards Bromley/Orpington.

One of the more recently converted Brewers Fayre public houses, on the fringes of Sevenoaks. It is quite apparent that a lot of thought has been put into supplying the type of entertainment demanded by the modern toddler. The family entrance is at the side of the main building, by the large car park, and from there you enter the main non-smoking dining area. Immediately to your left you will see the Charlie Chalk Fun Factory, which offers a variety of entertainment for children of all ages. For children up to four years of age there is a separate area with games tables, toys and a Wendy House; five- to ten-year-olds can, for a charge of 50p, play in the main Fun Factory, which is on two levels and incorporates slides, ropes and a variety of play equipment. For an extra 50p children can also play at one of the computer/video game consoles.

This whole area is supervised and children's toys, drinks and sweets can be purchased here.

The rear garden contains an outdoor playground with climbing frames, conventional slides and a 'commando'-type rope and tyre slide for the more adventurous. This area is enclosed and no food or drink is permitted here.

There are dining areas for smokers and non-smokers, and a main bar where children are not permitted. For those families who wish only to have a drink there is a grassed area at the rear of the pub, close to the play area, containing many picnic bench tables.

The whole building is tastefully decorated in a farmhouse style with oak tables, wheel-back chairs and tiled floors. The atmosphere is pleasant and the service friendly.

....

✕ (11.30am to 10pm; Sun from 12pm) £2–8: Teviotdale pie, vegetable crumble, gammon steak, chicken escalope, haddock & chips
Children: own menu
◗ Ale: Boddington's, Flowers, Old Speckled Hen and guests
Ⓟ Lots

Nr SEVENOAKS, KENT   **Map 3**
Ⓟ THE BULLFINCH, Riverhead
Tel: 01732 455 107
On the east side of Sevenoaks, just off the A25. Turn into Bullfinch Lane.

....

Reputedly built in the 1780s, The Bullfinch stands just below the level of the road and offers a quiet calm with its low beams, Gainsborough reproductions and collection of framed labels and stamps. There is a demarcation line between the family area and the bar, and the family area provides a variety of dining rooms and an excellent children's indoor play area. There are special baby-changing facilities, and four high chairs are available. The pub is open all day, but food is only served during the restaurant hours.

A lovely garden wraps itself round the inn. It is tree-filled and has a charming patio area with barbecue, family tables and umbrellas. There are several amusements for children – a climbing frame for older ones, and a bouncy castle, climbs, slides, bridges and tunnels for the younger ones.

....

✗ (12pm to 3pm and 6pm to 10pm) £2–9: prawn platter, mixed grill, Cajun chicken, lasagne, peppered steak
  Children: own menu
◻ Ale: Courage, Theakston's, John Smith's
Ⓟ Ample

Nr SEVENOAKS, KENT   Map 3
Ⓟ **CROWN POINT**, Seal
Tel: 01732 810 669
On the A25 east of Sevenoaks at Seal.

....

One of the major virtues of this pub is its very large garden, with a good expanse of lawn and terrace with bench tables, an adventure playground, tyre swings and a bouncy castle.

The family room is close to the garden and there is a bright and cheerful family dining area at the other end of the pub.

Good amenities are provided for families, including many high chairs and a nappy-changing unit. Food is available every day throughout opening hours and real ale fans are also well catered for, since there are usually six varieties on offer.

....

✗ (11.30am to 10pm; Sun from 12pm) £2–8: chicken Balti, vegetable crumble, fish dippers, sirloin steak, cheese omelette
  Children: own menu
◻ Ale: Boddington's and guests
Ⓟ Own car park

Nr SHEFFIELD, SOUTH YORKS   **Map 7**
P R THE KING'S HEAD, **Crosspool**
Tel: 0114 268 1203
On the A57 towards Manchester, between Broom Hill and Crosspool.

You can enjoy unrivalled views of the countryside, great vistas of rolling ground, gentle hills and distant church spires, from the gardens of the King's Head, which is housed in a substantial stone building.

The car park is terraced, and on the upper section is a small grassed and stone-flagged area with wooden picnic benches and tables and a small wooden climbing frame for the children. Although very near the road, a drink and a snack with such a view on offer is a real bonus on a sunny summer's day.

Immediately in front of the rear entrance is another sheltered stone-flagged patio with wooden tables and parasols, and another garden area has been made by the main entrance in the front of the building.

The main bar, an agreeable room with its low ceiling and wooden floor, has alcoves here and there and plenty of padded settles along with the wooden tables and chairs. There is also a family area here, decorated in similar style.

The restaurant has a small dining room on the ground floor and other areas on different levels. On the first floor there is seating on a small balcony area, which has a cast-iron Victorian fireplace; and down a short flight of stairs there is a long room with windows overlooking the car park and play area. Yet another room overlooks the valley and hills at the front of the building.

With its many recesses and nooks, the best use has been made of all the available space to ensure that you can find a quiet spot in which to settle for a drink or a meal.

The restaurant supplies free baby food and children's activity packs; there are baby-changing facilities and half a dozen high chairs.

....

✕ (12pm to 10.30pm) £2–13: Greek chicken salad, Normandy pork, ocean bake, king prawn salad, sirloin Oscar
Children: own menu
◐ Ale: Boddington's, Castle Eden, Marston's and guests
Ⓟ Own car park

SHOEBURYNESS, ESSEX   Map 6
Ⓟ THE SHOREHOUSE, Ness Road
Tel: 01702 292892
On the seafront at Shoeburyness, three miles beyond Southend Pier (the B1016).

....

A new development on the site of an old public house, The Shorehouse stands at the quiet end of the Southend seafront. It is three miles beyond the pier and the arcade area, but is within two miles of the Sea Life Centre and a mile and half from Southchurch Park where there is boating, amusements, tennis and even county cricket in July. The Shorehouse is opposite a coastguard station and a pleasant beach which affords glorious views across the Thames Estuary to the Kent coast.

The pub stands in front of a green open space where slides and climbs and benches and tables are already in operation. There are plans for this grass area to be fenced for the protection of children, and for this area to offer a host of entertainments such as magicians, Punch and Judy and a bouncy castle.

The interior of The Shorehouse is low-beamed and welcoming. There is Charlie Chalk's Fun Factory, with a large children's bar serving a host of sweets, drinks, crisps and gifts, alongside the family dining area. This area also boasts a Magic Roundabout, complete with Dougal, and a changing room where both men and women can deal with a baby. A supply of nappies, talc and baby cream is available at no charge.

Children are not restricted to this family dining area and may go anywhere in the pub until nine at night, for The Shorehouse holds a children's licence, but parents are encouraged to leave certain areas free for adults. Twelve high chairs are available, and there are tasters and half portions as well as the children's menu.

There are good facilities for the disabled, and, outside the standard menu, there is a willingness to provide for vegans and for those on special diets. Food is available at all times, and there are menus in French and German as well as braille.

....

✕ (11.30am to 10pm) £2–8: hot mushrooms, haddock & chips, turkey fillet, tagliatelle carbonara, vegetable crumble
  Children: own menu
◉ Ale: Boddington's, Flowers and guests
ℙ Plenty

SHOREHAM, WEST SUSSEX   **Map 3**
ℙℝ **ROYAL GEORGE**
Tel: 01273 591 904
On the A27 at Shoreham.

....

You cannot fail to see the Royal George, which presents a smart and cheerful face to the world. There are blue and white pillars in front of the white-painted façade, and an array of hanging baskets and window boxes of bright flowers adds to the fun.

The main bar, spacious and L-shaped, is complemented by a lounge bar with comfortable sofas and padded benches. This overlooks the appealing restaurant which benefits from its proximity to the neat garden and terrace with its nice display of bright flowers. The restaurant has a garden room atmosphere, with its high ceiling and flowery sun blinds, its brick pillars (and a couple of slender green pillars) and its large bay window.

High chairs are available and the restaurant is open all day on Sunday, when the lunches (just under £9 for two courses and just over £11 for three) offer good value.

....

- ✗ (12pm to 2pm and 6pm to 10pm; Sun 12pm to 10pm) £2–13: cod smokey, mixed grill, hot sesame chicken salad, fish & chips, steaks Children: own menu
- ◐ Ale: Bass, Wadworth's
- Ⓟ Own car park

SHREWSBURY, SHROPSHIRE   Map 4
Ⓟ Ⓡ The Oxon Priory
Tel: 01743 271 686
On the west side of Shrewsbury where the A458 meets the A5.

....

The vicar of the parish of Oxon, on the outskirts of this celebrated border town, would have been surprised, one feels, by the fate of his stately Victorian rectory. After a chequered history, it is now a large family pub and restaurant, poised at the junction where one road goes towards Welshpool and the other to Llangollen.

The accent is very much on the family market, with many high chairs available, a baby-changing facility, and a sizeable play area in the garden. The latter has a safe bark surface, and a bouncy castle appears during the summer. The garden is well tended and cheerful, with lots of shrubs and flowers and hanging baskets. Bench tables are set up on the terrace and the lawns.

The interior is spacious. There is an inviting lounge area, with a tiled fireplace and wood-panelled walls, in the old part of the building. The restaurant has big bay windows, a cheerful décor and plenty of pot plants; a second dining area has a high wooden ceiling and wooden panelling painted a bright green. There is a further restaurant area alongside. The restaurant hours are listed below but the pub is open all day and serves bar meals at all times.

....

✗ (12pm to 2.30pm and 5pm to 10.30pm; weekends 12pm to 10.30pm) £2–13: pâté, ocean bake, Louisiana chicken, sirloin steak, Normandy pork
   Children: own menu
◔ Ale: Boddington's, Flowers and guests
ℙ Own car park

SHREWSBURY, SHROPSHIRE   **Map 4**
ℝ GOOD LIFE, Barracks Passage, Wyle Cop
Tel: 01743 350 455
In the town centre, near the Lion Hotel.

....

This excellent vegetarian restaurant offers a warm welcome to families, and has no fewer than four high chairs available. You can also cope with changing a baby, since a pull-down shelf is provided in the Ladies.

The restaurant is housed in a fine 14th-century timbered building just around the corner from the Lion Hotel, in one of the most attractive parts of the old town, where timber-framed Tudor houses alternate with stately Georgian buildings.

There are two very attractive rooms in which you can settle to enjoy the wholefood cooking. All the dishes are prepared on the spot, and there is always a hot dish of the day and a good range of salads from which to choose.

....

✕ £1–3: home-made soup, five-bean cheese pot, savoury flans and quiches
Children: smaller portions
Open Mon to Fri 9.30am to 3.30pm; Sat 9.30am to 4.30pm; closed Sun
No credit cards accepted
🅿 Public car park nearby

Nr SHREWSBURY, SHROPSHIRE   Map 4
🅿🆁 BRIDGEWATER ARMS, Harmer Hill
Tel: 01939 290 377
On the A528 about six miles north of Shrewsbury.

....

This fine old sandstone pub stands four-square on the road north to the delightful little town of Ellesmere.

The Bridgewater Arms has been transformed into a very extensive family pub and restaurant, with a good array of facilities which include a large family dining area (no-smoking) and a little play area for tiny children, plenty of high chairs, a children's menu, and a nappy-changing unit. Outside there is a children's adventure playground, safely enclosed, and a bouncy castle.

One of the merits of the pub is the amount of space inside. It is a pleasant, open-plan interior with Laura Ashley-style wallpaper, richly patterned carpets, comfortable furniture, and wood panelling, glass screens and cheerful prints on the walls.

....

✗ (11.30am to 10pm; Sun from 12pm) £2–8: onion bhajis, chicken
  Balti, sirloin steak, vegetable moussaka, haddock & chips
  Children: own menu
◻ Ale: Boddington's, Marston's, Whitbread
ᴘ Lots

Nr SIDMOUTH, DEVON   **Map 1**
ᴘ **THE BOWD INN**
Tel: 01395 513 328
On the A3052 at Bowd Cross (junction with the B3176).

....

This is a classic English pub, with a thatched roof crowning its smartly
painted white walls, and with tubs of bright flowers around the entrance.
Inside, the archetypal style of an old inn is continued with black beams
and pillars, wooden settles, bow windows, huge open fireplaces and
copper pans and horse brasses.

The family room is off the main bar through some glass doors and is
in the same style as the rest of the pub: there is good wooden furniture
and prints on the walls. An alternative for families is the very attractive
dining room on the other side of the pub.

The garden has loads of space with plenty of bench tables, some of
them under wooden canopies. There is an excellent play area with slides,
seesaws and climbing frames.

....

✗ (12pm to 2pm and 6pm to 9pm) £2–12: plaice & chips, steaks,
  lamb curry, scampi & chips, crab salad
  Children: own menu, half portions
◻ Ale: Bass, Boddington's, Courage
ᴘ Own car park

SISSINGHURST, KENT
Map 3
Ⓡ **G**RANARY AT **S**ISSINGHURST **C**ASTLE **G**ARDEN
Tel: 01580 713 097
Off the A262, north-east of Cranbrook.

....

The wonderful gardens were created by Harold Nicolson and his wife, Vita Sackville-West, and are now in the care of the National Trust.

You can use the restaurant without paying the entrance fee and the National Trust try to look after families by providing high chairs and baby-changing facilities. There is a changing table in the Ladies by the main ticket office close to the restaurant.

The Granary is housed in an old barn, with many of the original pillars and beams still in place and plenty of new ones, too. It is all very attractively laid out and there are views of the gardens and the gatehouse from the restaurant.

....

✗ (12pm to 5.30pm, Tues to Fri; Sat and Sun from 10am; Easter to Oct) £2–6: smoked salmon, filled jacket potatoes, vegetarian dish of the day, chicken terrine, Lancashire hotpot
Children: half portions
Ⓟ Own car park

Nr SITTINGBOURNE, KENT
Map 3
Ⓟ **L**ADY **H**AMILTON, **Queenborough**
Tel: 01795 666 094
Off the A249 north of Sittingbourne. Head for Sheerness Docks. The Lady Hamilton is situated on the roundabout, two miles from Sheerness.

....

This road junction has long been the site of an inn, and the Lady Hamilton takes its name from the mistress of Lord Nelson who spent much of his time in the area when not engaged against the French. There is ample parking, and one is first struck by an inviting, colourful children's play area, a garden with a bouncy castle, slides and climbs, and benches at which the family can eat and drink.

From the garden steps you will enter the family room, which is tastefully decorated with posters attractive to children. In one corner of this spacious room is a play area which does not intrude upon the diners. The play area boasts a Postman Pat van, a Wendy House, a ball pool and other amusements. There is also an array of children's merchandise, and there is a special room in which father or mother can attend to the baby, and a toilet for the disabled.

The main bar, separated from the family room, recalls in its decoration the period of Nelson and Lady Hamilton. There are some interesting pictures and mementoes, and 'period' alcoves are lined with books. A total redecoration is planned, but the historical sense is to be maintained.

The Lady Hamilton is popular with users of the continental ferries, but this area, which Dickens used in some of his novels, has its own attractions, not least the Elmley Bird Sanctuary which is about two miles away.

There are seven high chairs on the premises and food is served throughout the day until 10pm.

....

✖ (11.30am to 10pm) £2–8: oriental prawns, Teviotdale pie, lasagne verdi, haddock & chips, steaks
   Children: own menu
◑ Ale: Boddington's, Flowers, Fuggles and Marston's
🅿 Ample

SLYNE, nr LANCASTER, LANCS   **Map 8**
🅟🆁 Cross Keys
Tel: 01524 823 166
On the A6.

....

This imposing stone building, built in 1830 according to the carving on the façade, has a distinct baronial air and faces down the main road towards Lancaster, a couple of miles away.

It is a spacious and welcoming family pub and restaurant, which is open throughout the day. The restaurant is shut during the afternoon but sandwiches and snacks are always available. High chairs and booster seats are provided and there is a nappy-changing unit. The children can have fun in the enclosed play area (with a safe bark surface) at the side of the pub.

The interior is nicely designed and has a number of rooms on different levels. The bar area stretches along the front of the building and has booths with curved settles. On a lower level, there is a large dining room. It is plushly decorated and has an open fireplace, wooden beams and square cottagey windows. Prints and china plates adorn the walls, and wall cupboards hold a variety of ornaments. Alongside there is a small dining room, and the family dining room is at the other end of the pub. There are lots of colourful prints on the walls – of teddy bears, carousels, clowns and horses. Toys and puppets and a wooden parrot are scattered about.

The Cross Keys is a welcoming family pub with a pleasant atmosphere.

....

✕ (11.30am to 2.30pm and 5.30pm to 10pm; weekends 12pm to 10pm) £2–8: moules marinières, chilli con carne, salmon steak, mixed grill, lemon chicken
   Children: own menu
◻ Ale: Theakston's and guests
Ⓟ Own car park

SNETTISHAM, NORFOLK Map 6
Ⓟ Ⓡ ROSE AND CROWN INN, Old Church Road
Tel: 01485 541 382
Just off the A149 on the north side of the village.

....

This ancient pub, of 14th-century origin, presents a lively face to the world, with a wealth of bright flowers adorning its front. You wouldn't guess that there is so much space inside, but there are three excellent bars, an attractive restaurant and two interconnected family rooms Several high chairs are made available.

The front bar is a delightful room with heavy black beams, which have an array of cooper's and carpenter's tools, a tiled floor and a huge open fireplace. Another smaller bar leads through to the pleasantly decorated restaurant; and there is a very comfortable back bar with a large brick fireplace.

The Garden Room is the larger of the two family rooms, spacious and bright and with a peaked pine roof, brick walls, tile floors and bentwood furniture. Windows look out to the attractive walled garden with its immaculate lawns, flowers and willow trees. To one side there is a large play area with swings, two wooden forts and a play house. It has a safe bark surface. There are some guinea pigs and caged birds here.

The other room, the Garden Bar, also looks out to the garden on one side. Both rooms have baby-changing facilities.

The Rose and Crown has three double bedrooms, each with its own bathroom. The pub also has a cottage in the village which is let on either a bed-and-breakfast or a self-catering basis.

....

✕ (12pm to 3pm and 6pm to 10pm) £2–12: smoked salmon, steaks, leek & Stilton bake, mixed grill, tagliatelle carbonara
   Children: own menu, half portions
◗ Ale: Adnams, Bass, Bateman's, Shepherd Neame and guests
Ⓟ Own car park

SOLIHULL, WEST MIDLANDS   **Map 4**
ⓅⓇ THE BARN, Hockley Heath
Tel: 01564 783 196
Near Junction 4 of the M42 and on the A3400 at Hockley Heath.
....

The pub's name is a fair description of this vast roadhouse-style establishment on the outskirts of Birmingham. The main part is a tall A-frame building and it has been converted by the Beefeater chain into a family pub and restaurant. Baby-changing facilities are available in two areas and there are several high chairs on the premises.

The theme of the restaurant is things agricultural and there is even a representation of a farmhouse inside; its roof goes towering upwards. Above the bar, farm wagons and wagon wheels are suspended from the ceiling. A number of rooms and alcoves are clustered around the building, including four little rooms built like cellars. It's all very comfortable, with padded wooden settles; and the brick walls and nice wooden tables create an agreeable atmosphere – if you ignore the wilder flights of fancy of the designer.

The garden is a pleasant option on a summer day; there is a good stretch of lawn and some pretty trees. The children have their own sizeable play area with slides and climbing frames.

✕ (12pm to 2.30pm and 5pm to 10.30pm; weekends 12pm to 10.30pm) £2–13: Greek dip, Normandy pork, steaks, salmon fillet, seafood tagliatelle

Children: own menu

◖ Ale: Bass, Boddington's, Castle Eden, Wadworth's

Ⓟ Own car park

SOLIHULL, WEST MIDLANDS   Map 4
Ⓡ **NOTCUTTS GARDEN CENTRE, Stratford Road**
Tel: 0121 744 4501
By the junction of the A34 and Exit 4 of the M42.

....

This is the flagship of the Notcutts garden centre group and is a most impressive place. Everything you could ever need for your garden, your patio or your window box is here, plus a great deal more besides.

This includes an excellent restaurant where you can get hot and cold food throughout the day. It is kept in pristine condition and a table, once vacated, is instantly cleared and cleaned by the efficient staff.

The terrace, with its cast-iron furniture, is a pleasant place to have a drink or a snack on a summer day, and there is a little children's play area at one end, with swings and a rocker placed on a safety surface.

An enterprising range of food is served here, in generous portions, at competitive prices. High chairs are made available and there is a baby-changing facility in the disabled toilet.

....

✕ (9.30am to 5pm) £2–5: roast of the day, chicken curry, lasagne, cauliflower cheese
   Children: own menu, half portions
Ⓟ Ample

SOUTH WIRRAL, MERSEYSIDE   Map 8
ⓅⓇ **BURLEYDAM, Childer Thornton**
Tel: 0151 339 8101
On the A41 towards Chester – and a mile from Junction 5 of the M53.

....

This massive Victorian brick pile (built in 1830) was owned by the Bibby family of shipbuilders. There are towering mature trees at the front and a few tables on a terrace. The garden at the rear also has many fine trees, and a display of shrubs and flowers, and there is masses of space on the immaculate lawns. Bench tables are set out on the lawns and the large terrace, and for the children there is a play unit and a bouncy castle.

The rooms inside the Burleydam have the impressive proportions you would expect of such a building and, despite its conversion to a family pub and restaurant, some of the original features remain: a splendid hall with a fine wooden staircase and fireplace, for example.

The high-ceilinged bar has padded settles along the walls, and upstairs there is the first of the many eating areas, a room (with a large brick fireplace) which stretches away to the back of the building. A great big Fun Factory has been positioned here and the children have their own soft drinks and snack bar. Other restaurant areas include a conservatory room which overlooks the garden; an extensive room with wooden pillars and beams and a central fireplace; and two other delightful rooms, one with the original wooden fireplace.

It is an imposing and very interesting building and has excellent facilities for families, including about two dozen high chairs and nappy-changing facilities. A Travel Inn is attached to the Burleydam.

✕ (11.30am to 10pm) £2–8: onion bhajis, fish pie, tagliatelle carbonara, vegetable moussaka, chicken escalopes
 Children: own menu
◻ Ale: Boddington's, Castle Eden, Flowers
Ⓟ Own car park

SOUTHAMPTON, HANTS   Map 3
Ⓟ Ⓡ **BASSETT, Burgess Road**
Tel: 01703 790 604
On the A35 between the University and the Hospital.

There is masses of space in this archetypal Brewers Fayre pub. Although it is designed on the open-plan principle, it is cleverly organized to give the impression of many rooms on different levels. It is decorated in an appealing way with bright flowery wallpaper, and with screens of wood and glass. Long padded benches, sofas and comfortable chairs complete the furnishings, and lots of quiet rooms and alcoves are tucked away, including a conservatory room which is a no-smoking area.

The facilities for families are comprehensive and include a pram and buggy park, a Toddlers' Corner, and nappy-changing rooms. Charlie Chalk's Fun Factory has a wide range of playthings, including a ball swamp and video cartoons.

Out of doors there is a terrace and a garden with bench tables and a play area with a safe bark surface; all are safely enclosed.

Food is available all day and every day, and it all adds up to a pub which is accurately trained on the family market.

....

✕ (11.30am to 10pm; Sun from 12pm) £2–8: fish dippers, vegetable crumble, sirloin steak, chicken escalopes, fish pie
Children: own menu
🍺 Ale: Boddington's, Wadworth's
🅿 Ample

SOUTHAMPTON, HANTS   Map 3
🅿🆁 FLEMING ARMS, Swaythling
Tel: 01703 584 358
Close to Junction 5 of the M27; adjacent to Swaythling railway station.

....

The exterior of this pub and restaurant (part of the Beefeater chain) belies its size, which is considerable.

The bar is agreeable and has some comfortable sitting areas, including an alcove with a long padded settle and a lounge up a few stairs. Beyond the bar, there is an outdoor play area with a wooden fort and a slide.

The restaurant is housed in two rooms, and the top room, with its high ceiling, brick walls and wooden pillars and panels, is especially congenial.

There are high chairs here and the bar is open all day and serves bar snacks.

....

✕ (12pm to 2.30pm and 5pm to 10.30pm; all day at weekends) £2–13: Greek chicken salad, prawn sundae, ocean bake, steaks, fillet of haddock

Children: own menu
- Ale: Boddington's, Flowers and guests
- Own car park

SOUTHAMPTON, HANTS — Map 3
PR THE BALMORAL, Nursling
Tel: 01703 732 262
Close to Junction 3 of the M27 on Romsey Road (A3057).

This attractive old pub was built of brick with weatherboarding above and has been expanded to make a sizeable pub and restaurant.

There is plenty of space in the bar, which sports a wooden ceiling, plaster walls, and wooden pillars. The restaurant is in much the same style, with lots of wood to be seen. Old advertising signs brighten the walls and there are some pretty windows at floor level. High chairs are made available in the restaurant.

One of the rooms leads out to the garden, where there are several bench tables, a wooden play unit on a safe surface and a bouncy castle. Beyond lies a Travel Inn which provides accommodation at reasonable prices.

✕ (12pm to 2.30pm and 5pm to 10.30pm; all day at weekends)
£2–13: Cajun prawns, pork satay, fillet steak, chicken tikka masala,
salmon fillet
Children: own menu
◻ Ale: Boddington's, Flowers and guests
Ⓟ Own car park

Nr SOUTHAMPTON, HANTS   **Map 3**
ⓅⓇ **ALMA INN, Lower Upham**
Tel: 01489 860 227
North-east of Southampton, on the B2177 at Lower Upham.

This attractive low-slung pub, built from flint and brick, is only a stone's
throw from the Marwell Zoo.

The Alma has a sizeable bar area on two levels. The well-proportioned
room has bay windows and is nicely furnished with an array of padded
settles and comfortable chairs. The no-smoking restaurant area is in the
same style and has a wooden ceiling, cheerful lampshades of coloured
glass, and wooden pillars and screens.

It is an excellent spot for families, since food is available throughout
the day. There are several high chairs and a mother and baby room.
In addition, there is a small play area inside the pub and a substantial
play unit outside with a safe bark surface. Adults can sit on the lawn
alongside or on the small terrace.

✕ (11.30am to 10pm) £2–8: onion bhajis, fish pie, sirloin steak,
chicken masala, vegetable crumble
Children: own menu
◻ Ale: Boddington's, Flowers and guests
Ⓟ Own car park

Nr SOUTHAMPTON, HANTS — Map 3
ⓅⓇ HEATH HOTEL, Dibden Purlieu
Tel: 01703 842 275
On the A326 near Beaulieu.

Dibden Purlieu sounds more fun than Southampton – and it is, since it is very close to all the attractions which Beaulieu has to offer.

The Heath Hotel is a substantial Victorian building which offers exceptional facilities for families: an enclosed outdoor play area with a fort and slides and a Wendy House; a large no-smoking family restaurant with a play area at one end with plenty of toys and a ball swamp; several high chairs; and baby-changing facilities.

The interior is appealing, with its wide windows, brightly coloured décor, wood panelling and comfortable furniture.

The Heath has the great advantage for families of being open, and serving food, throughout the day.

✕ (11.30am to 10pm; Sun from 12pm) £2–8: onion bhajis, cheese omelette, steaks, plaice & chips, vegetable moussaka
   Children: own menu
◑ Ale: Boddington's, Flowers and guests
Ⓟ Own car park

SOUTHEND-ON-SEA, ESSEX — Map 6
ⓅⓇ THE SILVER JUBILEE, 629 Rayleigh Road, Eastwood
Tel: 01702 522 357
Rayleigh Road runs parallel to the A127.

The Silver Jubilee is set back off the road and offers a leafy retreat for the drinker and diner. There is a large, well-tended garden which is backed by a stream and contains a small ornamental lake. There are a host of benches and tables under the trees, and for children there are slides, climbs, rockers and bouncing animals. An added attraction is that the Emerald Petanque Club have their ground in this garden so that one can enjoy the delightful diversion of watching a game of boule here on a summer evening.

The atmosphere is warm and friendly, with photographs and decoration suggesting Victorian times. Under low beams there is a long bar, and the restaurant area, which is on two floors, is behind the bar.

There is a designated children's area, but they may dine anywhere in the restaurant. Five high chairs are available, and there is a special room with changing facilities which can be used by mothers and fathers.

As well as a children's menu and half portions, baby food is available at no charge. The pub is open all day and bar food is served at all times (restaurant times below).

X (12pm to 2.30pm and 5pm to 10.30pm) £2–13: Greek dip, Normandy pork, steaks, salmon fillet, three-bean feast
  Children: own menu, half portions
◗ Ale: Boddington's, Flowers, Morland's, Marston's
P Spacious car park

STAINES, MIDDLESEX   **Map 3**
P SWAN HOTEL, **The Hythe**
Tel: 01784 452 494
Close to Staines Bridge where the A30 meets the A320.

This stately 18th-century inn stands in a wonderful location overlooking the river and was once a haunt of the bargemen who plied the Thames.

The lounge bar has superb views over the water, as does the very spacious conservatory, where families are welcome to settle down for a meal or some refreshment. The various bars are just as sizeable and are furnished in a relaxing way, with padded seats and settles and wooden tables. Two large open fireplaces house roaring log fires during the winter months.

On warm days you can sit on the paved terrace which runs the length of the building. With its lovely river views and the abundance of bright flowers in pots and hanging baskets, it is a delightful spot.

It is an excellent inn for families since it is open all day, seven days a week, and food is available at all times.

....

✕ (12pm to 10pm) £2–9: steak, scampi & chips, turkey pie, chicken curry
 Children: own menu
◖ Ale: Fuller's
ℙ Some spaces in front and on street

STANDISH, nr WIGAN, LANCS   **Map 8**
ℙℝ **CHARNLEY ARMS**
Tel: 01257 424 619
Close to Junction 27 of the M6 at Standish.

....

This large brick pub, opened in 1993, has a pleasing design and is very well placed near the motorway. It was named in honour of Sir John Charnley, an eminent surgeon who worked at the nearby Wrightington Hospital.

The interior is divided into a series of connecting rooms so that there is no feeling of being adrift in too large a space. Extensive use has been made of wood – for screens, the ceilings and a number of bookshelves – and of skylights of coloured glass. There are several open fireplaces which are flanked by bookshelves, and the walls are decorated with an array of prints, of yachts and fishing boats and Olde England scenes.

The no-smoking lounge area is an inviting spot with its bay window and padded settles. There are corner cupboards with displays of china, potted plants and many pictures, including a colourful one of a hybrid pheasant. One end of the pub contains a conservatory room with a wooden ceiling, and a raised platform in the centre is occupied by several tables.

The terrace has plenty of bench tables, and there is a play unit. High chairs are available, as are nappy-changing facilities. The Charnley Arms is open throughout the day and serves food at all times. A traditional Sunday lunch is good value at less than a fiver (£2.75 for children).

It is an excellent modern pub with all the facilities a family needs, and is run by efficient and friendly staff.

....

- ✗ (12pm to 10pm; Sun until 9pm) £2–9: oriental spring rolls, sirloin steak, rainbow trout, broccoli & hazelnut bake, mixed grill
  Children: own menu
- ◖ Ale: Greenall's, Stones
- ℗ Own car park

_____

STANTON ST JOHN, OXON   **Map 5**
℗ STAR INN
Tel: 01865 351 277
Just off the B4027 east of Oxford. There is a sign to the pub.

....

The original part of this pleasant stone pub dates back to 1720, and a modern addition combines well with it. Inside you cannot really see the join.

The pub has a spacious lounge bar with a flagstone floor and a large inglenook fireplace. It is an agreeable place to be, with some good wooden tables and plenty of pewter to be seen. Down the stairs in the older part there is a comfortable public bar, and alongside you will find a spacious family room, which is a no-smoking area.

A great asset is the sizeable enclosed garden which has a sandpit, a climbing frame and some swings. On the verge of the car park there is another large grassy area where children can play.

It is a charming and civilized pub with no fruit machines or juke boxes, and the music is kept at an unobtrusive level; there is a choice of real ale and of freshly cooked food, including vegetarian dishes.

....

✕ (12pm to 2pm and 7pm to 10pm) £2–8: crispy garlic mushrooms, chicken Kiev, pork in beer, winter vegetable casserole, sirloin steak
Children: own menu, half portions
◑ Ale: Hall & Woodhouse, Wadworth's
ℙ Own car park

STEYNING, WEST SUSSEX   **Map 3**
ℙ STAR INN, 130 High Street
Tel: 01903 813 078
At one end of the High Street.

....

We were not surprised to learn that the Star was Sussex Pub of the Year in 1994 and 1995, since it is a most attractive and welcoming place, a flat-fronted 18th-century brick building which was once a home run by the Quakers for waifs and strays.

You enter a very smart lounge bar with a large wooden farmhouse table on one side, and two alcove rooms. The ceilings are unusually decorated with walking sticks.

Through the businesslike public bar with its slate floor, you will come to the excellent family room, partitioned off by old beams and a little stable door. There are comfortable padded benches, a low brick fireplace and a beamed ceiling; adjoining this room is a play room with a collection of toys and some teddy bears.

The pretty garden at the side of the pub has a high flint wall with climbing plants on one side and a little stream on the other. In between there is a paved area and some lawn with tables and chairs. Across the car park there is another enclosed grassy area with more seating and a children's play area.

The pub is open throughout the day from 11am to 11pm on Saturdays.

....

✗ (12pm to 2pm and 7pm to 9.30pm) £2–10: cottage pie, sirloin
steak, plaice & chips, salmon & broccoli pasta
Children: own menu

◗ Ale: Boddington's, Flowers, Fuller's, Wadworth's

🅿 Own car park

STIPERSTONES, SHROPSHIRE   Map 4
Ⓗ **TANKERVILLE LODGE**
Tel: 01743 791 401
Off the A488 south of Shrewsbury. The brochure has clear directions.

This is a lovely and unspoilt part of Shropshire, made famous by
Mary Webb's novels, *The Golden Arrow* and *Gone to Earth*. It
also provided the setting for Malcolm Saville's adventure stories for
children.

Roy and Sylvia Anderson have a wonderful setting for their accommodation, which comprises four bedrooms in an extension to their own
house, the original part of which was an 18th-century hunting lodge.
Three of the bedrooms have twin beds and the other a double, and

they are all bright and clean and comfortably furnished. They are fairly compact in size but there is a good-sized sitting room on the ground floor (with a colour television) and a pleasant dining room with pine furniture. The charges are extremely modest (approximately £16 per person for bed and breakfast).

Across the lovely secluded garden, surrounded by flowers and greenery, there is Ovenpipe Cottage, the self-catering accommodation. It was once a pottery and an art gallery and the living area is on the first floor in order to take advantage of the many windows.

It is a delightful spot, on the site of the old Tankerville Mine and with the Devil's Chair looming above. All around is the magnificent Shropshire countryside and from the road above you can see for miles across the rolling fields to the hills beyond. It is only a short walk to the Stiperstones Inn, which serves food all day and every day, and the menu includes vegetarian and vegan dishes. There is a shop and a post office attached to the inn.

Nearby: All of south Shropshire is at your feet: the Long Mynd, much of which is owned by the National Trust, the Stiperstones Nature Reserve (with the famous Devil's Chair) and Carding Mill Valley are nearby, and golfers should know that Church Stretton golf course, designed by the incomparable James Braid, is a charming course on the hills. The children will be keen to see the Acton Scott Working Farm Museum near Church Stretton and Powis Castle. Lake Vyrnwy is also within easy reach.

Further south are the Clun villages – 'the quietest places under the sun' – Ludlow with its famous castle, and the Clee Hills. And don't forget Buildwas Abbey, the Roman City at Wroxeter and Wenlock Priory. Coarse fishing and horse riding can be arranged nearby.

....

✗ Dinner (7pm) £9: courgette & mint soup, Shropshire fidget pie, raspberry pavlova, cheese
£ Low
Facilities: 1 cot
4 rooms

Open all year
No credit cards accepted

P Own car park

STOCKPORT, GREATER MANCHESTER   **Map 8**
P R MIDLAND HOTEL, **Marple Bridge**
Tel: 0161 427 2370
On the A626 by the river in Marple Bridge.

....

No doubt this was once a traditional pub in its pleasant location by the water, and it has now been much extended to become a large family pub and restaurant. The long bar has wide cottagey windows and the restaurant has been constructed on a number of different levels. There are four or five rooms with padded settles and some quirky colour schemes; some of the walls have been rag-rolled and have friezes. An eclectic choice of prints and china plates decorates the walls, and there are screens of wood and coloured glass, and some open fireplaces.

It's a bright and welcoming place with good facilities for everyone, including families. Food is available throughout the day, and there are high chairs and baby-changing facilities. There are two play areas, one for young children indoors and another outdoors at the back of the pub by the car park.

....

✗ (1.30pm to 10pm) £2–8: oriental prawns, Teviotdale pie, sirloin steak, lasagne verdi, fried scampi
   Children: own menu

◗ Ale: Boddington's, Flowers

P Own car park

STOKE GABRIEL, nr TOTNES, DEVON Map 1
Ⓗ GABRIEL COURT HOTEL
Tel: 01803 782 206
Go to the village and you'll find a signpost to the hotel.

We are always happy to visit this very pretty 16th-century manor house. It's an elegant, white-painted building with an ornamental balustrade and a square tower, in a quiet village between Paignton and Totnes. It is set in three acres of lovely, tranquil sloping land which boasts one of the oldest pink magnolias in England, ancient yews, an old-fashioned knot garden, a vegetable garden and an orchard just made for visiting youngsters to play in. There's also a heated outdoor swimming pool, a croquet lawn and an outdoor play area.

The kitchen uses local produce as much as possible – fruit and vegetables from the garden, salmon and trout from the Dart, poultry and venison from nearby farms and woods. There are separate meal times for children, who are not allowed in the dining room in the evenings.

Nearby: This part of Devon has many attractions for visitors, especially families. There is an array of excellent beaches surrounding the busy resort of Torquay and many places to visit, including Compton Castle, Buckfast Abbey and its neighbour, the Dart Valley Railway. Further afield, the children can visit the Dartmoor Wildlife Park and the National Shire Horse Centre. The ruins of Berry Pomeroy Castle, haunted, of course, are not far from the hotel. Golf is available and trips on the River Dart can also be arranged.

✗ Dinner (from 7.30pm) £22: egg baked with cream & cheese, soup, fresh Dart salmon, pudding and cheese
   Children: high teas
   £ High
✓ Best Bargain Break: £232 per person, 4 nights – dinner, b&b
   Children: cot £7; £12 from 3 to 10 years; £15 thereafter
   Facilities: plenty of cots and high chairs; baby-listening to every room

19 rooms, 5 sets interconnecting
Open all year
P Own car park

Nr STOKE-ON-TRENT, STAFFS   **Map 4**
P R **ASHBANK HOTEL, Bucknall**
Tel: 01782 302 378
On the A52 (A524) at Bucknall.

....

The road signs still read A52 but the road is marked A524 on some maps. Suffice it to say that the pub is not very far from Alton Towers, which is still Britain's best theme park. The Ashbank is a substantial sandstone building which stands four-square at the top of a hill. From its windows you have splendid views of the countryside.

When we visited, a children's party was in full swing in the Fun Factory, a sizeable room with an array of play equipment (including a ball swamp) at one end of the building. One of the restaurant areas extends along one side, and the large windows overlook a paved terrace with bench tables and the garden. This part of the pub has cheerful decorations, which include lots of prints on the walls, and several booths with wooden screens.

The bar area is in much the same style and has a few alcoves with comfortable padded benches and a variety of wooden tables. On one of the fireplaces there are photographs of the local football team, which is sponsored by the Ashbank.

This pub and restaurant is aimed at the family market and provides high chairs and a nappy-changing unit. It is open throughout the day and serves food at all times. The extensive lawned garden is safely enclosed and has plenty of bench tables, a play unit on a bark surface and, in summer, a bouncy castle.

....

✕ (11.30am to 10pm) £2–8: oriental prawns, sirloin steak, vegetable crumble, steak & kidney pie, salmon fillet
Children: own menu

⊡ Ale: Boddington's, Marston's, Green Bullet
ℙ Own car park

STONHAM ASPAL, SUFFOLK   Map 6
ℝ **STONHAM BARNS, Pettaugh Road**
Tel: 01449 711 755
On the A1120 east of its junction with the A140.

....

What was originally a garden centre has expanded apace in the last few years and is now a crafts centre with shops selling farm produce, flowers, clothing, pine furniture and antiques, picture frames and so on. There is even a golf range at one end of the centre, and a pets' corner where children can, under supervision, feed the animals.

The restaurant has three eating areas; the smallest one, near the self-service counter, is nicely furnished with pine tables, and there is a large conservatory alongside; in addition, there is a spacious restaurant in the original barn. All the food is freshly made on the premises and is offered at reasonable prices.

If a baby needs a change of nappy, facilities are provided in the Ladies.

....

✗ (10am to 5.30pm; until 4.30pm in winter) £2–5: curried egg mayonnaise, beans on toast, omelettes, all-day breakfast, filled jacket potatoes
  Children: own menu, half portions
ℙ Lots

STOULTON, nr WORCESTER, HEREFORD & WORCS

Map 4

Ⓗ **CALDEWELL HOUSE, Pershore Road**

Tel: 01905 840 894

On the A44 south-east of Worcester.

The house is very well positioned for travellers and tourists since it is about three miles from Junction 7 of the M5 south of Worcester. It is a handsome house, with a Georgian façade and some Victorian additions, with its history on display inside, and a little museum. There is loads of space surrounding the house: a huge and well-maintained front lawn where you can play ball games, swings for the children, and a lawn where you can play croquet in the lovely and secluded rear garden. There is a miniature steam railway in the grounds, and the owners arrange special railway weekends.

Any family will enjoy the surroundings, which include several acres of woodland and a small lake; and there are farm animals – sheep, a donkey, and hens – to befriend.

The various rooms are generous in size and include two very large rooms at the front of the house: each can accommodate a double and a single bed and has plenty of room for a couple of easy chairs as well. The two rooms at the back of the house are delightfully secluded and look out over the garden. One of them has its own *en suite* bathroom and has a connecting door to a twin-bedded room. They can be used as a self-contained family suite.

The public rooms include a sitting room and a stately and charming dining room with wide windows on to the gardens.

Caldewell House has a relaxed charm of its own, excellent facilities in tranquil surroundings, and offers excellent value.

Nearby: For holiday makers there is a multitude of choices nearby: Bredon Hill on one side and the Malvern Hills on the other; further afield the Cotswolds and the Wye Valley; and quite close at hand Worcester Woods Country Park, Hanbury Hall, the Avoncraft Museum, Spetchley Park and Eastnor Castle. Music lovers might be interested in Elgar's birthplace (on the west side of Worcester).

✗ Dinner (by arrangement) £8
   Children: half portions
   £ Low
   Children: cot free; half price up to 12 years
   Facilities: 1 cot and 1 high chair; baby-listening by arrangement
   4 rooms, 1 family, 1 set interconnecting
   Open Mar to Dec
   No credit cards accepted
   Unlicensed
Ⓟ Ample

Nr STOURBRIDGE, WEST MIDLANDS   Map 4
Ⓟ Ⓡ THE BADGERS SET, Hagley
Tel: 01562 883 120
Near Junction 3 of the M5, on the A456 at Hagley.

This is another of those roadhouses which seem to have been so popular in the Midlands from the 1950s onwards. It is now a family pub and restaurant with a Travel Inn alongside.

The children are well provided for here, since there is an extensive garden at the rear with a play unit and a bouncy castle, a pets' corner (with chickens, rabbits, ducks, geese, a sheep and a pig), and a discovery trail. They also have their own serving point for snacks and soft drinks – it's called Toad's Tuck Shop. There are bench tables on the lawn for the adults.

There's loads of room inside the Badgers Set. The bar area is comfortable and the very large restaurant has a high peaked roof and is constructed on two levels. Wooden screens divide the rooms into more intimate booths and there are alcoves here and there. High chairs are available and there is a baby-changing facility.

....

✗ (12pm to 2.30pm and 5pm to 10.30pm; weekends 12pm to 10.30pm) £2–13: pork satay, ocean bake, three-bean feast, steaks, Indonesian chicken
  Children: own menu
℗ Ale: Bass, Boddington's, Flowers
ℙ Ample

STOW BARDOLPH, NORFOLK   **Map 6**
ℙ **HARE ARMS**
Tel: 01366 382 229
Off the A10, two miles north of Downham Market.

....

This lovely Norfolk village has a pub to match: a pub which has been a focal point of village life since it was built during the Napoleonic Wars.

It is a large and most attractive brick building, partly covered in ivy, and a spacious garden, with plenty of bench tables amongst the flowers and bushes, runs along one side. A smashing place to sit at peace on a summer day.

There is a good-sized conservatory at the front of the pub, and families are welcome to park themselves there. It is a pleasant room with half a dozen tables and decorated with several old advertising signs. Does anyone remember Rajah cigars? Many will remember Wincarnis. The Old Coach House, which is a function room, is also available for family use on Sundays.

Further inside you will find a very attractive, spacious bar, its walls adorned with brass artefacts of all kinds, with china plates and even some hickory-shafted golf clubs. Leading off the bar there is the restaurant, a handsome and beautifully proportioned room with some interesting decorations including portraits on wood of Queen Victoria and other royals.

It's a delightful inn, with an excellent reputation for its food, which includes a traditional Sunday lunch.

....

✕ (12pm to 2pm and 7pm to 10pm) £2–10: Lynn shrimps, lasagne, game pie, cod Mornay, beef goulash
　Children: small portions
◻ Ale: Greene King, Rayment's
ℙ Own car park

STOW-ON-THE-WOLD, GLOS　　　　　　　　Map 4
Ⓗ FOSSE MANOR HOTEL
Tel: 01451 830 354
On the A429, just to the south of Stow-on-the-Wold.

....

This privately owned hotel is housed in a stately Victorian manor house, its walls covered in Virginia creeper. It has the great bonus for families of a large garden, which runs to about seven acres and provides loads of space for children to play and for adults to relax. A play area is laid out on the smooth lawn at the front of the hotel and has a sandpit, swings and a slide, and there is a croquet lawn. A pleasant terrace lies at the back of the hotel and overlooks a quiet, enclosed garden with lawns and a pond; giant chess is laid out here.

The public rooms, spacious and comfortable, include a very pleasant lounge with lots of easy chairs and sofas, a large bar and a bright and cheerful dining room with wide windows on to the garden. The family bedrooms offer plenty of space and lovely views.

The Fosse Manor is an excellent family hotel in a superb location in the heart of the Cotswolds where there is much to enjoy.

Nearby: The Cotswold Farm Park, Birdland and the model village at Bourton-on-the-Water, the Folly Farm waterfowl sanctuary and the Cotswold Wildlife Park are all within easy reach, as are Sudeley Castle, Sezincote, and Chedworth Roman Villa. The hotel staff can arrange riding, fishing and clay pigeon shooting, and there are several golf courses in the vicinity.

⋯⋯⋯

✖ Bar snacks (12pm to 2pm and 6pm to 9.30pm) £2–10: ravioli, chicken tikka, venison steak, grilled salmon, pork & cider sausages;
Lunch (12.30pm to 2pm) £13: hot oriental prawns, grilled pork chop, pudding or cheese;
Dinner (7.30pm to 9.30pm) £18: Cornish scallops, chicken with sun-dried tomatoes, pudding or cheese
Children: own menu, half portions
£ High

✓ Best Bargain Break: £59 per person per night – dinner, b&b
Children: free
Facilities: 4 cots and 4 high chairs; baby-listening system
20 rooms, 3 family, 2 sets interconnecting
Open all year excluding Christmas week

ℙ Own car park

STRETTON, nr OAKHAM, LEICS   Map 7
Ⓡ RAM JAM INN
Tel: 01780 410 776
On the A1, about 9 miles north of Stamford.

....

This old pub, familiar to anyone who has travelled up the A1, maintains the best traditions of the English inn. The stone front of the inn remains but behind it is a restaurant which offers food from 7am onwards. The various menus offer a really enterprising choice of food at competitive prices; ignore all those ghastly fast-food places on the Great North Road and have some real food and good coffee at the Ram Jam Inn.

As you enter there is a snack bar, where breakfasts and other meals are served; down the stairs is a large bar area with a tiled floor, some sofas in one corner, and a glass dome over the centre; and at the far end are two dining rooms, smartly turned out with coral-coloured walls, polished wood floors and moulded ceilings.

Off the bar area there is a patio with a few tables and chairs, a stretch of lawn, and the open countryside of Rutland beyond.

There are seven comfortable and well-furnished bedrooms, including a family room. All but one of them overlook the orchard and the garden; despite the proximity of the A1 you will be assured of peace and quiet.

....

✕ Bar snacks (7am to 10pm) £2–7: falafel with salad, corned beef hash, rabbit stew, grilled Rutland sausage, fresh pasta of the day;
   Dinner (7pm onwards) £17: fresh linguini, noisettes of lamb, warm treacle tart with ice cream
   Children: own menu
   Open all year
◖ Ale: Ruddles
Ⓟ Own car park

STUDLAND, DORSET
⊞ KNOLL HOUSE HOTEL
Tel: 01929 450 450
On the B3351 east of Corfe Castle and north of Swanage.

Map 2

....

The Ferguson family have owned the Knoll House since 1959 and adhere to their philosophy of holding the balance between the differing requirements of their guests: on the one hand it has a location and an array of facilities which appeal greatly to families (and it continues to be one of our favourite family hotels), and on the other it also has many regular guests who are unencumbered by children. The philosophy is easy to express but difficult to achieve; in our opinion the Fergusons achieve it with style and aplomb.

Everyone is well looked after here. The children have their own dining room, with decent wooden furniture and cheerfully decorated with animal murals and colourful blinds. As well as their breakfast the children can have their lunch (there is an excellent menu which includes dishes such as grilled fish and roast beef) at 12.30 and are then supervised in the well-equipped play room (Wendy House, playpens, video cartoons, toys, etc) while the parents have their meal in peace. Similarly, children under 8 are not permitted in the dining room at night, but have high tea from 5 o'clock.

The facilities within the hotel and the 100 acres of grounds are extensive and include a heated swimming pool and paddling pool, safely enclosed, with a terrace, lawn and bar; a huge play area shaded by tall pines, with a pirate ship and a wonderful and ingenious 'Hag' adventure playground; and a par-3 golf course and two hard tennis courts. Indoors there are games such as table tennis, pool, table football, etc. Finally the well-designed leisure centre has a small indoor pool, a fitness room with serious equipment, a sauna, steam room and solarium, and a health juice bar. This is primarily a place for adults, but children are allowed in from 11am to midday, and for an hour in the afternoon if the weather is foul.

There is a feeling of spaciousness in the hotel, not least in the dining room where the tables are set well apart and a wall of windows overlooks the gardens. Similarly, the family suites offer plenty of space, with separate single or twin bedrooms for the children.

The location of the hotel, with its expansive grounds, encircled by National Trust land, and with one of the best beaches in Britain on the doorstep, is outstanding. It is a top-class family hotel in a superb holiday area.

Nearby: The beaches in this area are splendid, and indeed the Studland beach, with over three miles of sand, is one of the best and cleanest in Britain. Behind it lies the Studland Heath Nature Reserve, and its neighbour, Swanage Beach, is also clean and sandy. The Swanage Railway is on the doorstep, as is Durlston Country Park and Corfe Castle. Brownsea Island is delightful and has many sandy beaches, too. Sightseers can easily reach the Tank Museum at Bovington, Hardy's cottage and the Tutankhamun Exhibition at Dorchester; and the children will enjoy a visit to the Sea Life Centre at Weymouth.

✗ Lunch (1pm onwards) £15: hors d'oeuvres, soup, grilled whole local plaice, pudding or cheese;
Dinner (7.30pm onwards) £17: creamed smokies with prawns, roast Dorset lamb, pudding, cheese
Children: own menu
£ High
✓ Best Bargain Break: £770 per family of 4, 5 nights – full board
Children: a sliding scale depending on age
Facilities: plenty of cots and high chairs; baby patrol from 7.30pm to 11pm
80 rooms, including 30 family suites
No credit cards accepted
Closed Nov to end Mar
🅿 Own car park

STURRY, nr CANTERBURY, KENT   **Map 3**
P R PUNCH TAVERN, Calcott Hill
Tel: 01227 710474
Between Canterbury and Herne Bay on the A291.

Two miles north of the town of Sturry, the Punch Tavern is in an ideal spot, halfway between the beautiful city of Canterbury and the popular seaside resort of Herne Bay. There has long been a coaching inn on this site where now there is a most welcoming family pub. There is a children's licence so that youngsters may go anywhere in the house, although there are areas where adults are able to find privacy.

There is a large garden with family benches and a play area with climbs, swings, slides and seesaw animals. The interior is low-ceilinged and welcoming and decorated with relevant pictures and models of Punch and Judy, and extracts from the once-famous magazine, *Punch*. There is a light and pleasant conservatory with a large dining area and a play car and other children's amusements, but an inside play zone is being developed and will be open by the end of 1995.

Eight high chairs are available, and a mother and baby room. There is a children's menu and food is served at all times. It is a spacious and airy place where families receive a real welcome.

✕ (11.30am to 10pm) £2–8: oriental prawns, chicken Balti, turkey fillet, sirloin steak, lasagne verdi
Children: own menu
◔ Ale: Boddington's, Castle Eden, Flowers, Wadworth's
P Ample

SUMMERCOURT, CORNWALL
Map 1
P THE LONDON INN
Tel: 01872 510 281
Off the A30 to the south of Newquay.

The pub is housed in a small white building which was once two cottages owned by the Trewithen Estate and built *circa* 1650. It was converted by the brewery in 1944. Beyond the large car park you will see a grassed area on which there are two or three picnic tables, and there is also a covered area with wooden settles and benches and more picnic tables; plants and flowers in hanging baskets and tubs are scattered about.

Inside the pub there is an enclosed area specifically set aside for family groups; as with the rest of the pub this has wooden tables and wheel-backed chairs and is cosily lit with coach lamps.

This area and the main bar have brick walls, wooden partitions and cladding and a beamed ceiling. It is fully carpeted throughout and is a quiet place in which to eat and drink. Cornish cream teas are served during the afternoon.

✗ (12pm to 3pm and 7pm to 9.30pm) £2–7: plaice & chips, ham & eggs, seafood platter, mixed grill
Children: own menu, half portions
◖ Ale: Tinners
P Own car park

SUNDERLAND, TYNE & WEAR
Map 9
P R THE WESSINGTON, Castletown
Tel: 0191 548 9384
At the junction of the A19 and the A1231. Turn towards Sunderland.

This is a very large, recently built Brewers Fayre pub with excellent facilities for families. The single-storey brick building houses a comfortable and spacious interior which is easy on the eye: brick pillars, wooden screens and panelling, and cheerful wallpaper.

385

The family dining room has wide windows on to a terrace with many bench tables, and there is a play area alongside with a good array of things on which to slide, climb and swing (it has a safe surface).

Charlie Chalk's Fun Factory has a comprehensive selection of toys and games, including a ball swamp, roundabouts and a big slide. Tables and chairs are set out for the adults.

All these facilities are augmented by the provision of plenty of high chairs, baby-changing facilities and a children's menu. The pub is open all day and food is always available.

....

✗ (11.30am to 10pm; Sun from 12pm) £2–8: hot mushrooms, Teviotdale pie, vegetable moussaka, gammon steak, haddock & chips
  Children: own menu
◑ Ale: Boddington's, Castle Eden
Ⓟ Own car park

Nr SUTTON COLDFIELD, WEST MIDLANDS   Map 4
ⓅⓇ **BASSETTS POLE, Canwell**
Tel: 0121 308 0987
Just north of Sutton Coldfield where the A38, A453 and A446 converge.

....

As you can imagine, this is a very busy roundabout and, if you have had your fill of motorways and main roads and the playful antics of juggernaut drivers, you might pause and refresh yourselves here. Families are well regarded; high chairs and a mother and baby room are available and there are play areas both inside and out.

The pub is a large and stately building, its façade painted cream. The garden, mostly lawned and with several shady trees, has bench tables, and there is a play unit for the children and, in summer, a bouncy castle.

The roomy bar area is divided into three areas and is congenial with its brick pillars, padded benches and bright décor. One part of the restaurant has a high-peaked wooden ceiling and miniature farm wagons are suspended from it. The family dining room (no-smoking) also has a colourful look, with rich green paint laid over wooden panelling and bunches of barley, wheat and lavender decorating the beams. There is a small indoor play area, but by now a Fun Factory will have taken its place.

....

✴ (11.30am to 10pm) £2–8: oriental prawns, chicken Balti, Teviotdale pie, steaks, tagliatelle carbonara
  Children: own menu
◖ Ale: Boddington's, Flowers, Marston's
Ⓟ Own car park

SWAINSTHORPE, nr NORWICH, NORFOLK   Map 6
Ⓟ THE DUN COW
Tel: 01508 470 637
Five miles south of Norwich on the A140.

....

One of the wooden beams in The Dun Cow has engraved upon it Dr Johnson's message: 'Claret is the liquor for boys; port for men; but he who aspires to be a hero must drink brandy'. In fact, it is believed that a roadhouse stood on the site of The Dun Cow some hundred years before Johnson ever uttered those words with a smile.

The present pub is a solid, welcoming place, standing alone at the side of the road and noble and dignified enough to attract the cameras of passing tourists, for whom it has the aura of a typical English country pub. There is a pleasant garden at the rear and side which offers children slides, swings, a seesaw and a mysterious artificial tree with a house to which one must climb. There is a bouncy castle, family benches and a small patio area.

There is a light and attractive family dining room which looks out on to the garden, and two high chairs are available.

....

✴ (11am to 2.30pm and 6pm to 10.30pm) £2–11: Italian mushrooms, swordfish, sirloin steak, chicken Kiev, seafood tagliatelle
  Children: own menu

🍺 Ale: Ansells, Flowers, Tetley's
🅿 Own car park

SWINDON, WILTS   **Map 2**
🅿🆁 **RUNNING HORSE**
Tel: 01793 523 903
Near Junction 16 of the M4. Follow the sign to the town centre.

The theme of this family pub and restaurant is the horse; there is, for example, a model of a carousel suspended from the high vaulted ceiling of the restaurant. It's an unusual room on two levels, with elongated brick walls and wooden panelling, and an eclectic choice of decorations: jugs and plates, prints, china figures and a penny farthing cycle. There are several high chairs and baby-changing facilities.

The bar, on the ground floor, is well turned out, with its brightly coloured lampshades, padded benches, nice fireplaces, bookshelves and ceiling fans.

There is a small terrace at the rear of the pub beside a stream. Over a little bridge a lawn has plenty of bench tables, and a play area has been set up for children (plus a bouncy castle in summer).

✕ (12pm to 2.30pm and 5pm to 10.30pm; weekends all day)
£2–13: prawn sundae, fillet steak, chicken tikka masala, ocean
bake, provençale nut Wellington
Children: own menu
◖ Ale: Arkell's
Ⓟ Own car park

SYDLING ST NICHOLAS, nr DORCHESTER,   Map 2
DORSET
Ⓗ LAMPERTS FARMHOUSE
Tel: 01300 341 790
Off the A37 and the A352 north of Dorchester.

The village of Sydling St Nicholas nestles in a beautiful and unspoilt
valley, surrounded by fields and woods. The attractive farmhouse, built
about 400 years ago of brick and flint under a thatched roof, stands
hard by the approach road to the village, about three miles from the
A37, the Dorchester to Yeovil road.

The bedrooms are nicely furnished and have their own bathrooms;
the family room has an antique brass double bed and an unusual old

389

Swedish pine bed which can be adjusted to suit the size of the child. There is plenty of room for a cot or another bed.

The comfortable lounge has an inglenook fireplace with all the fittings for smoking bacon still in place. Board games, cards and toys are available. Meals are taken at the huge pine table in the farmhouse kitchen.

One wing of the farmhouse has been restored as a cottage for two people and a child (a cot is available). The charming bedroom is under the eaves and the sitting room has french windows which lead out to the garden. The rent varies from £120 to £200 a week.

The spacious garden is safely encircled by hedges and there is loads of room for children to play on the lawns. Mrs Bown is delighted to have families to stay, and the children can meet the farm's many animals – cows, chickens, ponies and dogs. There is much to do and see in the immediate vicinity.

Nearby: The attractive port of Weymouth is not far away. It has an excellent sandy beach, from which dogs are banned. Lodmoor Country Park is close to the beach, as is the nature reserve at Radipole Lake. This is Thomas Hardy country, and his cottage is nearby; also within easy reach are the Tutankhamun Exhibition, Maiden Castle, Athelhampton and T. E. Lawrence's cottage, Clouds Hill. The children may enjoy the Sea Life Centre at Weymouth.

....

✕ Dinner (6.30pm to 8pm) £10
    Children: half portions
    £ Low
    Children: cot £2; half price thereafter
    Facilities: 1 cot and 1 high chair; baby-listening by arrangement
    2 rooms, 1 family
    Open all year
    No credit cards accepted
    Unlicensed
P Ample

TALKIN, nr BRAMPTON, CUMBRIA   **Map 8**
P HARE AND HOUNDS
Tel: 016977 3456
In the centre of the village. Three miles off the A69.

This traditional black and white village inn is set high in the Cumbrian countryside. It is a truly unspoiled pub with an interior which has probably not changed much over the years. The monks who once used it as a stopping place on their journeys from Armathwaite to Lanercost Priory would recognize it.

The main bar is a cosy affair with black beams, rustic furniture, and the renowned stained-glass coats of arms. In winter, you will find a log fire in the stone fireplace. The family room, at the back of the pub, is very much in character, its walls scattered with various curios, and there is a pool table.

There is a small walled garden at the side of the pub, with some tables and chairs, sun umbrellas and many flowers.

The pub is close to Talkin Tarn and Hadrian's Wall, and it is a wonderful area for walking and other outdoor pursuits.

✗ (12pm to 2pm and 7pm to 9pm) £1–10: chilli prawns, fillet steak, rainbow trout, venison in red wine, chilli con carne
   Children: own menu, half portions
◑ Ale: Jenning's, Boddington's and guests
P Across the road

TAMWORTH, STAFFS   **Map 4**
P R THE LADYBRIDGE
Tel: 01827 54414
On the A4091 roundabout, near the Snow Dome.

Tamworth was the Saxon capital of Mercia, and a 12th-century castle (with many newer additions) still stands. The Ladybridge is something of a contrast, a huge purpose-built pub and restaurant, with a steep roof lined with dormer windows. There is a Travel Inn alongside.

Paved terraces with bench tables encircle the building and an enclosed grassy area has a play unit. By now, an indoor play area for young children will have been added to the many facilities for families: there are a number of high chairs on the premises and baby-changing facilities.

The very large bar area has reminders of the Potteries, such as a fireplace which resembles a kiln. A great deal of timber has been used to furnish the interior; the pillars have been made from old reclaimed pieces and there is an array of wooden beams. The restaurant circles the building and has been constructed on various levels. The large bay windows form alcoves here and there and it all hangs together well. The Ladybridge is open throughout the day and serves food at all times.

....

✗ (12pm to 10.30pm; Fri and Sat until 11pm) £2–13: prawn sundae, beef & Boddington's pie, seafood tagliatelle, gammon steak, Southseas kebab
Children: own menu
◖ Ale: Boddington's, Flowers, Marston's
Ⴒ Plenty

TAUNTON, SOMERSET   Map 2
Ⴒℝ **THE WHITE LODGE**
Tel: 01823 321 112
From Junction 25 of the M5 head into Taunton on the A358. The White Lodge is just off the main road – on the B3170 to Corfe.

....

Behind a white-painted façade with bay windows, there is an interesting stone building and you have to look hard to see that part of it is a modern extension; it's difficult to see the join.

On one side of this family pub and restaurant there is an attractive lawned garden with several trees, an abundance of shrubs and a small play unit for the children. On the far side of the car park there is a Travel Inn.

The very attractive interior includes an extensive bar with a beamed ceiling, some wood panelling, curved settles and a few bookshelves. It stretches down one side of the building and there is a nice low-ceilinged pubby area at one end.

The restaurant is a congenial spot. One of the dining rooms has wooden screens topped with coloured glass, several booths and wide windows on to the garden. There is also a conservatory room which overlooks the garden. The *pièce de résistance* is a superb high-ceilinged room with mouldings of green, blue and gold around the ceiling and a central rose with a chandelier.

The essential facilities for families are provided: high chairs and a baby-changing unit. The pub is open all day and the restaurant hours are shown below.

....

✗ (12pm to 2.30pm and 5pm to 10.30pm; weekends 12pm to 10.30pm) £2–13: Greek dip, three-bean feast, ocean bake, salmon fillet, sirloin Oscar
Children: own menu
ᗡ Ale: Boddington's, Flowers and guests
ℙ Own car park

Nr TELFORD, SHROPSHIRE

Map 4

P R MADEBROOK HOUSE

Tel: 01952 588 620

Off the A442 near Sutton Hill. Follow the signs for Iron Bridge Gorge.

This family pub and restaurant is nearer Ironbridge than the utilitarian 'new town' of Telford. The former town has a fine collection of museums which commemorates the industrial heritage of the area, and Madebrook House is only a stone's throw from these.

The cream-coloured building has a distinct Twenties look to it and was originally a farmhouse. It has been extended to accommodate a substantial restaurant, which is divided into three main areas, one of which overlooks the beautiful garden, with its fetching array of shrubs and flowers and immaculate lawn.

The other two eating areas are welcoming, with their cheerful décor, various prints on the walls and, with a nod to the area's industrial past, a good array of china plates on display. High chairs are available in numbers and there are two baby-changing facilities.

As well as the superb garden, there is a terrace at the front of the pub and, to one side, a children's play unit and a bouncy castle. Food is available throughout opening hours.

✘ (12pm to 10.30pm; Fri and Sat until 11pm) £2–13: pork satay, scampi, three-bean feast, seafood tagliatelle, steaks
Children: own menu
◑ Ale: Boddington's, Flowers, Marston's
℗ Ample

THURLESTONE, DEVON   Map 1
Ⓗ **THURLESTONE HOTEL**
Tel: 01548 560 382
In the centre of the village.

This has long been a favourite hotel of ours and on our various visits we have always found that the Grose family, who have owned and run this hotel since 1896, when Margaret Amelia Grose took a lease on the farmhouse, get most things right. When we last stayed we had a delightful room which overlooked the gardens and the sweep of Bigbury Bay, and we found the staff as friendly and efficient as always. The food was of excellent quality and cooked with skill.

All this makes a pretty good starting point for a family holiday. But in addition, this hotel, which is in one of the loveliest spots in south Devon, has wonderful facilities, including two hard tennis courts, two squash courts, a badminton court, a swimming pool and a play area with a climbing net, swings, a playhouse and a slide. The well-designed indoor pool has a paddling pool for very young children. There is also a fitness room. With table tennis and snooker, an excellent par-three course at the hotel and golf at Thurlestone and Bigbury, all aspiring superstars are catered for wonderfully well.

On a practical level, playpens are provided at both swimming pools and there is a well-equipped laundry room (washing and drying machines, ironing board and iron).

Good news for real ale fans: the baby-listening service extends to the hotel's pub next door.

Nearby: There are plenty of sandy beaches all along this stretch of coast, including one at Thurlestone. Inland, you can visit the National Shire Horse Centre and the Dartmoor Wildlife Centre, Buckfast Abbey and the adjacent Dart Valley Railway, and the castles at Compton and Totnes.

．．

✕ Light lunch (12.30pm to 2pm) £3–8: open sandwiches, smoked salmon, sirloin steak, beef Stroganoff;
Dinner (7.30pm to 9.30pm) £25: smoked salmon mousse, soup, medallions of pork loin, pudding and cheese
Children: own menu, half portions
£ High

✓ Best Bargain Break: £68 per person per night – dinner, b&b
Children: free up to 2 years; £15 to 12 years (includes breakfast and high tea)
Facilities: 6 cots and 6 high chairs; baby-listening lines to all rooms
Open all year (except for a week in Jan)
68 rooms, 15 family, 3 sets interconnecting

⌂ Ale: Bass, Palmer's, Wadworth's

🅿 Own car park

TIDEFORD, CORNWALL　　　　　　　　　　　Map 1
🆁 HESKYN MILL
Tel: 01752 851 481
By the A38 west of Saltash. Look for the sign and take the turning to St Germans.

．．

The old mill wheel is still attached to the wall of this beautiful stone building, and inside you can see the rest of the machinery on each floor. Downstairs, there is a small bar and under the low beams a nice mixture of wooden tables, sofas and settles and a wood-burning stove. The restaurant is up the open wooden staircase and is another delightful room, with a mix of differing wooden tables.

You will always find fresh Cornish fish on the menu; indeed, the owners try to use local sources for their food whenever possible.

There is a little terrace by the front door and lawns at the back where you can sit on warmer days.

....

✗ Lunch snack menu (12pm to 2pm) £3–12: fish soup, game pie, fish of the day, rack of lamb, fillet of salmon;
Dinner (7pm to 10pm) £18: baked aubergine, medallions of pork, pudding or cheese
Children: small portions
Closed Sun and Mon
⬭ Ale: St Austell
🅿 Own car park

TIVERTON, DEVON   **Map 1**
Ⓡ **KNIGHTSHAYES COURT**
Tel: 01884 254 665
Just off the A396 north of Tiverton.

....

All the confidence of the Victorian age went into the flamboyant style of this mansion, built in the 1870s to the design of the architect William Burges. The richly decorated interior has been restored and there are some notable paintings by Constable and Turner on display, as well as a Rembrandt self-portrait.

Knightshayes Court is the home of Lady Heathcoat Amory, formerly Joyce Wethered, who is reckoned to be the greatest of all lady golfers. One of the glories of the place is the gardens, which are immense and beautiful. The immaculate lawns, fine trees and arrays of flowers and shrubs make it interesting at any time of the year.

The restaurant was constructed in the old stable block, built in the same Gothic style as the main house, and the National Trust shop and a garden shop are also here. The restaurant is spacious and attractively designed; the two rooms have polished brick floors, stone walls with wood panelling and wooden tables, smartly painted red. You can get something to eat here throughout the day, while lunches are served from 12 till 2pm, and there are plenty of high chairs. Hot and cold meals are available.

The lavatories are roomy and the Ladies has a chair and plenty of space, alongside the washbasins, on which you can change a baby.

....

�еж £1–6: Devon pâté, fresh trout, ploughman's, cream teas
Children: half portions
Open Easter to 31 Oct; gardens 10.30am to 5pm; house 11 am to 5.30pm (4.30 in Oct); closed Fri
Ⓟ Ample

Nr TONBRIDGE, KENT   **Map 3**
ⓅⓇ **GATE INN, Hildenborough**
Tel: 01732 832 944
North-west of Tonbridge off the B245. The pub is next to Hildenborough railway station.

....

It is hard to believe that this warm and welcoming public house with its smart, predominantly wooden interior was once a fish and chip restaurant. It stands next to the station and overlooks a golf range and the farmland beyond. There is a delightful wooded garden with swings, springy cats and dogs, seesaws and a climbing frame. From the garden one walks into the family room with a small Charlie Chalk fun area and changing facilities where both mother and father can attend to a baby. The interior of the pub has recently been refurbished, and there are plans to develop a fun room for children.

The Gate Inn holds a children's licence so that children may go anywhere in the pub, but the area away from the main dining area is a smoking area for adults. There is both a children's menu and other options, while six high chairs are available.

....

✖ (11.30am to 10pm) £2–8: fish dippers, Teviotdale pie, turkey fillet, vegetable moussaka, chicken Balti

Children: own menu
ⓒ Ale: Boddington's, Flowers, Fremlin's
ⓟ Ample

TORMARTON, nr BADMINTON, AVON   Map 2
ⓟ COMPASS INN
Tel: 01454 218 242
Half a mile north from Junction 18 of the M4 – take the first right turn off the A46 going towards Stroud.

This fine old creeper-covered pub of 18th-century origin is in a useful spot – only a minute or so from the motorway. The main bar, with a good selection of real ale, leads down to the food bar. On from there is a huge glass-roofed orangery which is always pleasantly warm and bedecked with hanging plants. Children are welcome in the food bar or the orangery. A patio and a lawned garden offer pleasant spots to sit on summer days.

There is always a good display of food here, from the cold buffet to the daily specials, and it is served seven days a week. There is also an excellent vegetarian menu. The pub is open throughout the day and it is good to report that food is available at all times – from breakfast at 7.30 in the morning until 10.30 at night.

✗ (7.30am to 10.30pm) £2–7: fresh poached salmon, chicken curry, dressed crab, lasagne, ratatouille au gratin
Children: own menu, half portions
ⓒ Ale: Archer, Bass, Smiles
ⓟ Own car park

TORQUAY, DEVON   Map 1
Ⓗ CRAIG COURT HOTEL, 10 Ash Hill Road
Tel: 01803 294 400
Not far from the town centre and close to Castle Circus.

This well-maintained hotel is in a handsome Victorian building with spacious public rooms which include a comfortable lounge whose bay windows look out over the gardens, the town and the bay. There is a bar alongside. A secluded lawned garden sheltered by trees is a real sun trap, and you can enjoy panoramic views from the little terrace, shaded by a canopy, above the garden. Swings and a seesaw have been installed for the children.

The brightly decorated bedrooms have ample space and include two family rooms, one with a double and two single beds and the other with a double bed and bunk beds for two children. These have their own bathrooms, as have four of the other bedrooms.

The hotel faces south and is in a reasonably quiet road, yet it is within walking distance of the beaches, the main shopping centre and most of the attractions of the town. This comfortable and moderately priced hotel is a good base for a holiday in this part of the world, which has so much to offer to families.

Nearby: There is a host of things to do and see in this popular resort, with a wide selection of beaches – Blackpool Sands, Paignton, Anstey's Cove, Oddicombe Beach, Ness Cove, and Dawlish Warren, to name but a few. There are many other attractions for the holiday-maker: museums at Brixham, Torbay and Dartmouth; the Dart Valley railway; castles at Totnes and Compton; Buckfast Abbey; and the Dartmoor Wildlife Park and the National Shire Horse Centre near Plymouth.

✗ Dinner (6pm) £9: 4 course menu
   Children: own menu, half portions
   £ Low
✓ Best Bargain Break: £66 per person, 3 days – dinner, b&b
   Children: £3 up to 3 years; half price to 11 years; 25% off from 11 to 14 years

Facilities: 2 cots and 2 high chairs; baby intercom
10 rooms, 2 family
Open all year
No credit cards accepted
P Own car park

TREBARWITH STRAND, nr TINTAGEL, CORNWALL   Map 1
Ⓗ **OLD MILLFLOOR**
Tel: 01840 770 234
Off the B3263, south of Tintagel. Take the road to Trebarwith Strand.

Idyllic is the adjective which immediately springs to mind as, from the road above, you gaze down at this delightful 16th-century house with its leaded windows. It is set in ten acres in a little valley and the garden is appealing and peaceful. You can sit at the bench tables and look around you at the wooded slopes with their profusion of ferns and flowers, trees and trailing greenery. A small stream meanders through the garden and, when the rain comes, rushes through, so you must keep an eagle eye on your offspring.

Keep a wary eye on them too, and on where you place your own feet, when you approach the house, because the entrance can only be reached down a steepish gravel path and some steps. You must park your car in the spaces provided on the roadside.

The inside of the house lives up to its surroundings. The living room has four wooden dining tables and the sitting area is furnished with comfort and style; there are deep armchairs and a sofa on which to relax, and a beautiful old padded wooden settle. The three bedrooms, one of which is a family room, are lovely high-ceilinged rooms and are quiet and peaceful. The Old Millfloor is a no-smoking house.

This is definitely the place to 'get away from it all', and for a very reasonable price too.

Nearby: Down the road is the little beach of Trebarwith Strand, with Gull Rock rising impressively from the sea. You must exercise care on this beach as the rising tide can cut off the unwary. There are many alternatives nearby: for example, Crackington Haven, Harlyn Bay and Constantine Bay. There are superb walks along the coastal path. There are many attractions within easy reach, especially around Newquay: the zoo, the Lappa Valley Railway, Dairyland Farm Park and the lovely house at Trerice. The Tropical Bird Gardens at Padstow, Tintagel Castle, Pencarrow and Bodmin Moor are not too far away.

✖ Dinner (7pm to 8pm) £11
   Children: high teas
   £ Low
   Children: free if sharing with parents
   Facilities: 2 cots and a high chair
   3 rooms, 1 family
   Open Mar to Oct
Ⓟ Spaces on the road above

TRENT, nr SHERBORNE, DORSET   Map 2
Ⓟ **ROSE AND CROWN**
Tel: 01935 850 776
Four miles north-west of Sherborne off the B3148.

A couple of decades ago this was a farmhouse, built from two 15th-century stone cottages, which stands up a short drive in this delightful village. Anyone who enjoys real pubs will feel at home here, because the Rose and Crown has not been messed about by insensitive 'designers'. It has retained its simply decorated bar with a tiled floor, open fire, low ceilings and curved settles. The pub houses a collection of antique brass and copper cooking utensils.

To the right of the entrance, you will find a small family room, with a stone-flagged floor, a large fireplace and an early Victorian dresser. An alternative for families with older children is the attractive conservatory dining room. There is a varied choice of real ales to be had here, and some very interesting food, especially Creole and Cajun dishes from Louisiana, which was the landlady's home.

Outside, the skittle alley borders one side of the garden, with plenty of bench tables on the lawn, and there is a climbing frame for the children. There is a good display of flowers and you will have a lovely view over the hills of Blackmore Vale and the Elizabethan Compton House. The village church is only about fifty yards away. Both the church and Compton House were used as hiding places by Charles II when he was on the run from Cromwellian soldiers. The story is documented in Samuel Pepys' diaries.

It is agreeable to report that there is a total absence of music and games machines here – it's a very charming pub, and long may it remain so.

✗ (12pm to 2pm and 7pm to 9.30pm) £2–10: bouillabaisse, warm duck salad, barbecued chicken, Indonesian pork satay with peanut sauce, beef & Burgundy casserole
Children: own menu, small portions
⌒ Ale: Oakhill, Wadworth's and guests
ℙ Own car park

TRING, HERTS   **Map 5**
ℙℝ THE CROWS NEST
Tel: 01442 824 819
On the A41 between Tring and Aston Clinton.

This sturdy old pub has a steeply overhanging roof with dormer windows; an array of greenery and hanging baskets of flowers enliven the façade, and there is a small patio to one side with a few bench tables. Adjoining the Crows Nest is a Travel Inn.

The front of the pub belies the great amount of space inside. The pleasant bar has a plethora of wooden beams and pillars, and the windows are small and cottagey.

The back of the pub has been greatly extended to accommodate a very large restaurant. The Crows Nest motif has been liberally interpreted, and there is a ship's mast in the middle of the restaurant. It finishes with a skylight and there are oars and nets, and prints and photographs of nautical scenes. There is a lot of wooden panelling to be seen, a huge brick fireplace and twin skylights with ship's lanterns beneath.

It's all good fun but, if you like a good view while you dine, head for the conservatory at the back. You can see for miles and miles over rolling countryside towards Mentmore and beyond.

Immediately below there is a very large lawned garden and terrace. It's a lovely place to eat and drink on a sunny day. To one side another section of lawn includes a play unit, and an old rowing boat has also been placed here for the children.

....

✕ (Mon to Fri 12pm to 10.30pm; weekends until 11pm) £2–13: Greek dip, salmon fillet, three-bean feast, fillet steak, Indonesian chicken
Children: own menu

🍺 Ale: Boddington's, Flowers and guests

🅿 Own car park

TRURO, CORNWALL   Map 1
P **HERON INN, Malpas**
Tel: 01872 72773
Off the A30 from Truro.

....

Malpas is a little village set next to the estuary on the A30 leading out
of Truro. The Heron Inn is a long white and blue building by the side
of the road with a splendid outlook over the yacht basin and to the hills
above the estuary. On a sunny day you may eat or drink either on the
flagstoned raised terrace that fronts the pub or on a strip of public land
immediately across the road from the pub itself which looks directly
down the estuary.

Although children are allowed in all areas of the pub, to the left of
the entrance there is a small dining area surrounding a large stone-built
fireplace, alongside which there is a small separated area containing
electronic games and a pool table. The main bar is a long room which,
once again, has a large stone-built fireplace at one end. It has velvet bench
seating at either side with chairs and tables in rows adjacent to these. It
is a fairly modern beam-ceilinged pub with plenty of brass, plates and
bric-à-brac which enhances its country feel.

....

✗ (12pm to 2pm and 7pm to 9pm) £2–8: range of hot and
   cold dishes
   Children: own menu
◷ Ale: Tinners
P Own car park

TRURO, CORNWALL   Map 1
P **WILLIAM IV**
Tel: 01872 73334
In the town centre.

....

A hundred yards up from the main square, this cream and red
Victorian-style building is unmissable. It has a small car park at

the rear but the entrance is extremely narrow and easily missed! The Victorian theme continues inside with a large oval bar area in the centre of a large room. There are two raised seated areas at the front corners of the pub and one to the rear, next to which is a games area with various machines and a pool table.

This pub was built over the foundations of a 15th-century monastery and it is said that the ghost of a hooded monk is still in residence.

Families are welcome to use the food bar and the modern conservatory. With its tiled floor, comfortably padded wood furniture, wooden panelling, wrought-iron railing and greenery, it is an extremely pleasant place on a sunny day.

Beyond the conservatory, there is a small flagstoned patio area which has a terraced grassed picnic area alongside. These two areas are enclosed and are safe places for children to sit or play. There are wrought-iron tables and chairs, picnic tables and benches in abundance, and the many varieties of plants provide a garden setting right in the middle of the town.

....

✗ (11.30am to 2.30pm) £2–5: chicken goujons, scampi, vegetable pasta, burgers, omelettes
   Children: half portions
🍺 Ale: Tinners
🅿 Own car park

TUNBRIDGE WELLS, KENT   **Map 3**
🅿🆁 **THE OLD WEST STATION**
Tel: 01892 545 949
One and a half miles from the centre of town. Go south on the A26, past the Pantiles. There is a sign for a superstore and the pub is next to Sainsbury's.

....

The Old West Station is exactly what it says, a former railway station which, until the days of Dr Beeching, served the west of the town. It is now a delightful pub/restaurant which retains all the decoration and mementoes of the age of the steam train. There is the ticket office, a carriage which is part of the dining area, the old waiting room and the station master's office. The old buffet is now a long, attractive bar which maintains the railway-station theme. It is a place of fascination which is exciting to explore, with its reminders of past fares and once-frequent trains.

Children are not allowed in the bar, but they are welcome everywhere else, and they have their own special waiting room. One of the old waiting rooms is a family dining area, and there are baby-changing facilities and provision for the disabled.

Bar food is served whenever the pub is open, which is 10am to 11pm, and early-morning coffee has become very popular. The restaurant is open all day on Saturdays, and there are special menus for children as well as half portions. Five high chairs are available.

A long, charming veranda (once the platform) overlooks the car park, and it has a 'Palm Court' air. At present, there is no garden, but plans are in hand to develop a garden area in the near future.

The whole place has a delightful aura of times past.

....

✕ (12pm to 2.30pm and 5pm to 10.30pm; weekends 12pm to 10.30pm) £2–13: prawn sundae, sirloin steak, Indonesian chicken, seafood tagliatelle, three-bean feast
Children: own menu

🍺 Ale: Boddington's, Flowers, Fremlin's
🅿 Own car park

TWYFORD, BERKS   Map 5
🅿🆁 HORSE AND GROOM
Tel: 01734 403 136
On the A4 between Maidenhead and Reading (opposite Kennedy's Garden Centre).

This is a charming pub, several centuries old. Long and low-slung, with a steep and uneven roof with dormer windows, its façade is enlivened by climbing roses and many hanging baskets of flowers. The main bar is in the original building and advertises its great age with ancient pillars and beams and a nice marble and tile fireplace.

The lounge leads through to the restaurant, which is housed in an extension and is massive. One of the rooms has a high wooden ceiling, brick walls and wood panelling, and the main dining area is in much the same style. There are prints and copper artefacts on the walls, wood and glass screens and colourful lamps.

Families are very much to the fore here, and high chairs and a baby-changing facility are made available.

The garden at the rear is a pleasant spot, with shady trees on the lawns and several bench tables. There is a children's play area too.

....

✗ (12pm to 2.30pm and 5pm to 10.30pm; weekends 12pm to 10.30pm) £2–13: Greek dip, ocean bake, Indonesian chicken, peppered steak, seafood tagliatelle
  Children: own menu
Ⓒ Ale: Boddington's, Brakspear's
Ⓟ Own car park

TWYNING GREEN, nr TEWKESBURY, GLOS   Map 4
Ⓟ **VILLAGE INN**
Tel: 01684 293 500
Off the A38 three and a half miles north of Tewkesbury.

....

Once upon a time, when they played cricket on the village green, you could have sat in the shade of the huge plane tree – because in those days of fond memories the summer sun always shone brightly – and cooled the inner man with a few glasses of beer from this pub a few yards away. A handsome pub indeed, long and low and painted cream, and with dormer windows in the steep roof. In the 17th century it was three cottages, one of which was a bakery, and it has an agreeable interior with low ceilings and wooden beams.

The family room is at the back of the bar, is painted cream, and has highly polished tables and bucket seats; just beyond is the skittle alley, which is buffed like the sheen on a guardsman's boots. Outside, a vine-covered arbour (with a barbecue at one end) overlooks a beautifully kept lawned garden, which is enclosed, and has a rocking horse, some other toys for young children, and bench tables. This is a pub of great charm, which suits the attractive village well.

....

✗ (12pm to 2pm and 7pm to 9.30pm) £2–5: plaice & chips, pie, beef provençale, pork & chicken curry, Twyning sausages
  Children: half portions

� Ale: Boddington's, Flowers and guests
P Own car park

Nr WARRINGTON, CHESHIRE   Map 8
P R THE HOLLOW TREE, Stretton
Tel: 01925 730 733
Adjacent to Junction 10 of the M53 at Stretton. It is signposted from the A49.

The building is a classic 18th-century country house on three storeys, and the extension at the back fits in well. There is masses of space here, especially in the extensive garden, which is a delight with its well-maintained lawns and lovely mature trees. Bench tables with parasols are scattered about, and there is an excellent play area for the children.

The main bar area is housed in the original building and is a splendid place to linger over a drink or a meal. You can sit by one of the large windows and admire the views, and you would not know that the motorway is so close. There are alcoves here and there with comfortable chairs and padded benches, some wood panelling, lots of prints on the walls and shelves with china and pewter arranged on them.

The very large restaurant is broken up into a number of different areas. A dresser acts as a partition for one dining room which has a brick fireplace, and there are other small rooms, including one under a sloping wooden roof. A small-scale carousel is a focal point for the restaurant, and the no-smoking family dining areas are at one end. There are padded settles and brick fireplaces and the larger room has lots of toys on high shelves, and hung from the rafters of the tall ceiling. A representation of a Ferris wheel will also amuse the children. There is an indoor play area here with a ball swamp and other equipment.

Nappy-changing facilities and several high chairs are available. The Hollow Tree is a well-equipped and welcoming family pub and restaurant in a delightful location.

✗ (12pm to 2.30pm and 5.30pm to 10pm; weekends 12pm to 10pm)
£2–9: moules marinières, Cajun chicken, steak & kidney pudding,
seafood pie, peppered steak
Children: own menu
◊ Ale: Theakston's
▣ Ample

Nr WARRINGTON, CHESHIRE   Map 8
▣▣ LITTLE MANOR, Thelwall
Tel: 01925 261 703
*Off the A50 to the east of Warrington. Take the road into Thelwall
village.*

....

As you enter the grounds of the Little Manor you will see a parade
of towering trees and a stretch of immaculate lawn encircled by banks
of shrubbery. It is a suitable setting for this stately 18th-century
country house, a delightful, low-slung building with bay windows and
a conservatory at one side.

The owners are making a play for the family market with the provision
of high chairs in the restaurant and a sizeable play area which has been
placed in what was probably once the coach house.

Inside there is plenty of space, and the restaurant, smartly decorated
with a pale and flowery Laura Ashley-style wallpaper, occupies one end
of the building. There is a glass roof at one side of the dining room,
and wooden panelling on the lower walls.

There is a comfortable lounge between the restaurant and the bar,
which is huge and contains a variety of easy chairs and an expanse
of padded benches along the walls. A stately carved wooden fireplace
dominates one wall and there is also a conservatory room.

....

✗ (12pm to 2.30pm and 5.30pm to 10.30pm; weekends 12pm to
10pm) £2–5: cheesy chips, Cumberland sausage, garlic & herb
chicken, steak & kidney pie, mushroom & Stilton bake
Children: own menu

Ⓓ Ale: Boddington's, Flowers
Ⓟ Own car park

WATERGATE BAY, CORNWALL   Map 1
Ⓗ WATERGATE BAY HOTEL
Tel: 01637 860 543
On the B3276 north of Newquay.

....

This self-contained family hotel is not too far away from the busy resort of Newquay. Not that you need venture there, since there are loads of facilities at the hotel itself, including a sandy beach, part of which actually belongs to the hotel. The coastal footpath runs close by.

The garden has swings, sandpits, a junior 'assault course' and a trampoline, and many activities are organized for the children here and on the beach. In addition, there are Punch and Judy shows, fancy dress parties, swimming galas, table tennis and other sporting competitions, and conjurors every week. Adults have dancing and entertainments most evenings.

Indoors, there is a spacious play room for young children with plenty of toys and games, a slide and a pirate ship; this is supervised. Alongside, there is a pool table for older children. The snooker room is confined to adults or children supervised by adults. In addition, there is a tennis court, and a separate sports hall which has skittle alleys, a fitness room, a squash court and a court on which to play badminton, short tennis, etc adjoins the hotel. There is a putting green on one of the terraces which overlooks the bay and loads of room for families to relax, including a lounge or quiet room for adults only.

The Coffee Shop (open from 10am to 6pm) offers a good range of snacks and dishes of the day. It overlooks the outdoor swimming pool and paddling pool, and alongside it is a small indoor pool.

Nearby: Newquay itself is a busy and lively resort and, apart from Watergate Bay, there are many safe, sandy beaches in the near vicinity. There are many places to visit. Children will certainly be interested in the zoo, which has a large play area and a leisure centre attached to it, with swimming pools, squash and tennis courts and a golf driving range. There is a leisure park at St Agnes, a farm park (Dairyland) near Newquay and a World in Miniature at Goonhavern, five miles from Newquay. Add the Lappa Valley Railway and the Elizabethan manor house at Trerice, and there is something for everyone.

....

✖ Coffee shop (10am to 6pm) £1–4: soup, salads, ploughman's, hot dish of the day, filled baked potatoes;
Dinner (7pm to 8.30pm) £15: smoked mackerel pâté, roast leg of lamb, pudding and cheese
Children: own menu, half portions
£ Low

✓ Best Bargain Break: £27 per person per night – dinner, b&b
Children: free at certain times; 25% of adult rate up to 3 years; 50% from 4 to 7 years; 66% from 8 to 10; 75% from 11 to 14
Facilities: as many cots and high chairs as required; baby-listening system to every room
57 rooms, 27 family, 17 sets interconnecting
Open Mar to Nov

◷ Ale: local brew

ℙ Ample

_____

WELLS, SOMERSET   **Map 2**
Ⓡ **CLOISTER RESTAURANT**
Tel: 01749 676 543
In the cathedral cloisters alongside the book shop.

....

Calm and contentment should pervade your soul as you sit in this restaurant which is situated on one side of the cathedral cloisters. The arched roof is beautifully traced in carved stone, and through the mullioned windows, also framed with carved stone, you can see the cathedral, which is one of the great glories of church architecture.

The room is long and narrow, and the double row of plain wooden tables, overlooked by memorial plaques on the walls, maintains the ecclesiastical air.

The food concentrates on salads, snacks and hot dishes of the day, and there is always a good choice of cakes and pastries. It is all reasonably priced, and the profits go to the cathedral – so dive in.

The toilet block includes space for changing babies; there is a pull-down shelf and paper towels are provided.

....

✕ (10am to 5pm; Sun 2pm to 5pm) £2–4: jacket potatoes, quiches, salads, hot dishes of the day
   Children: smaller portions
   Closed for 2 weeks at Christmas
   No credit cards accepted
ⓅP Public car park

WELLS, SOMERSET   Map 2
Ⓡ THE GOOD EARTH, 4 Priory Road
Tel: 01749 678 600
On the A371 west of the cathedral, a few hundred yards from the High Street.

....

When you have uplifted your soul by gazing at the magnificent cathedral in this lovely town, attend to the inner self at this attractive wholefood restaurant. It is based in a series of bright and airy rooms with pine floors and solid oak tables and benches. You can also eat in a little paved courtyard with barrel tables and chairs.

There's a pleasing ambience to this restaurant, and the prices are very pleasing too – a substantial three-course meal will set you back around £5. A baby can be changed in the Ladies, where there is a table, and paper towels are supplied.

The wholefood store which is a part of the Good Earth has a full range of unrefined foods: newly baked bread, stoneground flour, local cheeses, free-range eggs, sugar-free jams and so on.

....

✕ (9.30am to 5.30pm, Mon to Sat) £1–3: soups, pizza, jacket potato
with cheese, dish of the day (e.g. mushroom & cashew nut pie, or
cauliflower cheese), salads
Children: own menu, half portions
🅿 Pay & display

Nr WELLS, SOMERSET Map 2
⊞ GLENCOT HOUSE, Glencot Lane, Wookey Hole
Tel: 01749 677 160
*North-west of Wells off the A371. Follow the signs for Wookey Hole. The
hotel is signposted.*

Glencot House is a stylish Victorian mansion in a splendid location
in 18 acres of gardens and parkland alongside the River Axe. There is
plenty of space for children to play and for adults to relax. It is a quiet
and peaceful place.

The building has been faithfully restored during the last few years
and the interior decorated and furnished with great care. There is lovely
oak panelling throughout the house and fine views through the large
mullioned windows. The library is a comfortable and quiet room and the
spacious lounge has an unusual patterned wood ceiling; the bay windows
overlook the gardens and the river, and there is a vast inglenook fireplace
which can seat six people with ease. A charming little bar with a veranda,
and a stately dining room, oak panelled and with a splendid chandelier,
complete the picture. Antique pieces abound and some discretion must
be exercised by younger children. The bedrooms have been furnished
and decorated in varying styles and to very high standards, and many
of them have idyllic views across the gardens to the water. Plenty of
space is provided for guests and especially so in the family rooms.

The extensive gardens are a delight, and guests can fish for trout in
the river and play croquet on the lawn. Indoors, there is a small plunge
pool and a sauna, a full-size snooker table and table tennis.

Glencot House is an outstanding hotel in a superb location, where
families are made very welcome.

Nearby: The charming city of Wells with its great cathedral is just over a mile away, and the famous Wookey Hole Caves are just down the road. The Mendips offer superb walks and you can take in both Cheddar Gorge and Ebbor Gorge. The nature reserve at the Chew Valley Lake is of great interest, as are the Tropical Bird Gardens north of Frome. Nunney Castle, the Fleet Air Arm Museum, Montacute House, Ham Hill Country Park, Cricket St Thomas Wildlife Park and the cities of Bath and Bristol are all within easy reach.

....

✕ Dinner (6.30pm to 8.45pm) £19: tomato & Stilton tart, peppered sirloin steak, pudding
   Children: own menu, half portions
   £ Medium
✓ Best Bargain Break: £80 per person, 2 nights – dinner, b&b
   Children: cots free; extra bed £10
   Facilities: 2 cots and 2 high chairs; baby-listening
   12 rooms, 2 family, 1 set interconnecting
   Open all year
Ⓟ Own car park

_____

WEST ANSTEY, YEO MILL, nr SOUTH MOLTON, DEVON   Map 1

Ⓗ **PARTRIDGE ARMS FARM**
Tel: 01398 341 217
Off the B3227 east of South Molton.

....

Once a coaching inn, where the last pint was served in 1905, the farm has been in the same family since the early years of this century. It now consists of 200 acres, and sits on the southern slopes of Exmoor. The charming building dates back to the 14th century and has rough-cast walls, painted pale pink, with honeysuckle climbing over them, and the lawned gardens sport several apple trees and a lily pond.

The cosy sitting room has comfortable chairs and a sofa, a large stone fireplace with a wood-burning stove, and paintings of wildlife and hunting scenes adorn the walls. There are no fewer than three charming dining rooms: one has a huge open fireplace decorated with old farm implements and cider jars and the low ceiling is cross-hatched with wooden beams; the next room has another open fireplace and a long wooden table; and the third dining room also contains a small bar, which has been kept as it was in the 19th century.

Everything overlooks the encircling farm land and guests are welcome to wander around among the cows, sheep, geese, dogs, cats and ponies. The farm, by the way, has its own stretch of trout fishing.

All of the bedrooms are pleasing. One has a four-poster, one double bedroom has a separate room with bunk beds, and there is a family room with a double bed and two bunk beds. Most of the rooms have their own bathrooms.

Partridge Arms Farm is run entirely by the Milton family and is a most appealing and welcoming place to stay in the heart of the Devon countryside.

Nearby: You are not too far from the north Devon and Somerset coastal resorts, including Woolacombe Sands and Croyde Bay. The whole of Exmoor is also at your feet – lovely for nature lovers, walkers, and pony trekkers. There is much else for the holiday maker within easy reach: the nature reserve at Braunton Burrows and the Exmoor Bird Gardens; the Maritime Museum at Appledore; Arlington Court; the Dartington Glass factory; Watermouth Castle and the Combat Vehicles Museum near South Molton.

✕ Dinner (7.30pm) £8
  Children: own menu, half portions
  £ Low
  Children: nominal charge up to 5 years; then according to age
  Facilities: 2 cots and 2 high chairs
  7 rooms, 2 family, 1 set interconnecting
  Open all year

No credit cards accepted
🅿 Ample

WEST BEXINGTON, nr DORCHESTER, DORSET Map 2
Ⓗ **MANOR HOTEL**
Tel: 01308 897 616
Signposted off the B3157 coastal road between Bridport and Weymouth.

....

This 16th-century stone manor house has a marvellous position in a small village in the lee of rolling downland overlooking Chesil Beach and Lyme Bay – popular for fishing but dangerous for swimming. There is safe swimming to be had at Weymouth's sandy beach, which is also patrolled by lifeguards during the summer season. Rowing and motor boats can be hired, and there are traditional children's attractions such as Punch and Judy shows and a children's beach club.

The hotel's interior is handsome, with its Jacobean panelling and flagstone floors, and the owner, a racing fan, has a multitude of paintings and prints of the sport of kings on the walls.

The appealing restaurant, with large windows overlooking the terrace and gardens, has a huge inglenook fireplace decorated with horse brasses and copper kettles and pans. There are two very comfortable lounges with fine views.

On the floor below you will find a splendid bar; it has a real pubby feel to it with its wooden tables, recessed window seats, whitewashed walls, beamed ceiling and horse brasses and harness. Up some steps is a large conservatory that can be used by families; it opens on to a lawned garden with bench tables. The bar always has a good choice of real ales.

We looked at several bedrooms, all decorated and furnished in fine style; a family room (with a double and a single bed) at the top of the house is particularly attractive with its sloping ceilings and terrific views.

The gardens include a lawned area in front of the hotel with bench tables, and a bigger stretch, overlooking the sea in the distance, which has a children's play unit.

418

Nearby: You are on the verge of the lovely Dorset countryside, made famous by Thomas Hardy. His cottage can be seen near Dorchester. The Tutankhamun Exhibition is near there too, as is Athelhampton, the Tank Museum at Bovington Camp, T. E. Lawrence's cottage (Clouds Hill) and Maiden Castle. Nature lovers will head for Abbotsbury, with its famous swannery, and the Sea Life Centre at Weymouth.

✕ Bar snacks (12pm to 2pm and 6.30pm to 10pm) £4–13: crab pancake, liver & bacon, Dover sole, game pie, rack of lamb;
Lunch (12pm to 2pm) £15: crab & prawn salad, chicken supreme, pudding;
Dinner (7pm to 10pm) £20: moules marinières, roast rack of lamb, pudding or cheese
Children: own menu, half portions
£ High

✓ Best Bargain Break: £113 per person, 2 nights – dinner, b&b
Children: half price for under-10s
Facilities: 5 cots and 5 high chairs; baby-listening system
13 rooms, 1 family
Open all year

◯ Ale: Wadworth's, Palmer's, Eldridge Pope

ℙ Own car park

WEST BRIDGFORD, nr NOTTINGHAM · Map 7
ℙℝ **THE WOLDS**
Tel: 0115 981 0050
On the A60 in the centre of West Bridgford.

This is a substantial building built of red brick, its main entrance flanked by two large bay windows. A stone terrace with picnic benches and parasols runs along the front of the pub.

The bar area stretches across the front of the pub. It has oak beams and wooden floors and the general theme is hunting and drinking;

mugs and flagons of all shapes and sizes adorn the walls and ceiling. To the right of the entrance is the main family room, and a separate raised area occupies one of the massive bay windows that are a feature of this pub. This is duplicated at the other end of the building and a long bar stretches between.

The restaurant is at the rear and has another massive semicircular bay window. Farmhouse-style tables and chairs are complemented by a pair of comfortable leather wing-backed armchairs which are positioned in front of a stone fireplace. There is a musical theme in this room; 78-rpm records and musical instruments decorate the wood-beamed ceiling. To the right of this bar is the main dining area, a long room on various levels. It is light and airy and decorated with a plethora of Tiffany glass lamps and windows.

At the rear of the pub there is an enclosed grassed garden area with many bench tables. Plenty of high chairs are provided, plus baby-changing facilities, and food is served throughout the day.

....

✕ (11am to 11pm; Wed and Sun until 9pm) £2–13: steaks, rack of ribs, Cajun salmon, plaice & chips, chicken Provençale
   Children: own menu, half portions
◐ Ale: Greenall's, Shipstones, Tetley's and guests
🅿 Own car park

WEST BUCKLAND, nr BARNSTAPLE, DEVON   Map 1
Ⓗ HUXTABLE FARM
Tel: 01598 760 254
Off the A361 east of Barnstaple. The farm entrance is opposite West Buckland School.

....

This is a delightful listed building which dates back to the 16th century, a Devon longhouse built of stone and with climbing jasmine over the walls. The house has been restored with care by the owners, and antique furniture complements the original features. The sitting room has fine proportions and looks on to an enclosed garden; it is a comfortable and very inviting room with a wood-burning stove and some pleasing corner cupboards. There are games and a good selection of books. Across the corridor, with its ancient black beams and screen panelling, there is a splendid dining room which has a large open fireplace with a stove, a dresser and a lovely wooden table around which the guests gather to enjoy Jackie Payne's excellent food (and home-made wine). The extensive gardens provide most of the produce used in the house. Children have their own small dining room for breakfast and high teas.

There is a games room in the garden, with table tennis and darts, and a quarter-size snooker table and lots of toys. There is loads of room for children to play, and swings, slides, a sandpit, Wendy House and see-saw are set up in the garden. Sheep are reared on the 80 acres of farmland and children are welcome to help to feed the pet lambs, rabbits, chickens and pygmy goats.

The bedrooms are furnished and decorated to a very high standard and are full of character, with views over the tranquil gardens and encircling countryside. The family rooms are very spacious, especially a secluded one on one side of the house which has a double and two single beds and a bathroom. The two bedrooms in the converted barn also have loads of space. A laundry room is available.

This welcoming and well-equipped farmhouse offers an excellent base for a family holiday.

Nearby: The coastal resorts of north Devon are fairly close and there are some excellent beaches to visit, especially at Woolacombe and Croyde Bay. The natural splendours of Exmoor are close and the Exmoor Centre near Dulverton is a good starting point for walks. The Tarka Trail runs past the entrance to the farm. There is much else to see: Braunton Burrows, one of the largest nature reserves in Britain; Arlington Court; Watermouth Castle; Exmoor Bird Gardens; the Maritime Museum at Appledore; Dunster Castle, Combe Sydenham Hall and Rosemoor Royal Horticultural Garden.

✗ Dinner (7.30pm) £12: herb & liver pâté, lamb korma, pudding and cheese

Children: own menu
£ Low
Children: cot £6; extra bed £9
Facilities: 2 cots and 2 high chairs, baby alarms provided
6 rooms, 2 family
Open all year except Christmas
Unlicensed
P Ample

WEST HUNTSPILL, SOMERSET   Map 2
P CROSSWAYS INN
Tel: 01278 783 756
On the A38 just south of Highbridge.

This pub is not very far from the M5 between Bridgwater and Burnham-on-Sea (Junction 22 or 23). Built in the 17th century, it is quite a large place and looks very smart with the lower half of the façade painted white and a tiled upper half. Inside, there are several rooms around the bar which have their fair share of wooden beams, exposed brickwork, wooden tables and settles. There is an open fireplace with a stove at one end of the main bar and an alcove with wooden settles formed into booths.

Families are welcome in a high-ceilinged room with plenty of tables and chairs, and a skittle alley at one end. Several high chairs are available.

For warm days, there is a little patio by the entrance as well as a quite large enclosed grassy garden with fruit trees and plenty of bench tables.

The pub has three bedrooms, two of which are family rooms with bathrooms. The cost is a very reasonable £34 per room.

✕ (12pm to 2.30pm and 6.30pm to 10pm) £2–10: whitebait, sirloin steak, vegetable bake, beef & mushroom pie
Children: own menu, half portions

Ⓓ Ale: Eldridge Pope, Flowers, Smiles and guests
Ⓟ Own car park

WEST RUNTON, nr CROMER, NORFOLK   Map 6
Ⓗ LINKS COUNTRY PARK HOTEL
Tel: 01263 838 383
West of Cromer on the A149. The hotel is close to the railway station.

The Links Hotel has a commanding position in West Runton. It stands halfway up a gentle hill leading to the Shire Horse Centre and looks away to the surrounding countryside. Some two miles from the attractive seaside town of Cromer, the hotel has a delightful sandy beach within a few hundred yards.

The local shellfish is one of the hotel's specialities and it has other attractions, including its own nine-hole golf course, an all-weather tennis court, a heated indoor swimming pool and other leisure facilities.

The Links Hotel dates from the time of Queen Victoria, but while retaining the quiet calm and relaxing atmosphere of that era, it offers all the comforts and luxuries of the 1990s. Indeed, an aura of calm greets you on entering the hotel, for there is a large lounge with armchairs and couches where you may drink tea or something stronger. There is an attractive bar, and the two rooms of the restaurant maintain the air of calm and relaxation with their turquoise-coloured walls and subtle lighting. Three high chairs are available, and there is a children's menu as well as half portions.

Lunch is not served in the restaurant, but is available in the Grill Room, known as the Fairways Bar, which is adjacent to the hotel; it looks over the golf course.

The hotel has forty rooms, and ten of these are the garden rooms, set around a garden area where children may play. There are six sets of interconnecting rooms in the main hotel, and three family rooms, as well as fourteen rooms which can be used as family rooms. The bedrooms are comfortable and elegant and maintain the calm and relaxing atmosphere.

Nearby: No doubt the children will want to visit the Shire Horse Centre, and there are many other attractions, including Felbrigg Hall, Blickling Hall and the North Norfolk Railway. The beaches are plentiful and the wildlife fascinating. This area of Norfolk has many fine golf courses: Sheringham, Brancaster and Hunstanton especially.

....

✕ Lunch (12pm to 2.30pm) £2–7: fried scampi, sirloin steak, vegetable lasagne, turkey schnitzel, burger;
Dinner (7.30pm to 9.30pm) £19: avocado & crab salad, braised rib of beef, pudding or cheese
Children: own menu, half portions
£ High

✓ Best Bargain Break: £119 per person, 2 nights – dinner, b&b
Children: free up to 16 years
Facilities: 4 cots and 3 high chairs; baby-listening on several lines
40 rooms, 3 family, 6 sets interconnecting
Open all year

🍺 Ale: Adnams, Webster's

🅿 Own car park

Nr WESTERHAM, KENT   **Map 3**
🅿🅁 **SPINNING WHEEL**
Tel: 01959 72622
On the A233 towards Biggin Hill.

....

This modern, low-slung brick pub sits just outside Westerham and offers a fine array of facilities for families. There is a very large no-smoking family dining room which has a play area with blackboards and toys and a Postman Pat van. The pub provides food throughout the day until 10 o'clock, and has several high chairs and a nappy-changing facility.

The family room leads out to an enclosed garden with many bench tables and a children's play unit, made of wood and placed on a safe bark surface.

There is a great feeling of space and light in the rest of the pub, where the emphasis is on comfort and a cheerful décor. Good wooden tables and comfortable padded benches and chairs, a richly patterned carpet, wood panelling and stained-glass skylights, and mullioned windows all add up to a welcoming interior. The large scale of the pub is tempered by dividing it into different rooms, with alcoves set here and there.

....

✗ (11.30am to 10pm; Sun from 12pm) £2–8: hot mushrooms, gammon steak, fish pie, chicken escalopes, tagliatelle carbonara
  Children: own menu
◐ Ale: Boddington's, Flowers
𝖯 Own car park

Nr WESTON-SUPER-MARE, SOMERSET   Map 2
Ⓗ PURN HOUSE FARM, **Bleadon**
Tel: 01934 812 324
Off the A370 south of Weston-super-Mare. Turn opposite the Anchor Inn at Bleadon. (The owners suggest leaving the M5 at Junction 22 to avoid heavy traffic around Weston-super-Mare.)

....

Weston-super-Mare is a busy place, but you will find peace and quiet at this handsome, creeper-clad 17th-century farmhouse situated at the foot of Purn Hill at the western end of the Mendips. There are splendid views of the surrounding countryside and across to the Bristol Channel.

There are excellent facilities for families, including four family-sized rooms, high chairs and cots. The bedrooms have plenty of space, especially the four family rooms, which have double beds and either one or two single beds for the children. The family room on the top floor under the eaves is charming, and there is a family suite on the ground floor which has a double bed and a second bedroom through an archway which can accommodate either a single bed or bunk beds.

Much of the food served by the friendly owner is grown on the farm's 700 acres, and visitors are welcome to walk around and watch the various farming activities. Children must of course be supervised. There is a games room (The Cave) with pool, table tennis, darts and board games, and there are plenty of books and information about the locality.

The large lawn is encircled by a drive and there is a rockery and a small garden pond. You can sit in the sun in a secluded walled area and even have a picnic there, perhaps in the shade of the ancient weeping ash tree.

Nearby: There is plenty to do and see in the area. Guests can fish in the River Axe which flows through the grounds of the farm, and trout fishing can be had at Chew Valley and Blagdon Lakes; riding and pony trekking can be arranged at local riding schools. Nearby attractions include Cheddar Gorge, Wookey Hole Caves, Wells and Glastonbury, and the East Somerset Railway near Shepton Mallet. There are plenty of sandy beaches within easy reach: at Uphill, Burnham and Berrow, for example.

✗ Dinner (6.30pm) £7
  Children: half portions
  £ Low
  Children: half price under 3 years; two thirds price 3 to 11 years
  Facilities: 2 cots and 2 high chairs; baby-listening system
  6 rooms, 4 family
  Open all year except Christmas
  No credit cards accepted
  Unlicensed
Ⓟ Own car park

Nr WESTON-SUPER-MARE, SOMERSET   Map 2
P THE FULL QUART, Hewish
Tel: 01934 833 077

Two miles from Junction 21 of the M5, on the A370 towards Bristol.

....

The pub is housed in a long, low, white-painted building set back from the side of the A370. You enter into a small, low-ceilinged bar, with fireplaces at both ends.

To the right of the main bar is the family room, with tapestries on the wall, and furnished with padded wooden settles, stools and small tables.

Passing back through the main bar area, you enter a larger seating area which is dominated by a huge stone-built, kiln-shaped fireplace. Padded settles hug the walls, together with wooden tables and chairs. Large hand-carved beams are a notable feature and these, as well as the walls, are festooned with equine bric-à-brac, with the odd pistol or old rifle dotted here and there.

Adjacent to this area is another large seating area, behind which is the main restaurant (which is for non-smokers only) where families are very welcome. There is also a small balcony area in this section where families may enjoy a quiet drink.

Leading out from the restaurant area, and adjacent to the car park, is a patio with many bench tables. To the right there is an enclosed children's play area with swings, slides and climbing frames. Alongside is an enclosed adventure/commando-type trail – just the place for children to play in order to ensure a quiet journey home! A grandstand view of a Great Western Railway main line can be had from the back of the pub.

The pub is open all day from Monday to Saturday.

....

✗ (12pm to 2pm and 6pm to 10pm; Sun from 7pm) £2–9: whitebait, chilli con carne, steaks, gigot of lamb, hazelnut & mushroom pie
 Children: own menu

◌ Ale: Bass, Butcombe's, Flowers, Royal Oak

P Plenty

Nr WESTON-SUPER-MARE, SOMERSET Map 2
P R HOBBS BOAT, **Bridgewater Road, Lympsham**
Tel: 01934 812 782
On the A370, three miles south of Weston-super-Mare.

When we visited the Hobbs Boat one sunny lunchtime, the garden was packed with children enjoying the adventure playground and the bouncy castle, while the adults looked on and enjoyed their food and drinks.

The large indoor playroom was just as popular and it has an array of things for children to crawl on or under, to ride on and fall on, including a ball swamp. Alongside there is the family eating area (no-smoking) and there are several high chairs and a nappy-changing facility.

The pub is divided up into alcoves and rooms on different levels and this masks its size. Smart wallpaper, richly coloured carpets, wooden furniture and padded benches and chairs make this a comfortable and appealing pub/restaurant with excellent family amenities.

✗ (11.30am to 10pm) £2–8: fish dippers, steak & kidney pie, sirloin steak, chicken escalopes, fillet of salmon
   Children: own menu, half portions
Ͻ Ale: Bass, Boddington's, Flowers
P Own car park

WESTONBIRT, nr TETBURY, GLOS Map 4
H HARE AND HOUNDS HOTEL
Tel: 01666 880 233
On the A433 south-west of Tetbury.

The gardens of this attractive Cotswold stone building, part of which started off as a farmhouse in the early 19th century, are a major attraction: ten acres of delightful gardens, with wide and smooth lawns, beautifully kept flower beds and hedgerows, and grand mature trees. There is also a shady walled garden outside the bar, with several bench tables.

Other facilities include two hard tennis courts, a croquet lawn, a squash court, table tennis and snooker; and down the road is the famous Westonbirt Arboretum, which is open every day of the year.

A full range of meals can be found here, and there is a small area off the main bar where families can park themselves, as well as in the lounge areas. The three-course Sunday lunch offers pretty good value.

Nearby: The Arboretum is very close to the hotel and there is a variety of places to visit within a reasonable radius: Berkeley Castle, the Wildfowl Trust at Slimbridge, Lydeard Country Park, Corsham Court and Sheldon Manor. The Cotswold Water Park provides all sorts of water sports and has a nature reserve and an adventure playground.

....

✖ Bar snacks (12pm to 2.30pm and 7.30pm to 9.30pm) £2–10: smoked trout, sirloin steak, game pie, poached salmon;
Lunch (12.30pm to 2pm) £11: egg & prawn mayonnaise, supreme of chicken, pudding or cheese;
Dinner (7.30pm to 9pm) £17: fresh asparagus, soup, escalope of venison, pudding or cheese
Children: own menu, half portions
£ High

✓ Best Bargain Break: £98 per person, 2 nights – dinner, b&b
Children: free to age 16
Facilities: 3 cots and 2 high chairs; 5 baby-listening lines
30 rooms, 5 family, 2 sets interconnecting
Open all year

◑ Ale: Courage, Wadworth's

ℙ Own car park

WEYMOUTH, DORSET   Map 2
Ⓗ **Streamside Hotel, 29 Preston Road**
Tel: 01305 833 121
On the A354, just before the sea front.

....

The hotel was built in the 1930s in mock-Tudor style. The black-and-white façade, ablaze with flowers in tubs, window boxes and hanging baskets, is a cheerful sight. You will find a fresh, attractive interior and the Tudor theme is continued with beamed ceilings.

The garden has both lawned and terraced areas, with plenty of picnic tables, chairs and bench tables. It overlooks a nature reserve. There is a swing in the garden. Indoors, there is a pool table, table tennis and darts.

Nearby: Weymouth has one of the safest beaches in the area (patrolled by lifeguards throughout the summer), a broad sweep of sand which is overlooked by the fine Georgian houses on the esplanade. Dogs are rightly banned from the main beach areas. At the back of the beach is Lodmoor Country Park and nature reserve. There is a Sea Life Centre in the town and many attractions within an easy drive: the Tutankhamun Exhibition, Hardy's cottage, the Tank Museum at Bovington Camp, Athelhampton House, Corfe Castle and the Swanage Railway.

....

✕ Bar snacks (12pm to 2pm) £2–6: Cumberland sausage, grilled trout, minute steak, brunch, salmon fishcake;
Dinner (7pm to 9pm) £10: pork & liver terrine, poached salmon, pudding
Children: own menu, half portions
£ High
✓ Best Bargain Break: £68–86 per person, 2 nights – dinner, b&b
Children: cot £4; £7 from 4 to 7 years; £12 from 8 to 12 years
Facilities: 2 cots and 2 high chairs; baby-listening to each room
15 rooms, 4 family
Open all year
Ⓟ Own car park

WHITBY, NORTH YORKS
Map 9

Ⓡ TRENCHERS, New Quay Road
Tel: 01947 603 212

In the town centre, opposite the tourist information office.

....

This family-owned restaurant looks so neat and clean, with its white-tiled floor and green bench seats. The fresh flowers enhance the modern décor, and it is a very popular spot with locals and tourists alike. This area of the town is being redeveloped.

The menu is extensive and includes many different fresh fish dishes. The premises were recently extended and the restaurant can now seat nearly 200 people.

The excellent facilities for families include many high chairs, breast-feeding facilities, and a changing mat and child seat in the Ladies. The children's menu offers a good choice, including chunky cod, cold roast ham, cottage pie and fisherman's casserole.

....

✗ £1–6: prawn salad, cottage pie, cod, haddock, plaice, sole, etc
   Children: own menu, half portions
   Open 11am to 9pm, mid-Mar to Nov
Ⓟ On street

WHITEWELL, nr CLITHEROE, LANCS
Map 8

Ⓟ INN AT WHITEWELL
Tel: 01200 448 222

Off the B6478. Six miles north-west of Clitheroe.

....

Down the winding lanes of the Forest of Bowland you will find this classic country inn alongside the village church. It is a solid stone manor house, parts of which date back to the 14th century, and was once the house of the Keeper of the Forest.

The interior is a mixture of dark antique and country pine furniture, and the east wing of the house is an art gallery, with a studio on the top floor. The enterprising landlord sells high-quality shirts, sweaters and shoes; and he is also a wine merchant, which ensures a very comprehensive list. An interesting choice of bar food is always offered here, and is all cooked on the spot; it's jolly good value, too.

There is a comfortable and attractive public bar and families just calling in for a drink or a snack can use a spacious room just in from the main door which has lots of tables and easy chairs and is attractively kitted out with antiques and hunting prints on the walls.

From the rooms at the back of the building and from the garden you have delightful views of wooded hills and the River Hodder below, where the landlord has several miles of fishing.

There are eleven *en suite* bedrooms, either double or twin.

....

✗ (12pm to 2pm and 7.30pm to 9.30pm) £2–10: savoury pancakes, Coniston smoked trout, fisherman's pie, Cumberland sausage
  Children: half portions
Ⓓ Ale: Boddington's, Marston's
Ⓟ Own car park

WIDECOMBE IN THE MOOR, DEVON   Map 1
Ⓟ OLD INN
Tel: 01364 621 207
North of Ashburton on the minor roads, and can be reached from the A38 or the B3212.

....

This famous village has a pub to match. It is part of a row of 14th-century stone buildings which also house gift and craft shops. It has several rooms with thick stone walls and lots of oak, and the family room has a large open fire, a floor of worn flagstones, oak benches and settles.

Children are also welcome in the long, narrow dining room which has several tables and padded bench seats, and in the other eating areas within the pub.

The way to the car park is not immediately obvious – take the road to the right of the stone buildings and the car park is on your left.

Next to it is a large grassy garden with a tiny brook, picnic benches and a terrace.

There's a good choice of food at reasonable prices, with daily specials, several vegetarian dishes and a Sunday lunch for around £5.

....

✕ (11am to 2pm and 6.30pm to 10.15pm) £2–10: Moorland smokie, turkey & ham pie, steaks, beef in red wine, bean casserole
   Children: half portions
◑ Ale: Usher's
ℙ Own car park

Nr WIGAN, GREATER MANCHESTER   **Map 8**
ℙℝ **VALE ROYAL HOTEL, Orrell**
Tel: 01942 223 700
On the B5206, close to Junction 25 of the M6.

....

This still has the look of a traditional village pub, with a façade which is brick on the ground floor and cream-painted pebbledash above, but it has been expanded by the Brewers Fayre group into a sizeable family pub and restaurant. It has a pleasant lounge bar with an open fireplace and padded settles ranged along the walls. The decorations include wall lights with shades of coloured glass, prints and black-and-white photos.

The dining areas are in the same style, their wide windows framed by colourful curtains. The family restaurant (no-smoking) has a wall of windows on to the garden. The various areas are divided by screens of brass and wrought iron – a sensible piece of design.

The terrace has bench tables, and there is a good-sized play unit on a safe bark surface.

....

✕ (11.30am to 10pm) £2–8: hot mushrooms, fish pie, steak & mushroom pudding, tagliatelle carbonara, chicken escalopes
   Children: own menu

🍺 Ale: Boddington's and guests
🅿 Ample

WIGHILL, NORTH YORKS   Map 9
🅿 WHITE SWAN INN
Tel: 01937 832 217
Off the A684. Look for the Wighill sign two and a half miles east of Tadcaster.

Located in a charming village, it is well worth straying off the main roads to stop off at this ivy-clad pub, with its terraces at front and rear.

It is a delightful 'pubby' place which is made up of five small, low-ceilinged rooms, all of which are well furnished, partly with antique pieces. There are log fires in all of them. Two of these rooms can be used by families: one is a most attractive room with a beamed ceiling and plenty of space; the other is a pretty little snug with padded benches around a wooden table. In addition there is a pleasant restaurant.

There is an enterprising choice of food here, available at all times except Sunday and Monday evenings, a good selection of wines, much wider than most pubs, and of real ales. Sunday lunch is good value at around £8, and the three-course dinner (from Tuesday to Saturday) costs under £12.

It all adds up to a welcoming pub with good facilities for families.

🍴 (12pm to 2pm) £2–11: game pie, haddock & chips, fresh salmon, wild boar pie, sirloin steak
   Children: small portions
🍺 Ale: Stone's, Tetley, Theakston's, Younger's
🅿 Own car park

WILMSLOW, CHESHIRE
Map 8

P R BODDINGTON ARMS, Racecourse Road
Tel: 01625 525 849
On the A538 near the centre of the town.

This is an extraordinary creation, a vast and modern brick pub with a pagoda-style roof and white statues flanking the portentous entrance. It's way over the top, a splendid example of 1980s kitsch, and the interior adds to the fun.

The bar area is conventional enough, very spacious but with several alcoves divided by screens of wood and glass. The huge restaurant has subdued lighting and the walls are littered with prints of Olde England. Crossed broadswords frame a coat of arms. Wide windows in the main dining area look over the garden and there is a central area flanked by four pillars of wood and glass. A heavy chandelier hangs above the table set for eight people; maybe King Arthur and a retinue of knights are regular visitors.

The Boddington Arms has excellent facilities for families – lots of space for a start, plus high chairs and baby-changing units. The garden is also on the grand scale; sweeping lawns surround the building with mature trees on the boundaries. The menu is extensive and includes three-course specials at £6.99 and £9.99.

✕ (12pm to 2.30pm and 5.30pm to 10.30pm; weekends 12pm to 10pm) £2–12: fresh salmon mayonnaise, steak Diane, haddock & chips, Barnsley chop, Mexican bake
Children: own menu
D Ale: Boddington's, Castle Eden
P Ample

Nr WINCHESTER, HANTS   **Map 3**
Ⓟ Ⓡ CAPTAIN BARNARD, Otterbourne
Tel: 01962 712 220
On the A31 at Otterbourne.

....

This is a very large, purpose-built brick pub with wooden cladding on the upper storey of the façade. There are two gardens, one at the front of the pub which is aimed at the adult customers and a large enclosed area at the rear of the pub where there is a substantial children's playground and several rides.

There is loads of space inside the Captain Barnard, all carefully divided up into a series of rooms and areas by the skilful use of wooden and stained-glass screens and timber-covered pillars. The wood panelling and many prints on the walls add to the fun and the pub is very nicely furnished with wooden tables and padded benches and chairs.

It is an excellent family pub with food on offer throughout the day, high chairs and a nappy-changing facility, a family dining room where smoking is denied, and a little indoor play area for the children.

....

✗ (11.30am to 10pm; Sun from 12pm) £2–8: hot mushrooms, steak & kidney pie, fried scampi, fish pie, chicken Alexandra
  Children: own menu
Ⓓ Ale: Flowers, Strong's
Ⓟ Own car park

WIRRAL, MERSEYSIDE   **Map 8**
Ⓟ Ⓡ GLEGG ARMS, Gayton
Tel: 0151 342 1982
At the junction of the A540 and the A5137.

....

The black-and-white façade of this ancient building suggests an interesting past, and it is known that William III stayed here in 1689 on the way to the Battle of the Boyne. The house was then known as Gayton Manor and the interior still exhibits a fine array of low beams and wooden pillars and panelling. One of the rooms off the bar, which will shortly receive a children's licence, has been built from the old stable and is a splendid spot with its plaster walls and vaulted ceiling.

The same style is evident throughout this much-extended pub-cum-restaurant. There are many alcoves, and nooks and crannies, and emphasis is firmly placed on brick walls, wooden pillars, low beams and open fireplaces. There is a good collection of militaria on the walls: battle-axes, swords, pikes, shields and a crossbow. The original dungeon is still there, close to a conservatory room with a sloping wooden ceiling. This is a lovely spot to have a meal since it overlooks the terrace garden. High chairs are available and there are baby-changing facilities. There is a Travel Inn attached to the Glegg Arms.

The garden is a delight, its well-tended lawns encircled by mature trees. There are many bench tables and three play units for the children. On the sunny day on which we visited, there were many families enjoying themselves outside.

....

✖ (12pm to 10.30pm) £2–13: prawn sundae, beef & Boddington's pie, haddock & chips, sirloin steak, seafood tagliatelle
   Children: own menu

⓪ Ale: Boddington's, Flowers and guests
Ⓟ Ample

WIRRAL, MERSEYSIDE   **Map 8**
ⓅⓇ OLD QUAY HOTEL, Neston
Tel: 0151 336 4343
On the B5134/5 at Neston.

This is a massive modern pub and restaurant, built from brick, in a superb location looking across marshland to the River Dee and the Welsh hills beyond. This stretch of land has a great variety of plant life and wildlife and is a haven for foxes, badgers and wading birds. You can sit on the terrace in front of the pub and enjoy the view, while the children can amuse themselves on the play unit.

If you happen to stop at the Old Quay Hotel during a summer weekend there should be some cricket to watch on the adjoining Neston ground – the wicket and the outfield looked to be in immaculate condition.

The interior of the pub is of spacious open-plan design. Brick pillars and screens break it up, and the various lounge and eating areas are built on different levels. Part of the restaurant has a wall of windows overlooking the marshland and the water. Excellent facilities for families include high chairs, baby-changing facilities and the availability of food throughout the day.

✖ (11.30am to 10pm) £2–8: oriental prawns, chicken Balti, steak & kidney pie, vegetable crumble, tagliatelle carbonara
Children: own menu
⓪ Ale: Boddington's, Castle Eden, Flowers
Ⓟ Lots

WITHYPOOL, SOMERSET   Map 2
Ⓗ **Westerclose Country House Hotel**
Tel: 01643 831 302
Off the B3223, south-west of Minehead. The hotel is signposted in the village.

The hotel sits just above a pretty village in nine acres of fields and lawns – plenty of space in which the children can roam. It is an agreeable, white-painted building, which began life as a hunting lodge in the 1920s (it was built by the Nicholson gin family) and has now assumed the mantle of a very comfortable and relaxing hotel.

If peace and quiet is what you seek, this is an excellent place to be, surrounded by lovely countryside and with the whole of Exmoor, its moorland teeming with wildlife, to explore.

We were impressed by the standard of the public rooms. There are two spacious lounges; one doubles as the reception area and the other has a good selection of books and a writing desk. They are nicely decorated and well furnished. The large conservatory is another agreeable place to sit; it is a comfortable spot and the bar is alongside. There is also a little terrace outside the windows.

We looked at several bedrooms, which have been decorated in a stylish and attractive way. They include a nice little single room which would suit an older child, and a splendid family room with a double bed built in an ingenious way against an old wooden pillar. This room also has a sofa bed.

The gardens around the hotel are well maintained, with smooth lawns and mature trees. There are lots of animals in evidence – cats, chickens and donkeys – which should please the children; and the hotel has stables, so you can arrive on horseback, if you wish.

It is clear that the owners have put a great deal of care into this very appealing hotel, where families will be welcomed and where they will be very comfortable. There is, by the way, an excellent vegetarian menu, and the Sunday lunch is marvellous value at under £12 for three courses.

Nearby: The hotel is right in the middle of Exmoor, a wonderful place to explore on foot or horseback. Birdwatching is a favourite pastime here and fishermen are very well catered for. The Exmoor Centre is just down the road at Dulverton. You can reach the coast to the north quite easily. If you like to see the sights there is plenty of choice: Combe Sydenham Hall, the West Somerset Railway, Dunster Castle, Fyne Court, Gaulden Manor, Knightshayes Court and Orchard Mill are all within easy reach.

....

✘ Bar snacks (12.30pm to 2.30pm) £3–9: smoked fish pâté, Exmoor trout, spicy bean casserole, steak & kidney pie, pork casserole;
Dinner (7.30pm to 9.30pm) £19: gratin of leeks & prawns, roast rack of lamb, pudding & cheese
Children: own menu
£ Medium

✓ Best Bargain Break: 5% discount from Sun to Thurs Oct to Mar
Children: free up to 3 years; £20 for an extra bed
Facilities: 2 cots and 2 high chairs; baby-listening system
10 rooms, 1 set interconnecting, 2 family
Open Mar to Dec inclusive

P Own car park

WIX, nr MANNINGTREE, ESSEX   Map 6
Ⓗ NEW FARM HOUSE, Spinnels Lane
Tel: 01255 870 365

The village is off the A120 west of Harwich. In Wix take the road to Mistley and Bradfield and there is a sign to New Farm House.

This large modern farmhouse is very well equipped to welcome families, especially if they are using the nearby Harwich ferries. Of the twelve rooms, five are family sized; we looked at several of them and they were spacious and comfortable. The six bedrooms in the annexe all have their own bathrooms and the family room there has a double bed and two bunk beds. As well as a large and comfortable lounge with a television, there is a quiet lounge where guests can read or write. There are facilities to make tea and coffee in all the rooms, and a small kitchen which guests can use.

The garden is not only large but immaculately maintained, with smooth lawns, a pond and a rockery. There is plenty of space to enjoy and, even better for youngsters, there is a large grassy paddock with swings and a slide, goalposts and masses of room for other games.

Nearby: Wix is surrounded by open farming country and there are delightful walks to be done, perhaps to the lovely Mistley, which has the largest population of mute swans in Britain. Castle House, the home of Alfred Munnings whose paintings are on show there, is at nearby Dedham, while Flatford was the home of John Constable, and children can feed the ducks at Flatford Mills. Other local attractions include Beth Chatto Gardens, St Osyth's Priory, the wildlife sanctuary at Fingringhoe Wick, Abberton reservoir which is a great haven for birds of all varieties, and the zoo near Colchester.

✘ Dinner (6.30pm to 7.30pm) £9: soup, roast beef & Yorkshire pudding, fruit flan, cheese
   Children: half portions
   £ Low
✓ Best Bargain Break: £84 per person, 3 nights – dinner, b&b
   Children: free up to 5 years; £9 from 5 to 12

Facilities: 4 cots and 2 high chairs; baby-listening system
12 rooms, 5 family
Open all year
P Own car park

WOKING, SURREY   **Map 3**
P R THE SURREY
Tel: **01483 474 312**
On the A324 on the west side of Woking.

....

This purpose-built pub and restaurant opened early in 1995. Constructed from brick and wood, it has the appearance of a Swiss chalet and is easy on the eye. There is a garden and a terrace at the front with a few bench tables, partly shaded by trees, and a children's play area has been placed there. At the side of the pub there is another larger terrace with wrought-iron furniture.

The well-designed interior has low ceilings in the bar area and expanses of padded benches; the brick walls are decorated with prints and old photographs. The main restaurant area has wide windows under a high wooden ceiling with skylights. It's a bright and welcoming place and the large open fireplace at one end adds to the atmosphere.

Beyond the restaurant there is a toddlers' play area with a ball swamp and lots of other equipment. The Surrey is very much aimed at the family market and high chairs and baby-changing facilities are available. It is useful to know that the pub is open throughout the day and provides food at all times.

....

✗ (9am to 10pm) £2–9: prawn platter, seafood pie, peppered steak, lasagne, lemon chicken
Children: own menu
🍺 Ale: Courage, Theakston's
P Own car park

WOKINGHAM, BERKS
Map 5

🅿🆁 Yᴇ Oʟᴅᴇ Lᴇᴀᴛʜᴇʀ Bᴏᴛᴛʟᴇ, **Barkham Road**
Tel: 01734 784 222
On the west side of the town, on the B3349.

....

A first sight of this well-proportioned brick building gives no clue to its size but the pub has a series of rooms which stretch on towards the extensive gardens at the rear. There is plenty of space here under the low ceilings and the design encompasses brick walls, open fireplaces, good wooden tables and padded settles.

The family dining room (a no-smoking area) overlooks the terrace and the gardens. The brick walls and paved floor complement the old wooden pillars and the ranks of wooden ceiling beams. Alongside there is another large dining room under a vaulted ceiling.

The garden is a great bonus for families and it was very busy when we visited one summer lunchtime. There is a rolling expanse of well-manicured lawn with many bench tables and sizeable paved terraces at both front and rear. The enclosed play unit has a safe bark surface and will keep the children amused.

....

✗ (12pm to 10pm) £2–9: moules marinières, chilli con carne, haddock
& chips, peppered steak, vegetable lasagne
Children: own menu
🍺 Ale: Courage, Theakston's
🅿 Lots

WOLLATON VALE, nr NOTTINGHAM, NOTTS
Map 7

🅿🆁 Pʀɪᴏʀʏ Tᴏʙʏ Hᴏᴛᴇʟ
Tel: 0115 922 1691
On the A52 west of Nottingham.

....

This substantial building houses a pub, a restaurant and a hotel with over thirty bedrooms. It is certainly in the family market, since high chairs are provided, as are baby-changing facilities. The main bar is divided into a number of smaller areas and is agreeable with its padded settles and wooden furniture.

You can enter the main restaurant, which also has a small bar area, from either the pub or the hotel or through a separate entrance in the car park. The small bar in the restaurant has padded armchairs and sofas in which to relax and have a drink prior to eating. The restaurant is split into six different areas. It is comfortably furnished in mock-Regency style with themes in the different rooms ranging from country cottage to sporting.

Pub food is available throughout the day and the restaurant hours are shown below. The Sunday Special – two courses for £7.50 – is good value.

....

✗ (12pm to 2.30pm and 5.30pm to 10.30pm; Sun all day) £2–13: tiger prawns, lemon sole, fillet steak, fish & chips, mushroom strudel
   Children: own menu, half portions
◌ Ale: Bass and guests
🅿 Own car park

WOLVERHAMPTON, STAFFS   Map 4
🅿🆁 BRADMORE ARMS
Tel: 01902 341 472
South-west of Wolverhampton. Take the A449 (to Kidderminster) and then the B4161 (signed to Compton).

....

The Bradmore Arms is housed in a stately brick building with huge bay windows which help to brighten the interior, which has a colourful décor – a rich mixture of claret, green and yellow. It's an open-plan design with plenty of wood panelling and a variety of prints on the walls.

The main dining area has a central fireplace, a sizeable table in one of the bay windows and a comfortable settee in the other. The family dining room (a no-smoking area) is at the other end of the pub and has a play area, with a ball swamp and other equipment, for younger children. There are several high chairs and a nappy-changing facility.

At the front of the pub, the lawn and terrace is an appealing option on a summer day and the play unit will keep the children occupied.

✕ (11.30am to 10pm) £2–8: onion bhajis, tagliatelle carbonara, vegetable moussaka, steak & kidney pie, turkey fillet
   Children: own menu
◯ Ale: Boddington's, Flowers, Marston's
P Own car park

WOODBRIDGE, SUFFOLK   Map 6
P **CHERRY TREE, Ipswich Road**
Tel: 01394 382513
Follow the sign from the A12 to Woodbridge, local route. The inn stands on the right just outside the town itself.

Do not be deceived by the rather unattractive exterior; the Cherry Tree is a delightful inn. It dates back over 400 years and has some of the original low beams, and the wooden tables and bar have a rural charm and warmth which is welcoming. It is generally accepted that the inn is haunted, and the landlord has no doubt that it is.

Children are welcome anywhere within the public house when they are eating, and high chairs and a children's menu are made available.

There is a pleasant garden with swings, climbs, rides and family benches and tables, and it has recently been fenced for added safety. There are plans to build an extension to the pub itself, but its character will be preserved.

✕ (11am to 2pm and 6.30pm to 9.30pm) £2–7: king prawns, broccoli & cream cheese bake, chicken Kiev, haddock & chips, sirloin steak
   Children: own menu, half portions
◯ Ale: Adnams, Flowers, Tetley
P Own car park

WOODHAM WALTER, nr MALDON, ESSEX   Map 6
P R THE BELL, The Street
Tel: 01245 223 437
West of Maldon, off the A414.

....

Very much off the beaten track, but easy to find, The Bell is an Elizabethan inn in a sleepy village three and a quarter miles from Hatfield Peverel. The Bell is on the left in a hollow just as you enter the village. One of many buildings that plastered up windows in the 18th century in an attempt to evade the iniquitous Window Tax, the pub consists of a lounge bar with irregularly shaped alcoves on various levels, old timbers and beams. A small, neatly decorated restaurant is up a few steps from the bar and has a parlour atmosphere, but food is served throughout the pub, and children may dine anywhere away from the bar area. There are two high chairs for younger children.

There is a delightful small, secluded garden at the rear of the pub with a stream, and opposite is a recreation ground with swings and pleasant walks.

....

✕ (12pm to 3pm and 6.30pm to 11pm; except Mon pm) £2–8: plaice & chips, steak & kidney pie, prawn curry, steaks, vegetarian dishes
   Children: half portions
◔ Ale: Friary Meux, Adnams and guests
P Small car park

WOOLACOMBE, DEVON   Map 1
H DEVON BEACH HOTEL, The Esplanade
Tel: 01271 870 449
On the coast road.

....

The hotel is housed in a substantial building, painted white with a blue trim, and stands high above Woolacombe Bay with its sheltered sandy beaches. It has an indoor heated swimming pool and a games room with a pool table, table tennis and various machines.

The views from the hotel windows are magnificent: a panorama of sand, rocks and sea that you can also enjoy from the sun terrace. Most of the bedrooms have the same view, and those we looked at were nicely decorated and functional. There are plenty of family rooms, and the Devon Beach is a decent, reasonably priced hotel.

The hotel also has a penthouse apartment which can accommodate up to seven people. The lounge and one bedroom have sun terraces and every room has lovely views out to sea. The terms, which include linen, heating, etc., range from £200 to £500 per week for four people (an extra person is charged at £50 a week).

Nearby: The beaches are wide and sandy; lifeguards patrol both Woolacombe and Croyde Bay during the summer. There is a great range of other attractions within easy reach: Watermouth Castle and Arlington Court; the nature reserve at Braunton Burrows and Exmoor Bird Gardens; the Exmoor Park Centre; Dartington Glass; and the Combat Vehicles Museum near Barnstaple.

✘ Bar snacks (12.30pm to 2pm) £2–5: ploughman's, jacket potatoes, salads, scampi & chips;
Dinner (7pm to 8.15pm) £11: salmon ramekin, soup, roast turkey, pudding and cheese
Children: own menu, half portions
£ Medium
✓ Best Bargain Break: £31 per person per night – dinner, b&b
Children: from £5 to £20 per day (including meals)
Facilities: as many cots and high chairs as needed; baby-listening system in every room
32 rooms, 17 family, 2 sets interconnecting
Closed Jan/Feb
Ⓟ Car park

WOOLACOMBE, DEVON   **Map 1**
Ⓗ WOOLACOMBE BAY HOTEL
Tel: 01271 870 388
In the centre of town.

This resort has a magnificent stretch of beach and a lovely setting amid rolling hills. The stately seaside hotel is in pristine condition both inside and out and has some fine public rooms, including comfortable lounges, a welcoming, high-ceilinged restaurant, two bars with real ale, and very agreeable and well-furnished bedrooms, many of them with sea views. The bathrooms are of very high quality.

The array of facilities includes a sizeable indoor pool with paddling pool (galas are organized for children), a steam room, jacuzzi and sauna, three squash courts, including a glass-backed court, table tennis and pool, a new and very well-equipped fitness room and an aerobics studio, and a very congenial snooker room with wood panelling and a high ceiling (for adults only).

The children have their own spacious play area indoors with table tennis, pool, amusement machines, big-screen videos and lots of organized activities. There is also a new crèche area for young children.

Everyone can enjoy the large outdoor swimming pool with its flume slide, around which there are lots of reclining seats. In addition the hotel has two hard tennis courts, an expansive stretch of grass in front of the hotel which runs down to the sea, and a play area to the side which has croquet, swingball, and a pitch and putt course. The hotel also has a motor yacht which can be chartered.

All kinds of games and sports are organized during the summer, and entertainments – dances and discos in the large ballroom – are laid on in the evenings.

The bistro and coffee shop is open all day for meals and snacks, and serves a three-course menu in the evening for around £10. The full dinner menu in the restaurant is excellent value, too.

The Woolacombe Bay is an impressive hotel in a delightful location and has all the amenities any family could desire. For holiday makers who prefer self-catering, the hotel has nearly forty apartments; the rents vary from £150 to £1160 a week.

Nearby: Woolacombe has a three-mile stretch of sands and there are other excellent beaches nearby, including Croyde Bay and Saunton, where there is a superb golf course. If you are interested in the natural world you should visit Braunton Burrows, one of Britain's largest nature reserves, and the Exmoor Bird Gardens should also appeal to children. Watermouth Castle is great fun for youngsters, while the adults will perhaps favour a visit to Arlington Court. The beauties of Exmoor are not far away and the Exmoor Centre near Dulverton is a good starting point for walks.

....

✕ Bistro (10am to 10pm) £1–4: selection of hot & cold snacks;
Dinner (7.30pm to 9pm) £17: 7-course menu, eg, hors d'oeuvres, soup, seafood vol au vent, roast venison, cheese, fruit
Children: own menu, half portions
£ High

✓ Best Bargain Break: £105 per person, 2 nights – dinner, b&b
Children: free up to 2 years; from £10 to £25 thereafter
Facilities: as many cots and high chairs as required; baby-listening to every room
61 rooms, 27 family, 11 sets interconnecting
Open mid-Feb to Dec

◖ Ale: Bass

🅿 Own car park

WORFIELD, nr BRIDGNORTH, SHROPSHIRE Map 4
H OLD VICARAGE HOTEL
Tel: 01746 716 497
Off the A454 east of Bridgnorth.

This large red-brick house was built in 1905 and was bought from the Church Commissioners by Mr and Mrs Iles over a decade ago. It is a small and very comfortable hotel; there are some fine antique pieces, and the walls display watercolours and engravings. The lounge bar, with its wide windows, is a relaxing place to have a drink, as is the splendid and spacious conservatory, full of plants and with excellent views of the countryside. The main dining room looks out to the gardens and there is also a small private dining room.

Hotels often claim that their bedrooms are individually designed, and this is certainly true at the Old Vicarage, where the rooms are very smartly furnished and decorated in fine style. The four rooms in the Coach House merit special mention since they have the extra luxuries of jacuzzi baths and double shavers. They are spacious and extremely comfortable and the ground-floor rooms (one of which is superbly equipped for disabled guests) have their own little gardens. It is no surprise to learn that the hotel is one of the very few in Britain to be placed in the de luxe category by the AA.

The hotel garden is safely enclosed and has spreading lawns and several mature trees. There is plenty of space for children to play and adults can try their skills on the croquet lawn.

Nearby: South Shropshire is a lovely part of the world with many attractive villages and towns: Church Stretton and the Carding Mill Valley, Clun with its castle, Ludlow and Bridgnorth, which has a motor museum. Within an easy distance you can visit the Ironbridge Gorge Museum, the Severn Valley Railway, Wilderhope Manor, the Safari Park at Bewdley, Wyre Forest and the Aerospace Museum at Cosford. You can play golf at Worfield at half price and Patshull Park is an alternative venue.

✕ Lunch (12pm to 2pm) £18: smoked salmon & avocado salad, entrecôte of beef, pudding;
Dinner (7pm to 9pm) £24: terrine of chicken & sweetbreads, fillet of brill, pudding or cheese
Children: own menu, half portions
£ High
✓ Best Bargain Break: £119 per person, 2 nights – dinner, b&b
Children: babies free; up to £15 thereafter (includes meals)
Facilities: 1 cot and 1 high chair; baby-listening system
14 rooms, 1 family
Open all year
Ⓟ Own car park

WORKSOP, NOTTS   Map 7
ⓅⓇ **THE ASHLEY**
Tel: 01909 530 915
North of Worksop town centre on the A60.

This converted Victorian house has been extended at the side and rear to provide for the large dining areas and many other facilities which a family pub and restaurant requires. At the back of the pub and adjacent to the car park is an enclosed area containing a small stone-flagged terrace with wrought-iron tables and chairs. Alongside there is a grassed area with bench tables and a play area with a large climbing frame and other equipment – on the day we visited there was also a bouncy castle in operation.

The family entrance is at the side of the building, and here the children will find a Charlie Chalk's play area. To the left is the main family dining area, which is non-smoking. There is a corner set aside for the tiny tots with suitable play equipment and a TV set. There are other machines and toys available in this part of the restaurant.

Farmhouse pine and Tiffany glass is the order of the day in this pub, and it is a light and cheerful place. The main bar, an extensive room, is furnished in the same style.

Children are allowed in all areas of the pub except the bar. There are two baby-changing facilities and plenty of high chairs.

....

✗ (11.30am to 10pm) £2–8: onion bhajis, chicken Alexandra, steak & mushroom pudding, lasagne verdi, sirloin steak
  Children: own menu
◐ Ale: Boddington's, Castle Eden, Flowers, Marston's
Ⓟ Own car park

WORSLEY, GREATER MANCHESTER   Map 8
Ⓟ🅁 COCK HOTEL
Tel: 0161 790 2381
Close to Junction 13 of the M62. Take the A575 north towards Walkden.

....

Do not be put off by the utilitarian appearance of this substantial brick-built pub, which is located next door to an Esso service station. It may look like a typical suburban boozer but the interior is far from that.

The large bar area is inviting and very comfortable; there are lounge areas with padded settles, and a sizeable skylight of coloured glass adds to the ambience. In addition there is a real bar (the vault) for drinkers, and it has a dartboard.

You will notice a remarkable selection of lush wallpapers in the pub; in the agreeable and spacious lounges which have a good array of settees and padded wall benches. There is more extravagant wallpaper in the restaurant too, as well as lots of prints on the walls and a big cabinet with a display of china. The *pièce de résistance* is a statue of a nymph in the main dining area. The other room is a splendid conservatory which overlooks the terrace. High chairs are available and there is a baby-changing unit. Food is served throughout the day.

The terrace at the rear also contains a good-sized play unit which is very popular with the children.

....

✗ (11am to 10pm) £2–12: fresh salmon mayonnaise, beef Madras, haddock & chips, fillet steak, mushroom & Stilton bake
   Children: own menu
◑ Ale: Boddington's, Flowers
℗ Ample

WORSLEY, GREATER MANCHESTER   Map 8
ⓅⓇ THE MOORINGS, Boothstown
Tel: 0161 702 6251
West of Junction 13 of the M563 – just off the A572. There is a sign to the pub.

....

The Bridgwater Canal runs past this family pub and restaurant and there is a mooring basin here for canal boats and other pleasure craft. It's a fine setting and this pub, pleasingly built of brick in 1994, takes full advantage of it. A series of terraces, with bench tables, overlook the water, as does the dining area, which runs the length of the building on one side.

The décor is lively; there are brick fireplaces, plush wallpapers, several skylights of coloured glass, prints on the walls and occasional standard lamps. There are many alcoves, including a no-smoking conservatory room with splendid views to all quarters. One end of the pub has a high, vaulted wooden roof with sets of florid chandeliers, and there are alcove rooms on either side.

The family market is much in the owners' sights, and high chairs and baby-changing units are made available. A sizeable play unit has been placed on one of the terraces. Food is available at all times.

This is an interesting modern pub in an attractive setting.

....

✗ (11am to 10pm) £2–8: mushroom & cheddar bake, haddock & chips, beef Madras, Cumberland sausage, spicy vegetable salsa
Children: own menu
◻ Ale: Boddington's, Flowers
ℙ Ample

WORTHING, WEST SUSSEX   Map 3
ℙℝ THE DOWNLANDS
Tel: 01903 234 085
On the A27.

....

This is one of those large, red-brick roadhouses of 1930s vintage, which went out of fashion for a while. But The Downlands has now been transformed into a hefty family pub and restaurant. When we called in, some refurbishment was about to begin.

At present there is a sizeable bar on two levels, an agreeable spot with wood panelling here and there and Laura Ashley-type wallpaper. The restaurant is in much the same style, though bright and light by virtue of its wide windows.

The facilities for families with small children are excellent; there are high chairs, and baby-changing facilities in the Ladies. The pub is open throughout the day, as is the restaurant at weekends, when the Sunday lunch is good value.

....

✗ (12pm to 2.30pm and 5pm to 10.30pm; weekends 12pm to 10.30pm) £2–13: Normandy pork, Indonesian chicken, salmon fillet, three-bean feast, beef & Boddington's pie
Children: own menu

🍺 Ale: Boddington's, Flowers and guests
🅿 Own car park

WREA GREEN, LANCS   **Map 8**
🅿 **THE GRAPES**
Tel: 01772 682927
On the B5259 south of Junction 3 of the M55.

....

This archetypal village pub sits alongside the church of St Nicholas with its tall spire, and the expansive village green spreads out before both buildings. In many English villages pubs and parsons are close neighbours.

The Grapes is a building of regular proportions and is smartly painted cream. It is very much a traditional layout: two rooms around the bar with padded wall benches, and with prints and displays of china plates on the walls.

It was busy when we visited one lunchtime, as was the attractive restaurant at the back of the pub. Families are made very welcome and high chairs are provided. We noticed that colouring pads are given to young customers, and there is a baby-changing unit in the disabled toilet.

The pub is open throughout the day and the restaurant's hours are shown below.

....

🍴 (12pm to 2.30pm and 5.30pm to 10.30pm; Sun 12pm to 10.30pm)
£2–13: coronation chicken, halibut au poivre, lasagne, barbecued loin of lamb, steaks
Children: own menu
🍺 Ale: Boddington's, Theakston's
🅿 Own car park

YORK, NORTH YORKS   Map 9
P THE BLACK BULL
Tel: 01904 411 856
On the A1079, about two miles east of York city centre.

Look for a large red-brick building on the right hand side of the road as you travel eastwards. The interior is divided into three main parts with a sizeable dining room at one end, a long bar area in the middle and a lounge/family area at the other end which links through into the hotel at the rear. The lounge has a number of leather wing-backed settees, padded bosun chairs, and wooden tables. This theme is continued in the bar and the dining room, which has hacienda-style alcoves at the rear. Since the pub is called the Black Bull there is a head of that species mounted on the wall in the bar, in addition to hunting, racing and farming prints and bric-à-brac. High chairs and nappy-changing facilities are provided.

At the rear of the building there is a small enclosed grass patio with wooden picnic tables and a play frame with swings and a slide.

The hotel is at the back of the pub, a modern building with very spacious bedrooms at reasonable prices.

✗ (12pm to 2pm and 7pm to 9.30pm) £2–12: seafood cocktail, swordfish steak, rump steak, garlic & coriander chicken, mushroom & cashew tagliatelle
   Children: own menu, half portions
P Ale: Tetley's
P Ample

YORK, NORTH YORKS   Map 9
R BETTYS CAFE TEAROOMS, 6–8 St Helen's Square
Tel: 01904 659 142
In the city centre.

The famous Bettys chain of North Yorkshire tearooms and restaurants is a firm favourite of ours and has set out to cater with style for all their customers, including families.

456

Mothers with babies or small children can dine here with the knowledge that the Ladies offers changing facilities, a playpen and disposable nappies. There are also bibs, beakers, plates and spoons for young children, plus both a toddlers' and a children's menu. They'll even heat up your own baby food if you ask them. There are no fewer than six high chairs on the premises.

The ground-floor café looks out, through walls of glass, on to the busy St Helen's Square, and below there is a tranquil, wood-panelled dining room.

On Sundays the various breakfasts are very popular and you can eat at leisure, browse through the Sunday papers, and listen to the piano.

....

✕ (9am to 9pm) £1–7: Masham sausages, haddock & prawn croustade, rarebits, haddock & chips, rosti with bacon
   Children: own menu, half portions
Ⓟ Public car parks nearby

YORK, NORTH YORKS   Map 9
Ⓡ TAYLOR'S TEA ROOMS, 46 Stonegate
Tel: 01904 622 865
In the city centre.

....

The wonderful aroma of freshly ground coffee greets you as you enter this agreeable tearoom and coffee shop. You'll find the restaurant on the first floor and the first thing which confronts you is an array of different teas and coffees, and an interesting display of unusual and ancient teapots. If you fancy some Mountains of the Moon or some Tippy Assam, this is the place.

The café comprises four interconnected rooms with windows which overlook busy Stonegate. It's a relaxing place in which to enjoy one of the array of snacks and meals or a traditional Yorkshire afternoon tea (ham or chicken sandwiches, sultana scone with cream and a Yorkshire curd tart).

Mothers with babies can relax here since there is a separate changing room, with a shelf and changing mat and a chair. Nappies, bibs and beakers, and baby foods are also provided.

The only music to reach your ears is the occasional strains of a busker from the pedestrian precinct below.

....

✗ (9am to 5.30pm) £1–7: scrambled eggs on toast, rarebits, omelettes, breakfast grill, raclette & ham Florentine
  Children: half portions
  Closed Christmas, Boxing Day and New Year
  Unlicensed
Ⓟ Public car parks nearby

Nr YORK, NORTH YORKS   **Map 9**
ⓅⓇ **The Starting Gate, Dringhouses**
Tel: 01904 707 151
On the A1036, near York Racecourse.

....

This modern sandstone building sits opposite the Forte Posthouse on the A1036 just beyond York Racecourse.

At the rear of the building there is a small grassed area on which, when we visited, there was a bouncy castle and some bench tables. Adjacent to this is a wood-chipped area with a climbing frame and other play equipment; both areas are safely enclosed.

The modern exterior belies the old-fashioned design inside, which is modelled on a barn. The first things that strike you are the beams, the rough brickwork and the wattle-and-daub effect. As you enter the main bar the room opens out into a pillared vault, in the centre of which is a stairwell up which climbs a huge mock beech tree complete with branches and leaves. Although there is a small section downstairs for eating, the main dining room is upstairs where there is a gallery leading round the stairwell and over the bar, and it continues around to the other side of the pub. There are alcoves at either end and a small secluded area under the gables.

Prints and posters relating to the York Racecourse are in evidence, as are sundry brass and copper artefacts and riders' silks. High chairs are provided and food is served throughout the day (bar snacks when the restaurant is closed).

....

✕ (12pm to 2.30pm and 5pm to 10.30pm; weekends all day) £2–13: pork satay, ocean bake, chicken pasta, sirloin Oscar, three-bean feast
   Children: own menu, half portions
◑ Ale: Boddington's, Castle Eden, Marston's and guests
🅿 Own car park

SCOTLAND

Map 11

ARDENTINNY, STRATHCLYDE
P ARDENTINNY HOTEL
Tel: 01369 810 209
In the village at the end of the A880.

You will find this cheerful, whitewashed inn on the shores of the busy Loch Long. It was built in 1720, and was on the drovers' route to Glasgow from the Highlands. The surroundings are delightful as you look across the water to the mountains beyond. You can sit on the terrace and admire the views; and a lawn, sheltered with trees and hedges, goes down to the edge of the loch. There are moorings if you should arrive by boat.

A room next to the bar serves as a family room, or you can head for the spacious buttery. There are bar lunches and suppers, and the restaurant, which has two high chairs, is open for dinner. The menus concentrate on 'Taste of Scotland' dishes.

The Ardentinny is open all day, and on Sundays food is available throughout opening hours. But please note that the hotel is closed from 1 November to mid-March.

✕ (12pm to 2.30pm and 6pm to 9.30pm; Sun all day) £2–10: haddock & chips, venison & mushroom pie, grilled salmon steak, fillet steak
Children: half portions
P Own car park

ARDKINGLAS, ARGYLL, STRATHCLYDE
R LOCH FYNE OYSTER BAR
Tel: 01499 600 236
On the A83 at the head of Loch Fyne.

The oyster bar is housed in an old farm building and its character is retained. The timbered roof is draped with nets, the walls are whitewashed and the furniture is natural wood, with some padded benches in booths. There are lovely views over the loch.

The accent is on informality. The customer can have a quick snack or tuck into a series of courses in any order he pleases. All the food is produced by the owners, who have their own oyster beds and their own smokehouse.

There are some non-fish items, such as smoked venison; and there is a shop alongside the oyster bar.

There is a baby-changing unit in the disabled toilet.

....

✕ (9am to 9pm; until 5pm in winter) £2–13: oysters, smoked mussels, dressed crab, smoked chicken, fresh salmon
   Children: small portions
Ⓟ Own car park

AUCHTERHOUSE, nr DUNDEE, TAYSIDE
Ⓗ THE OLD MANSION HOUSE
Tel: 01382 320 366
Follow the hotel sign from the B954 north of Muirhead.

....

The original part of this stylish and beautifully maintained building dates from around 1450, when the tower formed part of a large courtyard castle. Additions were made in the 16th century and, amongst the interior decorations, there is an unusual pendant ceiling which graces the dining room and part of the reception area. It was a present from the Earl of Marr to the Countess of Buchan and is a rarity. The interior is superb, with its stone walls and floors, antique furniture, huge open fires and a marvellous Jacobean vaulted ceiling. The house has been owned by some notable families, including the Strathmores and the Earls of Buchan, and William Wallace is said to have stayed in the house. Hence the tower to the east is named 'Wallace's Tower'.

Facilities include a squash court, grass tennis court, heated outdoor swimming pool and croquet lawn. The eleven acres of garden are a delight to the eye and comprise a series of secluded lawns and flower beds with sheltering yew hedges, huge trees, and woodland to explore beyond a fast-running burn.

The bedrooms are decorated and furnished in excellent style and there is a sizeable family suite which contains a four-poster bed, a separate single room and a bathroom. Another family room runs above the dining room and has a bathroom at one end and a shower room at the other; it is very large, probably about the length of a cricket pitch.

Bar food is available morning and evening and on a warm day you might sit out in the courtyard. The chef will cook 'whatever they want' for the children. The food is of an extremely high quality.

In the first edition of the *Family Welcome Guide* we wrote of The Old Mansion House as 'an exceptional place, whether for a quick drink or a longer stay', and that judgement is as appropriate as ever.

Nearby: Fishing and shooting can be arranged via the hotel and there are some great golf courses within reach – Carnoustie, St Andrews, Rosemount and Gleneagles, for example. You are well placed for sightseeing with Camperdown Wildlife Centre on the doorstep; the McManus Galleries in Dundee, Glamis Castle, Scone Palace, and J. M. Barrie's birthplace are within a reasonable distance.

....

✕ Bar snacks (12pm to 2pm and 7pm to 9.30pm) £2–12: poached salmon, steaks, fried fillets of sole, medallions of pork, roast of the day;
Lunch (12pm to 2pm) £15: curried chicken & melon cocktail, escalope of pork, rhubarb & ginger fool;
Dinner (7pm to 9.15pm) £24: smoked Tay salmon, medallions of venison, sticky toffee pudding
Children: half portions
£ High
No Bargain Breaks
Children: free to age 12
Facilities: 2 cots and 2 high chairs; 3 baby-listening lines
6 rooms, 1 family, 1 suite

Open all year except Christmas
P Own car park

BALLACHULISH, HIGHLAND
H BALLACHULISH HOTEL
Tel: 01855 811 606
On the A828 on the south side of Ballachulish Bridge.

The hotel has a superb position alongside Loch Linnhe and is overlooked by the hills of Ben a' Bheithir. It is a grand building in the Scottish baronial style, with curved Gothic windows and pointed gables. The public rooms are just as interesting. The cocktail bar is decorated in blue and its windows look out over a terrace and the loch; children can have their meals in here if they wish. The restaurant sits alongside, elegant with its deep blue and gold furnishings. It has the same enchanting views over the loch to the hills; in the evenings you can watch the slow setting of the sun. The public bar has been refurbished as the Ferry Inn and specializes in seafood dishes. Finally the lounge is a spacious and comfortable room, with plenty of easy chairs and sofas, a grand piano, oil paintings, and log fires in winter.

We looked at several bedrooms and were impressed by the high standards which have been set. The rooms are spacious and very comfortable, with furniture and decorations which are easy on the eye. Many of the rooms, including twenty new bedrooms, have the benefit of loch views.

There is a garden with a lawn and it contains a little slide for younger children. You can enjoy the magnificent views and plan your next walk. All guests can take advantage of the excellent leisure facilities at the nearby Isles of Glencoe Hotel.

There is a relaxed atmosphere at this excellent hotel, where all members of the family are made very welcome.

X Bar meals (12pm to 10pm) £2–10: smoked Loch Leven salmon, vegetable Stroganoff, Scotch sirloin steak, venison & mushroom casserole;

466

Dinner (7pm to 9.30pm) £22: smoked Glenuig trout & spinach terrine, supreme of pheasant, Drambuie trifle, cheese
Children: own menu, half portions
£ High
✓ Best Bargain Break: £90 per person, 2 nights – dinner, b&b
Children: free up to 16 years
Facilities: 6 cots and 6 high chairs; baby-listening system
54 rooms, 4 family
Open all year
Ⓟ Own car park

BALLACHULISH, HIGHLAND
Ⓗ **ISLES OF GLENCOE HOTEL**
Tel: 01855 811 602
Close to the A82, about a mile west of the village of Glencoe.

....

This splendid hotel opened a couple of years ago and is under the same ownership as the Ballachulish. It has its own distinctive style, built with a definite Scandinavian look, and has an unrivalled situation, right on the shore of Loch Leven with the dramatic pass of Glencoe behind. It gives the impression of almost being afloat. There are two lochside harbours and nearly two miles of water frontage, with an abundance of water sports available.

The bright and airy and very comfortable bedrooms are notably spacious, and many have spectacular views of the loch. The family rooms have bunk beds in addition to doubles or singles; and most of the other bedrooms can accommodate an extra bed or a cot without strain.

The dining room, with its metal rafters and rattan ceiling awnings and views over the water, reflects the relaxed style of this excellent hotel, a style which is aided in no small part by the youthful and cheerful staff. A conservatory restaurant has recently been added to the facilities.

A great bonus for guests is the leisure centre with its compact pool (with a wave machine and a jacuzzi), paddling pool and sauna. There is a little play area off the reception area for young children, and the hotel is located in several acres of parkland.

This is an exceptionally appealing family hotel.

Nearby: This is an unrivalled area for walking, and the hotel can advise you on the various routes. Fishermen have a choice of loch, sea or river, and all sorts of water sports can be arranged. Hill climbing, pony trekking and golf are all available, and the leisure centre at Fort William has a swimming pool, squash and tennis. Glencoe and Ben Nevis are close, and the children will enjoy a visit to the Sea Life Centre north of Oban. In the winter the area is a popular ski centre. A new attraction, Highland Mystery World, opens next door to the hotel in the spring.

....

✖ Bar meals (10am to 10pm) £2–14: mussels Portugaise, garlic chicken collops, steak and stout pie, sirloin steak, sweet & sour king prawns; Dinner (7pm to 10pm) £18: game pâté, poached Loch Leven salmon, pudding or cheese
Children: own menu, half portions
£ High
✓ Best Bargain Break: £99 per person, 3 nights – dinner, b&b
Children: free up to 2 years; £12 from 2 to 7; £20 from 7 to 16
Facilities: 6 cots and 6 high chairs; baby-listening system
39 rooms, 9 family
Open mid-Feb to Dec
Ⓟ Own car park

CLACHAN SEIL, BY OBAN, STRATHCLYDE
Ⓟ Tigh-an-Truish
Tel: 01852 300 242
Twelve miles south of Oban on the B844.

....

This long and low 18th-century whitewashed pub is situated in an idyllic setting next to the famous 'Bridge over the Atlantic Ocean', built in 1791, which connects Seil Island to the mainland of Scotland. There is an agreeable L-shaped bar with wood-panelled walls, and families are welcome to use another room alongside. The pleasant garden has tables and chairs where you can sit and admire the bridge and Seil Sound (weather permitting).

The summer menu varies slightly each day, but there's always something fishy; in the winter it's more limited, with things like 'toasties' available. Special children's meals will be prepared by request and charged accordingly, and there is a high chair in the pub.

The pub is open throughout the day during the summer months, and snacks are available during the afternoon.

....

✕ (12pm to 2pm and 6pm to 8.30pm) £2–7: local salmon & oysters, lasagne, sea food pie, steak & ale pie
  Children: special meals on request
🍺 Ale: McEwan's
🅿 Own car park

COMRIE, TAYSIDE
Ⓡ TULLYBANNOCHER FARM FOOD BAR
Tel: 01764 670 827
Just west of Comrie on the A85.

....

There is plenty of room for children, both inside and out, at this large café and craft centre, which is surrounded by woodland and hills. The café itself has a simple lay-out, high-ceilinged like a barn, and with an array of long wooden tables and benches. There is an excellent choice of hot dishes and salads, and of home-made cakes and pastries.

A table and a chair are stationed in the Ladies for the benefit of mothers with small children, and paper towels are also provided.

A large grassy garden at the front, with several picnic tables, will attract you on summer days, and there is loads of room for the children to play.

It is a lovely spot to stop for a meal or a snack, and has the added attraction of having a craft and gift shop and a garden centre on the site. Exhibitions of local paintings are also held throughout the summer.

....

✗ (9am to 9pm, Easter to mid-Oct) £2–10: local trout, venison casserole, haddock & chips, steak & Guinness pie, sirloin steak
Children: own menu, half portions
No credit cards accepted
ℙ Own car park

CUMBERNAULD, STRATHCLYDE
ℙℝ **BROADWOOD FARM**
Tel: 01236 737 556
Close to the junction of the A80 and A73, on the B8048 at the Craiglin roundabout.

....

This is a very recently built pub and restaurant, on a busy roundabout and adjacent to a retail park and Clyde's football stadium (currently shared by Airdrie Football Club, much to the distaste of the local supporters).

The Broadwood Farm was very busy with families when we visited one Saturday lunchtime; and it has the space and facilities to cope, since there are plenty of high chairs and nappy-changing facilities, and the children can use up their energies in the Fun Factory, which has a soft drinks bar and a lounge for the supervising adults.

Unencumbered adults might opt for the lounge at the other end of the pub, an agreeable wood-panelled room with an open stone fireplace and padded settles. In between there is an extensive bar area and a number of dining areas, broken up by stone pillars and a central stone fireplace. A circular conservatory room with a wooden domed ceiling is an interesting feature of the pub.

....

✗ (11.30am to 10pm) £2–8: onion bhajis, fried scampi, chicken Alexandra, Teviotdale pie, tagliatelle carbonara
Children: own menu

Ⓟ Ale: Boddington's, Castle Eden, Flowers and guests
Ⓟ Lots

Nr DUNOON, STRATHCLYDE
Ⓟ **COYLET INN, Loch Eck**
Tel: 01369 840 426
On the A815.

A friendly welcome awaits you at this 17th-century coaching inn. There is a small lounge where you may take the children and, on busy days, the dining room with dark oak tables and chairs is also put to use for families. You have a good view of the loch from this room, which is decorated with old china pieces and copper pans and has a dresser.

Alongside the road is an attractive grassy garden surrounded by trees, and across the road is the splendid Loch Eck, with towering hills behind.

✕ (12pm to 2pm and 5.30pm to 10pm) £1–6: chicken liver pâté, ploughman's, langoustine prawns, trout
Children: half portions
Ⓟ Ale: Deuchars, McEwan's, Younger's
Ⓟ Own car park

EAST KILBRIDE, STRATHCLYDE
ⓅⓇ **NEW FARM**
Tel: 01355 267 177
Just south of East Kilbride on the A726.

From the car park the impression is of a large suburban bungalow, and you would not guess at the great amount of space inside the pub/restaurant.

471

It is a rambling place on several levels, and the décor is designed to persuade you that you have entered an old country inn: there is a plethora of wooden ceiling beams, stone and timber pillars and wood panelling. The main dining area is very large and has an excellent view, through its wide windows, of the local golf course.

The conservatory room overlooks a paved terrace with several bench tables, and there is a children's play area here. An indoor play area for small children is also available.

When we visited, the New Farm was heaving with its Saturday lunchtime family trade, and it has all the facilities (high chairs, nappy-changing unit and play areas) needed to cope with it well – not least friendly and helpful staff. The restaurant is open all day and serves food at all times, and for the beer drinker, a good choice of real ales is available.

....

✖ (11.30am to 10pm) £2–8: prawn cocktail, chicken Balti, turkey fillet, steak & kidney pie, vegetable crumble
Children: own menu
◑ Ale: Boddington's, Flowers, Marston's and guests
ℙ Own car park

EDINBURGH, LOTHIAN
Ⓗ THRUMS HOTEL, 14 Minto Street
Tel: 0131 667 5545
Not far from the city centre, on the south side, off the A7.

....

The hotel is very convenient for the centre of Edinburgh and is in an area with many small hotels and guest houses. It has been constructed from two large Georgian buildings, in which many of the original features have been retained. The comfortable and well-decorated lounge has plenty of sofas and easy chairs and the large bay window gives it a bright appearance. The six family rooms have plenty of space and are attractively decorated.

An agreeable aspect of this hotel is its dining room, since part of it is housed in a conservatory, which in its turn looks out to the sizeable lawned garden with its pretty borders of flowers. It is a peaceful retreat away from the city bustle. There is also a stretch of lawned garden at the front.

Nearby: Edinburgh is a fine city with much to see and do: the famous Castle, the Palace of Holyroodhouse, the National Gallery, Huntly House Museum, the Museum of Childhood, the Royal Botanic Garden, and so on. Within easy reach are many other attractions: the Almondell and Calderwood Country Park and Beecraigs Country Park; and the city is surrounded by castles – at Dirleton, Hailes, Tantallon and Lauriston, for example.

✗ Lunch (12pm to 2pm) £7: soup, fish of the day, pudding;
Dinner (5.30pm to 8pm) £12: prawn cocktail, sirloin steak, pudding
Children: own menu, half portions
£ Medium
Children: cots free; half price up to 12 years
Facilities: 2 cots and 2 high chairs, baby-listening
14 rooms, 5 family
Open all year except Christmas and New Year
Ⓟ Own car park

EDINBURGH, LOTHIAN
ⓅⓇ **CRAMOND BRIG**
Tel: 0131 339 4350
On the west side of Edinburgh, on the A90 at Cramond Bridge.

This substantial stone roadhouse has long been a familiar landmark to anyone travelling to or from the Forth Bridge road.

If you enter from the car park side you will find a pleasant conservatory room and then a congenial bar, with a dining area in one of the large bay windows which are a feature of the building. Tucked away around a corner there is a quiet lounge with wood-panelled walls, an open fireplace and plenty of comfortable seats.

The bar area extends along the front of the building and includes a couple of alcoves – one with a table for six diners and the other with a couple of tables. On a half-landing there is a pleasant dining room with wide windows on to the garden.

The family section is concentrated at one end of the pub and primarily comprises a brightly decorated dining room. There are lots of toys on shelves, and the various decorations include a red wooden aeroplane and balloonists hanging from the ceiling. There is a small indoor play area (taken up by a ball swamp) and a sizeable outdoor play area in a garden which has a lawn and a terrace.

High chairs and a baby-changing unit are available in this agreeable family pub and restaurant.

....

✕ (12pm to 10pm) £2–9: prawn platter, chilli con carne, salmon steak, seafood pie, lemon chicken
Children: own menu
◲ Ale: Theakston's and guests
℗ Own car park

EDINBURGH, LOTHIAN
Ⓡ HENDERSONS SALAD TABLE, 94 Hanover Street
Tel: 0131 225 2131
Off Princes Street and on the corner of Thistle Street and Hanover Street.

....

A shop, wine bar, bistro and restaurant are encompassed in Henderson's, which is much more spacious than you would guess from outside, and is a real warren of rooms and alcoves. On the ground floor, fruit and veg and wholemeal bread from their own bakery is sold; and down the stairs you will find an attractive self-service vegetarian restaurant with pine tables. The choice of food is comprehensive, with a very large range of salads. The emphasis is very much on wholefoods, fresh salads and crunchy vegetables, complemented by some toothsome desserts.

There is also a very pleasant, spacious, low-ceilinged wine bar (with live music throughout the week, including jazz and classical), a separate no-smoking room, and two very snug alcoves with arched roofs (the old pavement cellars).

If you need to change or feed a baby, there is a pull-down shelf, a chair and paper towels in both the Ladies and Gents toilets.

....

✖ (8am to 10.45pm, Mon to Sat; bistro open Sun lunch) £1–4: vegetable curry, lentil stew, ratatouille, mushroom savoury, stuffed aubergine
  Children: half portions
☐ Ale: Belhaven
Ⓟ Meters

EDINBURGH, LOTHIAN
Ⓡ Scottish National Gallery of Modern Art, Belford Road
Tel: 0131 556 8921
North-west of the city centre – well signposted. The No. 13 bus goes to the door.

....

A formidable collection of 20th-century paintings and sculptures has been built up in this neo-classical building, which once housed John Watson's school.

The great names are well represented: Epstein, Nash, Moore, Hepworth, Sutherland, Dubuffet, Leger, Picasso, Giacometti, Magritte, Matisse, Braque, Miro, Paolozzi, and so on.

Most children will have fun looking at the amazing shapes and colours – and so will the adults; anyone with imagination will enjoy trying to interpret the remarkable paintings and sculptures.

The café has been in the *Family Welcome Guide* for many years and offers an interesting choice of salads, snacks and hot meals. It is a bright and attractive place and has a terrace with a sculpture garden for summer days. High chairs and a nappy-changing unit are provided.

The National Gallery of Scotland and the Scottish National Portrait

Gallery are both in the centre of Edinburgh and are also well worth a visit (entry is free). The latter also has an excellent café.

✕ (10.30am to 4.30pm; Sun from 2pm) £1–4: quiches, salads, home-made soups, filled baked potatoes, cheesy egg croissant
Children: half portions

Ⓟ Own car park

FOCHABERS, GRAMPIAN
Ⓡ BAXTERS
Tel: 01343 820 393
On the A96, one mile west of Fochabers.

The self-service restaurant is part of the visitor centre run by the famous Scottish food manufacturers. It is a bright and well-furnished place, which offers excellent value for money. There is a very good choice of fresh foods, a marvellous cup of tea, and lovely views of the Spey Valley through the wide windows.

The Visitor Centre is well designed, with shops which sell speciality foods, cooking utensils and craft goods. There are also guided tours of the factory at regular intervals, and the tour guides are multilingual.

There are several high chairs on the premises; and good facilities in the Ladies for dealing with babies – chairs, a baby-changing table and paper towels, for example.

The agreeable patio area has plenty of bench tables and cheerful parasols and overlooks the landscaped gardens and a field with Highland cattle. There is a lovely rose garden too.

This is a well-organized and pleasant place to visit, with very friendly and helpful staff, who retain their poise even on the busiest and hottest of days.

✕ (9.30am to 6pm; weekends from 10am; until 5pm in winter) £2–6: soup, filled jacket potatoes, Lossiemouth scampi, grilled Spey salmon, Baxters pancakes

Children: own menu, half portions
No credit cards accepted
🅿 Own car park

GIFFORD, LOTHIAN
🄷🅿 TWEEDDALE ARMS HOTEL, High Street
Tel: 01620 810 240
Six miles or so south of Haddington, on the B6355.

We have long been fans of this very attractive 17th-century coaching inn, situated in a smart village to the south-east of Edinburgh. It is a long, white-painted building, smartly furnished, and the baskets of dried flowers hanging on the walls and ceilings add a cheerful touch.

In the last few years it has expanded to become a medium-sized hotel without losing its character as an inn. The long and spacious bar area is a most agreeable and welcoming place, nicely furnished with padded chairs and benches. When we last visited, it was fun to see a family gathered there for lunch, complete with small child in a high chair. Across the corridor there is a very smart lounge, scattered with sofas and easy chairs; an open fire adds to its charm, as do some interesting oil paintings. The attractive dining room has French windows on to an enclosed garden.

We looked at several rooms, including an excellent family room, and found the standards of comfort and decoration to be of a high standard.

Families are welcome anywhere in the inn to eat and drink, and on summer days you might head for one of the two pretty walled gardens, where there is plenty of space and the added bonus of a climbing frame, a swing and a trampoline for the children. There is also a huge stretch of village green at the front of the pub.

There is an excellent choice of food on the bar menu, as well as a full restaurant menu in the evenings and at Sunday lunchtimes. In common with many of the pubs and hotels in Scotland, the bar is open throughout the day.

....

✕ Bar meals (12pm to 2pm and 7pm to 9pm) £2–8: spaghetti Bolognese, smoked salmon, escalope of turkey, sirloin steak, lamb Madras;
Dinner (7pm to 9pm) £19: smoked trout fillet wrapped in smoked salmon, soup, breast of duck, pudding or cheese
Children: own menu, half portions
£ Medium

✓ Best Bargain Break: £80 per person, 2 nights – dinner, b&b
Facilities: 3 cots and 3 high chairs; plug-in baby alarm
18 rooms, 3 family

◖ Ale: Greenmantle, Ind Coope Burton and guests

🅿 On the street

INCHBAE, nr GARVE, HIGHLAND
Ⓗ **INCHBAE LODGE HOTEL**
Tel: 01997 455 269
On the A835 north-west of Garve.

....

The journey to Inchbae Lodge is a joy in itself, through some of the loveliest glens in the Highlands and passing Loch Garve and Rogie Falls. Six miles from the nearest village, Inchbae is a remote former Victorian hunting lodge, now a charming and informal hotel with a well-deserved reputation for good food.

The hotel sits alongside the River Blackwater and there are magnificent views of the heathered hills in every direction, with Ben Wyvis towering over the scene. If you value peace and tranquillity, Inchbae is the place for you, and it is an ideal base for a country-loving family who want to tour the Highlands.

The seven acres of grounds, which include an island on the River Blackwater, are not 'gardened'; they are mowed by tractor and provide a lovely setting for the hotel. The children will love the freedom and all the space. Younger children should be supervised, however, since there is an unfenced pond, but there are safe play areas in an enclosed part of the grounds.

Guests can fish in the river at the bottom of the garden, and the children can make friends with the various animals: pet rabbits, chickens, sheep, dogs, cats and cattle. If the weather is inclement all sorts of games and puzzles are available in the hotel.

Nearby: Many types of outdoor pursuits can be arranged – fishing, clay pigeon shooting, hill walking, golf and riding – and the area is a prolific one for wildlife. From Garve station you can take a trip by train to the Kyle of Lochalsh and then over the sea (a short ferry trip) to Skye for the day. If you fancy some sightseeing in other directions you can visit the Corrieshalloch Gorge, the Beinn Eighe Nature Reserve, and the Torridon Mountains Centre; near Inverness you can see the Loch Ness Monster Exhibition, Urquhart Castle, Cawdor Castle and the battlefield of Culloden.

✖ Bar snacks (12pm to 2pm and 5pm to 8.30pm) £2–10: sweet pickled herring, sirloin steak, fillet of haddock, haggis, casserole of the day; Dinner (7.30pm to 8.30pm) £20: seafood platter, soup, roast grouse, pudding
  Children: own menu, half portions
  £ Medium
✓ Best Bargain Break: £85 per person, 2 nights – dinner, b&b
  Children: free of charge
  Facilities: 3 cots and a high chair; baby-listening system
  12 rooms, 3 family
  Open all year except Christmas
  No credit cards accepted
🅿 Own car park

INVERNESS, HIGHLAND
Ⓡ **Theatre Restaurant, Eden Court Theatre, Bishop's Road**
Tel: 01463 221 723
Follow signs to 'town centre and castle' and then to 'Eden Court'.

We were alerted to this restaurant by one of our readers, and it is an ideal place for families in this famous city. It has several high chairs, a well-equipped mother and baby room, and excellent freshly cooked food.

It is a bright, airy and spacious restaurant and through the huge windows you have splendid views of the River Ness. It is in the grounds of the Old Bishop's Palace and the theatre complex also houses an excellent shop which sells Scottish arts and crafts.

The garden is delightful, with large and immaculate lawns, rose beds and mature trees. You can sit here and look over the river to the castle.

The restaurant offers excellent value in a lovely setting. There is always a good vegetarian option and a fine choice of herbal teas, and the local fish soup, cullen skink, is a meal in itself.

✖ (10am to 8.30pm; closed Sun) £2–7: cullen skink, smoked salmon, roast chicken, fish & chips, vegetarian dish of the day
Children: half portions
Ⓟ Car park behind theatre

KELSO, BORDERS
Ⓗ **Ednam House Hotel, Bridge Street**
Tel: 01573 224 168
Go to the centre of town and look for the hotel sign.

This splendid and stately hotel offers real value to families at a time when many hotels overcharge disgracefully for mediocre service and facilities. Although none of the rooms are specifically designated as family rooms, most of them have ample space for a cot and an extra bed.

It's a grand Georgian mansion, built of sandstone in 1761 – a noted fishing hotel which was once owned by the Duke of Roxburghe. The beautiful interior retains its 'ducal' air with lots of carved wood and ornate plasterwork (in the main lounge there is a relief of Zeus chasing Aurora); and the dining room has recently been refurbished to splendid effect. The three acres of gardens have a croquet lawn, and a long balustrade overlooking a lovely stretch of the Tweed. It is handy for the town (once described by Sir Walter Scott as the most beautiful in Scotland) and many places of historic interest – and the staff will arrange other activities for you and your children: riding, golf, fishing, etc.

Nearby: There are numerous interesting places to see in the locality including the remarkable Floors Castle and the ruins of Kelso Abbey. There are abbeys at Dryburgh and Jedburgh also, and Sir Walter Scott's house, Abbotsford, is not far away. Bowhill, Traquair House, Dawyck Botanic Garden, Kailzie Gardens and Neidpath Castle are all within easy reach.

....

✕ Bar lunches (12.30pm to 2pm; not Sun) £2–5: smoked trout, grilled sole, steak & kidney pie, vegetable crumble;
Dinner (7pm to 9pm) £17: smoked haddock, soup, pot-roasted duck, pudding or cheese
Children: high teas, half portions
£ High

✓ Best Bargain Break: £86 per person, 2 nights – dinner, b&b
Children: free up to 8 years; sliding scale thereafter
Facilities: 3 cots and 2 high chairs; baby-listening system
32 rooms
Closed Christmas and New Year

P Own car park

KILMAHOG, BY CALLANDER, CENTRAL
P LADE INN
Tel: 01877 330 152
On the A821 one mile north of Callander.

Just outside the attractive town of Callander you will find this agreeable country pub. It is spacious inside, with plenty of seating, and families are welcome to use a light and airy room which is down a few steps from the main pub and looks directly out to the garden. This has several tables and is bordered with shrubs, tubs of flowers and two ponds with goldfish. It's a congenial place to be on a summer day.

You will receive a friendly welcome from the staff, and the home-made food is freshly cooked, served in hearty portions and is very good value. Just the thing to set you up either before or after exploring the Trossachs. There are two high chairs on the premises and the pub is open all day.

- ✕ (12pm to 3.15pm and 5.30pm to 9.15pm) £2–12: lasagne, fish pie, lamb chops, sirloin steak, haddock & chips
  Children: half portions
- ◑ Ale: Flowers, McEwan's, Martin's and guests
- P Own car park

KINCRAIG, HIGHLAND
R LOCH INSH CHALETS AND BOATHOUSE RESTAURANT
Tel: 01540 651 272
Off the B9152 (it's parallel to the A9 north of Kingussie). Follow the signs to Loch Insh Watersports.

This restaurant, built from natural stone and old telegraph poles, has a superb position on the shore. Loch Insh is a great centre for water sports, including canoeing, sailing, windsurfing, raft-building and salmon and trout fishing. You can also hire mountain bikes, and there is an artificial ski slope, an adventure park and a fitness trail.

There's a grassy and sandy area by the water's edge or you can seek the shade in the woods behind where tables are also set up. Dogs are banned from the picnic area – another very sensible idea.

There's a good choice of fresh salads on the various menus (snacks, bar meals and à la carte), and the children's menu includes a drink and ice-cream. Barbecue stands are available and you can use them on the shore. Beach barbecues are held throughout July and August.

There are six log cabins for hire, very well equipped and spacious and with the bonus of the beautiful surroundings. The weekly rentals vary from £280 to £710 and short breaks are available at most times of the year.

✕ (10am to 10pm) £1–12: filled jacket potatoes, burgers, sirloin steak, venison casserole, Loch Insh salmon
Children: own menu, half portions
Open Jan to end Oct and New Year week
🅿 Own car park

LOCHWINNOCH, STRATHCLYDE
🅿Ⓡ THE MOSSEND
Tel: 01505 842 672
On the A760 close to its junction with the A737.

This roadside pub and restaurant is presentable, in its coat of pebbledash covered in white paint, and offers fine facilities for families: plenty of space inside, high chairs, a baby-changing unit, and a sizeable Fun Factory with its own soft drinks and snack bar.

That's a pretty good start and it is a congenial place for anyone, whether with a family group or not. The extensive bar area overlooks the garden and includes a lounge area at one end with a bay window. Comfortable padded settles are ranged around the walls.

At the far end you will mount a few steps to the open-plan restaurant, with its large windows. Screens of wood and coloured glass form booths, and there is a round table for eight diners in one corner.

The conservatory room is a pleasant spot from which to admire the views of the distant loch and the low-lying hills.

Below there is a paved terrace and an enclosed lawned garden with a play unit and a bouncy castle.

✕ (11.30am to 10pm) £2–8: oriental prawns, chicken masala, fillet of salmon, sirloin steak, vegetable moussaka
　Children: own menu
◖ Ale: Boddington's, Flowers and guests
ℙ Ample

MILNGAVIE, STRATHCLYDE
Ⓡ THE FAMOUS COFFEE HOUSE, Findlay Clark Garden Centre, Boclair Road
Tel: 01360 620 700
On the B8049 just south of junction with the A807; look for the Findlay Clark Garden Centre.

The largest garden centre in Scotland houses an excellent coffee shop in a conservatory, which is smartly decorated with trellis and curtains on the walls, pictures (for sale), basket-weave chairs, and naturally lots of potted plants.

The whole place, with a vast gift and garden accessory area indoors, is laid out in a spacious and attractive way, and there is a very wide range of food available: snacks, salads, hot dishes and pastries.

There are plenty of high chairs here, and nappies can be changed in the disabled toilet.

✕ (10am to 5pm) £2–5: cheese & bacon quiche, cannelloni, open sandwiches, chicken tikka masala, spaghetti carbonara
　Children: half portions
　No credit cards accepted
ℙ Own car park

Nr NAIRN, HIGHLAND
Ⓗ Ⓟ **COVENANTERS INN, High Street, Auldearn**
Tel: 01667 452 456
Two miles east of Nairn, just off the A96, on the edge of the hamlet of
Auldearn.

The inn has quite a history since the rebel Covenanters fought the Battle
of Auldearn with the Duke of Montrose in 1645 in what is now the car
park. The building began life as a mill and a brewhouse in the 17th
century and it is good to report that the original character of the place
is still apparent.

The lounge bar, for example, has sandstone walls, a low, oak-beamed
ceiling, oak tables and settles, and a wood-burning stove. It is a warm and
welcoming spot. Families are made welcome here, too. Older children
and adults can use the snooker table and the dartboard, and younger
ones are not forgotten, since there is a play area and a good selection
of toys. Another dining area/lounge has a conservatory.

On sunny days you can sit on the paved terrace where there are several
bench tables. There is a small children's play area with a wooden fort,
climbing frame, a slide and swings.

Nearby: There are some fine sandy beaches in the area, including
Burghhead, Nairn and Findhorn, which is a good surfing centre. There
are some fascinating places to visit within an easy drive: Cawdor Castle,
the Highland Wildlife Park, the battlefield of Culloden, Urquhart
Castle, the Loch Ness Monster Exhibition and Brodie Castle. Golfers
have a good choice of courses, including the championship links at
Nairn, and fishing, horse riding and water sports are all readily
available.

✗ Bar snacks (12pm to 2pm and 5pm to 9pm) £2–10: smoked venison,
  pickled herring, langoustines, roast pheasant, fillet steak
  £ Medium
✓ Best Bargain Break: £25 per person per night – dinner, b&b
  Children: free up to 14 years
  Facilities: 1 cot and 2 high chairs; baby-listening to all rooms

8 rooms, 2 family
Open all year
P Own car park

NEWCASTLETON, BORDERS
R **THE COPSHAW KITCHEN**, 4 North Hermitage Street
Tel: 013873 75250
On the east side of the main street, the B6357.

This restaurant used to be a grocer's shop and is now divided into two parts: the plain and simple tea room and the restaurant, which is also an antique shop. There is a huge old dresser on one side and shelves on the other, all inundated with antique china and bric-à-brac. The menu is the same in each although you pay a bit more in the restaurant – but the prices are very reasonable.

At the front is a shop where there are further antiques and second-hand goods for sale, and more antiques up the stairs. The snack menu and children's menu serve as one and the same; quite right – why should the children always get the fish fingers?

The proprietor will provide a chair in the small Ladies for a mother wishing to breast-feed a baby.

In the winter you should check the opening times, which may vary a little.

X (9.30am to 5.30pm every day; Wed to Sat 7pm to 9pm; weekends only Jan to March) £2–9: egg mayonnaise, haddock & chips, steaks, lasagne, game pie
Children: own menu, half portions
P Own car park

ONICH, nr FORT WILLIAM, HIGHLAND
Ⓗ **ALLT-NAN-ROS HOTEL**
Tel: 01855 821 210
Just east of Onich village on the A82.

Beautifully situated by Loch Linnhe, this hotel was once a Victorian manor house, and it has lovely views of the mountains and towards the Isle of Mull. You can take particular pleasure in these from the lounge and nicely decorated dining room. The bedrooms offer plenty of space, especially those with bay windows overlooking the loch.

There is a large, rambling garden at the front and the side of the hotel, and you have superb views of the loch. It has terraced lawns and trees, a stream and pond, benches and picnic tables and a shady lawn at one side.

Nearby: Any form of water sport can be arranged, and some tuition to accompany them. The area is a fisherman's paradise: for salmon or trout, sea fishing or coarse. Walking, climbing, golf and pony trekking can all be arranged and there is a leisure centre in Fort William. If you fancy some sightseeing, Glencoe and Ben Nevis are close, and the West Highland Museum is in Fort William. The children will certainly enjoy a visit to the Sea Life Centre near Oban.

✗ Dinner (7pm to 8.30pm) £20: guinea fowl terrine, collops of pork, pudding or cheese
Children: own menu, half portions

£ High

✓ Best Bargain Break: £150 per person, 3 nights – dinner, b&b

Children: £5 to age 3; £8 from age 4 to 12; £16 from age 13 to 16

Facilities: 3 cots and 3 high chairs; baby-listening through the phones

21 rooms, 3 family

Open all year except Nov

🅿 Own car park

PEEBLES, BORDERS
Ⓗ Ⓡ **CRINGLETIE HOUSE HOTEL**
Tel: 01721 730 233
Two and a half miles north of Peebles on the A703.

This delightful hotel has been recommended in the *Family Welcome Guide* from its first edition onwards and has always been a favourite of ours. The house was built in 1861 for the Wolfe Murray family, one of whose ancestors, Colonel Alexander Murray, accepted the surrender of Quebec on the death of General Wolfe in 1759.

Cringletie is a most appealing and distinguished sandstone mansion and shows all the exuberance of the Victorian age, with its high windows, pointed towers and tall chimneys. It is set in nearly thirty acres of beautiful gardens against a background of gentle hills. You can certainly relax in such a setting, and the children can make use of the play area. There is also a new all-weather tennis court, croquet lawn and putting green.

The public rooms are elegantly furnished and well proportioned, and there is an interesting choice of food; it is not surprising that the hotel has been recommended in the *Good Food Guide* for twenty years. A couple of acres of kitchen garden ensures that the ingredients for your meals are fresh.

Nearby: You are only about twenty miles from Edinburgh with its many attractions. Almost on the doorstep you can visit Neidpath Castle, Kailzie Gardens, Traquair House, Dawyck Botanic Garden and the John Buchan Centre. You are surrounded by lovely countryside if you like walking; and horse riding, fishing and golf are all readily available.

....

✗ Lunch (1pm to 1.45pm) £15: spiced tomato soup, escalope of pork, pudding or cheese;
Dinner (7.30pm to 8.30pm) £25: devilled crab, soup, medallions of beef, pudding or cheese
Children: half portions
£ High
✓ Best Bargain Break: £57 per person, per night – dinner, b&b
Children: cot £3.50; £8–15 thereafter
Facilities: 3 cots and 3 high chairs; baby-listening
12 rooms, 2 family
Open early Mar to 1 Jan
Ⓟ Own car park

PEEBLES, BORDERS
Ⓗ PEEBLES HOTEL HYDRO
Tel: 01721 720 602
Off the A72 (Peebles to Galashiels).

A gigantic Victorian spa hotel, in thirty acres of grounds, whose portals you need never leave because everything you want is on site. The huge chandeliers, glass-domed roofs, and miles of corridor hark back to a more expansive age.

The many and varied facilities include an excellent fenced-in children's playground, a 'commando course' for older children, two squash courts, badminton, three hard tennis courts, a volleyball court, a pitch and putt course, a putting green and an indoor heated pool in the leisure centre, which has been named 'Bubbles'. Sensibly, there is a playpen in the Ladies' changing room.

There is a vast games room with three table tennis tables, two snooker tables (for over-18s only), table football and space invaders, and in addition a play room which is supervised and has toys, a slide, a rocking horse and a video. On most days the hotel has a number of full-time children's supervisors; and there are masses of events organized right through the day for children and for adults; plus dances at least twice a week.

Nearby: There are dozens of golf courses and excellent places to walk, ride and fish. Within easy reach you will find Kailzie Gardens, Traquair House, Neidpath Castle, the John Buchan Centre, Dawyck Botanic Garden, Bowhill and Sir Walter Scott's house at Abbotsford.

✗ Bubbles (12.30pm to 10pm) from £1.25: quiche, salads, dish of the day, vegetarian dish;
Lunch (12.45pm to 2pm) £13: cold buffet, pudding or cheese;
Dinner (7.30pm to 9pm) £18: lamb samosa, fresh local trout, pudding or cheese
Children: high teas, half portions
£ High
✓ Best Bargain Break: £118 per person, 2 nights – dinner, b&b

Children: from £5 to £17 (includes breakfast and high tea)
Facilities: plenty of cots and high chairs; baby-listening via the
telephones
137 rooms, 26 family
Open all year
�‍ Ale: Greenmantle
P Own car park

ROCKCLIFFE, DUMFRIES & GALLOWAY
H **BARON'S CRAIG HOTEL**
Tel: 01556 630 225
Follow the sign to Rockcliffe from the A710.

This delightful granite-built hotel, with its unobtrusive modern
additions, stands in lovely grounds overlooking the Solway and Rough
Firth. From the elegant dining room and the airy, high-ceilinged lounges
you have splendid views of the water and the wooded hills.

The hotel is set in a dozen acres of woodland, with immaculate lawns
and colourful displays of flowers, especially when the massed ranks of
rhododendrons are in full bloom. You can sit here at peace or perhaps
take some gentle exercise on the putting green.

Nearby: This is a most attractive and unspoiled part of Scotland and
there are miles of sandy beach around Southerness. In the vicinity of
the hotel there is plenty to do in the way of sailing, fishing, golf (at
Southerness, for example), wind surfing, horse riding and walking. If
sightseeing is on the agenda there is plenty of scope: Threave Garden,
Caerlaverock Castle and the nearby nature reserve, Broughton House
and the Gem Rock Museum at Creetown.

✗ Bar lunches (12.30pm to 2pm) £2–10: chicken liver pâté, goujons
of chicken, smoked salmon, sirloin steak;
Dinner (7pm to 9pm) £20: smoked salmon, braised duck breast,
pudding or cheese

Children: own menu, half portions
£ High
✓ Best Bargain Break: £57–67 per person per night – dinner, b&b
Children: free
Facilities: 3 cots and 3 high chairs; baby-listening line
22 rooms, 4 family
Closed end Nov to Easter
🅿 Own car park

SEAMILL, STRATHCLYDE
🅿🆁 WATERSIDE INN
Tel: 01294 823 238
On the A78 just south of Seamill.

The name of this family pub and restaurant is an accurate description of its location, alongside the waters of the Firth of Forth and with a view to the neighbouring Farland Head. You can take a ferry from nearby Ardrossan to the Isle of Arran.

The Waterside Inn is a sprawling roadside hostelry, with a spacious interior and excellent amenities for all members of the family. It is open throughout the day and serves food at all times, and has high chairs in numbers, plus nappy-changing facilities.

The bar has a traditional pubby atmosphere, owing to the beamed ceiling and wood panelling and the padded settles along the walls. There is a good choice of real ales.

A large stone fireplace is a feature of the restaurant, which is divided into three or four separate areas. There are delightful views of the ocean from one side.

You can also enjoy the seascape from the extensive lawned garden or from the terrace. A children's play area occupies one side of the garden and a bouncy castle is set up in summer.

✕ (11.30am to 10pm) £2–8: fish dippers, haddock & chips, gammon steak, lasagne verdi, marinated lamb steak

Children: own menu
Ⓓ Ale: Boddington's, Flowers and guests
Ⓟ Lots

SELKIRK, BORDERS
Ⓗ PHILIPBURN HOUSE HOTEL
Tel: 01750 20747
Where the A707 and the A708 meet, just out of the town.

The house dates back to 1751, and not long before that date the Covenanters and the Royalists did battle at Philipbaugh, which lies in the field only a short distance away. It became a hotel in 1972 and specializes in family holidays.

In the rambling but well-kept grounds (for which the hotel won an award a couple of years ago) you will find a heated swimming pool, a pets' corner, a trampoline and a badminton court. Inside there are two games rooms.

Adults who prefer a less active outdoor existence will find plenty of peace and quiet on the spacious back lawn, which has a number of bench tables and garden chairs.

There is a very flexible system of eating arrangements here. A quick-bite menu served from 6pm is a favourite with older children while the comprehensive children's menu is served from 5.30pm at prices ranging from under £1 up to £9.

The management and staff make a big effort to keep their guests happy and the hotel will arrange a nanny for the odd morning or afternoon, given reasonable notice.

Nearby: If you are the active type you can go walking, fishing or pony trekking and there is a fine selection of golf courses. There are many attractions within reach – Abbotsford (Sir Walter Scott's home), Bowhill, Traquair House, Floors Castle, the abbeys at Dryburgh and Melrose, and Kailzie Gardens.

✕ Bar snacks (12pm to 2pm and 7pm to 9.30pm) £2–13: croute
Bengal, salmon fishcakes, Tiroler grostle, croque monsieur, roasted
quail;
Dinner (7.30pm to 9.30pm) £23: sole & salmon terrine, soup, rack
of Border lamb, Italian trifle or cheese
Children: own menu, half portions
£ High

✓ Best Bargain Break: £110–140 per person, 2 nights – dinner, b&b
Children: various reductions up to 15 years
Facilities: 6 cots and 6 high chairs; baby-listening system
16 rooms, 11 family
Open all year

Ⓟ Own car park

TWEEDSMUIR, BORDERS
Ⓟ CROOK INN HOTEL
Tel: 01899 880 272
On the A701 a mile north of Tweedsmuir.

A very scenic drive awaits you, from whichever direction you approach
this roadside inn, which is said to be Scotland's oldest licensed
premises (1604).

A smartly painted building greets you, with the curved windows of
a 1930s extension on one side. It certainly does not look out of place,
nor does the cheerful tartan carpet which covers the ground floor of
the inn.

Families can use the large conservatory off the main entrance and it
is well furnished with tables and chairs. The adults can also enjoy a
superb bar in the old part of the building. It has a stone floor, plastered
stone wall and a huge central fireplace. A nice spot for a few draughts
of Greenmantle. It is the Willie Wastle bar, and a framed copy of the
famous poem by Burns hangs in the hall.

Make sure that you visit the Ladies or the Gents before you leave –
to see the Art Deco mirrors and tiles which are still in place.

There are two gardens to enjoy on a summer day: across the road a large and shady lawned garden; and alongside the pub another large stretch of lawn with bench tables and a climbing frame. The Crook Inn is open throughout the day.

If you fancy some fishing you can buy a permit at the Inn to fish for trout on the Tweed.

....

✗ (12pm to 9 pm) £2–10: smoked trout mousse, haddock & chips, sirloin steak, poached salmon, steak pie
  Children: own menu
Ⓓ Ale: Greenmantle
Ⓟ Own car park

TYNDRUM, CENTRAL
Ⓡ **CLIFTON COFFEE HOUSE**
Tel: 01838 400 271
On the A82.

....

On a main tourist route, this is a busy and efficient restaurant with a craft centre and food shop which offers a wide range of products, including Scottish whisky, shortbread, preserves, cashmere, pottery and other souvenirs.

The restaurant is large, well organized and sparkling clean. The pine ceilings, bright Formica-topped tables and many plants and flowers add to the welcoming atmosphere.

The lavatories for the disabled have shelves ideal for nappy-changing, and the owner will find a quiet spot for a mother wishing to breastfeed her baby. The staff are very happy to warm bottles and baby food.

There is an excellent range of freshly cooked food, both hot and cold, served in generous portions at reasonable prices. A good enough recommendation for anyone and especially for families on the move.

....

✕ (8.30am to 5.30pm) £1–7: tuna salad, fresh salmon salad, steak pie, kedgeree, Hebridean leek pie
Children: half portions
Closed early Jan to 1 Mar
🅿 Own car park

WALES

Map 10

ABERAERON, DYFED
® THE HIVE ON THE QUAY, Cadwgan Place
Tel: 01545 570 445
In the town centre.

....

This delightful café is situated on a converted coal wharf between the two harbours; the inner harbour has been pedestrianized to a large extent. Half the restaurant is in a stone building and the other half in a conservatory. You can eat in the courtyard.

It is a most attractive place, amid colourful and neat cottages, and above the restaurant you will find a honey-bee exhibition. Another attraction is the Aeron Express which starts nearby. The replica of a device originally built in 1885, it is an aerial ropeway which takes people across the harbour. The sea aquarium is also nearby and will appeal to the children.

All the food is freshly home-made with an emphasis on Welsh recipes; the salads are always interesting and the bread and cakes delicious (they are made from organic flour and free-range eggs). It is good to report that the children's menu is not the usual dreary fish fingers and chips, but a proper offering of soup, salads and hot savoury pancakes. The honey ice creams are an absolute delight, whatever age you are, and there is also a range of honey fruit sorbets, all made from fresh fruit, and yoghurt ices. Across the courtyard there is a fresh fish shop and the restaurant therefore has a wide range available.

If you wish to change a baby there is a shelf in the Ladies.

....

✗ £1–7: cracked crab salad, local prawns, spinach & cream cheese cannelloni, hot savoury pancakes;
Dinner (6pm to 9.30pm) £8: smoked salmon, Aberaeron huss, honey ice cream
Children: own menu, half portions
Open 10.30am to 5pm May, June and Sept; 10am to 9.30pm July and Aug; closed end Sept to spring bank holiday

🍺 Ale: Wadworth's
🅿 Ample street parking

ABERDOVEY, GWYNEDD
Ⓗ **HARBOUR HOTEL**
Tel: 01654 767 250
On the sea front.

Here is a hotel which makes a special effort to make all members of the family feel at home. It is a charming Victorian property which has been restored in a stylish and comfortable way. Amongst the nine rooms are three smart and comfortable family suites, which comprise two separate bedrooms and a bathroom. Three of these are especially quiet, since they are at the back of the hotel.

Their family restaurant, Rumbles, is open all day from 10am and offers a good range of food, including vegetarian dishes, main courses and snacks at reasonable prices. The hotel dining room is reserved for the adults in the evenings, and the basement wine bar offers an excellent choice of food, wines and beers.

Nearby: There are five miles of sand on the doorstep, and a public play area a hundred yards away. There are many other excellent beaches nearby, and the lovely Aberdovey golf course just up the road, with concessionary rates for guests. There are many attractions within reach including the Centre for Alternative Technology, the Coed-y-Brenin Forest, the Llanfair Slate Caverns, the Maes Artro Tourist Village, steam railways at Talyllyn, Fairbourne and the Vale of Rheidol, and Portmeirion to the north.

....

✕ Rumbles (10am to 10pm) £1–9: plaice & chips, seafood platter, spicy vegetable chilli, lamb cutlets, steak;
Dinner (from 7.30pm) £15: king prawns, rack of Welsh lamb, pudding or cheese
Children: own menu, half portions
£ High

✓ Best Bargain Break: 5% discount for 2 nights; 10% for 3 nights; 15% for 7 nights
Children: £5 under 3 years; £12.50 from 4 to 9; £20 from 10 to 15 years
Facilities: 3 cots and 3 high chairs; baby-listening system to all rooms
9 rooms, 3 family
Open all year

🅿 Public car park opposite hotel

ABERDOVEY, GWYNEDD
Ⓗ **TREFEDDIAN HOTEL**
Tel: 01654 767 213
On the A493 west of the village.

....

This appealing hotel has an enviable position just outside Aberdovey and overlooks the lovely Aberdovey golf course, a great favourite of Bernard Darwin, who wrote: 'about this one course in the world I am a hopeless and shameful sentimentalist and I glory in my shame.'

The hotel naturally offers its guests concessionary rates there. Beyond the links you can see the sandy sweep of Cardigan Bay.

Apart from the golf, a vast expanse of beach, and the sea, there is plenty more at the hotel: a large and well-designed indoor heated pool with a separate paddling pool for children (the area is surveyed by closed-circuit television); an all-weather tennis court; a 9-hole pitch and putt course, table tennis and pool in the games room; a children's play room; and a snooker table. The hotel also has its own speed boat, and water skiing can be arranged.

There is a play area for children up above the hotel and alongside the tennis court. It has a large wooden climbing frame, a swing and a slide, and a safe surface underfoot.

There is a stretch of garden in front of the hotel, and a putting green. It's a lovely place to sit on a summer's day and look across the links below to the vast expanse of sea.

It is an excellent hotel in a very pleasant seaside resort. In addition, the hotel has a house, a bungalow and a flat for rent on a self-catering basis from £240 to £500 a week.

Nearby: There are long stretches of beach on which to laze, and a wide choice of water sports: sailing and canoeing, wind surfing and water skiing. Railway enthusiasts have plenty to see: the Vale of Rheidol, Fairbourne and Talyllyn railways. Castle Nant Eos is worth a look, as is the Corris Craft Centre. Pony trekking can be done in the vicinity, and river, sea and lake fishing are available.

....

- ✗ Lunch (12.30pm to 1.45pm) £8: tuna & olive salad, cold buffet or hot dish of the day, pudding or cheese;
  Dinner (7.15pm to 8.30pm) £16: egg & prawn mayonnaise, ravioli Parmesan, poached fillet of lemon sole, pudding and cheese
  Children: high teas, half portions
  £ Medium
- ✓ Best Bargain Break: £82 per person, 2 nights – dinner, b&b
  Children: cots £9; extra bed £21 (includes breakfast and high tea or dinner)
  Facilities: 6 cots and 6 high chairs; baby-listening

46 rooms, 7 family, 3 sets interconnecting
Closed Jan/Feb
🅿 Own car park

ABERGAVENNY, GWENT
Ⓗ🅟 LLANWENARTH ARMS HOTEL
Tel: 01873 810 550
On the A40 towards Brecon.

The hotel is more or less halfway between Abergavenny and Crickhowell, and sits in a splendid position above the River Usk. It is a large roadside inn and hotel which has its origins in the 16th century but has been substantially altered and extended in the last two decades.

This is a hotel which has excellent facilities for families, who will find a spacious restaurant alongside the bar, and there are several high chairs available. Down a few stairs there is a sizeable conservatory where they are also welcome to settle. It is appropriately furnished with cane furniture, and from here you have a lovely view of the river below – down a steep bank which is crowded with bushes and small trees. On warmer days you can sit on the paved terrace which has the same views

503

of the Usk Valley. The hotel has two stretches of salmon and trout fishing which are available to guests.

Nearby: This is a lovely part of Wales and you could do no better for scenery than to follow the Usk south. There are a great number of castles to see. The ruined one at Abergavenny has a museum on site; Tretower Castle; Raglan; and the three castles of Gwent which form a triangle – Grosmont, Skenfrith and the White Castle. The area is a splendid one for walkers, golfers, fishermen and horse riders, and plenty of other sports are available.

....

✗ Bar snacks (12pm to 2pm and 6pm to 9.30pm) £3–13: smoked chicken breast, poached salmon, mushroom Stroganoff, loin of pork; Dinner (6pm to 10pm) £18: fresh crab cocktail, rack of lamb, loin of pork, pudding or cheese
Children: own menu, half portions
£ Medium
✓ Best Bargain Break: £49 per person, 2 nights – b&b
Children: half price
Facilities: 2 cots and 4 high chairs; no baby-listening
18 rooms
Open all year
⌂ Ale: Bass, Ruddles
Ⓟ Own car park

Nr ABERYSTWYTH, DYFED
Ⓟ **HALFWAY INN, Devil's Bridge Road, Pisgah**
Tel: 01970 880 631
On the A4120 between Devil's Bridge and Aberystwyth.

....

One of the finest views, of the Rheidol valley surrounded by hills, awaits you at this appealing old pub – a long, white-painted two-storey building. Just down the road are the well-known Mynach Falls, and it is a lovely part of the world.

Even lovelier for real ale drinkers when they see the stillage in the bar; it holds four barrels and the licensee will serve over 40 different ales during the course of a year. It is a nice bar too, with a slate floor, stone walls, scrubbed wooden tables and pews and huge wooden beams.

Families can use a spacious room alongside; it has plenty of tables and comfortably padded bench seats, and through a window you can see the trickle of a small waterfall. A small snug, with one table, is off to one side.

There are tables outside the pub, and up above it a long grassy terrace where the children can play. The views from here will delight you.

The pub is open throughout the day during the summer months and there is music on Friday evenings.

....

✕ (12pm to 2pm and 7pm to 9pm) £2–11: sirloin steak, chicken & ham & mushroom pie, Brie & broccoli pithivier, plaice & chips, spaghetti Bolognese
Children: own menu, half portions
◯ Ale: Felinfoel and a range of 40 brews
ℙ Own car park

Nr BEREA, nr ST DAVID'S, DYFED
Ⓗ Cwmwdig Water Guest House, Groesgoch
Tel: 01348 831 434
Off the A487 a few miles north-east of St David's.

....

The house is less than a mile from the Pembrokeshire coastal path, and guests are therefore well set for excellent walks in the area. The guest house was converted from a 17th-century farmhouse and its adjacent barns, and offers very comfortable accommodation in rooms which mostly have views towards Abereiddy Bay.

The useful facility of a small kitchen is provided so that you can make snacks and drinks, and there are two sitting rooms: a large one with a beamed ceiling, an open fire and a good selection of books, and a smaller television room. There is a separate dining room and a small

505

bar. We stayed here recently and were impressed by the excellent value offered; the food was particularly good, cooked with skill and generously served. The restaurant is open for coffee, light lunches and afternoon tea, as well as dinner.

Nearby: Pembrokeshire has so much to offer the holiday-maker, and the lovely town of St David's is just five miles away. There are many good beaches along the coast; Abereiddy Bay and Whitesand Bay are close, and the latter is particularly good for surfing. Children will no doubt be keen to visit the Wildlife Park at Cardigan, and there is a Marine Life Centre near St David's. There is quite a choice of museums and castles: at Scoton Manor, Haverfordwest, Pembroke, Manorbier, Tenby, and so on.

✗ Dinner (7pm) £10: pear & cheese salad, steak paprika, pudding and cheese
  Children: half portions
  £ Low
  Children: babies free; £3.50 from 2 to 5 years; £7 from 5 to 7; £10.50 from 8 to 12 years
  Facilities: 3 cots and 3 high chairs; baby-listening system
  13 rooms, 2 family
  Open all year except Christmas
Ⓟ Ample

BETWS-Y-COED, GWYNEDD
Ⓗ Ty Gwyn Hotel
Tel: 01690 710 383
On the A5 just south of Waterloo Bridge.

This handsome stone hotel, partly built in the 16th century, was one of our earliest finds for the *Family Welcome Guide* and remains a firm favourite. It has a stylish interior with antique furniture scattered about, comfortable armchairs, highly polished oak furniture and old prints on the walls.

There are several rooms in which to settle, including a very attractive beamed lounge with comfortable chintzy armchairs and a small room alongside with a lovely carved antique pew. You can eat bar meals here or in the bar itself, most appealing with its low-beamed ceiling, polished oak furniture and old cooking range set in a huge fireplace. Wherever you look there are antiques and bric-à-brac – china, prints, lamps, brassware and other curios; it is a fascinating place.

The bedrooms are beautifully furnished and decorated in varying styles and include two superb family rooms at the top of the building under the rafters. One has a four-poster bed and a separate children's bedroom and has the advantage of a little balcony; and the other also has a four-poster and a single bed for a child. Several of the other rooms can easily accommodate an extra bed or a cot.

You will find some excellent food here, both in the bar and in the charming, low-ceilinged restaurant – there is always a good selection of fish dishes, and the three-course Sunday lunch is a real bargain at under £12. The hotel is very much a family affair. It is owned and run by the Ratcliffe family, which is one of the keys to its great charm and individuality.

Nearby: Four main valleys converge at this town, which is the gateway to the beauties of the Snowdonia National Park. The great mountain is not far away and you can travel close to its summit on the mountain railway, which starts at Llanberis. Enthusiasts can also sample the Ffestiniog Railway. There are many attractions within easy reach, including Gwydyr Forest and the Cwm Idwal nature trail, the slate caverns at Blaenau, and Portmeirion. The north coast can be reached quickly, and there are many sandy beaches; Llandudno, for example, a traditional seaside resort with a pier, donkey rides, Punch and Judy shows, etc, plus the Great Orme Country Park.

✕ Bar snacks (12pm to 2pm and 7pm to 9.30pm) £2–12: marinated herring, cottage pie, Welsh lamb chop, sirloin steak, aubergine & mushroom Stroganoff;

Dinner (7pm to 9.30pm) £17: moules marinières, rack of Welsh lamb, pudding or cheese

Children: own menu, half portions

£ Low

✓ Best Bargain Break: £69–110 per person, 2 nights – dinner, b&b

Children: free up to 3 years; 75% off from 4 to 6; 50% from 7 to 12; 25% from 13 to 16

Facilities: 2 cots and 1 high chair

12 rooms, 1 family

Open all year

◗ Ale: Theakston's

ℙ Own car park

BODFARI, CLWYD

ℙ **DINORBEN ARMS**

Tel: 01745 710 309

Follow the signs to Tremeirchion from the A541 – it's by the village church.

This black-and-white 17th-century pub is very busy, especially at weekends, but has a family room, the Garden Room, and several high chairs. There is a grassy enclosed play area with a swing nearby.

The gardens are terraced, with ponds and alcoves and plenty of seating, and indeed won a pub garden award a few years ago.

The smorgasbord is only served at lunchtimes and is so popular on Sundays that it is impossible to provide ordinary bar meals as well. It is advisable to book, or you might go hungry. We think that it is excellent value at £8.50 for adults and between £1.75 and £4.25 for children, depending on their age. At other times, there is a wide-ranging selection of bar meals.

✖ Lunch (12pm to 2.30pm) smorgasbord
  Dinner (6pm to 10.30pm) £13: carvery (and daily specials)
  Children: own menu, half portions
🍺 Ale: Ruddles, John Smith's, Webster's
🅿 Own car park

Nr BRIDGEND, GLAMORGAN
🅿🆁 THE WATERMILL, Ogmore Road
Tel: 01656 650 562
On the Bridgend to Ogmore by Sea road, the B4524.

This pub was never a watermill – but a charming stone farmhouse whose origins go back to the 14th century.

Inside the designers have done their best to create the illusion that it was a mill and the five floors of the restaurant march up to the building's rafters. It is agreeably done, with brick walls, some wooden panelling and booths in which to sit. The watermill motif is emphasized by the wooden wheel on one of the walls.

There is a spacious bar which leads out to a garden at the rear. The lawn has several bench tables and a barbecue area, and customers can gaze upon open countryside from here. The children's playground has a safe surface. An unusual feature is the presence of a crazy golf course alongside the car park – a great attraction in the summer months.

There are nappy-changing facilities, and high chairs are provided. Families will also welcome the fact that food is served from noon throughout the day until 10.30pm.

....

✕ (12pm to 10.30pm) £2–13: pork satay, three-bean feast, minted lamb steak, seafood tagliatelle, fillet steak
  Children: own menu
◖ Ale: Boddington's, Brain's, Flowers
ℙ Ample

CAERPHILLY, GLAMORGAN
ℙℝ THE CROSSWAYS
Tel: 01222 888 850
On the A468 just east of Caerphilly, close to Bedwas.

....

This very large purpose-built pub is on the edge of an industrial estate and is a useful place for families because of its excellent facilities: plenty of high chairs, baby-changing facilities and play areas for the children. It serves food throughout the day until 10pm.

The Crossways is well designed and makes the most of the space at its disposal. Substantial brick pillars are a feature of the bar area and the central room has a splendid vaulted roof with huge cross-beams. Thereafter the pub is cleverly split up into a variety of rooms and alcoves on different levels; some have wood-panelled walls and there is a small room with walls painted a deep red. Flagstoned floors and wooden ceilings add to the fun.

The family restaurant (a no-smoking area) is at one end of the building. There are bay windows here and another room leads to the Fun Factory with its ball swamp and a myriad of things on which to jump, slide and climb. There is a kids' bar which serves soft drinks and snacks.

The large lawned garden has lots of bench tables and a play unit with a safe bark surface.

....

✗ (11.30am to 10pm) £2–8: woodland melon, steak & mushroom pudding, lasagne verdi, gammon steak, fillet of salmon
   Children: own menu
◑ Ale: Boddington's, Flowers and guests
℗ Plenty

CHEPSTOW, GWENT
ℙℝ **PIERCEFIELD, St Arvans**
Tel: 01291 622 614
On the A466 in the village of St Arvans.
....

Smartly painted in cream, this large pub is not far from Chepstow racecourse and contains excellent facilities for families.

There is loads of space inside, as is apparent as soon as you enter and see the bar stretching along one side of the pub. There are several interconnected areas and the occasional alcove, and the wood panelling and good-quality carpets give the whole place a comfortable look.

The family eating area is very welcoming, with wooden tables and chairs and curved padded settles, and is no-smoking territory. There is a children's play area, with a ball swamp and other items, at one end. Nappy-changing facilities are provided, as are several high chairs.

Outside you will find a large lawned garden with some shady trees. There are bench tables here and it is safely enclosed; the well-equipped children's play area has a bark surface and there is also a bouncy castle.

Its facilities make the Piercefield a very useful family pub and it has the extra bonus of providing food and drink throughout the day.

....

✖ (11.30am to 10pm; Sun from 12pm) £2–8: onion bhajis, roast chicken, plaice & chips, steak & kidney pie, turkey fillet
   Children: own menu
🍺 Ale: Bass, Boddington's, Flowers and guests
🅿 Plenty

CRICCIETH, GWYNEDD
Ⓡ MOELWYN RESTAURANT, Mona Terrace
Tel: 01766 522 500
By the sea front off the A497.

....

The hotel/restaurant is housed in a Victorian building which is framed with creeper. It is bright and welcoming and the dining room itself is smartly decorated with patterned wallpaper and pink tablecloths. There is an excellent range of food on offer here, including a special menu for children and smaller portions of most dishes. The restaurant is open every evening, and for lunch on Sundays and during the peak holiday periods. It offers splendid value at around £9 for a lunch of three courses.

From many of the windows you have superb views of Cardigan Bay, the hills, and in the distance Harlech Castle, and especially so from the small garden, which is a delightful place to sit on a summer's day. The public rooms include a charming bar and lounge with a bay window and a residents' lounge on the first floor; it has a video machine, table football and a piano. There are six bedrooms, decorated and furnished to a very high standard, and all with their own bathrooms. Most of them have delectable views of the bay and are very comfortable.

512

✗ Dinner (6.30pm to 9.30pm) £14: smoked Welsh trout roulade, escalopes of pork, pudding or cheese
Children: own menu, half portions
Ⓟ On the street

CWMBRAN, GWENT
ⓅⓇ **Ashbridge Inn**
Tel: 01633 876 678
Off the A4051 on the northern edge of Cwmbran.

The original part of the building was once a farmhouse and later it was transposed to a coaching inn on the Abergavenny road. It retains its charm with its steep roof and dormer windows and has been expanded to make a spacious family pub and restaurant.

The design is open plan but broken up into a number of areas by wood and glass screens. A central eating area has a high vaulted ceiling which is dominated by a heavy chandelier; at one end a wooden prancing horse is poised above the tables. Wide windows at the side of the pub give a conservatory effect.

Charlie Chalk's Fun Factory, with its ball swamp and sundry other

513

amusements, will keep any child amused, and there is also a small play area for very young children. With lots of high chairs, a nappy-changing unit and the availability of food throughout the day until 10pm, this pub is very much aimed at the family market.

A paved terrace runs along the front and side of the Ashbridge and there are plenty of bench tables. The play unit has a safe bark surface and a bouncy castle is set up during the summer.

....

✖ (11.30am to 10pm) £2–8: prawn cocktail, steak & kidney pie, haddock & chips, chicken escalopes, vegetable crumble
Children: own menu
℗ Ale: Boddington's, Flowers, Wadworth's and guests
Ⓟ Plenty

Nr CWMBRAN, GWENT
ⓅⓇ **THE GATE, Llanfrechfa**
Tel: 01633 875 155
On the B4236 north of Newport.

....

An attractive building which was once a coaching inn, the Gate has steep roofs and a weatherboarded upper storey, whereas the ground floor is painted white as a contrast.

The interior is very appealing. The main bar has a good stone fireplace, a low and heavily beamed ceiling, padded settles and easy chairs; and the adjoining lounge area is designed in the same style, with padded settles and nice wooden tables.

The restaurant area was constructed in the old stables, whose high-peaked wooden roof and rafters remain as delightful features. The area is laid out on two levels, with alcoves here and there.

On warmer days you might elect to sit on the terrace at the front of the pub. From there, or from the lawned garden, you could keep an eye on the children, who can enjoy the playground (safely enclosed) with its swings, slide and climbing frames.

This is an excellent family pub and restaurant, where high chairs and baby-changing facilities are provided.

....

✗ (12pm to 2.30pm and 5pm to 10.30pm; all day at weekends) £2–13: Greek dip, steaks, chicken tikka masala, fried scampi, beef & Boddington's pie
Children: own menu
◖ Ale: Boddington's, Brain's and guests
🅿 Lots

DOLWYDDELAN, GWYNEDD
Ⓗ **ELEN'S CASTLE HOTEL, Dolwyddelan**
Tel: 01690 750 207
On the A470 south-west of Betwys-y-Coed.

....

This charming stone hotel, its walls hung with ivy and Virginia creeper, dates back to the 18th century and was once part of the Earl of Ancaster's Welsh estate. It was once a village alehouse and later a coaching inn.

It is a comfortable and relaxing hotel with a welcoming little bar, with an ancient stove, in what was once the kitchen; the game hooks are still in place. The lounges are comfortably furnished, and the bright dining room has windows on to the garden.

The bedrooms are furnished and decorated in a functional and unfussy style and this is reflected in the very reasonable prices.

It is a pleasant place to relax, especially in the large and attractive garden alongside the hotel. It is safely enclosed and rises on three levels, each separated by rambling roses and flower beds. Children can play in an adjoining field, which contains the legendary Roman well, which is reputed to have healing qualities.

Nearby: The hotel is situated in the lovely Lledr Valley in the middle of the Snowdonia National Park. It is a splendid spot for walkers, climbers and fishermen. The hotel is a starting point for many walks, including the popular one to the summit of Moel Siabod. Fishermen can try their luck for trout and salmon in the nearby river, and coarse fishing is also available to hotel guests. Pony trekking can also be arranged locally. Dolwyddelan Castle, built in the 12th century by Llywelyn the Great, is well worth a visit, as are Gwydir Castle, Gwydyr Forest with its many walks, and the Cwm Idwal Nature Trail. Bodnant Garden and the Great Orme Country Park are close, and you can easily reach the sandy beaches of the north coast.

....

✘ Bar snacks (11.30am to 2pm and 6pm to 9pm) £2–9: liver & herb pâté, poached halibut, bulghur wheat & walnut casserole, sirloin steak, grilled Conwy plaice;

Dinner (6.30pm onwards) £12: egg & prawn mayonnaise, noisette of lamb, pudding

Children: own menu, half portions

£ Low

Children: free up to 3 years; half price from 4 to 8; three quarters from 9 to 14

Facilities: 2 cots and 1 high chair; baby-listening system

10 rooms, 2 family, 1 set interconnecting

Open all year

🅿 Own car park

GLYN CEIRIOG, nr LLANGOLLEN, CLWYD
Ⓗ **GOLDEN PHEASANT HOTEL**
Tel: 01691 718 281
On the B4500 west of Chirk.

This traditional country hotel, run by the same family for nearly half a century, is a welcoming sight. Set in the beautiful Ceiriog Valley, the hotel has its own flower-filled garden, two tiled patios and a play area for the children, and it includes a swing, a slide and a climbing frame. There is also a paddling pool, a pets' corner and an aviary.

Inside, two comfortable lounges look down the lovely Ceiriog Valley. The splendid Pheasant Bar has dark wooden settles, stuffed game birds in glass cases, many items of militaria, an old stove with the original tiles on the fireplace surround, and a fine, carved wooden mirror. A lovely place to have the odd tincture or two.

At lunchtimes and in the evening you can eat from the bar menu and the dining room offers a full menu. If you are keen on country pursuits, such as fishing and shooting, the hotel provides excellent facilities; and they have their own riding centre as well.

We looked at several family bedrooms, attractively decorated and with plenty of space. The sight of the peaceful hills from their windows was yet another bonus.

Nearby: This is a lovely part of the Border country and naturally there are interesting castles to see, at Chirk and Powis, for example. The mansions of Erddig and Plas Newydd are worth a visit, and the Llangollen Steam Railway will take you on a trip through the delightful Dee Valley. Pistyll Rhaeadr and the Lake Vyrnwy Visitor Centre are both within easy reach.

✕ Bar snacks (12pm to 2.30pm and 7pm to 9pm) £2–5: lasagne, chilli con carne, sweet & sour pork, gammon & egg;
Lunch (12pm to 2.30pm) £12: soup, grilled Ceiriog trout, bread & butter pudding;
Dinner (7pm to 8.30pm) £15: prawn & tuna salad, roast local pheasant, pudding or cheese

Children: own menu, half portions
£ High
✓ Best Bargain Break: £79 per person, 2 nights – dinner, b&b
Children: free up to 18 years
Facilities: 3 cots and 2 high chairs; baby-listening to all rooms
15 rooms, 5 family
Open all year
Ⓟ Own car park

GLYNARTHEN, nr CARDIGAN, DYFED
Ⓗ PENBONTBREN FARM HOTEL
Tel: 01239 810 248
Off the A487 north of Cardigan. There is a sign on the road.

Great care has been exercised in the conversion of these old stone farm buildings. The bedrooms, most of which can take an extra bed and a cot, have been built in what were once the stables, the granary and the barn. The three family rooms are on the ground floor and contain a double and a single bed, and a bathroom. They are attractive rooms under their sloping roofs and look out to the countryside. The whole project has been done in a stylish and charming way and it deservedly won an award as an outstanding farm conversion.

The public rooms are on either side of the courtyard. There is a very pleasant and comfortable restaurant, with stone walls, pine tables, a wood-burning stove, a grandfather clock and a fine Welsh harp. Alongside is a spacious lounge, very light by dint of its skylight, and French windows lead out to a small terrace.

Mr and Mrs Humphreys have an interesting museum, which contains an old farm tractor, pottery and many other artefacts; there is also a nature trail on the surrounding land.

Nearby: The hotel is in a marvellous spot for walking, riding and fishing; and there are some excellent beaches nearby – Penbryn, Tresaith and Mwnt, for example. There is a wildlife park at Cardigan, and a splendid stretch of coastline leads down to St David's with its famous cathedral.

✗ Dinner (7pm to 8pm) £12: smoked fish terrine, Welsh lamb cutlets, pudding
  Children: own menu, smaller portions
  £ Medium
✓ Best Bargain Break: £80 per person, 2 nights – dinner, b&b
  Children: free up to 16 years
  Facilities: 2 cots and 2 high chairs; baby-listening on 2 lines
  10 rooms, 3 family
  Open all year
🅿 Own car park

HAY-ON-WYE, POWYS
Ⓡ **THE GRANARY, 20 Broad Street**
Tel: 01497 820 790
In the town centre.

The café is situated near the clock tower in this appealing town, whose position on the borders of England and Wales has ensured more than its fair share of bloody mayhem over the centuries. It's peaceful enough now and the town has become a notable centre for second-hand books. There are numbers of interesting antique shops, too, and the River

Wye, which meanders past the town, is a particularly alluring stretch of water.

The restaurant certainly was a granary (and also a wool collection warehouse in its time), as the machinery and pulleys which are still in place will confirm. It's a relaxed and welcoming place, with an excellent choice of freshly cooked food available, including an extensive vegetarian menu. Whenever we visit it is busy – a testament to the quality of the food and the reasonable prices.

There are several high chairs and, if you need to change or feed a baby, facilities can be made available.

....

✕ (10am to 5.30pm; until 9pm during Easter and summer holidays)
  £2–6: leek au gratin, rogan josh, beef in Guinness, spicy pork
  Children: half portions
◯ Ale: Bass, Hancock's
ℙ Plenty on the street except on market day (Thursday)

HOLYWELL, CLWYD
Ⓗ **GREENHILL FARM**
Tel: 01352 713 270
On the Holywell to Greenfield road, almost opposite the Royal Oak.

....

This is a most attractive farmhouse, built of stone on a timber frame in the 16th century, and the façade is a mass of bright flowers during summer. The original beams and pillars are much in evidence in the comfortable lounge, which also has an open fire and a little alcove with window seats. The dining room was built about a century later and is notable for its partly oak-panelled walls and the sturdy beams on its ceiling.

The bedrooms are delightful, also with their share of oak beams and pillars, and with fascinating views of the estuary. The rooms are spacious, especially the family room which has a double bed, two bunk beds and its own bathroom. All the rooms are now equipped with televisions.

From the farm you will have superb views of the Dee Estuary and

Hilbre Island; and just beyond the Island you will perhaps be able to see the great golf course at Hoylake. You can sit on the spacious lawns and admire it all, and the children can head for the play area with its swings, slide, Wendy House and climbing frame. Guests are welcome to roam the 120 acres of the farm, which supports a herd of pedigree cattle. If the weather is unkind there is a games room with snooker, darts, toys and board games. On a more utilitarian front, the Jones family also provide a washing machine and dryer.

This is a wholly delightful place to stay, full of charm and character. A large family could occupy all three bedrooms and the prices charged are very reasonable indeed.

Nearby: There is much to see in this part of the world. The Greenfield Valley Heritage Park is on the doorstep, and there are castles to see at Rhuddlan, Ewloe and Flint. Just a bit further on you can visit Loggerheads Country Park (near Mold), and there is a sports and water centre in Holywell, and the Sun Centre in Rhyl.

....

✕ Dinner (6.30pm) £8: home-made soup, steak & kidney pie, pudding
Children: half portions
£ Low
Children: cot £2; half price up to 10 years
Facilities: 1 cot and 1 high chair, baby-listening can be arranged
3 rooms, 1 family
Open 1 Mar to 31 Oct
No credit cards accepted
Unlicensed
🅿 Ample

KEESTON, nr HAVERFORDWEST, DYFED
Ⓡ KEESTON KITCHEN
Tel: 01437 710 440
On the main A487 – not in the village.

Converted from an old farm cottage, this roadside restaurant is cosy and welcoming and has a little sheltered terrace by the front door. Coffee is served from about 10.30am and a good selection of reasonably priced snacks is served at lunchtime. (On Sundays a traditional roast lunch is served.) There's plenty to suit a young palate and, if required, half portions are available, as they are for dinner.

The owners can find some space in their own accommodation where a mother could feed or change a baby.

The owners have two self-catering flats available in the house next door, and these can be booked for single nights as well as longer periods. In addition, there is a twin-bedded room with bathroom and living room, to let.

✕ Lunch (12pm to 2pm) £1–5: Welsh rarebit, vegetarian lasagne, salade niçoise, spicy chicken;
Dinner (7pm to 9.30pm) £15: mushrooms stuffed with cream cheese, lamb cutlets in filo pastry, fresh fruit meringue
Children: own menu, half portions
Ⓓ Ale: Bass (during the summer season)
Ⓟ Own small car park

LLANDUDNO, GWYNEDD
Ⓗ ST TUDNO HOTEL, The Promenade
Tel: 01492 874 411
On the promenade opposite the pier.

We are firm fans of this excellent seaside hotel, which is furnished with great style and care, and welcomes all the family, from babies to grandmothers. The St Tudno sets a standard to which few hotels in the traditional seaside resorts aspire. It is not an inexpensive hotel, but it offers marvellous value for money.

Alice Liddel, Lewis Carroll's Alice, stayed at the hotel when she was eight and was no doubt pleased that it was situated opposite the pier and close to the beach, where there are donkey rides and Punch and Judy shows.

The hotel has a small indoor heated swimming pool near the coffee lounge, which, like all the public rooms, is elegantly furnished and comfortable. The Garden Room restaurant is particularly appealing, with its dashing wallpaper and hand-painted panels, and has the benefit of being air-conditioned and a non-smoking area. It is a lovely setting in which to sample the excellent food, which has a deserved reputation for quality, based as it is on the best available local produce. Older children can join their parents for dinner, but the younger ones are served high tea in the coffee lounge at 5.45pm. They have a varied menu too; fish fingers appear on it, but they are home-made, as are the beefburgers which are made from sirloin steak.

We looked at several bedrooms, all furnished and decorated in fine style and many with lovely views over the bay. The family rooms are spacious, especially a top-floor room under a sloping ceiling; it contains a king-size bed and a double bed which pulls down from the wall.

St Tudno is a most impressive family hotel, which is run with great style and sympathy.

Nearby: Llandudno has its own long and sandy beaches and there are many others to enjoy along the coast. The Great Orme Country Park rises nearly 700 feet from the sea and has a wide variety of wildlife. You can reach the top on foot, by car, cable car or Victorian tramway. There are several castles in this part of Wales: Conwy, Penrhyn and Gwydir – and Bodnant Garden is a wonderful sight. The children will no doubt like to visit the Welsh Mountain Zoo, Gwydir Forest and the Cwm Idwal Nature Trail. There is also a dry ski slope and a toboggan run about half a mile away.

✘ Bar lunches (12.30pm to 2pm) £3–8: local plaice, Welsh rarebit,

prawn omelette, black pudding & bacon salad, poached local
salmon;
Dinner (7pm to 9.30pm) £28: quail & mushroom tart, soup, saddle
of Welsh lamb, hot coconut & rum tart, Welsh farmhouse cheese
Children: own menu, half portions
£ High
✓ Best Bargain Break: £123–174 per person, 2 nights – dinner, b&b
& Sunday lunch
Children: £10 for cots; from £15 thereafter (including breakfast)
Facilities: 4 cots and 4 high chairs; 4 baby-listening lines
21 rooms, 4 family, 2 suites
Open all year
Ⓟ Own car park

LLANDUDNO, GWYNEDD
ⓅⓇ CRAIGSIDE INN
Tel: 01492 545 943
On the B5115 next to Little Orme.

You will have a fine view of the bay and of Great Ormes Head from the
garden of this pub and restaurant. It is a sizeable lawned area and includes
a terrace with bench tables, a children's play unit and, in summer, a
bouncy castle.

The substantial stone building has excellent amenities for all members
of the family. There are high chairs and baby-changing facilities; and
on the first floor the Fun Factory has a great array of playthings (ball
swamps and so on) and a snack and soft drinks bar.

The bar area is a congenial place for the adults to settle. There
are comfortable padded benches and up a few steps there is another
lounge. The restaurant has a series of rooms under a high ceiling.
They are separated by wooden screens and the colourful wallpaper
adds to the fun. The conservatory room overlooks the terrace and the
play area.

✗ (11.30am to 10pm) £2–8: oriental prawns, chicken Balti, vegetable crumble, Teviotdale pie, sirloin steak
Children: own menu
◻ Ale: Boddington's, Castle Eden, Welsh bitter and guests
Ⓟ Lots

LLANGOLLEN, CLWYD
Ⓡ **GALES, 18 Bridge Street**
Tel: 01978 860 089
In the town centre.

The renowned international Eisteddfod takes place each year in this picturesque town in the Dee valley; in the heart of lovely hilly country, it is guarded on one side by the famous Horseshoe Pass.

This restaurant has a catholic mixture of tables and chairs, some stout and splendid; there are pews from a church in the back room and from a chapel in the front. The rooms are panelled, with an even board floor and oak pillars and beams. It is all very appealing, classical music plays softly, and there are prints for sale on the walls.

The patio is enclosed by brick and trellis and there is a vine-covered arbour, with wooden benches and tables.

The building dates from 1775, though some parts are a bit older. It has great charm and atmosphere, and the food is reasonably priced. A mother could use a spare bedroom if she needs to feed or change a baby.

Gales has fifteen bedrooms, all with their own bathrooms.

✕ (12pm to 2pm and 6pm to 10pm) £1–5: mushroom & trout Mornay, tuna & tarragon mousse, beef & paprika pie, Hawaiian pork, spicy vegetable casserole
Children: small portions
Closed on Sundays
One high chair only
Ⓟ 11 spaces and on street

LLANHARAN, SOUTH GLAMORGAN
Ⓟ Ⓡ HIGH CORNER HOUSE
Tel: 01443 238 056
On the A473 in Llanharan.

This large Victorian pub, with prominent bay windows, has been converted to provide excellent family facilities. The interior is very spacious but a more intimate atmosphere has been provided by varying the level of the floor and by the use of alcoves here and there. There is an attractive fireplace at one side, and bright carpets.

The special family room is a no-smoking area, and has a children's play area, a nappy-changing facility and high chairs. Outside there is a small enclosed garden with several bench tables.

High Corner House has the extra bonus for families of being open all day with food available at all times.

✕ (11.30am to 10pm; Sun from 12pm) £2–8: hot mushrooms, sirloin steak, fried scampi, vegetable crumble, chicken masala
Children: own menu
Ⓓ Ale: Bass, Boddington's, Brain's, Flowers
Ⓟ Own car parking

LLWYNDAFYDD, DYFED
P CROWN INN
Tel: 01545 560 396
Off the A487 or the A486 near New Quay.

The Crown is only a couple of miles from the sea and is a very popular pub, especially on summer days, when the terrace and the beautiful landscaped garden (which has won several awards) are packed with families having food and suitably long drinks. The children can have a lot of fun in the playground with its slides and a climbing frame.

Your eye will be caught by the good proportions of this long and low 18th-century building, smartly painted white with black trimmings. There is plenty of space, too, in the family room which is off the main bar and has a good quota of tables, benches and so on.

There is always an excellent choice of freshly cooked food here, from both the bar menu and the *à la carte* restaurant menu. The emphasis is very much on fresh fish, meat and vegetables from local producers, and the dishes of the day are always enterprising. There's a good selection of real ales too.

✕ (12pm to 2pm and 6pm to 9pm) £2–9: garlic mushrooms, steaks, lamb pie, lasagne, pan-fried local plaice
  Children: own menu
🍺 Ale: Boddington's, Flowers and guests
P Own car park

MAENTWROG, BLAENAU FFESTINIOG, GWYNEDD
P THE GRAPES HOTEL
Tel: 01766 590 365
Just off the A487 as you turn into the village.

Wooded hills rise steeply across the road from this grey stone building dating from 1853, though there has been a hostelry on the site since the 13th century, and the ancient cellars still remain. Hanging baskets and window boxes brighten the façade. At the back the large veranda, safely railed along the front, overlooks a pretty garden with trees, shrubs and a small pond with a fountain (the garden is private).

The veranda room with its sliding window is an ideal place for summer meals and looks away to the hills. In addition, there is a sizeable family room alongside, a charming room with its stone walls, nice wooden tables and padded settles. The two bars are very appealing, with stone walls, wooden pillars and pews and a collection of pewter tankards. An old Wurlitzer juke box sits in the front bar. The whole place has a lovely atmosphere and families are made very welcome. Baby-changing facilities and three high chairs are available.

This pub has elected to open all day (except Sunday) and food is available most of the day. In the afternoon during summer, cold food is available on the veranda.

....

✗ (12pm to 9.30pm; Sun 12pm to 2pm and 7pm to 9pm) £2–9: rack of Welsh lamb, aubergine moussaka, beef en daube, local dressed crab, leek & ham bake
Children: own menu, half portions
⦹ Ale: Bass, Marston's, Stones and guests
ℙ Own car park

Nr MERTHYR TYDFIL, GLAMORGAN
ℙℝ PENTREBACH HOUSE, Pentrebach
Tel: 01443 693 616
On the A470 just south of Merthyr Tydfil.

....

This stately manor house was built in 1850 for an iron master who employed a minimum of ten servants to keep his home running smoothly. It's a lovely building, pristine in its coat of white paint.

From the car park you walk past a large and grassy garden with a number of beautiful mature trees. An adventure playground has been laid out with a safe bark surface and the adults might head for the relative comfort of the terrace which overlooks it.

The family restaurant is housed in a particularly attractive room at one end; it has its original stone fireplace and a lovely bay window with a curved settle beneath. Alongside, the Charlie Chalk Fun Factory has all the amusements a child might crave, plus a bar to serve soft drinks and snacks.

The adults have a choice of several other rooms. The bar has many alcoves and sitting areas under the wooden ceilings with their heavy cross-beams, one of which has the date of the house carved on it. There is plenty of wood panelling in evidence and it all adds up to a pleasant atmosphere.

Families are well looked after; there are plenty of high chairs and a nappy-changing facility. The pub is open all day and makes food available at all times.

....

✗ (11.30am to 10pm) £2–8: fish dippers, chicken Balti, sirloin steak, vegetable moussaka, tagliatelle carbonara
Children: own menu
◯ Ale: Boddington's, Flowers, Wadworth's
Ⓟ Plenty

NEW QUAY, DYFED
Ⓟ BLACK LION HOTEL
Tel: 01545 560 209
Follow the one-way system to 'Harbour and Beach'.

....

Of 17th-century origin, but added to in 1830, this stone hotel is close to New Quay harbour, down a narrow road. You can walk straight into one of the bars off the street, and very welcoming it is, with oak beams, lots of brassware and two fireplaces – one used as a 'sit-in' area, the other housing a wood-burning stove. There are two small rooms at each end, one of which houses a pool table and the other a bar-billiards table. The latter has windows which look out over the bay.

The dining room is dedicated to Dylan Thomas, who was a regular in the Black Lion in the mid-1940s. The comfortable room has a portrait of him and over fifty fascinating photographs.

The long and grassy garden, with several bench tables, has a fabulous position overlooking Cardigan Bay, the beach and the harbour, all ringed by protective hills. There is a children's slide here and an 'enchanted tree', and a boule pitch. Barbecues are laid on during the summer and there are Punch and Judy shows for the children at Saturday lunchtimes in July and August.

The pub is open all day from Monday to Saturday.

....

✖ Bar snacks (12pm to 2.30pm and 6pm to 10pm) £2–9: plaice & chips, steak and ale pie, spaghetti Bolognese, chicken dhansak, pizza

Children: own menu, half portions

🍺 Ale: Boddington's, Burton, Tetley's and guests

🅿 Own car park

NEWPORT, GWENT
P R **ROYAL OAK, Chepstow Road**
Tel: 01633 282 155
On the A48, as you enter Newport from Junction 24 of the M4.

....

This substantial roadside pub was built in the mid-eighties and has a spacious interior ideal for coping with a varied clientele, including family groups.

A conventional bar occupies one side of the building and there is also a large lounge bar with comfortable padded benches and a raised sitting area at one end. A food counter occupies one corner and beyond is the restaurant, an agreeable room with its brick walls, wooden pillars and beams, screens placed here and there and farming artefacts decorating the walls and ceiling.

There is a good range of food on offer, including a children's menu which is more enterprising than most – pasta, smoked chicken, cream Brie and courgette crumble, for example. The Sunday menu is good value at under £9 for two courses (just over £11 for three courses).

High chairs are available, and baby-changing can be done in the Ladies, where there is plenty of space.

On summer days customers can head for the terrace and the adjoining beer garden.

....

✗ (Mon to Sat 12pm to 2pm and 6pm to 10pm; Sun 12pm to 10pm) £2–11: cod smokey, mixed grill, steaks, fish & chips, sesame chicken
  Children: own menu
◯ Ale: Bass, Hancock's
P Plenty

PENALLY, nr TENBY, DYFED
Ⓗ PENALLY ABBEY HOTEL
Tel: 01834 843 033
Just off the A4139 west of Tenby.

....

This delectable 18th-century stone manor house, built on the site of an ancient abbey, sits high above the coast road and from its windows and gardens you can see Tenby golf course and Carmarthen Bay beyond. Indeed, the sandy beach is a ten-minute walk across the links (reduced green fees available).

The stone walls and gabled windows house some beautifully proportioned and spacious rooms, made even more interesting by the pointed arches of the windows and the doors; an unusual and very effective design. The highly attractive lounge has comfortable sofas and chairs, and a piano, and the elegant dining room has splendid views. The pleasant bar has a conservatory alongside which also takes advantage of the panoramic views out to sea.

If you fancy a swim, there is a small indoor heated pool; or you can relax in the five acres of mature lawns, garden and woodland. It is a lovely spot and has the added attraction of a ruined 13th-century chapel within its confines.

The owners try to keep a balance here between families and other guests, and most of the bedrooms are spacious enough to take extra beds and cots. Some of them contain sofa beds, and all the double rooms have splendid four-poster beds. We were greatly impressed by the care which has been exercised in furnishing and decorating the rooms; they are comfortable and stylish. The top floor contains two very attractive bedrooms; the double room has high wooden rafters and there is a twin-bedded room along a short corridor (plus two bathrooms). A family could use the rooms as a self-contained suite and enjoy great comfort and seclusion.

The old coach house has now been converted to form four rooms, and the high standards of comfort and decoration have been maintained. Each has a four-poster bed and a bathroom, and the rooms on the upper floor have terrific views over the bay.

There are several extra facilities which are unusual and welcome; for example, breakfast is served until 11 o'clock in the morning. Younger children (under 7) are encouraged to have their evening meals at 5 o'clock, so that the adults can linger undisturbed over their dinner.

The Penally Abbey is an exceptional hotel in a delightful part of Wales.

Nearby: Tenby is a busy seaside resort with sandy beaches, of which there is a wide choice, including Manorbier Bay, Barafundle Bay (owned by the National Trust) and Broad Haven. There are several castles to see: Pembroke, Tenby, Manorbier and Carew, for example; and the children will relish a visit to Manor House Wildlife Park. Caldey Island, with its abbey and Cistercian monastery, can also be visited.

✕ Dinner (7.30pm onwards) £22: crab thermidor, rack of Welsh lamb, pudding or cheese
  Children: half portions
  £ High
✓ Best Bargain Break: 10% discount from 1 Nov to Easter
  Children: free to age 6; half price from 6 to 14
  Facilities: 3 cots and 2 high chairs; baby-listening system
  12 rooms, 4 family
  Open all year
🅿 Own car park

PONTYPRIDD, GLAMORGAN
🅿🆁 **Upper Boat Inn, Rhydfelin**
Tel: 01443 842 050
Off the A470 south of Pontypridd. Take the turning for Rhydfelin.

This substantial pub, with its half-timbered façade, sits at a roundabout below the A470.

The restaurant has been designed on a number of different levels and the brick walls, wooden pillars and panelling, and glass screens are easy on the eye. The no-smoking family eating area leads out to a terrace at the back of the building where there are several bench tables, an adventure playground and, during the summer, a bouncy castle.

When we visited one lunchtime, the clientele was a good mix of locals, business people and families; but this Brewers Fayre outlet is especially welcoming to the latter. Apart from the many high chairs which are provided, there is a baby-changing facility in the Ladies; and the pub is open throughout the day and serves food at all times.

....

✗ (11.30am to 10pm) £2–8: onion bhajis, haddock & chips, vegetable crumble, turkey fillet, Teviotdale pie
Children: own menu
🍺 Ale: Boddington's, Flowers and guests
🄿 Own car park

RHOS-ON-SEA, GWYNEDD
🄿🅁 THE SHIP
Tel: 01492 540 198
On the B5115 between Colwyn Bay and Llandudno.

....

This presentable stone pub has a steeply pitched roof and the extension at the back marries in well. The enclosed lawned garden has several bench tables and would be a good spot to settle on a summer day, while the children enjoy the play area at the side.

Comfortable cane chairs and padded benches are the main feature of the lounge bar area, and there is a further large bar. This is very much the pub part of The Ship and also contains a pool table.

Up some stairs from the lounge bar, the main dining room is pleasantly furnished with cane-backed chairs and has colourful prints on the walls. On an upper level there is another dining area under a high ceiling. It is light and bright and French windows lead out to the garden.

High chairs are provided and the restaurant is open throughout the day on Sundays, when the lunch is good value at under £9 for two courses.

....

✗ (12pm to 2pm and 6pm to 10pm; Sun 12pm to 10pm) £2–11:
Greek dip, steaks, fish & chips, hot chicken salad, pasta Lucana
Children: own menu
🍺 Ale: Bass
🅿 Lots

RUTHIN, CLWYD
🅿🆁 YE OLDE ANCHOR INN, Rhos Street
Tel: 01824 702 813
On the A494.

Ruthin is an attractive old market town in the Vale of Clwyd and is
encircled by hills. A fine collection of architecture can be viewed –
from medieval to modern – and St Peter's church (14th century) and
the Elizabethan Nantelwyd House are especially notable.

The Anchor is an archetypal inn: it serves drinks, excellent food
in its restaurant and has fourteen bedrooms to let. An 18th-century
building, white-painted with black shutters and an array of flowers
in window boxes, it suits the town well. The spacious bar is an
appealing spot to settle over a drink or a meal. There are open
fireplaces with wood-burners at each end, and plush padded benches,
and the decorations include prints and black-and-white photographs of
bygone Ruthin days, copper pots and pans, and a collection of jugs
hanging from the ceiling beams.

The restaurant is a very congenial spot, a cool and low-ceilinged room
with a rich green carpet. All the food is cooked on the premises from
fresh ingredients: the owner bakes his own bread and makes his own
ice-cream, for example.

The same care has gone into the accommodation. The rooms are
all well appointed and very comfortable, and include two twin-bedded
rooms which can interconnect to make a family suite. Cots are available
and baby-listening can be arranged.

The Anchor is a welcoming inn with excellent facilities.

✕ Bar meals (12pm to 2pm) £2–5: mushroom provençale, steak sandwich, lasagne, omelettes;
Restaurant (12pm to 2pm and 6.30pm to 9.30pm) £15: mushrooms au poivre, chicken boursin, pudding or cheese
Children: small portions

◷ Ale: Bass, Worthington

ℙ Own car park

ST DAVID'S, DYFED
Ⓗ **WARPOOL COURT HOTEL**
Tel: 01437 720 300
Close to the centre of the town; the brochure has clear directions.

This hotel has been recommended in the *Family Welcome Guide* since the very first edition. It is an appealing place, built of grey stone, has extensions here and there, and was built in the 19th century as the St David's Cathedral choir school. It is a comfortable hotel and has a remarkable collection of 2500 antique armorial and pictorial wall tiles.

It is certainly not lacking in charm and it has a magnificent position on the unspoiled Pembrokeshire coast, adjoining stretches of which are owned by the National Trust. There are wonderful views of St Bride's Bay, especially from the large lawned garden, a delightful place to loll on a warm day. It is notable for the statuary dotted around.

There are excellent facilities here, including a covered and heated swimming pool, a gymnasium, a pool table and table tennis, an all-weather tennis court, a croquet lawn and an outdoor play area for children. Golf can be arranged at the nearby St David's Golf Club.

The hotel has a fine reputation for its food and puts a strong emphasis on fresh local produce, especially fish: crab, lobster, sewin and sea bass are caught nearby. A vegetarian menu is available, and local Welsh farm cheeses are served.

Nearby: There are lovely beaches here – Whitesand Bay, Newgale Sands and Marloes Sands, for example – and the Pembrokeshire coast path can be followed. The famous cathedral is within walking distance and the Marine Life Centre is just down the road. There is a wildlife park near Cardigan and another near Tenby; and lots of castles to see, including Carew, Tenby and Manorbier.

✕ Bar snacks (12pm to 2pm) £3–7: scrambled egg with smoked salmon, game sausages, steak sandwich, smoked haddock omelette; Lunch (12pm to 2pm) £17: fish mousse, steak & Guinness pie; Dinner (7pm to 9.15pm) £28: haddock & cockle fishcake, medallions of loin of lamb, pudding, cheese
Children: high teas, half portions
£ High
✓ Best Bargain Break: £126 per person, 2 nights – dinner, b&b
Children: free up to 14 years
Facilities: 3 cots and 3 high chairs; baby-listening system
25 rooms, 3 family
Open all year except Jan
◗ Ale: Bass
🅿 Own car park

SULLY, nr CARDIFF, GLAMORGAN
🅿🆁 THE CAPTAIN'S WIFE, Beach Road
Tel: 01222 530 066
Just off the B4267.

It is worth seeking out this expansive family pub merely for the views: the rocks, the seascape of Sully Bay and the island. You can lean on the sea wall and drink it in or, even better, grab a table on the terrace and enjoy it in comfort with a glass of Boddington's to sup.

The pub, long and low and painted white, has a wide frontage to the ocean and a garden to one side with an adventure playground.

Very much aimed at the family market, the interior has a number of good-sized rooms. Beyond the bar area there is a no-smoking family restaurant, which has a small play area for very young children. Another wood-panelled room looks on to the veranda and the garden. Here also is a Charlie Chalk Fun Factory (when we visited, a children's party was in full swing) with all sorts of amusements, including a ball swamp – and the children have their own bar for soft drinks and snacks.

There is loads of room for the adults, too, including a large room beyond the bar. Up above is a spacious restaurant under the rafters.

The Captain's Wife is open all day and serves food at all times. There are plenty of high chairs, and baby-changing facilities are provided.

....

✕ (11.30am to 10pm) £2–8: oriental prawns, chicken Alexandra, marinated lamb steak, vegetable crumble, sirloin steak
   Children: own menu
⊙ Ale: Boddington's, Flowers and guests
ℙ Lots

Nr SWANSEA, WEST GLAMORGAN
ℙℝ **COMMERCIAL INN, Killay**
Tel: 01792 203 980
On the A4118, about 3 miles west of Swansea at Killay.

....

If you are on your way to the Gower, this is an excellent place to break your journey, especially if you have children in tow.

The pub is open all day, provides food throughout most of its opening hours, and offers a full range of amenities for families. There is a special family room, which is a no-smoking area and has a play machine for children; high chairs are provided; and there is a nappy-changing facility. In addition the large, safely enclosed garden has a well-equipped play area on a bark surface and a bouncy castle. You can watch your darlings from the safety of the terrace.

The interior of the Commercial Inn is a cheerful and well-designed place, with a long L-shaped bar, wooden tables and chairs, padded benches, the occasional alcove, and pleasant stained-glass screens and windows. When we had lunch there it was busy and the staff coped cheerfully and efficiently with their many customers.

✕ (11.30am to 10pm; Sun from 12pm) £2–8: onion bhajis, tagliatelle carbonara, steak & kidney pie, fillet of salmon, marinated lamb steaks
Children: own menu
◐ Ale: Boddington's, Flowers, Marston's
Ｐ Plenty

Nr WREXHAM, CLWYD
ＰＲ THE BEECHES, Gresford
Tel: 01978 853 214
On the B5445 at Gresford, north of Wrexham.

A roadside pub on a large scale, The Beeches has become a family pub and restaurant in the Brewers Fayre chain and has a Travel Inn alongside. All the facilities required by a family are here, including high chairs, a nappy-changing unit and a children's menu; and food is available throughout the day from just before noon until 10pm.

The capacious bar and restaurant has an array of windows on to the garden and has been constructed on a number of different levels. The various areas have cheerful wallpaper, a variety of prints on the walls, padded settles and some large bay windows. The family dining area (no-smoking) has a play area for young children, and upstairs, there is a sizeable Fun Factory and a children's soft drinks bar.

The garden is safely enclosed and has bench tables on the lawns, plus a children's play area and a bouncy castle.

539

- ✕ (11.30am to 10pm) £2–8: onion bhajis, chicken escalopes, steak & kidney pie, vegetable crumble, lasagne verdi
  Children: own menu
- ◑ Ale: Boddington's, Flowers and guests
- ℗ Lots

INDEX OF ESTABLISHMENTS

Peebles Hotel Hydro, Peebles 490*†
Philipburn House Hotel, Selkirk 493*†

Scottish National Gallery of Modern Art, Edinburgh 475

Theatre Restaurant, Inverness 480
Thrums Hotel, Edinburgh 472
Tigh-an-Truish, Clachan Seil 468
Tullybannocher Farm Food Bar, Comrie 469
Tweeddale Arms Hotel, Gifford 477

Waterside Inn, Seamill 492

Wales
Ashbridge Inn, Cwmbran 513

Beeches, the, nr Wrexham 539
Black Lion Hotel, New Quay 529

Captain's Wife, the, Sully 537
Commercial Inn, nr Swansea 538
Craigside Inn, Llandudno 524
Crossways, the, Caerphilly 510
Crown Inn, Llwyndafydd 527
Cwmwdig Water Guest House, nr Berea 505

Dinorben Arms, Bodfari 508

Elen's Castle Hotel, Dolwyddelan 515

Gales, Llangollen 525
Gate, the, nr Cwmbran 514
Golden Pheasant Hotel, the, Glyn Ceiriog 517
Granary, the, Hay-on-Wye 519

Grapes Hotel, the, Maentwrog 527
Greenhill Farm, Holywell 520

Halfway Inn, nr Aberystwyth 504
Harbour Hotel, Aberdovey 500
High Corner House, Llanharan 526
Hive on the Quay, the, Aberaeron 499

Keeston Kitchen, Keeston 522

Llanwenarth Arms Hotel, Abergavenny 503

Moelwyn Restaurant, Criccieth 512

Penally Abbey Hotel, Penally 532*
Penbontbren Farm Hotel, Glynarthen 518
Pentrebach House, nr Merthyr Tydfil 528
Piercefield, Chepstow 511

Royal Oak, Newport 531

St Tudno Hotel, Llandudno 522*
Ship, the, Rhos-on-Sea 534

Trefeddian Hotel, Aberdovey 501*
Ty Gwyn Hotel, Betws-y-Coed 506

Upper Boat Inn, Pontypridd 533

Warpool Court Hotel, St David's 536*
Watermill, the, nr Bridgend 509

Ye Olde Anchor Inn, Ruthin 535

* *Hotels with swimming pools.*
† *Hotels with childcare facilities.*

READERS' COMMENTS

Please use this sheet to recommend establishments which you think should be considered for the next edition of the *Guide*. The basic facilities we look for are:

- hotels with cots, high chairs and a free baby-listening service
- pubs with facilities for families
- restaurants with high chairs

Comments, adverse or otherwise, are welcome about any of the current *Guide*'s entries.

To: The Editors, *Lex Family Welcome Guide 1996*, c/o Hamer Books Ltd., Freepost, London SW13 9BR

Full name and address of establishment: ....
....
....
....

Phone number: ....

Comments: ....
....
....
....
....

Name and address of sender: ....
....
....
....

We regret that we cannot acknowledge these forms, but they will be properly considered.

READERS' COMMENTS

Please use this sheet to recommend establishments which you think should be considered for the next edition of the *Guide*. The basic facilities we look for are:

- hotels with cots, high chairs and a free baby-listening service
- pubs with facilities for families
- restaurants with high chairs

Comments, adverse or otherwise, are welcome about any of the current *Guide*'s entries.

To: The Editors, *Lex Family Welcome Guide 1996*, c/o Hamer Books Ltd., Freepost, London SW13 9BR

Full name and address of establishment: ....
....
....
....

Phone number: ....

Comments: ....
....
....
....
....

Name and address of sender: ....
....
....
....

We regret that we cannot acknowledge these forms, but they will be properly considered.

READERS' COMMENTS

Please use this sheet to recommend establishments which you think should be considered for the next edition of the *Guide*. The basic facilities we look for are:

- hotels with cots, high chairs and a free baby-listening service
- pubs with facilities for families
- restaurants with high chairs

Comments, adverse or otherwise, are welcome about any of the current *Guide*'s entries.

To: The Editors, *Lex Family Welcome Guide 1996*, c/o Hamer Books Ltd., Freepost, London SW13 9BR

Full name and address of establishment: ....
....
....
....

Phone number: ....

Comments: ....
....
....
....
....

Name and address of sender: ....
....
....
....

We regret that we cannot acknowledge these forms, but they will be properly considered.

READERS' COMMENTS

Please use this sheet to recommend establishments which you think should be considered for the next edition of the *Guide*. The basic facilities we look for are:
- hotels with cots, high chairs and a free baby-listening service
- pubs with facilities for families
- restaurants with high chairs

Comments, adverse or otherwise, are welcome about any of the current *Guide*'s entries.

To: The Editors, *Lex Family Welcome Guide 1996*, c/o Hamer Books Ltd., Freepost, London SW13 9BR

Full name and address of establishment: ....
....
....
....

Phone number: ....

Comments: ....
....
....
....
....

Name and address of sender: ....
....
....
....

We regret that we cannot acknowledge these forms, but they will be properly considered.

READERS' COMMENTS

Please use this sheet to recommend establishments which you think should be considered for the next edition of the *Guide*. The basic facilities we look for are:

- hotels with cots, high chairs and a free baby-listening service
- pubs with facilities for families
- restaurants with high chairs

Comments, adverse or otherwise, are welcome about any of the current *Guide*'s entries.

To: The Editors, *Lex Family Welcome Guide 1996*, c/o Hamer Books Ltd., Freepost, London SW13 9BR

Full name and address of establishment: ....
....
....
....

Phone number: ....

Comments: ....
....
....
....
....

Name and address of sender: ....
....
....
....

We regret that we cannot acknowledge these forms, but they will be properly considered.

READERS' COMMENTS

Please use this sheet to recommend establishments which you think should be considered for the next edition of the *Guide*. The basic facilities we look for are:

- hotels with cots, high chairs and a free baby-listening service
- pubs with facilities for families
- restaurants with high chairs

Comments, adverse or otherwise, are welcome about any of the current *Guide*'s entries.

To: The Editors, *Lex Family Welcome Guide 1996*, c/o Hamer Books Ltd., Freepost, London SW13 9BR

Full name and address of establishment: ....
....
....
....

Phone number: ....

Comments: ....
....
....
....
....

Name and address of sender: ....
....
....
....

We regret that we cannot acknowledge these forms, but they will be properly considered.